W9-AQL-839

Education for Christian Living

RANDOLPH CRUMP MILLER
Professor of Christian Education
on the Luther A. Weigle Fund
The Divinity School, Yale University

Englewood Cliffs, N. J.
PRENTICE-HALL, INC.

LIBRARY OF CONGRESS
CATALOG CARD NO.: 56-6985

First printing . . . . January, 1956
Second printing . . . . August, 1956
Third printing . . . . June, 1957
Fourth printing . . . . May, 1959

PRINTED IN THE UNITED STATES OF AMERICA
23869

To

Elizabeth Fowlkes Miller

PREFACE

John Wesley once gave this advice to his ministers: "Wherever there are ten children in a Society, spend at least one hour with them twice a week. And do this, not in a dull, dry, formal manner, but in earnest, with your might. 'But I have no gift for this.' Gift or no gift, do it, else you are not called to be a Methodist preacher. Do it as you can, till you can do it as you would. Pray earnestly for the gift and use the means for it, particularly study the children's tracts." [1]

The church has not always shared John Wesley's concern for the Christian upbringing of children, although Christian homes have provided an atmosphere in which Biblical faith has come to life, and Sunday schools have flourished. Today's view of Christian education is broader than Wesley's, but the minister's personal responsibility is just as great. The *Methodist Discipline* says that "in each local church there shall be a church school for the purpose of discharging the church's responsibility for instructing and guiding its entire constituency in Christian faith and living."[2]

In this book we are concerned with the comprehensive educational program of the local church as it seeks to provide for all its people. Although children receive much of our attention, we try not to forget that everyone shares in the educational process.

The growing concern for theology has led to a consideration of its effect on educational theory and methods in the churches. I am convinced that an autonomous Christian education finds its source in theology, and that what we know of God and man in terms of Christian doctrine determines our objectives, our theory, and our

---

[1] *Minutes of the Methodist Conferences, 1744-1798* (London: John Mason), I, 63-69.

[2] *Doctrine and Discipline of the Methodist Church* (Nashville: The Methodist Publishing House, 1952), p. 226.

method. Because theology makes use of all the data of human knowledge within the perspective of a Biblical faith, the insights of modern knowledge and technique are used, but they are the servants of Christian goals rather than the masters of the Gospel. This, I think, is an important distinction that becomes clear within the body of this book.

The first part of the book provides a theological framework in which the significance of Christian education is seen in terms of its history, of modern secular thinking, and of theological developments. The needs of those who learn are examined according to age-group characteristics. In the second part, the impact of home, school, community, and church are discussed. The third part deals with methods, both as they are used in the classroom and as they are applied to worship. The fourth part is concerned with the practical problems of administration and organization.

I have kept in mind the needs of the student for the ministry, and I have included in brief form most of what he needs to know about Christian education. I have also provided information for the college student, for church school teacher or officer, for the busy pastor, and for the general reader.

In the section titled "For More Information," books and other publications are listed according to the subjects covered by the chapters, and they often contain points of view different from those expressed here. "A Basic Bibliography" comprises about fifty essential books that are in general agreement with the thesis of this book.

My own point of view has grown out of a lifelong interest in theology and in the philosophy of religion, combined with a practical concern for the educational work of the local church. From 1947 to 1956, I was on the Curriculum Development Division of my own church and worked with the members of the staff in formulating a point of view for *The Seabury Series* of lesson materials. During this time, I wrote *The Clue to Christian Education*[3] as an expression of the relation of theology to educational method.

The Rev. C. William Sydnor, Jr., executive secretary of the Curriculum Development Division of the National Council of the Protestant Episcopal Church, has read the manuscript, and to him and

[3] New York: Charles Scribner's Sons, 1950.

my other friends on the staff of the Curriculum Development Division I am deeply indebted. My colleague, Professor Paul H. Vieth, has provided many notations which have helped me immeasurably, and his insight has contributed to my own growth. My wife and six children provide a continuing laboratory for my "theology of relationships."

Acknowledgment of permission to quote copyrighted materials appears in the footnotes. In the case of quotations from various translations of the Bible, each passage is marked as follows:

KJ — *King James Version*

RSV — *Revised Standard Version* (copyright 1946 and 1952 by the Division of Christian Education of the National Council of Churches of Christ in the United States of America)

G — *The Complete Bible: An American Translation,* by Edgar J. Goodspeed and J. M. Powis Smith (copyright 1939 by the University of Chicago Press)

P — *The Four Gospels Translated into Modern English* and *Letters to Young Churches* (copyright 1952 and 1947 by The Macmillan Co.)

K — *The New Testament* in the translation of Ronald A. Knox (copyright 1944 by Sheed and Ward, Inc., New York)

PB — *Prayer Book* translation from the services of worship and the psalms (Seabury Press)

RANDOLPH CRUMP MILLER

TABLE OF CONTENTS

PART I: PRINCIPLES OF CHRISTIAN EDUCATION

PART ONE

Principles of Christian Education

CHAPTER I

THE SIGNIFICANCE OF RELIGIOUS EDUCATION

RELIGIOUS education has been a major concern of the faithful throughout human history. The young of all ages have been brought up to practice and to understand inherited traditions and ceremonies at least partly through religious training. Acquaintance with the major passages of holy writings has for many a youngster been his introduction to the teachings of great religious leaders. Careful training in the mores and morals of family, tribe, national religion, or denomination has led to religious character development.

Varying emphases in the philosophy and methods of education have served changing ends throughout the Christian tradition, depending on the dominant theology, the kind of authority associated with the Scriptures or the church, and the goals of the culture of the day. Today we need to understand Christian education within the framework of a twentieth-century theology, of a view of the authority of the Bible and church consistent with the best Christian scholarship, and of a culture that is predominantly secular in spite of its avowedly Christian nucleus. We must also get to know the available resources inside and outside the church in order to gain a practical, sound, adequate, and relevant theory of Christian education for today.

Today more people are realizing their need of Christian education. Adults are hungering for faith as a source of moral and spiritual stability in a world where the props have been knocked from under many secular assumptions. There is a growing concern for the teaching of religion on the levels of higher education and for the establishment of new college pastorates. The science of the care of the aged, under the name of geriatrics, is beginning to fire the interest of the churches in ministering to older people.

The churches, more clearly than any other group, are recognizing the need for community relationships on a scope broad enough to include family groups, and those separated from their homes, in a fellowship that is concerned with the redemption of all the people. Group dynamics has operated within a select circle as an experimental device, but its requirements of acceptance and appreciation of the personalities of all members of a group are being seen within the wider scope of the Christian fellowship. Here is a point of view that includes both the individual and the group, with recognition of the worth of the individual as an end in himself and with appraisal of the social process that is the means by which the individual truly becomes a person.

THE PURPOSE OF THIS BOOK

The purpose of this book is to lead all interested persons into an understanding of the theory, techniques, and administration of Christian education. The dedicated layman needs this information just as much as the professional religious educator, the college chaplain, and the local pastor. The college student needs knowledge of this kind even if he never intends to be a parent or to teach in the church school, for as a Christian he will find that unless he shares his faith he will lose it. The Christian parent finds that much of the responsibility for the Christian education of his children falls on his shoulders. Although it is true that Christian living is in itself the most contagious form of influence, it needs the guidance that comes from a sound understanding of the ways in which Christian faith may be most effectively shared. The proclamation of the Gospel in the light of his vocation, is the responsibility of every Christian, and this privilege may be sacrificed only at the cost of the loss of one's faith.

The leadership and responsibility for such a program must be shared by the entire congregation. Throughout its history the Sunday school movement has been guided by lay leaders, with assistance from professional, trained educators and the clergy. In addition a

Christian individual influences his friends and acquaintances at every point of daily life, whether he is teaching school, working in the bank, serving as a clerk in a store or gas station. The way the individual worshiper treats a new attendant at church is educational – for good or ill.

We need, therefore, a real understanding of Christian nurture in its broadest and most effective forms. We need to understand the church's task in the education of all its members, of potential members, and of the surrounding community. This involves a point of view, a program of action, and a ready knowledge of techniques for communication of the good news of Jesus Christ. In today's world, this is a complicated and difficult task, but the understanding of it is vital if the church is to be an effective agency for educating its members and through them reaching society with the impact of the Gospel.

THE NEED FOR A POINT OF VIEW

Christian education involves a point of view, for it is a particular kind of education. It is not secular education with a halo, although the Christian can ignore secular insights only at his peril. Christian education is concerned with the relevance of revealed Christian truth. Theology, which is the truth-about-God-in-relation-to-man, is the determining factor in the development of a philosophy of education, of techniques to be used, of goals to be attained, and of nature of the learners to be taught.

Theology tells us primarily about the nature of God and the nature of man and about the relations between them. What we think about God has much to do with the picture of the universe to be taught. What we think about man has much to do with our view of his teachability and of the goals that by God's grace may be achieved. What we believe to be God's requirements for men's behavior determines our goals of Christian ethics. What we believe about the ultimate hope of eternal life as a gift of a loving Father provides a perspective for education quite foreign to many non-Christian assumptions. What we believe about the church provides a view of the social process in which education takes place: a view that may prove quite strange to educators operating without reference to God's purpose to redeem man from his sins.

Our point of view involves us in theological thinking. As we have said, it is our purpose to impart Christian truth. We need a clearer understanding of the teaching of the Christian faith about the historical events recorded in the Bible and centering in Jesus Christ. If we believe the life and death and resurrection of Jesus Christ constitute the turning point of history, we will teach history in a different way from those who believe that Buddha, Socrates, or Karl Marx represents the crux of the time process.

What we think about the church makes a difference, too, for if the congregation is just a group of men assembled to reaffirm their beliefs with a musical accompaniment, their educational procedures cannot be a matter of life and death. But if the church is the Body of Christ, a fellowship of the Holy Spirit, which is the channel of God's grace by which men are redeemed, then what happens within this communion of faithful people is of ultimate significance.

What we think about the family in relation to God also makes a difference. If the relations of husband and wife and children have divine sanction, so that the family may be thought of as a cell within the larger organism that is the church, then the family unit has supreme importance in the church's program of education. Infant baptism and dedication then do not just involve an individual child; they place responsibility upon the parents and/or godparents and congregation to see that the process of nurture in faith symbolized by these acts is continued through the ministry of the parents.

Education in the church involves every person as a child of the heavenly Father, as a person for whom Christ died. Every Christian should grow in wisdom and in favor with man and God. Education "from womb to tomb" within the redemptive fellowship of the Body of Christ is our goal.

THE EDUCATIONAL APPROACH

Modern educational philosophies among secular and religious thinkers reflect many centuries of theorizing and experimenting, from Plato's time on down.

Observation and experimentation since 1900 have provided us with adequate data for judging the effects of various methods and practices. The emphasis in philosophy on pragmatism, which holds that whatever works is true, has led to the testing of many educational procedures. The new developments in psychology, including child and developmental psychology, the psychology of learning, the psychology of religion, and psychiatry, have provided insights into the human mind that were only guessed at in previous centuries. The study of the social process as the medium in which education takes place has altered our views concerning the relationship of teacher and pupil.

The common distinction has been between content-centered and child-centered education. As the emphasis shifted from the content to the child, the problems of motivation and interest were placed in a new light. Because the child did not have adequate resources within himself for solving his own problems and because of pressures for the achievement of traditional intellectual goals, some educators and many teachers and parents have tended to revert to the primary emphasis on content.

This problem has been brought into a new focus in recent years through the question of what is the relationship between content and method. For Christian theology this involves the relationship between God and man. The center of the curriculum is a twofold relationship between God and the learner. The curriculum is both God-centered and experience-centered, with theology standing behind the curriculum. The purpose of Christian education is to bring the individual into the right relationship with God and his fellows within the fellowship of the church and within the framework of the fundamental Christian truths about all of life.[1] These truths *are* theology, but theology becomes relevant only as the learner recognizes his basic needs in the perspective of God's activity in his experience. As the learner responds in faith and trust to God's love, he is brought into real and genuine membership in the community of love that is the church. These personal relationships with God and with our fellows are the environment in which Christian education takes place.

Christian theology is the primary source of Christian educational theory and procedure. Through the revelation of God, as we understand His mighty acts in history, we find a Christian interpretation of the nature of man and of the goals of the educational process. We use all the insights of modern science and theory in education, but

[1] See my *The Clue to Christian Education* (New York: Charles Scribner's Sons, 1950), p. 8.

the assumptions of the secularists about the nature of the world and of man are not our assumptions. We begin with the truth that is ours as Christians, and because all facts and observations are assumed to be consistent with the one area of truth and revelation which comes from God, we may then use the observations, experiments, and insights of non-Christians within the framework of Christian truth.

Too often it has seemed that theories of religious education have begun from a secular viewpoint with Christian theology as a footnote to a non-Christian perspective. It is our purpose to reverse this procedure and to use all secular insights as tools within the framework of Christian faith. The educational philosophy of John Dewey, for example, is of supreme importance to anyone dealing with educational processes, yet his theory of truth is unsatisfactory and his metaphysics is almost completely negative. A theological critique of his goals and methods enables us to make full use of the valuable contributions of America's most influential educator without sacrificing our Christian perspectives and goals.

ADMINISTRATIVE PROBLEMS

The combination of sound educational theory and effective educational procedures depends on adequate administrative techniques. Considering all the varieties of church administration in American Protestantism, we must use descriptive terms that are generally understood and must recognize that administrative programs provide for many different kinds of leadership even within one denomination. Furthermore, we must see how other human groupings contribute to religious development or hinder it.

(1) Most church schools are small, often with as few as twenty-five pupils. Yet there are many others with enrollments reaching five hundred or one thousand and more. Some are in the sole charge of the pastor; some have lay superintendents; others have professional directors of religious education; and still others have a roving missionary who attends one service a month and otherwise leaves the educational program entirely in the hands of lay people. We shall have to consider the different areas of responsibility in terms of such situations.

(2) The division of educational responsibility poses another problem. In some parishes there is a complete separation of church

and church school, with the minister responsible for the former and a lay superintendent responsible for the latter. In other situations there is still the idea that, although the pastor is in charge, the church school is the private domain of lay people; where this idea prevails, the pastor's authority is questioned and sometimes undermined. In larger congregations, a division of responsibility frees the pastor from taking part and places the authority in a minister of education (either an assistant minister or a professionally trained director of religious education). These arrangements are often unsatisfactory. The problem in such cases is to provide a unified program of education for every member of the congregation, with authority and mutual understanding centered in a central board or council headed by the pastor or the delegated minister of education.

(3) The theological position upheld in a specific congregation also makes a difference in what will happen. Not only are there the usual distinctions between various types of theology (including liberal, conservative, neo-orthodox, fundamentalist, and other labels) to be considered, but there are also the educational assumptions underlying these theological positions. If the educational goals and methods and assumptions about the nature of the learner are derived from a particular theology, the curriculum will vary with the dominant theological theory. The view of revelation with its theory of knowledge and truth will determine the kind of authority used, the emphasis on content, the choice of methods, and the desired ends. If truth is a matter of particular words found in the Scripture the emphasis will be different from that of a congregation which thinks of truth as a description of relationships between God and man in history. If God reveals himself by what he is recorded to have said, that will provide goals different from those resulting from the belief that God reveals himself by what he does. The crucial point of the nature of Christ will determine the kind of decision expected of learners. All these problems will affect the administration of the educational program of a congregation, for administration exists in terms of presuppositions and goals.

THE BIBLE

We can see more clearly the impact of theology on Christian education by looking at recent thinking about the Bible. There is a movement in theology to interpret the Bible as the record of

God's mighty acts in history. God's revelation is seen in the events recorded in the Bible. There is a historical and unfolding drama of redemption to be found in the Bible that is relevant to the Christian believer's decisions for living in today's world. In this record of God at work in history, we may observe the changing relationships between God and man as God seeks to bring man into the right religious adjustment.

Beginning with creation, we see God's purpose for the world. But man disobeys God by defacing the image of God within him, and so is cast out of the Garden of Eden. Man's relationship with God is thus broken by disobedience and rebellion, and in the tragedy of this separation from God man stands helpless. Man cannot by his own power be restored to God's presence.

But God enters into a covenant with his people, and promises that he will be their God if they will keep his law. The people of Israel become his people, and the story of the Old Testament in the law and the prophets tells how man failed to keep God's law. God's redemptive activity is present, but men do not "do justice, love kindness, and walk humbly with God" (Micah 6:8, G); they do not "let justice roll down like waters, and righteousness like a perennial stream" (Amos 5:24, G).

Because men do not or cannot keep God's commandments, the prophets look forward to a Messiah who will lead Israel to a new relationship with the heavenly Father. This expectation is fulfilled by the coming of Jesus Christ, who through his life and death and resurrection is the Redeemer. "For if while we were enemies we were reconciled to God by the death of his Son, much more, now that we are reconciled, shall we be saved by his life" (Rom. 5:10, RSV).

In our understanding of this central act in the drama of redemption, we have the crucial point in Christian education. And from this act comes the church as the Body of Christ, the fellowship of the Holy Spirit, the family of God – a redemptive and redeeming community of which we are members. It is within this community that we learn the good news of the Gospel and are committed to the God who gives us grace to work out our salvation. As we stand in faith and hope at this point in history (the twentieth century *Anno Domini* – the year of Our Lord), God stands over us in judgment, and there is a consummation both within the historical process and beyond it.

RELATIONSHIPS

If Biblical theology provides such a story of God at work in history,[2] certainly we can relate it to the education of children and adults in the church. With this dynamic view of revelation as an ongoing process (for God is not dead but is the Lord of history), we are not bound by fixed words or by historic formulations of the faith. The important factor in education is *relationships.* The language by which we communicate the truth of God at work in history and in the lives of men is the language of relationships.

The goal of a mature personality is integration resulting in wholeness of intent. This integration is often thought of in terms of beliefs and doctrines, moral standards, or social adjustment, all of which may be good and often are necessary to mental, moral, and social health. But they are not enough, and they are no substitute for essentially Christian integration.

Christian integration arises in the personal relationships between man and God and between man and man. It results from a right religious adjustment, by means of which the human person comes into the presence of a divine Person. It is more than an activity of the will or mind or emotions, for it involves the total personality in relation to God. It is personal communion within a community of persons.

The radical nature of Christian integration tells us much about the language of relationships. Often more is taught by attitudes and atmosphere than in actual words. There is an influence in worship, as the congregation comes into a new relationship with each other and with God, that is often more meaningful than the words themselves – for example the manner in which a mother treats a young child communicates the relationship of love when the word itself is still meaningless.

Most theological concepts arose originally as attempts to describe relationships. If we are correct in interpreting the Bible as a record of the mighty acts of God, the resulting ideas of God are descriptions of relationships between God and man in history. The creeds arose as

---

[2] See Bernhard Anderson, *The Unfolding Drama of the Bible* (New York: Association Press, 1953).

efforts to summarize the Biblical story. They are statements of faith in a God who did certain things—created the world, sent Jesus Christ and the Holy Spirit, inspired the founding of the church, and gave us the promise of everlasting life. Even the difficult doctrine of the Trinity takes on more meaning when we see it as a description of the ways in which men have known God at work in their midst.

REVELATION

Truth as we know it arises from our interpretation of events of experience. Revelation is that particular segment of truth that arises from the interpretation of our relationships with God. William Temple says that because all things are grounded in God's will, "all therefore is alike revelation; but all is not equally revelatory of the divine character. We find revelation at its highest where God finds occasion for unusual action . . . ." Revelation consists "in a coincidence of divinely guided events with minds divinely illuminated to apprehend those events, so that there" are "no 'revealed truths', but there" are " 'truths of revelation.' . . . The revelation is received in a living experience; all doctrines are inferences drawn from that revelation in the context provided by the rest of experience; and their spiritual value is not in themselves; it is in the directions which they offer for recovering the experience from which they spring."[3]

Theology lies behind the relationships that have educational value. But if Temple is right, "all doctrines are inferences," and their value is in the help they give in recovering the relationships so described. What is crucial is the personal relationship, and theology gives us the interpretation of that personal communion between man and God within the religious community.

The task of Christian education is to provide opportunities for the right kind of relationships and to interpret all relationships within the framework of the revelation of God in Christ. The desired goal is increased integration of the total personality as it is centered on the living God through the experiences provided by life in the family, church, and other religious groupings, and through the interpretation

---

[3] William Temple, *Nature, Man and God* (London: Macmillan & Co. Ltd., 1934), pp. 315, 499, 500. By permission of Mrs. William Temple and Macmillan Co. Ltd., London.

of experiences that do not lead in this direction. Through knowledge of the record of experience, through the sense of obligation to the ways of behavior identified as the will of God, through membership in the church, and through the sharing of the redemptive life as we see it revealed in the life and work of Jesus Christ, the Christian comes to maturity.

ECUMENICAL OUTLOOK

The theological base of Christian education is broader than that of the local parish or the denomination. There is a coming together in theology today. The varieties of theological thought are found within the denominations, most of which have their liberal and conservative wings. Among the churches that have been working together on theological issues, there is a great amount of fundamental agreement.

Although many forms of cooperation between the churches go back a century or more, the movement toward unity in both theology and action got its start in 1910, culminating in the World Council of Churches in 1947. In the United States, the Federal Council of the Churches of Christ in America (1905) combined with other agencies to form the National Council of the Churches of Christ in the United States of America in 1950. Religious educators, who had cooperated in many ventures in the nineteenth century, formed the International Council of Religious Education in 1922, and this became the Division of Christian Education of the National Council of the Churches of Christ in America in 1950. The new version of the Bible (1946, 1952) is a cooperative effort sponsored by this group and welcomed by almost all denominations.

Interdenominational cooperation has not meant that differences have been watered down. They have been recognized as what they are, as honest interpretations of the record of God's work in history. They are not insuperable barriers to Christian fellowship, worship, and cooperation, but are indications of the richness of the Gospel of Jesus Christ that cannot be contained by man-made theologies.

Ministers are being trained in many instances in interdenominational divinity schools, where they are expected to be loyal to their own denominations but also to have a greater appreciation of traditions other than their own. Leaders going on to graduate degrees are especially likely to be found attending such institutions.

In the field of religious education, this trend is especially noticeable. Though most congregations use the lesson materials of their own denomination, some of these materials are prepared from outlines by interdenominational experts. There are nondenominational publishers whose lessons have a wide sale among churches of a variety of denominations. Two or more denominations sometimes cooperate in preparing materials that are the official lessons for all their churches. Often it is discovered that materials prepared by one denomination are suitable in several others. There are many exceptions to this observation, but the point to be emphasized is that not theological indifference but theological unity makes this possible where it happens.

Certain trends in theology contribute to this "ecumenical" feeling. The most important is the newly developed concern for the nature of the church. A generation ago, many Protestants had forgotten the Reformation heritage of doctrine about the church. The church was a convenient meetinghouse or worship center for those who wished to gather. But among the Reformers there was a dynamic concept of the church as the Body of Christ, as a community of faithful people, a communion of saints. The church was the organism of Christ's Body whereby God's grace was channeled to men. This view has become prominent again among Protestants who think of the church as a redemptive and redeeming fellowship. The nature of the church and the quality of life in the church determine the kind of education that goes on.

Through the cooperative agencies of religious education, the common concerns of all are explored and experimental results are shared. The Religious Education Association (1903), in which Jews, Protestants, and Roman Catholics cooperate, works for all three groups. Their journal, *Religious Education,* is a valuable source of information for representatives of all religious faiths, dealing as it does with specific problems and common concerns. Here, for example, is to be found some of the best thinking on the place of religion in the public schools, the problem of religion and higher education, the philosophy of religious education, the place of the home in religious training, the significance of parochial and private schools, the significance of youth clubs, intercultural relations, leadership training, theology and religious education. Among Protestants, the significant cooperation is found in the Division of Christian Education of the National Council of Churches and its journal, *The International Journal of Religious Education,* which deals with Protestants' common concerns. A broader scope is covered by the World Council of Christian Education, which has a journal, *World Christian Education,* distributed in most countries.

A PHILOSOPHY OF CHRISTIAN EDUCATION

Philosophy is, literally, the love of wisdom. William James once called it "a stubborn attempt to think things through." It is more than sanctified common sense because it involves all of men's critical faculties. In terms of education it involves a view of the world, a critical examination of the nature and worth of man, and a careful scrutiny of the learning process.

Current educational philosophies are broken down into several groupings. John P. Wynne suggests a classification into three major divisions: educational authoritarianism, educational laissez faire, and educational experimentalism.[4] He writes that educational authoritarianism assumes that influences outside the learner are of primary significance and that external control is necessary for them to work. It sometimes takes the form of a carefully worked out philosophy, but more often the unconscious attitudes of teachers, parents, and pupils. It has a long history and much support, and many types of educational philosophy fit into this class.

Educational laissez faire, he says, is the opposite of this in assuming that education depends primarily on factors within the individual learners, making the development on inherent capacities the primary goal. This view also has historical roots, but it has not found its way into as many educational philosophies as has the authoritarian position. It has been strengthened by the romantic tradition and by certain discoveries in psychoanalysis.

Wynne says that educational experimentalism differs from the other positions by its emphasis on the interaction between the individual and his environment. It is not to be identified with progressive

[4] John P. Wynne, *Philosophies of Education* (New York: Prentice-Hall, Inc., 1947), pp. 4-11.

education, and yet it is related to it, receiving its best formulations in the writings of John Dewey, Boyd H. Bode, and William H. Kilpatrick. It is an attempt to combine the best elements of the authoritarian and laissez faire groups without being a synthesis of both. To achieve this there must be a new direction in educational thinking.

This same problem is faced in developing a philosophy of Christian education, which has also been beset by its traditionalists and progressives and which needs a new sense of direction. But, whereas the secular philosophers find their clue in a new philosophical system, the Christian educators find theirs in a new understanding of the place of theology in relation to the learning process.

Involved in the church's educational program are a number of theologies. The assumptions about the nature of man, his relationship to God, his ways of learning, his motivations and goals, his ultimate purpose in life, and his membership in the human community are theological assumptions. Unless they reflect a sound and critical theology of the church, and therefore stand for truth wherever it may be discovered, these assumptions may undercut any hope of effective Christian education.[5]

THE IMPORTANCE OF COMMUNITY

Marjorie Reeves emphasizes the importance of adjustment to the wealth of outside experience pouring in upon the learner. In the process of adjustment, the learner needs security, love, and guidance; for when these factors are lacking the results are a sense of chaos, insecurity, and meaninglessness. She says that certain experiences are vital: "that of belonging within a society which gives a stable framework of law and order; of meeting reliability or trustworthiness in the human beings who exercise control; of growing up within groups of persons which are not too large to be 'humanly assimilable'; of finding within these groups a significant personal part to play in the service of common purposes."[6] This means working in small groups, where there is no desire to exploit, dominate, or possess. This means a right

---

[5] See James D. Smart, *The Teaching Ministry of the Church* (Philadelphia: Westminster Press, 1954), pp. 66-67.

[6] Marjorie Reeves, *Growing Up in a Modern Society,* 3d ed. (London: University of London Press, 1952), pp. 17-18.

attitude of the community toward its young, so that their basic needs can be met. Within such a group, where they know themselves as persons among persons, the grace of God is at work to assist them in self acceptance and in the service of others. The tools of method and content become relevant in such experiences, and the young people grow in wisdom and in favor with God and man.

Secular and Christian educators agree on this need for the community in education, but the Christian assumes that God is at work in both secular and Christian communities, whereas the secularist may not refer to the theological issues at stake. Both, for example, stress the importance of groups outside of formal schooling, but the Christian thinks of the family as a Christian "cell" and of the other groupings of children and adults in terms of the words of Jesus: "Where two or three are gathered together in my name, there am I in the midst of them" (Matthew 18:20, KJ). Every gathering of Christian disciples in the name of the Master creates a redemptive and redeeming community, where broken relationships are healed and broken spirits are restored.

A Christian philosophy of education assumes that the church is the central institution of learning, but it also recognizes the limitations of the church as an inclusive community in the structure of society. Therefore, from the beginning, it has recognized the need for redemptive activities in other human groupings. The Old Testament stresses the significance of the family with its religious rituals and the responsibility of parents for bringing up children in the knowledge of the Law and the fear of the Lord. Until the rise of the Sunday school in the nineteteth century, the home was the basic institution for religious instruction.

Horace Bushnell's *Christian Nurture,* the most significant book of the nineteenth century in Christian education, assumed that a "child should grow up as a Christian and never know himself as being otherwise," and that this was the evangelistic and educational responsibility of the Christian home. Today, throughout the whole field of religious education, the duty of the parent as the primary teacher of religion is being restored to its former place of importance. The various kinds of schools, public, private, and parochial, are recognizing more clearly the importance of providing not only instruction in religion but also an environment in which faith flourishes. Informal groupings of boys and girls, of men and women, sponsored by churches,

Christian associations, and community agencies, provide opportunities for the interpretation of daily experience on Christian terms.

Marjorie Reeves suggests that when "the marks of true community" are to be found, individuals are nourished in terms of their personal needs. She does not mean "chance collections of persons" but "a truly educative community" that is "subject to the rule of law which is beneficent and consistent and – as far as possible – willingly accepted by each member. All the members of the society must treat each other as persons . . . . Each member must find a significant part to play in the life of the whole, the purpose of which he understands as fully as possible. . . . The group must contain an element of 'mixture,' so that there are tensions and differences to be experienced. . . . The group must serve some purpose bigger than the immediate self-interest of its members." [7]

The development of character comes from loyalty to a community, and most learners have a choice of social groups to which they must be loyal. The variation in standards and demands provides genuine conflict in the conscience, and the stronger loyalty rather than the higher ideal will normally win out. It is desirable, from the educational standpoint, for the learner to share in the life of as many communities as meet the requirements of the marks listed above, and to develop the strongest loyalty to the group with the highest relevant ideals.

METHODS

With such goals as these as the center of a philosophy of Christian education, and with theology considered in terms of both its truth and its relevance, we derive methods of learning that are consistent with the insights of theology into the nature of man, using the assistance of the discoveries of all the related sciences and arts of education. Child psychology, educational psychology, the sociology of learning, the psychology of religion, and psychiatry have contributions to make. What is desirable is an educational philosophy that is sound, adequate, and relevant from the standpoint of theology, psychology, pedagogy, sociology, and history, with a realistic appraisal of the resources for fulfilling these goals in today's world.[8]

---

[7] Reeves, *Growing Up in a Modern Society,* p. 35.

[8] See Gardner Monks, *Towards the New Curriculum: Specifications* (Greenwich: Seabury Press, 1949), pp. 40-47.

CHAPTER 2

HISTORICAL DEVELOPMENT OF CHRISTIAN EDUCATION

WE CAN imagine what education was like in Jesus' time. There was a synagogue school in Nazareth to which the young boy walked. These words, among many others, were learned by heart: "Hear, O Israel: The LORD our God is one LORD; and you shall love the LORD your God with all your heart, and with all your soul, and with all your might" (Deut. 6:4-5, RSV).

The boy's father was responsible for his learning the law. "And these words which I command you this day shall be upon your heart; and you shall teach them diligently to your children, and shall talk of them when you sit in your house, and when you walk by the way, and when you lie down, and when you rise" (Deut. 6:6-8, RSV). The boy learned the words, but he also saw the law being lived in his own home.

The family was the center of Jewish religious teaching. Books were not available, but the memory of the Jews was trained to recall the chief points of the Law and the prophets. Combined with this oral teaching was the following of the Jewish rituals in the home, which included reciting much of their Bible. Any child in a pious home was necessarily exposed to the central teachings in this manner.

There was also the synagogue, and the services there were chiefly teaching services. Sometimes connected with the synagogue was the elementary school, where a boy would learn the Hebrew alphabet and language and begin to study the Scriptures. Beyond this were the secondary schools and the academy. These schools may have flourished for one or two centuries before the time of Christ, and they were in the ascendancy in the first century, A. D.

This involves an understanding of the history tion, especially of the developments during the p We shall need to define education and Christian edu to look at the objectives and goals for all Christian lea have to see how the content is related to method by dynamic theology of relationships, and apply this to the of religious readiness. Because this process is going on alm where, we shall have to look at religious education in th school, and community, as well as in the church.

Against this background, methods become supremely impo There are many types of teaching, and we shall be concerned classroom response and the methods of stimulating, guiding, a assisting learners in seeing the relevance of Christian truth. Althoug the context will be chiefly in terms of the classroom, it will have wider implications for all educational situations, and there is special need for understanding methods of Christian worship.

ADMINISTRATION

Beyond the understanding of method is the administration of such a program in the local congregation. We shall need to see how the church is organized for Christian education with a comprehensive program reaching every member and with outreach to the community and to the world. We shall need to deal with the special groups: children, youth, young adults, married couples, families, adults, older people. Administration reaches out to the vacation church school and released time activities. The educational resources and lesson materials for such a program need careful selection, and leadership needs to be expertly trained. And in the end, we must find the means for evaluating the success of the educational program of the congregation.

This is our task. This book aims to help you in understanding more clearly the scope, aims, nature, means, and structure of Christian education.

Home, synagogue, and school system offered a well-rounded education to the Jewish boy of the first century. Later, when Jews were hounded and their synagogues and schools were closed, the Jewish family maintained the religious life, and education in the Torah continued.

EDUCATION IN JESUS' TIME

How Jesus was educated is open to conjecture. We may be certain that he was reared in a Jewish home, and thus was familiar with Jewish customs and teachings from his earliest years. It was his custom to attend the synagogue regularly. His close acquaintance with the Scriptures indicates that he must have had some formal schooling, for he was aware of the arguments used by the experts as well as with the content of the Scriptures and contemporary writings. He may have known Rabbinical Hebrew and Greek.[1] He also learned the carpenter's trade and probably knew well the economic conditions of the workmen of his day.

Jesus himself was known as a teacher. He used pithy, brief sayings and commandments; he used parables; he reflected the rhythm of Hebrew and Aramaic poetry. He varied his approach according to his listeners. Sometimes he was critical and hostile and even scathing with large crowds. He handled questions with piercing insight. He used fascinating stories with the curious listeners. He taught his disciples of the inner circle with intimacy.

He taught from a theological point of view, and his theology was always relevant, for it was in terms of the particular questions and needs of the group facing him. He found the "growing edge" of his hearers and led them on into richer and deeper loyalty to the Father. His parables were based on the life situations of the people, and they concluded with an appeal for action. Above all, he lived with the "disciples" (which means learners or apprentices), who learned not only from his words but also from the contagious radiance of his faith as he guided them into new adventures. In this sense, Jesus was

---

[1] See Chester C. McCown, *The Search for the Real Jesus* (New York: Charles Scribner's Sons, 1940), p. 136; Joseph Klausner, *Jesus of Nazareth* (New York: The Macmillan Company, 1925), pp. 234-35; John Wick Bowman, *The Intention of Jesus* (Philadelphia: Westminster Press, 1943), pp. 47-50.

a master teacher, whose methods are found in some present day educational philosophies.[2]

THE PRIMITIVE CHURCH

From the beginning there was a teaching church. On the first Pentecost, after some three thousand had been baptized, we read that "they devoted themselves to the teaching and the society of the apostles, the breaking of bread, and prayer" (Acts 2:42, G). The Gospels themselves grew out of the teaching and preaching of the fellowship. There was need to reinterpret the Hebrew Scriptures for Jewish converts and to show the meaning of the Gospel to those steeped in Greek culture.

Even before the Gospels were written, the apostles used at least five kinds of teaching: the Christian interpretation of Scriptures for converting and educating the Jews; the proclaiming of the Christian tradition, perhaps in the form of a brief creed learned as a preliminary to baptism; a similar teaching leading to a brief confession of faith; teaching the life and sayings of Jesus; moral instruction in "The Way" or in the two "Ways" of life versus death. Possibly there was separate instruction in the meaning of baptism and the Lord's Supper.[3]

Christian parents had responsibility for their families, and much teaching occurred in the home. "Fathers, do not provoke your children to anger, but bring them up in the discipline and instruction of the Lord" (Ephesians 6:4, RSV). Sherrill translates this same passage, "Nurture them in education and admonition of the Lord." [4]

The early church was aware of itself as a community of the Spirit. Inspiration in tongues was popular for a while, but soon dropped into the background as extravagance of emotion gave way to disciplined

---

[2] See Lewis J. Sherrill, *The Rise of Christian Education* (New York: The Macmillan Company, 1944), pp. 76-79, 85-86, 90-93. This is a full and accurate account of Christian education to A.D. 1400. See also Luther A. Weigle, *Jesus and the Educational Method* (Nashville: The Abingdon Press, 1939).

[3] See Lewis J. Sherrill, *The Rise of Christian Education,* pp. 144-53; also, Philip Henry Lotz, ed., *Orientation in Religious Education* (Nashville: Abingdon-Cokesbury Press, 1950), pp. 15-16.

[4] Lewis J. Sherrill, *The Rise of Christian Education,* p. 158; see *Interpreter's Bible,* X, 729-732.

thinking and conduct. The tradition loomed ever larger and soon became a written source of teaching. In the services of worship, there was the teaching portion known as the mass of the catechumens for those anticipating baptism, who left before the second part known as the mass of the faithful.

For several centuries, there was instruction outside the worship service to prepare men and women more carefully for baptism. There was opportunity to give instruction, to provide moral probation, and to offer a limited fellowship with other Christians. But as the Dark Ages came on, there was practically no formal instruction even during worship, and except for informal instruction by the priests, most knowledge came from a strange mixture of popular theology and superstition.

THE MEDIEVAL CHURCH

The monasteries had kept learning alive during the Dark Ages, especially through the copying and preserving of manuscripts. There were schools connected with the monastic orders, open to those who wished to become members. For the education of priests there were the schools associated with the cathedrals, offering the liberal arts plus special study in theology. By the close of the twelfth century, the universities had been founded and had become genuine centers of learning. At Bologna, for example, the great emphasis was on law, and at Paris the major subject was theology. Out of the teaching of such men as Peter Abelard (1079-1142) there developed a new concern for the place of reason, and though Abelard himself was not able to maintain a place in the church, his arguments became the center of later Scholasticism.

RENAISSANCE AND REFORMATION

The revival of learning associated with the rise of the universities was accelerated by the rediscovery of Aristotle through contact with the Arabs, and this in turn stimulated interest in Plato and Greek philosophy in general. The great synthesis in the *Summa Theologica* of Thomas Aquinas (1225-1274), whereby the Christian tradition and the philosophy of Aristotle were joined together in a system that today is the official position of the Roman Catholic Church, accelerated the interest in Greek and Roman culture.

In southern Europe, the Renaissance laid the foundation for the humanistic tradition in education, with its concern for esthetics, for the good life in this world, and for the wisdom of the ancients in Greece and Rome. It emphasized the rights of the individual and the goodness of the "natural man." It was a secular movement stressing the delights of living, the ideal of liberty, the free exercise of criticism, and, among those who found Christian morality too binding, a freedom from moral restraints. For education, the results were seen in the content of the curriculum, the rise of scientific thinking, and critical methods in the study of religion.

The Reformation was a rediscovery of Scripture, and was as radical in its way as the Renaissance rediscovery of Greek humanism. Centering in Martin Luther (1483-1546), who reacted against the moralism and legalism of Rome with its accompanying corruption, the New Testament faith of salvation by grace replaced the idea of salvation through merit. Luther was aided by the new means of communication and the printing press. Supported by the political and religious attitudes of the times, and building on the accumulated antipathy to Rome, he found himself the head of a new church. In 1555, the peace of Augsburg recognized the Protestant churches.

The impact of the Reformation is still being felt. Although the Reformers believed that all life should be controlled by the will of God, they made distinctions between church and state that led to these being thought of as separate spheres, and laid the groundwork for modern secularism.

The Protestant emphasis on the Bible as the people's book led to revolutionary changes in education. The Bible appeared in the languages of the people in Germany, Switzerland, England, and elsewhere. The vernacular appeared in the services of worship. It was essential that the people learn to read in order to understand God's Word, participate in the services, and read the writings of the Reformers. Preaching also revived and became a most effective tool of education. Teaching in the Christian family was encouraged, and small catechisms were prepared for children.

Most important of all was the establishment of Christian schools. Both Martin Luther and John Calvin (1509-1564) proposed plans for elementary, secondary, and university education. John Knox (1505-1572) made similar proposals in Scotland. The state was responsible along with the church for education, in Luther's view, and the tendency was to combine humanistic and religious education within one system for the whole of life. This impulse carried over into American life.

AMERICAN COLONIAL PERIOD

The dominant educational theory of early American life was a transplanted Protestantism. Although a service according to the Book of Common Prayer was held in Drake's Bay, near San Francisco, in 1579, the colonies of Virginia and Massachusetts were the first to be established. In New England there was a tendency to find the basis for civil law in Biblical moral codes, and the Bible was of course the supreme authority for one's beliefs. The law of the state required "that all masters and families do, once a week at least, catechize their children and servants in the grounds and principles of religion, and if any be unable to do so much, that then, at the least, they procure such children or apprentices to learn some orthodox catechism, without book, that they may be able to answer the questions that shall be propounded to them out of such catechisms by their parents or masters, or any selectman, when they shall have called them to a trial of what they have learned of this kind." [5] The sermons were long and authoritative in fields of theology, morals, and politics, and were the chief means of education.

During the first generation of life in New England, concern for religious education remained on a high plane. The urgent need for an educated clergy is marked by the founding of Harvard University in 1636, with William and Mary, Yale, and others following soon afterward. There were nine colleges before the Revolution. It should be noted that the universities of Mexico and Lima were established at even earlier dates under Roman Catholic auspices. Religious teaching was normally a part of the regular education of the young, and parents took their responsibilities seriously.

Conditions were not favorable to high educational standards. At-

[5] E. P. Cubberley, *Readings in Public Education in the United States* (Boston: Houghton Mifflin Co., 1934), p. 19.

tendance was irregular, and often the schools operated for only a few months out of the year. The effects of pioneer life, Indian warfare, political and ecclesiastical controversies, economic and agricultural difficulties, and exclusiveness in the churches led to a generation of parents who themselves had only a meagre education. Not all of the early settlers had been religious, and the influence of the indifferent was felt.

Until the Great Awakening in 1734, the decline in religious teaching had been serious. The general impact of the revival was good; but it did not last long, and there was another period of lethargy lasting until after the Revolutionary War. In the meantime, Baptists and Episcopalians had moved into New England, upsetting the monopoly of the Congregationalists.

The rise and fall of concern for religious education was experienced throughout the colonies. The same theological viewpoints were held, with children thought of as depraved beings even when they had been baptized. The Anglican colonies, especially Virginia, did not go in for sudden conversions, but they failed to meet the children's needs in either education or worship. In all the colonies, diversity of belief and the rise of denominations led to a religious pluralism that made religious teaching seem sectarian.

Before the War of Independence, most of the conditions that were to lead to the banishing of religious teaching from the schools were already in existence. The favored denominations were losing their supremacy, the identity of church membership and political rights was being broken down, and religious tolerance was becoming a political and educational necessity.[6]

RELIGIOUS EDUCATION IN THE UNITED STATES

The formation of a nation out of the thirteen colonies resulted in necessary changes in the pre-revolutionary pattern. Whereas each colony had a dominant religious tradition, the national picture was of variety. The religious freedom described in "The Bill of Rights"

---

[6] See George Stewart, Jr., *A History of Religious Education in Connecticut to the Middle of the Nineteenth Century* (New Haven: Yale University Press, 1924); Sandford Fleming, *Children and Puritanism* (New Haven: Yale University Press, 1933); Clifton H. Brewer, *A History of Religious Education in the Episcopal Church to 1835* (New Haven: Yale University Press, 1924).

made support of a particular sect unconstitutional, and this carried over to state laws. Even where there was a desire to support religious schools with public money, the rise of public schools made it impossible to pay for two competing systems.

There were probably four major causes for the elimination of religion from the curricula of most state supported schools. (1) The first was that the psychology of the Revolutionary War made the breaking of traditions particularly easy. The dominant religious force among the founding fathers reflected the deism of the times with its suspicion of the political power of the churches. In Europe religion and education had been closely related, and the reaction against a state church was strong among the colonists.

(2) The second was that the scope of America's educational interests widened to include many technical and cultural courses. Religion, not being in immediate demand, began to be neglected. The influence of the Renaissance was stronger than that of the Reformation, which assisted in the separation of church and state.

(3) The third factor was the rise of the frontier, with its hard life and its demands upon the initiative and ingenuity of the individual. Organized religion followed the frontier too slowly and was unable to meet the changing needs fast enough. The varieties of religion added to the confusion. Little known sects, with pentecostal leanings and working independently of the authorities, made large advances among the frontier folk.

(4) The fourth and probably determining factor was that denominational jealousies spread rapidly. The question of *what kind* of Christianity became more important than the *fact* of Christianity, and in 1827 Massachusetts passed a law forbidding the teaching of sectarian religion in the public schools. Later, when Roman Catholicism became a rival to Protestantism, the issue became even sharper. Contributing to the general breakdown of religious instruction in the schools was the rising secularism of the time. The significance of John Locke's philosophy as a basis for political action was recognized by church and state alike, and his educational theories were based on the role of reason. Jean Jacques Rousseau's romantic love of nature, combined with his view of the natural goodness of man, led him to suggest that religious training should begin at the age of fifteen or even later. Religious instruction, therefore, tended to be based on natural principles, and where the secularists were in

control traditional religious teachings were suspect. The secular public school began in the first part of the nineteenth century against this background, and because the churches were divided among themselves, they were impotent to do much about it. Horace Mann asked why a child should be taught about the future life when he needed to know so much to live fully in this one.

SUNDAY SCHOOLS

The Sunday School movement is generally associated with the name of Robert Raikes, of Gloucester, England, who in 1780 began gathering under-privileged children into his home on Sundays for instruction by paid teachers. Silas Todd had a similar program about the same time at Wesley's Foundry in London, where the main concern was learning to read the Bible. William Elliott, a Methodist in Virginia, conducted a program on his estate for white children, servants, and slaves before 1790. The Methodist Conference in Charleston, South Carolina, also had Sunday schools under way about this time. "The First Day or Sunday School Society" was organized in Philadelphia in 1791 under the leadership of Bishop William White to aid ignorant and lawless children, following the plan of Raikes. These schools were more philanthropic than religious, and when public and private instruction in secular subjects became more prevalent, they either lost their popularity or moved in the direction of religious instruction for all.

These early schools often were conducted throughout the day on Sunday, with time out for religious services. They gave instruction in reading and writing, and combined this with the use of a catechism and the Bible. Emphasis was on memory work, with no grading of materials in most instances, although some catechisms strove for simplicity of statement. The process was rather dull, and reward tickets were introduced as early as 1811 to stimulate interest.

The Sunday school became a useful tool for the instruction of all children, and by the end of the War of 1812 conditions were favorable for expansion. Various societies were organized, at first on a city basis, for the promotion of Sabbath schools. By 1824 the Sunday and Adult School Union was operating in 17 states with 723 schools, 7,300 teachers, and 49,619 scholars. This group became the

American Sunday School Union in 1824, and for the next 40 years it pioneered in establishing schools and preparing materials. By 1830, there were 6,000 schools and 400,000 scholars.

But denominational rivalries broke up the Union and it lost its effectiveness. As early as 1826 the Episcopalians were identifying their own schools with the local congregation on a denominational basis. The Presbyterians in 1846 began a movement to establish parochial and secondary schools and church-controlled colleges, with the movement petering out in 1870. The first Roman Catholic parochial school was erected in Philadelphia in 1782, and the system became official in 1829. By 1840 there were 200 parochial schools in operation. With the public school a lost domain, with parochial schools seemingly impractical for Protestants, and with the family having abdicated much of its responsibility, only the Sunday school remained.

By the time of the War between the States, certain principles had been established. The Sunday school was a lay enterprise based on nonprofessional teaching, it was for children of all social classes as far as any denomination avoided class consciousness, its age limits had been extended to the very young and to adults, and the time schedule had been reduced to one or two hours.

Although the Sunday school was now associated with the church, it was only an adjunct of parish life. The curriculum was specifically religious and the content was primarily the Bible. Unrestricted memorization of unrelated Bible passages, with the emphasis on quantity, became the rule. As time went on, there was some selection of passages by the teacher, and privately published lessons provided a degree of order and value in the content to be used. This was followed by a flood of denominational materials pointing in many different directions; and though for the most part this added to the confusion, it also pointed to a crude grading of material.

Between 1860 and 1900, the old Union having dropped into the background but continuing its existence, there was a renewal of the convention idea, which had begun about 1832. There were sessions in 1859, 1869, and 1872, and in 1875 the Canadians joined workers from the United States. A World Sunday School Convention began meeting in 1889; and though the official leadership is now in other hands, the convention idea is still effective for less official exchanging of information.

As early as 1831 there was a demand for the training of teachers, a movement that spread rapidly, although it did not reach the theological seminaries till 1906, when courses in religious education were first offered for the clergy. Out of the confusion came various kinds of uniform lessons (in 1873) and new teacher's helps. There was one lesson for all ages in all schools, with exposition of the lessons in all publications that cooperated. Though the uniform lessons are still available and have been improved, they have not been favored by professional educators for a long time. In some ways, the uniform lessons had been a backward step, although they had standardized content and made the educational process easier for the teachers.

In the early days of the Sunday school, children had been theologically characterized as sinners who could not hope for redemption until they were old enough to confess faith in Christ. They heard of the tortures of the damned, and were told that there was nothing they could do about it. Much of this theology was inhuman and psychologically dangerous, for it built up the attitudes of frustration and guilt without offering the hope of redemption. They sang,

> O what pleasure 'tis to see
> Christians in harmony agree!
> To teach the rising race to know
> They're born in sin, expos'd to wo.[7]

In 1846, Horace Bushnell (1802-1876) reacted strongly against this kind of teaching. Bushnell's *Christian Nurture* presented a sane and balanced view of the situation, but to his age he seemed a radical, and his position was vigorously opposed. His major thesis has been the guiding light of all modern religious education. It led to the emphasis on the needs of the child, to the insight that a child should be reached at his "growing edge," to the idea of the growth of the total personality as an integrated whole, to the concept of evangelism as a decision within the community of church and home, and to the place of the home as basic to Christian nurture. Horace Bushnell was the great emancipator of children from a devastating repression and overstimulated consciousness of guilt; he was the apostle of the normal

[7] Quoted by Clifton Brewer, *A History of Religious Education in the Protestant Episcopal Church to 1835* (New Haven: Yale University Press, 1924), p. 174.

child in a Christian home; and he believed that Christian beliefs could be stated simply and in terms of human experience.[8]

Although acceptance of Bushnell's ideas was slow in taking hold, he is rightly called the father of the religious education movement, and events in the twentieth century vindicated almost every point of his thinking.

Many lay leaders held out for uniform lessons; but by 1884 the professionals had had enough, and in 1892 the graded Blakeslee series appeared. As religious education moved into the twentieth century, conditions were such that new advances from many fields could be incorporated into the thinking of professional leaders and through them into the conventions and organizations.

THE TWENTIETH CENTURY

During most of the nineteenth century there were advances in Biblical scholarship, but owing partially to the uniform lessons and conservative lay leadership, none of this reached the educational programs of most churches. By the beginning of the new century many seminaries provided the new approach to the Biblical study, and some ministers were willing to pass it on to their congregations. New discoveries in manuscripts, more accurate translations such as the American Standard Version in 1901, and new theories concerning authorship, date, and situations of the Biblical writings led to a re-evaluation of the place of the Bible in religious education.

Because the Bible has always been the center of Protestant religious education, these new discoveries were greeted with apprehension, concern, or enthusiasm, the reaction depending to a great extent on the theology of the individual. Conservative response was strong enough to bar these studies from some lesson materials for over half a century, but very early in the century many books for lay people and church school lessons incorporated the findings of the Biblical scholars. A new view of the authority and use of the Bible arose, and when combined with the educational theories of the time, this led to

[8] Bushnell's "Dissertation on Language as Related to Thought and Spirit," which prefaced his volume on *God in Christ* (1851), is remarkably apt today. See also Sandford Fleming, *Children and Puritanism* (New Haven: Yale University Press, 1933), pp. 185-208.

a view of the Bible as a tool for gaining religious insight rather than as an end in itself.

CHILD PSYCHOLOGY

A second factor influencing Christian education was the rise of child psychology, with its vindication of Horace Bushnell's *Christian Nurture*. The growth of the child became a central factor in religious education, and no longer was the child thought of as a viper, a rattlesnake, or guilty of total depravity. Sin was not destroyed as a religious concept, except in extreme forms of thinking, but it was recast in terms of conscious intention. Further understanding of the capacity of the child led to a careful grading of the lessons. Disciplinary problems were understood in terms of what a child naturally does at a certain age. The psychology of adolescence threw new light on the emotional upheavals of conversion, on the tendency to withdraw from the Church, and on the "age of temporary insanity." Child psychology became a strong ally of the church, and no longer did Christian educators have to rely entirely on rule of thumb and intuitions in dealing with children.

PSYCHOLOGY OF RELIGION

The rise of psychology of religion as an influential discipline at the turn of the century was a third factor in the changes taking place in Christian education. Most influential was William James' *Varieties of Religious Experience* (1902), but the writings of E. D. Starbuck, George Stratton, George A. Coe, and many others helped to open new channels. The experiences of the mystic, the power of prayer, the effects of conversion, the nature of faith, and many other religious experiences were charted, catalogued, and understood better than before. Worship came in for careful scrutiny by James B. Pratt and Willard L. Sperry. Because the psychology of religion was based strictly on human experience of the divine, religion was seen more clearly in its relation to human beings. It became easier for the religious educators to align religious beliefs with experience, to center their teachings in the actual and potential experiences of the age groups, and to make more clear the relation between belief and action.

Theologians made use of these findings, with perhaps the most thorough study being Douglas C. Macintosh's *Theology as an Empirical Science* (1919), and this kind of theology found its expression in some church school lessons. Secular psychologists such as Freud and Jung dealt with these same problems from the standpoint of psychoanalysis, and their insights were in turn used by clinical psychologists of religion in the field of pastoral psychology. In recent years, such men as Basil Yeaxlee have traced the development of religion in the child with references to psychoanalysis but in terms of a well-rounded psychological understanding of religion as a development of the filial relationship. Yeaxlee's *Religion and the Growing Mind* (1939) brings religious education and psychology of religion together in a fruitful interpretation.

EDUCATIONAL PSYCHOLOGY

The fourth area of scientific discovery was in educational psychology. The theories of John Dewey, especially his idea of "education as a social process," were taken into the thinking of all competent religious educators. Dewey's most significant book was probably *Democracy and Education* (1916), and George Albert Coe followed the next year with his *Social Theory of Religious Education* (1917). Coe had learned from Froebel and Parker as well as from Dewey, and he emphasized the growing experience of the child within the social process. He built on the significance of religious experience as a means of leading the child to understand the meanings of life, and he was suspicious of indoctrination. The Bible became a sourcebook for the revealing and revaluing of religious values. This meant a psychologically rather than a logically ordered curriculum, for the psychology of the child in his social situation became the focal point from which materials were selected.

Development of this thinking continued among the leaders of the Religious Education Association and the International Council of Religious Education. The latter worked out its philosophy under the leadership of William Clayton Bower. His committee worked closely with a group of six outstanding leaders in the field of general education. The emphasis was on the enrichment of experience, on the use of subject matter to provide meaning and guidance for experience, and on the place of the church as an ideal community in which the learner participates. Activities of learning should be adapted to the learner, filled with problems that cause him to grow, shared in a social situation, and related to his other experiences. It was felt that a new curriculum was essential for achieving these goals.

Within this report was the theological assumption that what is Christian can be discovered through educational practices, rather than from what is already known. It was this assumption, rather than the educational policies, that led to difficulties later on.

By 1930 Paul H. Vieth, who was director of research and service, had developed seven objectives that were incorporated in the International Curriculum Guide published in 1932, *Book One: Principles and Objectives of Christian Education,* which summarized the seven volumes of the original report.[9]

LIBERAL THEOLOGY

As religious education came of age, it built on the foundations of new discoveries in psychology and Biblical studies, but it also was guided by the dominant theology of the period. William James not only influenced psychology and philosophy, but also wrote, "Let empiricism once become associated with religion, as hitherto, through some strange misunderstanding, it has been associated with irreligion, and I believe that a new era of religion as well as of philosophy will be ready to begin." [10] Until the mid-1930's it seemed as if James were right, for the great names of that period were empiricists, holding to the liberal doctrine that we can find truth by seeking it in experience, and that by being objective we can establish doctrine that is intellectually respectable.

No one who could be called "neo-Orthodox" appeared in Vergilius Ferm's two volumes on *Contemporary American Theology,* published in 1932-33, and in 1936 Henry N. Wieman and Bernard E. Meland spent only 18 pages on this movement in *American Philosophies of Religion.*

---

[9] See Harrison S. Elliott, *Can Religious Education Be Christian?* (New York: The Macmillan Company, 1940), pp. 56-62; William Clayton Bower and Percy Roy Hayward, *Protestantism Faces Its Educational Task Together* (Chicago: National Council of Churches, 1949), pp. 60-62, 206-209.

[10] William James, *A Pluralistic Universe* (New York: Longmans, Green and Co., 1909), p. 314.

Most of the religious educators grew up and developed their theological orientation in the hey-day of liberalism, as reflected in Coe's *What Is Christian Education?* (1929). In 1940, Harrison Elliott was making a strong battle against the inroads of the dialectical theology of Karl Barth and Emil Brunner and defending a positive and liberal faith in *Can Religious Education Be Christian?* (1940). But already the pendulum was swinging in a new direction, and the voices of Protestant theology echoed those of the Continental theologians. Theological questions that the religious educators could not answer were appearing in the religious journals, and H. Shelton Smith's *Faith and Nurture* (1941) lumped the theories of the liberal religious educators together with John Dewey's humanistic position.

THE CHANGING THEOLOGICAL CLIMATE

This changing theological climate has altered the emphases of some religious educators, has led to lesson materials more concerned with theology, and has caused a rethinking of the relation of theology to educational method. But though psychology of religion is no longer a subject in itself, having given way to the psychology of personality, clinical psychology, and pastoral counseling, the findings of child psychology and the psychology of learning are more significant than ever and need to be aligned more closely to the procedures of religious education. Biblical scholarship has continued to advance, and it is easier to see the relevance of the Bible for Christian education against the background of today's theology than in previous times.

The International Council of Religious Education was concerned with these changes, and a committee under the leadership of Luther A. Weigle brought out a revised statement of basic philosophy in 1940, *Christian Education Today.* After pointing to the extremes of theology, one of which placed the full responsibility on man whereas the other tended to deny the value of religious education, it said that religious education should seek a middle way. Although the International Council of Religious Education could not impose a theology on its member churches, it had the job of reinterpreting the Christian faith in terms of today's needs and experiences.

In 1944, a large committee began a series of meetings that led to reports, later summarized by Paul H. Vieth in *The Church and*

Christian Education (1947). These reports combined theological and educational insights and marked a significant advance in educational philosophy. "The foundations of Christian education are to be found in the nature and condition of man who is to be educated, in the faith which the church professes, and in the principles of education which define how learning takes place." [11]

In one form, the problem was stated as the relationship between content and method. An attempt was made to relate these in terms of a relevant theology that would bridge the gap in terms of the meaning of Christian living. It is just as important to have a sound theology behind the kindergarten lessons as behind the adult discussion program, and the problem is that of communication so that the Gospel comes alive in the lives of the members of the class.

James D. Smart thinks we should analyze the actual theologies underlying the confused curriculum resources of today, and then work toward a true theology. He has taken an important step in this direction in his *The Teaching Ministry of the Church.*[12] The understanding of community in its Christian context is essential if we are to understand clearly what the orders of life do to people.[13] The *Seabury Series,* derived from experimental teaching situations in which the emphasis is on family worship and the quality of life of the Christian community as the context in which Christian education takes place, is the first series of lesson materials to take these insights and to use them in a dynamic sense.[14]

RELIGIOUS EDUCATION

Courses in religious education became popular in most seminaries during the first half of the twentieth century. The kind of thinking emanating from George A. Coe, William C. Bower, and Harrison Elliott provided leadership that emphasized a liberal theology and progressive methods. Other leaders, including Luther A. Weigle,

[11] Paul H. Vieth, *The Church and Christian Education* (St. Louis: Bethany Press, 1947), p. 52.

[12] Philadelphia: Westminster Press, 1954; see pp. 61-67.

[13] See Howard Grimes, "Is Religious Education Obsolete?" in *Religion in Life,* Summer 1954, p. 384-395; Frederick W. Dillistone, *The Structure of the Divine Society* (Philadelphia: Westminster Press, 1951), especially chap. 12; Emil Brunner, *The Misunderstanding of the Church* (Philadelphia: Westminster Press, 1953),

[14] Greenwich: Seabury Press, 1955.

avoided extreme positions and always kept in mind the essential nature of the Christian heritage as received through the historic church. Weigle says:

> The heart of the Christian faith is the gospel—the good tidings of the kingdom of God. The gospel is not merely that the kingdom of God is in the future, near or far, but that the kingdom of God is here. God reigns, God acts. God manifests his will in the frustrations of human folly and wrong, as well as in the wisdom and strength to be gained by those who seek first his kingdom and his righteousness. . . . The Christian faith . . . holds that history has direction, and is moving under the hand of God toward a goal.[15]

> There is no real distinction between evangelism and Christian education, for "all that we do is within limits and by powers that are ordered and sustained by God."[16]

Men and women began to make religious education a profession, and this led to the demand for further training. Some were ordained ministers of education in churches; others were lay directors. Many found their way into the educational departments of denominations, worked for councils of churches, and entered interdenominational agencies. There were specialists in children's work, youth work, college work, young adults, adults, leadership training, and in work among specialized groups including the rural and isolated peoples. Special skills were needed, and in some cases training beyond what the seminaries offered was obtained in schools of education.

Churches strengthened their denominational departments of religious education. They improved their lesson materials and other educational resources. They put leadership training teams in the field. They brought in specialists to help with particular problems.

Although the Sunday morning hour is not to be belittled when we count the numbers of boys and girls who learned all they know of Christ under strict time limitations, dissatisfaction with the traditional Sunday hour has led to various kinds of expanded programs. More church schools now open at 9:15 A.M., which allows time for an adequate worship service and a class period of from 40 to 50 minutes. Others make use of the 11 o'clock hour for their worship, and have an hour or more instruction before church. Some have used "unified plans" between the hours of 10 and 12, and some have,

---

[15] Luther Allan Weigle, *Jesus and the Educational Method* (New York: Abingdon Press, 1939), p. 115.

[16] *Ibid.*, pp. 119-120.

because of geography, been simplified to just one hour for everyone. Spectacular results have been obtained with a special program for high school students, running on Sundays for two to three hours in the late afternoon and evening; this plan utilizes the most effective members of the staff at a time when no other demands are made on them, and incorporates parental cooperation into preparation of an evening supper.

Use of time other than that provided on Sunday is illustrated by week-day classes, vacation church schools, and summer conferences.

Another recent development is leadership training. The major problem in the Protestant church school is that teaching is in the hands of the laity. This function of the priesthood of the laity is a great resource, but often lay people are untrained in theology, educational theory and method, and the knowledge of children. These lacks have hampered the educational effectiveness of the church within the narrow limitations of available time, and the inadequacy of the teachers has been reflected in the "crutches" provided to make teaching "easy" in many series of lessons.

Experiments in recent years have re-established Horace Bushnell's thesis of the significance of the Christian home. When Hugh Hartshorne and Mark May published their *Studies in Deceit* (1928), it showed that there was very little correlation between Sunday school attendance and ethical decisions. But the research of Ernest M. Ligon has indicated a high degree of correlation between parental guidance and Christian character. A report of the International Council of Religious Education makes this point clear: "Perhaps if we had spent as much time and money in helping parents to do their job as Christian educators and in training pastors and key workers in the local Church as we have spent upon the production of new types of curriculum and the promotion of various schemes for raising the Church by its bootstraps, we should now be less alarmed." [17]

The concern for the family unit as central to the educational program of the church led to a rethinking of worship. Much worship had been of the assembly type, meeting informally in rooms by departments, led by lay superintendents. In some cases this was very effective, and in others it resembled the Tower of Babel. Three reactions against this should be noted. The first was to bring the children into

[17] Quoted in my *A Guide for Church School Teachers,* 2nd ed. (Greenwich: Seabury Press, 1947), p. 16.

the church for a genuine service of worship geared to their needs, either by departments or as a group. The second was to make the service an experience in family worship, intelligible to children of all ages but including parents. The third reaction was to make graded worship as effective as possible.

The interest in worship pointed anew to the pastor as one of the most important educators. When the service was moved to the church, often the pastor found himself responsible for the story or the sermonette, or for the entire service. In many cases, the minister began to see his responsibility to the children and established a relationship that brought children into a realization that the church is a redemptive community. The Eakins' *The Pastor and the Children* (1947) underscores this responsibility and makes even more important the pastor's training in religious education in seminary.

THE THRESHOLD OF A NEW AGE

The educator of today must be competent in educational psychology, developmental psychology, the sociology of learning, and many other scientific disciplines. But these studies, important as they are for insight and method, do not provide the goals, establish the truth, or describe the person we are to educate. For this we must turn to the theology of the church and, in the light of our own denominational loyalties and of the amount of freedom our denominations permit, work out our own salvation with fear and trembling. In the light of our personal faith and system of beliefs, the theology of our Christian maturity must guide us in selecting the goals and establishing the beliefs, and in relating both goals and beliefs to our scientific knowledge. Only by such a combination may we hope to become adequate educators within the Christian tradition.

CHAPTER 3

WHAT IS CHRISTIAN EDUCATION?

DEFINITIONS of education usually reflect a whole educational philosophy, involving descriptions not only of what happens in experience but also what goals are desired and what techniques are used. Education is a process whereby the accumulated wisdom of society is passed on to its members, and, at the same time, a process whereby members of a society reach out for new knowledge. Education may involve a general interpretation of the values of a culture, a specialized and limited appreciation of certain aspects of a culture, or intensified learning that in some respects may transcend a culture.

Plato (427–347 B.C.) believed that harmony of the soul is the goal of education. "Now I mean by education," he said, "that training which is given by suitable habits to the first instincts of virtue in children," [1] these virtues being implanted before they can understand the nature of them.

Behind the Greek concept was the assumption that a man could achieve virtue through knowledge. The impact of Christian thinking that man needs God's grace because he is a sinner made it clear that education by itself is insufficient. Thomas Aquinas (1225–1274) sought to bring these two views together, and his synthesis was maintained with only slight variations during the Renaissance and Reformation. Education was the imparting of knowledge through the symbols of the spoken and written word.

With the rise of naturalism and the sciences, leaders such as Johann Amos Comenius (1592–1670) began placing the emphasis on learning through the senses. John Locke (1632–1704), in his *Essay Con-*

---

[1] Plato, *Laws,* II, Sec. 653.

cerning Human Understanding, criticized all innate ideas. The full power of this educational insight was lost, however, because of the belief that the mind is passive.

Johann Pestalozzi (1746–1827) was one of the first to seek the meaning of education through observation. Jean Jacques Rousseau (1712–1778) placed the emphasis on feeling and doing. Friedrich Froebel (1782–1852) saw the significance of self-development in terms of more than intellect, and this led him to see that a child's play had educational value. He saw that a child went through "stages," and out of this view came the kindergarten.

The rise of empiricism in philosophy and psychology led to further insights. William James (1842–1910) insisted that experience is continuous and that the connectedness of events is as much a part of experience as the events themselves. "Education," said James, "in short, cannot be better described than by calling it *the organization of acquired habits of conduct and tendencies to behavior.*" [2]

John Dewey (1859–1952) used the insights of empiricism and instrumentalism in his now classic definition:

> Education is a constant reorganizing or reconstructing of experience. It has all the time an immediate end, and so far as activity is educative, it reaches that end—the direct transformation of the quality of experience. Infancy, youth, adult life—all stand on the same educative level in the sense that what is really *learned* at any and every stage of experience constitutes the value of that experience, and in the sense that it is the chief business of life at every point to make living thus contribute to an enrichment of its own perceptible meaning.[3]

Dewey is quite clear that education is based on personal experience.

> Everything depends upon the *quality* of the experience which is had. . . . Unless experience is so conceived that the result is a plan for deciding upon subject-matter, upon methods of instruction and discipline, and upon material equipment and social organization of the school, it is wholly up in the air. What is needed is a coherent *theory* of experience, affording positive direction to selection and organization of appropriate educational methods and materials.[4]

---

[2] William James, *Talks to Teachers* (New York: Henry Holt and Co., 1899), p. 29.

[3] John Dewey, *Democracy and Education* (New York: The Macmillan Company, 1916), p. 89.

[4] John Dewey, *Experience and Education* (New York: The Macmillan Company, 1938), pp. 16, 17, 21. Copyright 1938 by Kappa Delta Pi.

The learner exists in a community. "If education is considered as a process of growing up within the life of a group," says Marjorie Reeves, "it is immediately clear that this goes on all the time." [5] The impact of person upon person, even when mediated through books and projects, is the crucial point in all education. This personal element transcends our educational philosophies, so that we learn from great persons even when the philosophy is wrong.

LEARNING

Learning occurs when a person responds to a situation to achieve mastery of a problem, satisfaction of curiosity, relief of frustration, knowledge of facts, or insights into the meaning of life. Behind the process is some kind of motivation, and out of it come various degrees of satisfaction.

John Dollard and Neal E. Miller have approached the fundamentals of learning by considering drive, cue, response, and reinforcement. The drive is the motive, the cue is the stimulus, the response is an act or thought, and the reinforcement is the satisfaction or reward.

Every person has certain *drives* that must be satisfied. When one is deprived of satisfaction of these drives, they are strengthened and express themselves in various ways. Learned or acquired drives depend on the primary drives such as hunger, thirst, and reactions to pain and cold. The process of socialization provides many different combinations of drives and responses. The learned and primary drives often compete with one another.

The *cue* determines the response of the learner. It provides the when, where, and how of the learner's response. All kinds of combinations of cues are possible, and the pattern of the various cues determines the response. Unless a cue is noticed, it has no value, and therefore learning to notice is important. When the pupil has learned to pay attention, guidance is a real possibility.

The first *response* is crucial, for if it is correct it eliminates much trial and error. The selection of the right cue initiates the desired order of response, but this is not as simple as it seems, for the learner brings his own previous experiences to bear on his response. As he

[5] Marjorie Reeves, *Growing Up in a Modern Society* (London: University of London Press, 1952), p. 11.

learns, he alters the order of response, eliminating whatever does not bear directly on the goal. New patterns are developed, and novelty enters the process.

Strong motivation and stimulus are not sufficient in themselves. Even constant repetition does not lead to learning if the act or thought fails to give satisfaction. Even what has been learned moves toward extinction if there is no reinforcement, although it is easier to recall what has been learned than to learn something entirely new.

Reinforcement is whatever strengthens the tendency to respond to a stimulus. It may be decrease in pain or increase in pleasure. Attention, praise, and status are essential for every learner. The atmosphere and attitudes within the group prevent or provide reinforcement.

Learning is both conscious and unconscious, and the same principles apply to both. In many cases the learner does not see the connection between his behavior and the original stimuli, either because his responses were learned in infancy or because he picked up certain reactions, prejudices, and mannerisms without clearly connecting the response with the reinforcement.

The satisfaction must be immediate if the cue-response connection is to be strengthened. The present experience is life itself, a never-to-be-repeated opportunity to respond to a situation that makes life meaningful *now*. The mature teacher must see this connection, for only in this sense is the present a preparation for the future.[6]

There is no sure-fire method of establishing the right kind of relationship between teacher and pupils. Methods are tools that may be used, just as two sticks may be rubbed together to start a fire, but the condition of the sticks has much to do with whether a fire will occur no matter how skillfully they are rubbed. Many approaches are possible, but in the long run, interest increases as the pupil masters the subject matter and sees its relevance to his needs and to the questions he is capable of asking.[7]

THE CURRICULUM

"Curriculum," which originally meant a race course, is the path

[6] See John Dollard and Neal E. Miller, *Personality and Psychotherapy* (New York: McGraw-Hill Book Co., 1950), pp. 25-124. See also Neal E. Miller and John Dollard, *Social Learning and Imitation* (New Haven: Yale University Press, 1941), pp. 1-90.

[7] See Chapter 10.

traversed by pupil and teacher in reaching a desired objective. It may be a pathway over which many others have traveled, or it may be the opening of a road through new terrain. It may be going somewhere, or it may be aimless as it wanders through a maze toward an undefined goal. It has a heirarchy of values that is open to constant re-evaluation, and it has a theory of knowledge that stands or falls on the basis of an adequate philosophy.

The basic curriculum is the whole of life, but the term is normally restricted to learning experiences under some kind of control by a responsible institution. "The curriculum becomes all of the child's life for which the school is responsible." [8] William Clayton Bower formulated a definition, which the International Council of Religious Education adopted in 1930: *"the curriculum of Christian religious education is the experience of the learner under guidance."* [9]

Religious educators have accepted this interpretation, insisting that "method consists in bringing about those conditions under which enrichment and control of experience take place." [10] The subject matter for such a curriculum develops from experience, utilizing the actual situation as well as the past experiences of the learners and teacher. Systematized and recorded knowledge from the past is brought to bear on the concerns of the present, so that the curriculum becomes a means for living meaningfully *now* and in the future.

This means that we "teach not so much things as the meaning of things." [11] As far back as 1903, in *The Child and the Curriculum,* John Dewey wrote that the problem of the teacher differs from that of the scientist, for the teacher

> . . . is concerned with the subject matter of the science as *representing a given stage and phase of the development of experience.* His problem is that of inducing a vital and personal experiencing. Hence, what concerns him, as teacher, is the ways in which that subject may become part of experience; what there is in the child's present that is usable with reference to it; how such elements can be used; how his own knowledge of the subject matter may assist in interpreting the child's needs and doings, and determine the medium in which

[8] John S. Brubacher, *Modern Philosophies of Education* (New York: McGraw-Hill Book Co., 1950), p. 226.

[9] *International Curriculum Guide, Book I* (Chicago: International Council of Religious Education, 1932, 1935), p. 18.

[10] *International Curriculum Guide,* I, 21.

[11] John Dewey, *How We Think* (Boston: D. C. Heath & Co., 1933), p. 236.

> the child should be placed in order that his growth may be properly directed. He is concerned, not with subject matter as such, but with the subject matter as a related factor in a total and growing experience. Thus to see it is to psychologize it.[12]

There are no fixed points in such a curriculum, but it is alive. The order is psychological rather than logical, and the long-range planning is in terms of what normally happens to a child.

SIGNIFICANCE FOR CHRISTIAN EDUCATION

The developments we have been summarizing occurred within the field of secular education. They have arisen from psychological, sociological, biological, and philosophical insights and not from theology. Yet most of these ideas have been taken over by religious educators, because the ways of learning do not change with the subject matter.

The question here is the *source* of educational theory. If Christianity adopts secular theories without questioning them, it will be working for secular ends. Teaching based on an uncritical acceptance of Dewey's educational theory and view of the universe will point students toward a Dewey world-view rather than toward a Christian view of life.

Christian educational theory must not be a footnote to secular discoveries. The goals and values of Christian education are derived from Christian theology and not from secular methodology. From a theological perspective, educational theories and methods are to be evaluated and used within the framework of Christian faith.

This is not to belittle the discoveries and theories of secular educators, but to recognize their value in the light of Christian standards. Children, whether they are Christian or not, learn in the same way, respond to similar stimuli, have common interests, share the same capacities and faculties of mind, and develop along certain predictable lines. Christians can ignore such facts at their peril. Coe and Bower and Elliott are right in using Dewey's insights, even though the theological position of today is different from that of Coe's time.

---

[12] Reprinted from *The Child and the Curriculum,* by John Dewey, pp. 29-30, by permission of The University of Chicago Press. Copyright 1903 by University of Chicago.

Some religious educators have espoused the philosophy of secular education almost to the exclusion of Christian theology. A few have preferred a naturalistic point of view. The majority of Christian educators, however, have sought to keep abreast of developments in both theology and education and have attempted to develop a theory that uses the insights of both. This problem of rethinking both theology and educational theory is kept in focus throughout this book.[13]

RELIGION

There are some who say that religion cannot be taught.[14] Yet religion claims to be based on the truth of revelation and discovery, and therefore its knowledge is available to all who seek it. It is a way of living meaningfully that is learned within the community of believers. It is not philosophy, although it is subject to the critical evaluations of the philosophic mind. William Temple points out that "you can get out of philosophy just what you put in – rearranged no doubt, set in order and rendered comprehensible; but while the machine may determine the size and shape of the emergent sausage, it cannot determine the ingredients." [15]

Temple goes on to say that if you start with what is measurable, that is all you will get out of it. "Philosophy seeks knowledge for the sake of understanding, while Religion seeks knowledge for the sake of worship. The province claimed by both is the entire field of human experience." This leads him to his most important distinction: *"The primary assurances of Religion are the ultimate questions of Philosophy."* Religion, in its higher forms, is assured that "Spirit is a true source of all initiation of processes, . . . all existence finds its source in a Supreme Reality of which the nature is Spirit, . . . between that Spirit and ourselves there can be, and to some extent already is, true fellowship, at least such as is involved in our conscious dependence on

[13] See H. Shelton Smith, *Faith and Nurture* (New York: Charles Scribner's Sons, 1941) for a critical appraisal of the theology of religious educators.

[14] See my *A Guide for Church School Teachers* (Greenwich: Seabury Press, 1947), pp. 17-21, for reasons why religion can be taught.

[15] William Temple, *Nature, Man and God* (London: Macmillan & Co., Ltd., 1934), p. 13. By permission of Mrs. William Temple and Macmillan & Co., Ltd., London.

that Spirit." [16] This is quite an assumption on philosophical grounds, but all higher religions make this a primary assurance.

For the purpose of religious education, we need to look more closely at the nature of religion. Basil A. Yeaxlee is convinced that "religion is in the truest sense a correspondence between normal, healthy men and God as the final, living, personal Reality." Although there is no religious drive or impulse, we can properly speak of a *religious sentiment*. "Sentiment" in this context means a grouping of emotional tendencies around an object of consciousness in such a way that when one is aroused the others are aroused also. Emotions are closely related to propensities or instincts, and therefore the latter are also stimulated to action.

Yeaxlee believes that all factors of the personality are involved in such choices. These groupings of emotions and propensities may be integrated on both a small and a large scale, with a dominating sentiment in ultimate control. They may be grouped and regrouped in terms of loyalty to home, church, gang, college, vocation, political party, nation, and the United Nations.

Religion is a sentiment, and it must become a dominating sentiment on purely psychological grounds if the individual is to achieve personal wholeness, with security and health of mind and body, so that the values of man's creative work may be conserved.

> Religion thus involves and expresses the whole person in all his relationships. Thought, feeling and will, reasonable belief, disciplined and directed emotion, purposive conduct—all are bound up with it.[17]

This process is going on from birth to the end of life on earth, and religious education is concerned with the development of the total personality in its environment.

Approaching the origin of religion by means of the analysis of a number of theories, Bishop Henry H. Shires reaches the conclusion that there must be a principle of coherence. He writes:

> Religion is an affair involving all of man's powers, and the varieties of religious experience mean that will, or reason, or feeling may be paramount. *But none of these is the cohesive principle, and it is just here that the theories fail. The basic element which arises from the*

---

[16] *Nature, Man and God*, pp. 30-31, 35. Italics his.

[17] Basil A. Yeaxlee, *Religion and the Growing Mind*, 3rd ed. (Greenwich: Seabury Press, 1952), pp. 16, 27, 28.

> *interplay of these functions is faith, and the essence of religion is found in the commitment of the total self to divine power. . . .* Faith arises from religious experience, and religion arises in the individual and has arisen in history whenever men organize their experiences around a divine being which compels their faith.[18]

Shires, using a philosophy of religion, and Yeaxlee, using psychology, come to almost identical conclusions.

When men's personalities are integrated with God as the center, the results in terms of religious living are seen in their ethical standards, personal relationships, and concern for the welfare of all. Any personal religion that is strong enough to provide a master sentiment must express itself in social action, just as any yearning for social justice can be satisfied only by the power demonstrated in personal religious faith.

CHRISTIANITY

When we turn to the meaning of Christianity, we come up against difficulties similar to those met in defining religion. Not only does Christianity mean many different things today, but it has had a great variety of meanings in the past. One writer identifies eight different strands of primitive faith in the New Testament alone.[19] Another sees so many kinds of Christian faith that he concludes the best we can do is to formulate our own. The varieties of Christologies, in which Jesus is thought of as mere man at one extreme and as Logos at the other, provides no norm for defining Christianity. Views of the Bible, the church, authority, and ethics indicate that there is no such thing as Christianity in general but only particular Christianities.[20]

Although this position is based on a pluralistic interpretation of history, it serves as a warning to those who think they can define Christianity with any degree of accuracy and still satisfy the majority of its adherents. The church was split from its earliest days, even in

[18] Henry H. Shires, "An Inquiry into the Origin of Religion," in *Christianity and the Contemporary Scene,* ed. Randolph Crump Miller and Henry H. Shires (New York: Morehouse-Gorham Co., 1943), p. 72. Italics his.

[19] See Ernest W. Parsons, *Religion of the New Testament* (New York: Harper & Bros., 1939).

[20] See Arthur Cushman McGiffert, *Christianity as History and Faith* (New York: Charles Scribner's Sons, 1934), pp. 3-13.

Paul's time, and even the ecumenical movement does not promise organic unity of the churches.[21]

The creedal requirement of the World Council of Churches may provide a common ground for defining Christianity. Membership is based on the acceptance of Jesus Christ as God and Savior. This is the focal point of the Christian faith, and appears in many rituals of confirmation or confession of faith. Although the acceptance of Jesus Christ as Lord and Savior is open to many interpretations, it means that there is a personal relationship between the believer and the God of Jesus Christ. This loyalty to Christ leads to the integration of the believer. Men's broken relationships are restored by God's grace. The decision of the believer leads to the experience of power to obey God. Behind this grace-faith relationship lies a theology that guides the process and is essential for understanding the goals and purposes of Christian education.[22]

The Christian faith is a Biblical faith. But there are as many ways of looking at the Bible as there are of evaluating Jesus Christ. One way of getting beneath the differences is to look at the Bible as the story of man's redemption, as a drama of God's mighty acts in history, in which God is revealed as creator, giver of a covenant, lover of men who gave his Son for our redemption, founder of the church through the Holy Spirit, and the judge of history who stands beyond history.[23]

Christianity provides the means to make sense out of life. We accept the disordered chaos of history, the sins and frustrations and tragedies of men, and the pessimism and hopelessness of much of everyday life and turn all this into a world in which God is working out his purpose. Just as the prophet of the exile could make sense out of the Babylonian captivity,[24] and Hosea could make sense out of his wife's infidelity,[25] and the early Christians could make sense out of the crucifixion, so we can see that the world is God's. It may be foolishness to the Greeks and a stumbling-block to the Jews that God's Messiah died on a cross for the redemption of all mankind,

---

[21] See Henry Pitney Van Dusen, *World Christianity* (Nashville: Abingdon-Cokesbury Press, 1947), pp. 69-77.

[22] See my *The Clue to Christian Education,* pp. 18-36, for a fuller treatment of Christology as the focal point.

[23] See Bernhard Anderson, *The Unfolding Drama of the Bible* (New York: Association Press, 1953).

[24] Isaiah 52:13-53:12.

[25] Hosea 3:1-5.

but understanding why God sent his Son is the key that unlocks the door to salvation.

The Gospel is good news that the God who made us is a God of love as well as justice, that God is active in history and has intervened in history to do for man what man could not do for himself, that "God was in Christ reconciling the world to himself" (II Cor. 5:19, KJ, RSV), that the new life in Christ is experienced within the fellowship of the church, that the power of the Holy Spirit is available to us as grace and forgiveness and power and wisdom, that there is redemption unto eternal life, and that Jesus Christ has opened the door to the final triumph of good by freeing us from the power of evil and from the fear of everlasting death.[26]

THE CHURCH

The Christian faith as it exists today is found in the church. The institutional structure is not the church, but within the institution there is a fellowship of the Holy Spirit that flows from communion with Jesus Christ. The church has possession of a great truth: This divine-human society was founded by God through Jesus Christ and one dwells in this fellowship through faith, and yet a man cannot acquire this faith except as he is nurtured within the life of the fellowship.

Although the historic institution of the church seeks to be this kind of a fellowship, it fails because of the sinfulness of its members. The beloved community of Christ is a redemptive community, in which all members know themselves to be sinners in need of forgiveness, and are therefore willing to forgive others in the fellowship. It is this communion of persons with each other and with God that is the true church.

This true church is found within the local congregation but is not identical with it. The tragedy of the church — and its ineffectiveness as a religious educator — lies in its failure to be a church in this redemptive sense. The environment of Christian education is spoiled when the quality of life of the local congregation fails to rise to the level of redemptive activity throughout every aspect of parish life.

---

[26] See *Towards the Conversion of England* (Westminster: Press and Publications Board of the General Assembly, 1945), pp. 18-24.

The solution to this problem takes us back to the focal point. Christ is present in the true church. He is the Christ who was sent by the Father to pay the price of sin, who was born, crucified, and risen, and who lives in the church today. Because of Jesus Christ's redemptive activity in history, as revealed in the cross and resurrection, we know through faith that he continues to redeem us and all the world today.[27]

Whether we be children or adults, the life of the church can meet our fundamental needs. It can meet our ultimate requirement for love and acceptance as we are, by showing us the forgiving love of God in Christ. This may not always be evident in either the behavior or worship of a particular congregation, but the very existence of a fellowship of the Spirit (to whatever degree) releases God's power to those who are seeking the Lord where he may be found.

The structure of law and discipline for our lives is found in the teachings of the church as it reiterates the commandments of the law and the prophets. The requirements for justice and social righteousness, the threat of judgment on sinful men and nations, the prophetic hope of God's act in sending a Messiah to save men from their sins, and the simple summary that we must "do justice, and love kindness, and walk humbly with" our God (Micah 6:8, G), are found in the Word of God as it has been given in trust to the church.

Our freedom and the direction of our growth depend on our response in faith within the community to the grace of God, for it is God's grace that enables us "to walk worthy of the vocation to which" we "are called" (Eph. 4:1, KJ).

Finally, there is the need to believe in something beyond ourselves, and our only escape from the worship of devils, of material objects, or of the state lies in the God who demands our loyalty. We respond to him with reverence and awe as we come to see his mystery and holiness, and we have faith that we are justified not for anything that we do but through the mysterious grace of God who loves us.[28]

RELIGIOUS EDUCATION AND CHRISTIAN EDUCATION

One of the great religious leaders for a period of about 50 years

[27] See Emil Brunner, *The Misunderstanding of the Church* (Philadelphia: Westminster Press, 1953), pp. 9-73, for a brilliant description of the nature of the true church.

[28] See Chapter 5 for a detailed treatment of basic needs.

was George Albert Coe (1862–1951). He was working in the field of psychology of religion at the turn of the century, at the same time that William James, Edwin D. Starbuck, and George Stratton were doing their pioneering work. His approach to religion was in terms of values, and he thought of religion as the *revaluing of values* rather than as devotion to value. By combining old and emerging desires into a consistent whole, the religious man is integrated in terms of recognizing the value of values.

Coe had a high opinion of the worth of an individual person and believed that the learner can discover truth only by entering into the process of discovering it for himself. This means that he must question all traditional teachings and rediscover them in his own terms, not as abstract ideas but as answers to concrete questions. Coe answered the question of what Christian education is in these words, "It is the systematic, critical examination and reconstruction of relations between persons, guided by Jesus' assumption that persons are of infinite worth, and by the hypothesis of the existence of God, the Great Valuer of persons." [29]

The problem of method was important, for Coe believed that effective method and effective religion go together. "The religious education movement," he wrote, "was and must be a movement for the re-making of religion itself"; and "effective method in the teaching of religion must be directly derived from the nature of the religion to be taught." [30]

Religion does not contribute any new kind of value, Coe thought, but it operates on and within values to increase, organize, and perpetuate them. "The spiritual is present wherever persons are present; and whatever, from milk to roses, and from a game of tag to a pay envelope, gives colour or form to a personality, is a concern of any religion that would be realistically spiritual." [31] The right motivation for a social ethics that will remake society lies behind his concern at this point.

Coe was aware that religion in general did not affect changes in

---

[29] George Albert Coe, *What Is Christian Education?* (New York: Charles Scribner's Sons, 1929), p. 300.

[30] Coe, "The Elusiveness of Religion," *Religious Education,* XLVII (March-April 1952), 153. The whole issue is dedicated to Coe.

[31] George Albert Coe, "My Own Little Theatre," in Vergilius Ferm, ed., *Religion in Transition* (New York: The Macmillan Company, 1937), p. 116. The article is autobiographical.

personality or character. He was impatient with traditional theology and preferred to work in harmony with the Christian tradition but not within his inherited Methodist position. At this point, Coe did not go as far as some others. The Wiemans, in their *Normative Psychology of Religion,* defined "all education" as "the process of sharing effectively certain selected parts of the accumulated culture of society." They showed how this process was carried on in secular, moral, character, and theological education, and then wrote that "religious education carries on the process in such ways that the individual will develop loyalty to the absolutely supreme and inclusive value which is beyond all values known or conceivable through the present resources of society." [32]

This definition applies to any religion. There is nothing especially Christian about it. With the changing theological scene, there was growing dissatisfaction with such a view, and the leaders sought to define a specifically Christian education.

CHRISTIAN EDUCATION

This definition begins at a point different from that of the religious educators who were revaluing values. Operating from within the Christian tradition and with a degree of theological responsibility, it begins with the fact that we have a Gospel and that Christian education begins when we are confronted with it. It is education within a social process, but the community is the Christian home on the one hand and the church as a redemptive fellowship on the other. It involves the individual as he makes a personal decision, and it has an impact on society in terms of vocational responsibility. It is concerned with history because God chose to reveal his nature through historical events, and thus the past is essential for an understanding of the present and of our hope for the future. It begins and ends with personal relationships, not only in the formative influences that determine Christian character but also in the other attitudes of society that impinge upon our basic loyalties and sometimes destroy them. These personal relationships are between persons and persons, and between persons and God, and our love for God whom we have not seen

[32] Henry N. Wieman and Regina Westcott Wieman, *Normative Psychology of Religion* (New York: Thomas Y. Crowell Co., 1935), pp. 461-63.

depends on our love for our brothers whom we have seen. It is involved when men break their relationships with each other and with God, and when God's healing grace restores those relationships.[33]

Adelaide Case provides us with a good definition:

> Christian education is the effort to make available for our generation —children, young people, and adults—the accumulated treasures of Christian life and thought, in such a way that God in Christ may carry on His redemptive work in each human soul and in the common life of man.[34]

The center of Christian education is not man but God, and our task is to bring the individual Christian into the right relationship with the God of Jesus Christ and with his fellows, so that by grace the individual may do the task to which he is called. To come into such a relationship involves a decision, and thus Christian education is intimately concerned with evangelism. This means that we must confront every learner with Jesus Christ, so that he will put his trust in God through Christ, and by the power of the Holy Spirit live as Christ's disciple within the dynamic fellowship of a truly Christian church.[35]

It is impossible to escape the theological implications of a definition of Christian education. George A. Coe was right when he said that any effective method must be derived from an effective religion. Just as Coe's theology stood behind his educational assumptions and methods, so our theology must stand behind ours. *Theology is prior to the curriculum; for curriculum arises from the grace-faith relationship of the Christian community.* Our beliefs guide our actions and serve as the presuppositions for our goals and methods, and theology is simply our beliefs about God and man as we consider them relevant to our personal responsibilities and decisions.

THE PURPOSE OF CHRISTIAN EDUCATION

The purpose of Christian education is to lead each person into a decision to live as a Christian. His fundamental questions must be

---

[33] See Paul H. Vieth, *The Church and Christian Education* (St. Louis: Bethany Press, 1947), pp. 52, 59-60.

[34] Quoted by Dora P. Chaplin, *Children and Religion* (New York: Charles Scribner's Sons, 1948), p. 136.

[35] See my *The Clue to Christian Education,* p. 8.

answered. He needs to know who he is, who other people are, what the world is like, and where we are going. Each individual needs to know his own nature, and with the help of all that we know about man, he learns to know not only his own being but also what others are like.

The rich tradition of our religious heritage leads him to a deeper understanding of human relations. As he becomes a member of the community in which he discovers the records of God's mighty acts, the lore of tradition, and the redemptive power of Christ, he knows that this is God's world. As he begins to share in the Christian faith, he comes to the experience of grace that heals the relationships of the world.

The purpose of Christian education is to make men whole. The integration of personality is often sought in terms of ideals, beliefs, or social adjustment; and although goodness and knowledge and social acceptance may make a gentleman, they do not make a Christian. Much religious advice along these lines appeals to the person who thinks he can become a success by praying, or can achieve peace of mind through a right religious adjustment. Many church schools have turned out those who think they can be saved by keeping the law or by getting along with others, but actually all we have turned out have been Pharisees or Sadducees.[36]

It is essential that we recognize the radical nature of Christian integration. Integration occurs when relationships between persons are secure, when there is a personal encounter with God, when there is a society of persons in a dynamic community, when there is an organic relationship between a man and his environment. The goal of Christian integration is that maturity which feeds on the "solid food" of the Gospel, which "is for the full-grown" (Heb. 5:14, K). "Strong meat" (KJ) is our goal, and we are to leave the milk, which is for babes, behind.

This integration comes to pass within a community, and yet it happens to an individual – which means that we need always to recognize Whitehead's partial truth, that "religion is what a man does with his solitariness." Also, this integration occurs within a Christian community that is placed over against a non-Christian or semi-Christian or secular community that surrounds it.

---

[36] See Charles Duell Kean, *Making Sense Out of Life* (Philadelphia: Westminster Press, 1954), for a brilliant analysis of the Pharisee and Sadducee.

When a society is sufficiently Christian, Christian education is made less difficult. Marjorie Reeves suggests seven needs that society might provide:

> 1. The experience of comprehending the natural world as a universe of law and order which is 'given' to man and upon which he is dependent.
> 2. The experience of living in human societies which seek to express in their own life this same principle of reliable order and consistent law administered by trustworthy authority.
> 3. The experience of true personal relationships, of loving and being loved, and of working in groups which give direct contact of person with person, rather than in masses.
> 4. The experience of understanding and embracing one's daily work as a significant and worthy service to the community.
> 5. The experience of understanding that to which one belongs, and of entering into clear-sighted, critical membership.
> 6. The experience of being challenged to serve worthy purposes greater than oneself.
> 7. The experience of withdrawal into solitude.[37]

In some parts of the world, this is too much to ask of the society in which the church operates. The church is restrained, or persecuted, or forced underground, and there is little hope that social and moral conditions will change. But in other countries, the secular or semi-Christian culture is congenial to Christianity and there are points of contact. More than this, there is concern that the church should grow and become stronger.

Not only because the church needs certain freedoms in order to be effective, but because society needs these same characteristics in order to be healthy, the church often enters the social and political arena to achieve a greater stability for the family, protection of the sanctity of personality through due process of law, and an atmosphere in which human fellowship may be achieved across all artificial and racial lines. The Gospel is concerned with the whole of life and therefore the church must act to assure itself that society will not cripple men's souls and bodies.

A work written probably in the third century, known as "The Ad-

---

[37] Marjorie Reeves, *Growing Up in a Modern Society* (London: University of London Press, 1952), pp. 124-25.

dress to Diognetus," shows the interest of the early church in teaching and creating disciples.

> If you also desire this faith, receive first full knowledge of the Father. . . . The tree of knowledge does not kill, it is disobedience that kills. . . . There is neither life without knowledge, nor sound knowledge without true life. . . . For whoever thinks he knows anything apart from knowledge that is true and supported by life knows nothing, he is deceived by the serpent, because he did not love life.[38]

Christian education is concerned with this kind of knowledge on all levels of existence. The primary purpose is to bring persons into that redemptive community that is the true church. The corollary, which is of equal importance, is to bring the world outside the church within the scope of God's redemptive act in Christ, so that all mankind may benefit from the gift of the Gospel.

OBJECTIVES

In 1930, the International Council of Religious Education adopted a set of objectives. They were formulated by Paul H. Vieth and have appeared in all publications dealing with the problem during the intervening years.[39] Christian religious education seeks:

1. To foster in growing persons a consciousness of God as a reality in human experience, and a sense of personal relationship to him.
2. To develop in growing persons such an understanding and appreciation of the personality, life, and teachings of Jesus as will lead to experience of him as Savior and Lord, loyalty to him and his cause, and manifest itself in daily life and conduct.
3. To foster in growing persons a progressive and continuous development of Christlike character.
4. To develop in growing persons the ability and disposition to participate in and contribute constructively to the building of a social order throughout the world, embodying the ideal of the Fatherhood of God and the brotherhood of man.
5. To develop in growing persons the ability and disposition to participate in the organized society of Christians—the Church.

---

[38] "Address to Diognetus," 10:1, 12:2b, 4, 6, in Edgar J. Goodspeed, *The Apostolic Fathers* (New York: Harper & Bros., 1950), pp. 281-85.

[39] Paul H. Vieth, *Objectives of Religious Education* (New York: Harper & Bros., 1930); see also William C. Bower and Percy R. Hayward, *Protestantism Faces Its Educational Task Together* (Chicago: National Council of Churches, 1949), pp. 208-09.

6. To develop in growing persons an appreciation of the meaning and importance of the Christian family, and the ability and disposition to participate in and contribute constructively to the life of this primary social group.[40]

7. To lead growing persons into a Christian interpretation of life and the universe; the ability to see in it God's purpose and plan; a life philosophy built on this interpretation.

8. To effect in growing persons the assimilation of the best religious experience of the race, pre-eminently that recorded in the Bible, as effective guidance to present experience.[41]

Further research indicated how these objectives could be used with various age groups. They were guides to balanced goals for the development of lesson materials, for specific achievements within the church as it is organized for Christian education, and for the teacher in the classroom. The success of these objectives is demonstrated by the fact that they have not been revised, except for the addition of recognition of the place of the family in the program of Christian education.

For the teacher, these objectives are essential for measuring content and determining method, and are therefore adapted to the capacity of the learner. For the learner, these objectives are a basis for the purpose and motivation of learning activity, and therefore must be related to his basic interests for him to respond. Teacher and pupil may, therefore, share in common objectives, and by this cooperation the learning process moves in a desirable direction. "The concern of Christian education is to help persons, whether young or old, to live as Christians – to face the actual situations that their world presents to them, and to resolve the issues involved in terms of Christian values and purposes." Christian faith is "life with God, in response to His redeeming love as revealed in Jesus Christ his Son, and in the power of the Holy Spirit." [42]

Christian education, like Christian theology, is concerned "to reinterpret Christian faith in terms of the living experiences of our own

---

[40] This objective was added in *Christian Education Today* (1940).

[41] *Christian Education Today* (Chicago: International Council of Religious Education, 1940), p. 16; *The Curriculum Guide for the Local Church* (Chicago: International Council of Religious Education, 1945), p. 8. Original form in *Principles and Objectives of Religious Education* (Chicago: International Council of Religious Education, 1932), pp. 10-16.

[42] *Christian Education Today,* pp. 10, 16.

day, to discover its wider and deeper implications, and to bring it into effectual relation with the issues of contemporary living." [43]

These quotations indicate something of the responsible position of today's leaders in Christian education. Because the objectives are general statements, they need only occasional redefinition, but because men and their cultures are constantly changing, we must adapt both the content and the methods of Christian education to the needs of men, so that the redemptive love of God in Christ will always be relevant to the contemporary scene.

A new theological statement, followed by a new formulation of objectives was worked out by a committee under the chairmanship of Lawrence Little in 1956.

---

[43] *Ibid.*, p. 12.

CHAPTER 4

THEOLOGY AND CHRISTIAN EDUCATION

THEOLOGY is the truth-about-God-in-relation-to-man. It is the most significant of all truths for meaningful living. It is the source of our knowledge of what God has done for man and provides guidance for faith and action in the world. It stands behind the process of Christian education and tells us of the nature of God and man. Because it tells us about God and his world, it provides the content of education. Because it tells us about man, it is the source for our methods of teaching, including in its data the findings of science.

Theology originates in the activity of God and in the experience of men. Theology has arisen from history, and has been formulated as men speculated on the meaning of historical events. It has arisen in revelation, which is another name for discovery. For whenever a particularly revealing event is appreciated and interpreted by a particularly appreciative and illumined mind, there we have revelation.

The growth of the basic Christian doctrines may be interpreted in this way. The meaning of Jesus Christ arose from the attempt to interpret the event. Among the early disciples there was the memory of Jesus as he had appeared to them in their daily life in Palestine. They knew him and observed his actions and listened to his teachings. After the resurrection, they knew him still, and they experienced the closeness of his presence. The earliest records show that they were interpreting what Jesus' activities meant from the beginning of their experience, and we can trace somewhat accurately the insights that came to the disciples.

In his letters Paul struggled with this problem of interpretation, and the Gospels, all written after Paul's time, provide further evidence of the development of understanding. But the question of interpretation did not close with the New Testament. The earliest councils of the church struggled further with the problem, and a formula was agreed upon at Chalcedon in A.D. 451, which seemed at the time to account for the known facts. But still the church was not satisfied, and although the creedal statement in the Nicene Creed has not changed, men have continually reinterpreted the meaning of the creed.

Today, men are still looking for deeper insights into the meaning of Christ, based on the primary experience of the early church recorded in the New Testament, the continuing experience of the meaning of Christ throughout the history of the church, and the sense of the presence of Christ in the lives of men today. Thus, revelation and discovery come together in the recognition that God reveals himself through his own mighty acts in history and in the lives of men.

Even so formidable a doctrine as the Trinity can be traced in a similar fashion. Augustine, who was an accomplished theologian, recognized that one's experience of God is in terms of Father, Son, and Holy Spirit; but "when the question is asked, 'Three what?' human language labors under great poverty of speech. The answer is given, however, 'Three persons,' not that it might be expressed, but that it might not be left unexpressed." [1] The Trinity is an attempt to reconcile man's contradictory experiences of God at work in the cosmos, in history, and in his daily life. Concepts and language have not the richness to express it adequately, and the doctrine of the Trinity is the best we can do to represent man's experience in a formula. In other words, the doctrine of the Trinity is relevant to man's experience of God, and therefore we seek to discover its relevance for us in the relationships of daily life.

The doctrine of man, likewise, is not derived from an abstract concept but from man's experience of himself. Both the glory and the tragedy of man, seen as a child of God and as a sinner, is not the private property of the Genesis story of creation, although it is unfolded there in all the power of God's revelation through a story. But the insight found there is repeated by man everywhere throughout his history. Because we have the revelation of God through the Bible, we are more likely to discover and accept that truth in our own lives. And because the picture of man is true, man is likely to

---

[1] *On the Trinity,* V, 10.

reject it out of pure rebellion and refusal to see the truth, a rejection that in turn verifies the Biblical insight that man tends to rebel.

For theology to be relevant to Christian education, we need to see its significance at two levels: the adult level and the learner's level. Because theology provides the answer to man's basic questions about his existence and, therefore, guides him into a redemptive relationship with God within the fellowship of the church, we need to see how this happens at Christian maturity and also at the learner's level regardless of chronological age. The pastor, teacher, and parent, who are basically responsible for the education of children, youth, and adults, need a mature faith based on intelligent and relevant beliefs before they can become the means whereby this faith is imparted to those for whose education they are responsible.

BIBLICAL THEOLOGY

Although God reveals himself to some extent in all history and all creation, the Christian finds a special revelation in the Bible. Here we find theology in the concrete sense, for the Bible gives us a picture of God in relation to his people. It tells us of men's insights, of the history of a people who share all the sins of mankind, and of acts ascribed to God that we find offensive.

The Bible has been studied from every angle, and all the tools of modern science have been used to tear it to pieces and put it together again. The Bible is known as is no other book. But the chief thing to remember about the Bible is that it is a record of God's mighty acts in history by which he revealed himself to those who could appreciate it. When we read the Bible, it is as if we were in a theater watching the unfolding of a mighty drama; but the drama has taken place on the stage of history rather than before the footlights, and before we are through watching it we find that we are drawn into its full meaning as active participants.

The earliest participants in the drama of redemption did not know how the story would turn out. They had faith that Yahweh was a great and powerful deity, and they cried out for a Messiah to save them from their sins, but they could only see the basic principle and not the act. They saw something of the power of forgiving love in the story of Hosea and of the need for a suffering servant in the second Isaiah, and Habakkuk had told them that they would be made just by faith, but they could not unify these ideas in a person.

Our view of the drama is different, because the passing of time has brought us on the stage after God has acted in Christ to reconcile us to himself. We know that the ultimate outcome is not in doubt, for we belong to the church and read the Old Testament through the eyes of the New Testament. We have seen that the covenant made with Abraham and renewed in Moses and Jeremiah has been made anew through the death and resurrection of Jesus Christ. As Oscar Cullmann has put it, the victory is already won, and what we have to do is to conclude the battle; for D-Day has passed and V-Day is a certainty.[2]

We view the drama, then, from the standpoint of one who knows the conclusion of the matter. But we do not know it for ourselves. As in a life insurance company, which can tell how many people will die, we know that many will be saved, but we have no statistical evidence that will guarantee our personal salvation. The Bible pictures us as having the gift of salvation offered through faith in Christ, but offers us no guarantee that we will decide to accept it. The basic motif is that the lost will be found, the dead will rise again, the lonely and separated will be joined with God and their fellows, but that every man has the freedom either to accept or reject this possibility.

The Bible tells this story not in dogma or in theological propositions, but in terms of a drama. God has acted in history to provide us with the gifts of creation, the covenant, Christ, the church and the Holy Spirit, and the consummation of judgment and hope.

These five acts of the drama of redemption are not clearly marked out, and yet such a framework emerges from Bible study. We look at this drama as members of the church who have inherited the gifts of creation, covenant, and Christ. We see creation in the light of "In the beginning was the Word" (John 1:1) as well as of "In the beginning God created" (Gen. 1:1).

The Bible story is thrust into the present age. "God can be depended on, and it was he who called you to this fellowship with his Son, Jesus Christ our Lord" (I Cor. 1:9,G). This new relationship with God is possible because through Christ there was a new agreement, a new covenant between God and man. "For by grace have you been saved through faith; and this is not your own doing, it is the gift of

[2] *Christ and Time* (Philadelphia: Westminster Press, 1950), p. 84.

God – not because of works, lest any man should boast. . . . Therefore, . . . lead a life worthy of the calling to which you have been called" (Eph. 2:8,9; 4:1, RSV).

As we seek to be obedient to our vocations, we discover our continuing unworthiness. We know that the final act of the drama impinges on us in terms of God's judgment. We know that judgment faces us at death. We know that God stands beyond history as the ultimate judge of all creation. We face this judgment with hope, for it means "the act by which judgment is done; it also means that which is right, whether custom, the rights of the individual or group, the right in general, or simply justice." [3]

Because judgment is the act of a loving God, it is always redemptive, and only our refusal to accept God makes it retributive. The stiff-necked resistance of individuals and nations brings punishment to the fore, but we are capable by God's grace of entering into personal relations with God by which the breached relationships with our fellows are healed.

The Biblical faith in life after death is obvious. We have the *hope* of resurrection unto eternal life and the *fear* of damnation. "This is the testimony, that God gave us eternal life, and this life is in his Son. He who has the Son has life" (I John 5:11–12a, RSV).[4]

Reinhold Niebuhr summarizes this in brilliant fashion:

> The Christian church is a community of hopeful believers, who are not afraid of life or death, or present or future history, being persuaded that the whole of life and all historical vicissitudes stand under the sovereignty of a holy, yet merciful God whose will was supremely revealed in Christ. It is a community which does not fear the final judgment, not because it is composed of sinless saints but because it is a community of forgiven sinners, who know that judgment is merciful if it is not evaded. If the divine judgment is not resisted by pretensions of virtue but is contritely accepted, it reveals in and beyond itself the mercy which restores life on a new and healthier basis.[5]

---

[3] Millar Burrows, *Outline of Biblical Theology* (Philadelphia: Westminster Press, 1946), p. 173.

[4] See my *A Symphony of the Christian Year* (Greenwich: Seabury Press, 1954), pp. 12-18, for a fuller treatment of the five acts of the drama. For a different division, see Bernhard Anderson, *The Unfolding Drama of the Bible* (New York: Association Press-Haddam House, 1953).

[5] Reinhold Niebuhr, *Faith and History* (New York: Charles Scribner's Sons, 1949), p. 238.

This view of the Bible eliminates most of the educational difficulties at once. The drama tells the story of everyman. The basic relationships it describes are as true for a child as for an adult. The great events are those of our common experience. Every child is created, and in the experience of birth and early experiences as an infant he is faced with his creaturehood and his need for autonomy in the midst of dependence and security. He is faced by the rigidity of the adult world, the rule of law, and the dependability of discipline. He needs redemption, for he cannot save himself; and in his helplessness and reliance on his parents in whom he lives and moves and has his being, he must be saved from death if he is to live. Except he live in community, he cannot become a person; for community, communion, and communication go together. Through the community of home, school, and church channels are opened for the Holy Spirit. And from the time he is weaned, he faces judgment, even though it be only his mother's disapproval as he fails to perform according to her expectations.

The Biblical drama applies at every age, according to the capacities and experiences of that age. Because it is a true revelation of God at work in history, it is dynamic and relevant as God is at work in us. Although the language of the Bible, the chronology of history, and the implied metaphysics may open slowly to the growing child, the relationships of the Bible are eternally relevant from birth to death. The whole Bible is always relevant, even when particular parts of the Bible are not. The theology of the Bible is essential to Christian education long before any of its content can be understood.

At every moment, the child is in danger of rejection. This may come from his own rebellion when he has become able to make choices within the community, but often it comes from rejection by those in the community who are not full of grace. His parents, no matter how much they love him, will reject him from time to time. His brothers and sisters will treat him with cruelty, through indifference, ignorance, and wilfulness. Because none of us is capable of the constant practice of fellowship or participation or sharing (in the New Testament sense of *koinonia*), he will learn to reject us even before rejection is the conscious choice of his ego. Whether this be a psychological observation or a Biblical doctrine, it is a theological insight based on God's relationships with man. Every person, from the moment of birth to the moment of death, no matter how much he has grown in grace, still stands in need of redemption and under judgment. The Bible is therefore relevant to Christian education at every point in our existence.

THEOLOGY AND LIFE

Martin Buber gets at the problem of the relation of theology to life through what he calls the "I-Thou" relationship. He contrasts this with the "I-It" relationship. When we treat a person as a "Thou," we recognize that he is an end and not a means and, therefore, he is not to be used for our pleasure. But we get so mixed up that we use persons and serve things, whereas the proper relationship consists of serving persons and using things. When we use persons as things, we become estranged from them and, therefore, hurt ourselves as well as them.

God works through persons in relationship. This is both a theological and an educational insight. Herbert H. Farmer states, "God's purpose is such, and He so made humanity in accordance with that purpose, that He never enters into *personal* relationship with a man apart from other human persons." [6] When a man works through such relationships, he treats each other person as a "Thou" and therefore discovers the "eternal Thou" behind each person. The "new structure of personal relationship," which is the church, provides the environment in which God's power of salvation is appropriated through faith.[7] The covenant of which the Bible speaks is between *the people* and God, and Christian education takes place in a social process.

It is here that John Dewey's educational insights and the truth of the Gospel come together, for we learn to become persons in a group, and the nature of the group determines to a great extent the kind of persons we will become. The quality of life, which is the structure of relationships, is the crucial element in a theology of relationships, and the Christian sees God at work in the fellowship of the Holy Spirit.

The purpose of Christian education is seen more clearly: God stands at the center, and we are to use every means at our disposal to bring individuals into the right relationship with God and their fellows within the fellowship of the church. This basic loyalty carries over

---

[6] Herbert H. Farmer, *The Servant of the Word* (New York: Charles Scribner's Sons, 1942), p. 37.

[7] See Reuel L. Howe, *Man's Need and God's Action* (Greenwich: Seabury Press, 1953), pp. 19-30, 57.

into daily life and is interpreted in terms of one's vocation as he lives from moment to moment in relationship with his fellows everywhere.

Because this is a personal relationship, we must never lose sight of the individual. He is the person of worth in the community, and the maturity of his faith is the concern of all. When one is confronted by the living Christ and accepts him, he is moving toward that integration of personality that is the goal of religious education.

The integration of the Christian lies in the personal relationship between God and man. It flows from the divine-human encounter, the right adjustment, from trust in a God of grace. It is more than an activity of the mind, or will, or emotions, for it involves the total personality in relation to ultimate reality. This radical Christian integration is two-dimensional, for it involves adjustment to both God and one's fellows.

Modern studies in psychology emphasize this same concern for the total personality as it is related to the environment, and see that personal relations are more significant to mental health than orientation to values or beliefs. The Epistle to the Ephesians describes it as arriving "at real maturity — that measure of development which is meant by 'the fullness of Christ.' We are not meant to remain as children at the mercy of every chance wind of doctrine and the jockeying of men who are expert in the crafty presentation of lies. But we are meant to hold firmly to the truth in love, and to grow up in every way into Christ, the Head." God's "gifts were made that Christians might be properly equipped for their service, that the whole Body might be built up until the time comes when, in the unity of common faith and common knowledge of the Son of God, we arrive at real maturity." (Eph. 4:13b–15, 12–13a, P).[8]

Integration arises from an understanding of the Biblical treatment of faith and grace. The Christian faith insists on the priority of God's love, and our love is possible because he loved us first. God's grace is the free gift of his love, and our faith is the response that we make in trust to his grace. It is this faith-grace relationship that is in the foreground of Christian education; but the background is theology, which guides the process and points to the ultimate goals. The church provides an "atmosphere in which grace flourishes," but it cannot guarantee the decision of faith, which is an act of the individual.

---

[8] See my *Clue to Christian Education,* pp. 7-11.

These personal relationships, when seen in terms of Buber's "I-Thou," contribute to the answers to man's basic questions. Even a small child is asking "Who am I?" and "Who are you?" before he has found the words to express these questions. He learns them from the way he is treated by his parents and brothers and sisters in his home. He learns that he is what he is treated as; and he knows others by the way they treat him. He is learning a doctrine of man, as man is related to his fellows and to God, and this is either good or bad theology depending on what answers he learns. He is also asking, "What is the world like?" and "Where are we going?" His world is his home; and then it begins to expand, and his attitudes toward the expanding horizons of his own little world express what he thinks it is like and where it is going.

THEOLOGY AND THE UNDERSTANDING OF CHILDREN

Theology provides insights for our understanding of children, and theology provides the basis for the integration of children's personalities in their religious growth. The Christian view of man as a child of God and a sinner is developed in the Biblical story. Man is so disobedient, so selfish, so profoundly traitorous to the nature that God implanted, that he crucifies God's own Son. Here, in history, is the revelation of the truth about God in relation to man. Yet the man who is capable of crucifying the Christ is also capable of being the Christ. One historic incident reveals both the misery and the glory of man.

But Christian theology is never satisfied with analysis or diagnosis, but turns to the cure immediately. The reconciliation that comes in Christ is the heart of the matter. God has so acted that man will be saved if he turns to the Father. The relationship of faith and grace is the center of Christian evangelism and Christian nurture.

Many actions that are normal for children are abnormal for adults. Children pass through "stages," whereas adults commit sins. There is just enough truth in this facile statement to lull us into overlooking the dangers involved. For example, there are certain stages when children tell lies because the motivation lies in the activity of the imagination; but there are times when children tell lies when the motivation is to avoid an unpleasant situation. It takes a combination of developmental psychology and theology to evaluate such situations. The capacity for sin is present in the small child, but an understanding of intention makes it possible for adults to distinguish between sins, mistakes, and stages.

A noncritical theology makes the mistake of treating children as little adults and, therefore, makes no place for childish behavior patterns. A sound theology recognizes that all children are sinners and that they need the resources of the Christian fellowship, but it sees that God does not demand the same behavior of all people or all age groups. God does not expect children to act like adults but as faithful children. A sound theology also recognizes that each child is to be treated as an end in himself, for he has ultimate value in God's sight. The reason Jesus said, "Let the little children come to me," was that they are persons and not things; they are creatures of a loving, heavenly Father.

As the child is nurtured in Christian faith, he comes into knowledge of God as Father. But he has been learning of the meaning of fatherhood from birth, as his father has been a mediator of God's grace. Because human fathers are often such failures, it has been seriously suggested that we avoid the picture of God as a heavenly Father. If, as we assume, religious faith begins in the parent-child relationship and in attitudes, attachments, and repulsions, which are primarily emotional, the fatherhood role cannot be avoided either theologically or psychologically. Even a child of an unworthy father "clings to those few elements of good that persist in the most brutalized, callous, or indifferent parent, and in his fantasy world he will create a picture of fatherhood which is inspired by those elements of good, even if reinforced by what he sees and envies in the lives of happier children. It will be a picture of a father who commands reverence and evokes love – the kind of Father whom Jesus made known to men, and who is no fantasy." [9] It is no accident that in many church schools fathers are teaching in the nursery and kindergarten classes, for this is one means of associating the whole idea of religion with fatherhood, especially when a particular child needs a concept of a father other than his own.

THEOLOGY OF RELATIONSHIPS

The concept of the home as a Christian "cell," a community in

---

[9] Basil A. Yeaxlee, *Religion and the Growing Mind,* rev. ed. (Greenwich: Seabury Press, 1952), p. 87; see pp. 55-58, 85-87, 187-188.

miniature in which the relationships are those of love, law, growth, and the mystery of God's grace, is basic to an understanding of Christian education. As we trace the development of religion in the child, we see the importance of the home as the primary teacher of religious faith, primarily through the person-to-person relationships within the family circle. The atmosphere of the home provides the influences that educate the young child; the structure of the home provides the impressions of the earlier school years; the teachings of the home begin to have some effect on younger children and a greater effect on the older ones until they come to the "stage" of rebellion, which is a normal accompaniment of adolescence.

The home cooperates with the church and school and other community agencies in this process. Not for long are the parents the sole influence, but the danger is that they will abdicate their responsibility long before they have performed their full task. Normally, the school has no specifically religious functions, but through its relationships it may reinforce or damage the development of religious faith in home or church.

The church is the major fellowship of religious instruction, both through its influence on the primary fellowship of the home and through its continuing influence on individuals and society. The chief educational weapon is simply the quality of life in the local congregation. The child learns through participation in the activities of the church, and insofar as these activities are *redemptive* in bringing the impact of the Gospel into the life of the learner, Christian education is taking place.

The difference between the church and all other human groupings is that it is a unique community of the Holy Spirit. Its functions are marked off from others, in that it meets for worship, fellowship, instruction, pastoral work, missionary activity, and to express its world-wide nature. In each of these functions, it is a redemptive and sustaining fellowship, concerned with relationships between persons and between the group and the heavenly Father. Its sacraments are means of grace, its preaching of the Word is more than human opinion, its instruction centers on Christ as the focal point, its pastoral concern is with the total personality standing in need of redemption, its mission is to bring the good news to those who have not heard it, its ultimate goal is to be a fellowship of all mankind, transcending ecclesiastical, national, and racial boundaries.

Insofar as the local congregation seeks to be this kind of a community, the quality of its life will permeate every member, from birth to death, and it will seek the tools to do the job more adequately. Method is motivated by theology and is derived from the nature of man seen from the perspective of Christian faith.

> The Church exists for the purpose of re-enacting the Gospel story. Here, in Christian family and parish life, the divine love which accepts the unlovable and unworthy becomes a reality in experience, since the Christ of the Cross is here a continuing presence and power.

Canon Theodore O. Wedel also writes that "a child can understand the love story of redemption in the Bible. The words which constitute the Bible's vocabulary are comprehensible to children and adults alike if interpreted by the language of *relationship.*" [10]

This language of relationship is something prior to and deeper than words. It is illustrated by the child who learns to trust his mother because of her trustworthiness; it is the language of love that far transcends any words of the lovers, although we thank God for "words to tell our loving." Words, at best, are symbols of experienced relationships, especially the great words of religion: faith, hope, love, law, grace. The transformed Christian, who is reborn, who was lost and found, who was dead and is alive again in Christ, is a man experiencing a new relationship. By the power of God channeled through human activity, we are healed when our relationships are broken, and we are sustained in those rich relationships of love, which by God's grace are maintained.

Theology is relevant to life, and therefore to Christian education. The key words are always *relevance* and *relationship*. Irrelevant theology that does not help restore or sustain human relationships has no guidance for the educational process, but the relevant truth of the Christian revelation speaks to man in every condition, offering him the hope of a new relationship with God and his fellows, and ultimately with the hope of resurrection unto eternal life.

---

[10] Theodore O. Wedel, "Leadership Training in Christian Education," *World Christian Education* (2nd Quarter, 1952), p. 31. See also Reuel Howe, *Man's Need and God's Action,* pp. 65-76.

CHAPTER 5

GROWTH IN RELIGION

RELIGION emerges from within the natural relationships of a child. The attitudes, attachments and reactions of early childhood, which are primarily emotional, provide the raw material out of which a growing faith develops. The way in which basic needs are met is the crucial element all along the way, for the foundations are established by the emotional maturity, stability of relationships, and abiding faith of the parents.

Horace Bushnell, over one hundred years ago, put this as strongly as he could:

> The operative truth necessary for a new life may possibly be communicated through and from the parent, being revealed in his looks, manners, and ways of life, before they are of age to understand the teaching of words, for the Christian scheme, the gospel, is really wrapped up in the life of every Christian parent, and beams out from him as a living epistle, before it escapes from the lips or is taught in words. And the Spirit of truth may as well make this living truth effectual as the preaching of the gospel itself.[1]

In this chapter, we are attempting to understand the nature of growth in religion as it applies to persons in various age groups. The correlation brings us an understanding of what is called "religious readiness," which is the "growing edge" at which the learning process can be motivated. If we understand the basic needs of a person, see

[1] Horace Bushnell, *Christian Nurture* (New Haven: Yale University Press, 1947), p. 14. See also Elizabeth M. Manwell and Sophia L. Fahs, *Consider the Children – How They Grow* (Boston: Beacon Press, 1951), pp. 3-15; Basil A. Yeaxlee, *Religion and the Growing Mind* (Greenwich: Seabury Press, 1952), pp. 57-58; Lewis J. Sherrill, *Understanding Children* (Nashville: Abingdon Press, 1939, pp. 32-50.

the relevance of the Christian faith as it meets those needs, and provide the opportunity for the person to grow in that direction, he will respond in the light of his own motivation. There is no guarantee that a perfect combination of these elements will stimulate a desirable response, because any decision of faith depends upon the free choice of the individual and this cannot be coerced, but from an examination of the evidence we can promise increased likelihood of a desirable response.

Growth, as we understand it, is not simple change. Many changes are symptoms of simple rhythmic processes within the human organism, and others are instances of degeneration rather than growth. Growth involves an element of loss, but the gain predominates over the loss. A mature person has put away childish things, including some of the desirable elements of childhood, but genuine maturity always represents a net gain in spite of the losses. The achievement of a major purpose always means the sacrifice of minor values, but the net gain is growth. Richard C. Cabot defines growth as:

> . . . the production of novelty within the range of purpose without dominant self-destruction. Learning, experimenting, admiring, and sharing, exemplify growth. . . . Growth takes place in character, not toward character; in wisdom, not toward it. There is no goal which we approach. . . . Growth comes by the appropriation of the energies of the universe taken in both through our food and the air we breathe and through all that we learn from the world and from other people. Any one who does not turn away from reality and refuse to learn cannot help growing. The opposite of growth, therefore, degeneration, results from refusing to learn the lessons which cumulative experience teaches to all who do not refuse them.[2]

Men may refuse to grow, and therefore "education into religion" depends on the decision of the learner. "The growing edge of anyone's knowledge is at the point where his questions push out like the edge of a tissue culture." [3] The foods of growth are the answers to man's basic needs. As man grows as a complete personality, religion must minister to his total needs.

---

[2] Richard C. Cabot and Russell L. Dicks, *The Art of Ministering to the Sick* (New York: The Macmillan Company, 1936), pp. 377-78. See also Richard C. Cabot, *The Meaning of Right and Wrong* (New York: The Macmillan Company, 1933), chaps. 5 and 6.

[3] See *The Art of Ministering to the Sick*, pp. 13-19.

The total person may be analyzed in terms of his physical drives, his psychical urges, his mental aspirations, his social yearnings, and his economic stimuli. He is a complex of many different drives, and his needs are answered from many different directions in his environment. He responds to the opportunity to exercise control over his environment, he increases his self-control as he functions in many different relationships, and he becomes capable of deeper personal and social relationships within his environment. As the Christian way is seen to be relevant to his needs and his questions about the nature and value of life, he responds at his "growing edge."

Religious readiness in a person is what we understand by his "growing edge," the point at which he can reach out and make contact with the meaning of his world. When we confront him with the Gospel at the point where he can respond, in terms of relationships that are meaningful, in terms of concerns that are live options, in terms of answers to questions he is asking or of stimulating questions he is capable of asking, he *may* respond. This motivation, when supported by God's grace, leads him to grow in religious insight and feeling, involving his total personality as he participates in the life of the Christian community.

BASIC NEEDS AND THEOLOGY

The fundamental needs of man may be catalogued in various ways, but the basic catagories are love and acceptance, structure and order, growth, and a sense of mystery.

(1) Everyone needs *love and acceptance.* Spiritual as well as mental and physical health turns on satisfaction of the desire to be loved, for when one is accepted as he is within a community he has a sense of security. Security may be impersonal, and that is never sufficient; each person needs a security centered in friendly companionship and self-giving love; he needs to know that as a person he is accepted as he is and not as he ought to be. Growth in religion is moving through the need of receiving this kind of love into the compulsion to give it. As one grows toward Christian maturity, as he grows up in love, he finds that he is more and more a giver of love. To love and be loved, to accept and be accepted, to feel secure and give security, constitute the full satisfaction of this basic need.

None of us is capable of this, and life is a series of broken relationships needing to be healed. Selfish love alternates with love for others, or in cases of arrested development there is never any growth beyond self-love. The power of God's grace is necessary if man is to overcome his rebellion, which separates him from his fellows and from God. This sense of frustration is overcome when man knows himself to be loved by God. Knowing his imperfections and the strength of his self-will, he "comes to himself" in the knowledge that God loves him enough to have sent Jesus Christ as his Redeemer.

The problem of Christian education is to provide a Christian answer to these needs within the environment of the learner. Home, school, and other community organizations may or may not contribute to his "growth in grace," but it is chiefly the responsibility of the church as a "fellowship of the Holy Spirit." The need is met theologically by the doctrine that "God is love" (I John 4:8), but the relevance of this is in terms of the mediation of God's love through the ministry of persons.

(2) Everyone needs *a structure of law and order, a sense of discipline, a recognition of the place of moral values.* Here security arises out of the dependableness of life. A child needs the kind of world he can count on, and as we grow we need a skeleton for the body of our beliefs and actions. The moral law is fundamental to the structure of any society, operating in all of man's community activities and seen as essential to his political and international relationships as well as to his more intimate communities. Just as the Ten Commandments provided the heart of the old covenant between Yahweh and Israel in Moses' time, so they serve as the nucleus of civil and criminal law in Western culture today.

When law is broken, relationships between persons are shattered. Paul brings this out vividly:

> But if I do the things that I do not want to do, it is not I that am acting, it is sin, which has possession of me. I find the law to be that I who want to do right am dogged by what is wrong. My inner nature agrees with the divine law, but all through my body I see another principle in conflict with the law of my reason, which makes me a prisoner to that law of sin that runs through my body. What a wretched man I am! Who can save me from this doomed body? Thank God! it is done through Jesus Christ our Lord! (Romans 7:20-25a, G).

The problem of Christian education is to provide an understanding of the structure of law and order in the world. Both natural and moral law are involved here, and they are experienced in the process of growing up. The dependableness of relations in the home is the starting point, and maturity can be measured by the degree to which natural and moral law are obeyed. Insight into moral values comes from the theological realization that God is just and that he requires righteousness. And because of our failures, we face the judgment and mercy of God.

(3) Everyone needs *freedom to grow*. The individual has problems of physical, mental, spiritual, and social growth. "Full-grown men have a right to solid food, for their faculties are trained by practice to distinguish right and wrong" (Hebrews 5:14, G). The "strong meat" of the Gospel comes with maturity. So we pray,

> Our children bless, in ev'ry place,
> That they may all behold thy face,
> And knowing thee may grow in grace.[4]

The tragedy of life is that growth is frustrated at every level or, often, permitted to move in the wrong direction.

> Ground that drinks in frequent showers and produces vegetation that is of use for whom it is cultivated receives God's blessing. But if it yields thorns and thistles, it is thought worthless and almost cursed, and it will finally be burned (Hebrews 6:7-8, G).

The impact of life today on the growing personalities of children and adults often stunts and distorts them, in much the same way as the heathenish practice of foot-binding dwarfed the feet of little girls. Yet when curiosity and the desire for novelty are allowed freedom to operate, growth takes place.

God stands behind all growth that is worthwhile, and theologically we speak of God's grace as the free gift of himself as he forgives us, restores us to relationship with him, and provides the strength and guidance by which we grow to true maturity. The church stands as a community that seeks to be a channel of grace through person-to-person relationships.

(4) Everyone needs to *cultivate and deepen his sense of mystery*. When one lives on a horizontal plane, he becomes blind to the deeper

[4] F. Bland Tucker, in *The Hymnal 1940* (New York: Church Hymnal Corp., 1943), No. 504, stanza 2b.

and higher dimensions of life, but even a child does not live without a feeling of wonder and reverence. The mystery of love as communicated through his relationships with his parents is paralleled by a sense of wonder as he observes nature, and ultimately this becomes what Rudolf Otto called the sense of the *numinous,* of awe and reverence before the mystery of the ultimate reality.

This need for a mystery beyond one's self is often satisfied through superstitions, magic, astrology, and false religions. Devotion to various ideologies, surrounded as they are with rituals and intimations of the nature of reality, serves as a substitute for loyalty to the God of Jesus Christ.

The Christian mystery is faced through a challenge to one's faith. The risen Christ brings the Biblical drama of redemption into the arena of today's living, and man is confronted with a decision. The mystery of God's otherness is overcome through what God did in Christ. As one comes to the maturity of Christian faith, "that full measure of development found in Christ," so that he is no longer "blown about and swung around by every wind of doctrine through the trickery of men with their ingenuity in inventing error" (Eph. 4:13, 14, G), the basic needs of life are met, for then he knows himself loved and accepted and capable of giving love, subject to the law and capable of administering the law, growing into his own destiny and capable of being a channel of grace for others, and rooted and grounded in the unfailing mercy of the God of Jesus Christ and obedient to him.

HOW CHRISTIANITY MEETS BASIC NEEDS OF AGE GROUPS

The basic needs that the Christian religion can satisfy are universal, but they progress within themselves according to the developmental level of children and adults. The problem of growth in religion and the resulting religious readiness is understandable in terms of the needs of the various age groups. Many full-scale studies are available on the characteristics of children at different periods, but few of them deal systematically with the relation between needs and the Christian answer. All that can be done here, however, is to summarize the findings in such a way that they will have significance for the remainder of this book.

(1) INFANCY

The infant experiences love and acceptance as a result of parental attitudes. The stability of this relationship is the chief tool of Christian education during the first three years. Infant baptism or dedication is the means whereby the church ministers to the infant through the parents and godparents. What God does directly in the sacrament of baptism is not controlled by education. When the parents see the religious significance of these early experiences, they will understand that there is a "priesthood of parenthood," which is their responsibility. Processes of weaning and toilet training and experiences of sex are crucial, for at this level security arises from the sense of closeness to and approval by the mother, and this is the basis of all future teaching.

Discipline and law come to the infant primarily through the dependableness of the relationship. A mother who is consistent in meeting the basic needs of the infant provides a structure of security. A well-ordered home, geared to the capacities of the infant, provides a foundation for the later understanding of the moral law.

The growth of the infant is seen primarily as he learns to take solid foods, to walk, and to speak. The parent will be amazed as he thinks of God's grace at work through *his* child, and will understand more fully his ministry as a channel of God's grace, providing guidance and opportunity at the infant's growing edge.

The parents are interpreting God to the infant and young child through the only possible medium. Often parents do not understand, even when they themselves are religious, that here are the roots of religion; and therefore damage to the child's religious development may occur in these early years. The child's first acquaintance with wonder and mystery comes from his parents' love, and this is a two-way process as the parents regard him with awe. The father's attitude toward the mother, her attitude toward the father, and their prayers together provide an atmosphere in which the infant knows he is loved. This relationship of the child to his parents is the cornerstone of all religious teaching. The parents must be the mediators of God's grace, or else the child is unlikely to have any experience of God at all during his early days.[5]

---

[5] See Basil A. Yeaxlee, *Religion and the Growing Mind*, pp. 44, 48.

(2) THREE AND FOUR YEARS

The *pre-school* period, which we think of as the ages three and four, is often the time for attending a *nursery* school or play school. The child has experiences with the total family, plus those with many people outside the immediate circle of the home. Sometimes there is an experience of church during this period, with the warmth of the love and security of the church as a redemptive community being the primary educational experience. Although the mother provides the atmosphere of security and love, the father moves into a position of greater responsibility, for the child derives his belief in and acceptance of his heavenly Father from his experience of his human father. At this stage influence does the teaching, and instruction through words is almost useless, and for purposes of future instruction the influence of the father is crucial.[6]

Law to the pre-school child is the ways of the family. He is busy learning what is required of him, and the dependableness of routine is essential to his well-being. Right and wrong are what he finds pleases or displeases those in authority, and only constant repetition in a regular manner will build routine into a structure of law.

Growth for this age is primarily in terms of self-help, developing vocabulary, and learning through manipulation. The child is becoming part of a community, but he still operates from the perspective of his own ego. Respect for property is not likely to develop this soon, but he is learning to play alongside his peers. It is said that when nursery children cooperate, it is coincidence; they just happen to be doing the same thing at the same time.

The mystery of God is beginning to open up. The child may see his parents praying, or hear grace said at the table. He may see a baptism, or attend church. He hears references to God and Jesus simply by being part of a Christian community, and he knows that he is a member of that fellowship. The Biblical drama is coming alive not in words but through his relationships, for he has been created, has faced law on his own terms, is a member of a community in which he is forgiven and restored to relationship, and faces judgment through punishment or feeling lonely. He is sustained by God's act through Christ because he is a member of a Christian

---

[6] See Yeaxlee, *op. cit.*, pp. 55, 57, 87.

family. The language of relationships is one he can understand, and in time he will find the words to tell of these experiences.

By the time he is ready for church school, whether he begins at the age of two or five, a great deal has been accomplished by his parents. He may or may not have had the experiences that meet his basic needs. The chances are very good that only a small minority of children have the resources of the relationships we have described. The majority will not have known a consistent relationship of love and acceptance, and thus God's nature will have been misinterpreted at all these points.

Furthermore, because children differ in the progress of their learning, they will not all require the same methods for meeting these needs. At best, any listing of where children will stand at a given age is mere guess work based on statistics and observation, and therefore not necessarily applicable to a particular child. Children with all these various backgrounds normally are enrolled in churches with equally varied ideas of what Christian education is by the time they are in kindergarten.

(3) FIVE

The five-year-old relies primarily on his parents' love, and on security in the family as the chief cause of integration. He has the urge to relate to the parent of the opposite sex; male confronts female, and female confronts male. This may begin at an earlier stage, but in any event there will be some shifting back and forth as the child establishes himself as a person.[7]

He is beginning to see what right and wrong are, independent of his desire to please his parents. Sometimes he attends weekday kindergarten. He comes up against the rules of his church, begins to learn something about manners, and identifies himself with his own sex.

He starts to develop simple concepts and comes to a new appreciation of nature and pets. He begins to build ideas on his own experiences and elaborates them with fantasies. He tends to believe what he hears without any questioning.

He assimilates the attitude toward the mystery of religion shown

[7] See Lewis J. Sherrill, *The Struggle of the Soul* (New York: The Macmillan Company, 1951), pp. 34-37.

by others, and begins to appreciate the wonder of worship. He hears some stories about God and Jesus, and often confuses the two of them. Nature's wonders become a source for religious interpretation. He may experience the mystery of death, either through a pet or an older friend. Life is still pretty much a satisfying experience, without too much complexity, at this stage. The child is beginning to anticipate future experiences, although only over a short span. He is still impressed primarily by externals, such as the architecture of a church, the beauty or lack of it in the classroom, the tone of a teacher's voice, the confinement of too long worship services, and the atmosphere of kindliness or of harsh discipline that prevails.

(4) PRIMARY

The first three grades, ages six through eight, cover a period of great advancement. During this period the child must realign his adjustments to society. The home environment is still dominant, but school is now a serious business and his acceptance among his schoolmates and teachers is of great concern. He senses that the church is like a big family, and many congregations try to see that their "family nights" and other activities involve him as a fully accepted person. The family worship service, when he is included, is a reassuring experience and builds his sense of being wanted.

Sometime between the ages of four and eight, a child will begin to wonder about death.[8] The questions in his mind deal with his own sense of security. He discovers that people die; then that his mother or father might die, which upsets his equilibrium; and then that he will die someday, which often fills him with fear. This may become particularly poignant if a friend the same age should die, and besides the religious hope of eternal life it may be helpful to point out that the ages between seven and fourteen have the lowest death rate of any age group. He needs reassurance, and this comes by honestly facing the facts of death at about the first grade.

The primary child discovers the law of ownership and enjoys it as long as he is the owner. He needs to learn to respect the rights of

---

[8] See Arthur T. Jersild, *Child Psychology* 4th ed. (New York: Prentice-Hall, Inc., 1954), pp. 356-57. See Helen Parkhurst, *Exploring the Child's World* (New York: Appleton-Century-Crofts, Inc., 1951), pp. 184-207.

others, and this is more difficult. Right and wrong are now in the realm of law, and his developing conscience tells him when he has transgressed the law.

He is developing physical skills at a rapid rate, especially reading and writing. He knows himself as a growing self. Many new concepts are developing, although they are still in the realm of concrete experiences. Radio and television become part of his growing horizon. He will be shifting during this period from the realm of fantasy to the realm of fact, and will begin to ask, "Is it true?"

The mystery of baptism is a great assurance to the primary child. If he sees a baby baptized, and it is explained in his own terms as meeting the basic needs we have listed, it increases his understanding of the love of God. A class of first graders may spend two Sundays preparing to understand what happens to one of its members who is to be baptized, and then they witness the baptism and discuss it afterwards. Churches that do not have infant or child baptism may accomplish similar ends with the service of dedication, which has the value of stressing the responsibility of parents although it lacks the sacramental element. When children see one of their number accepted as "a child of God and an inheritor of the kingdom of heaven," they understand that God loves them and accepts them as they are, and that he expects them to be obedient to his laws as they grow in wisdom and faith.[9]

The primary child is ready to appreciate the mysteries of birth and death, especially as he moves from the fantasy to the factual stage. The particular experiences of the group are the significant element in opening up these topics. He is ready to hear stories about Jesus and God, although he lacks the sense of history and chronology necessary for perspective on the drama of redemption. He participates to a limited extent in the services of worship. The beauties of nature are appreciated as part of God's wonderful world, although there is a danger that nature will be treated sentimentally by the adults seeking to teach him. Chiefly, he needs to know that he is a full-fledged member of God's great family, and this comes more from relationships than from words.

---

[9] See Reuel L. Howe, *Man's Need and God's Action* (Greenwich: Seabury Press, 1953), pp. 51-61.

(5) JUNIOR

The junior is in the fourth, fifth, and sixth grades. Sometime between the ages of nine and eleven he moves out into the world and the beginnings of independence can be observed. Often there seems to be a break between the fourth and fifth grades, the fourth grader seeming closer to the third than to the fifth grader. For this reason some churches using a two-grade cycle place the third and fourth grades in the "lower junior" group and the fifth and sixth grades in the "upper junior" group.

The junior is developing social attitudes and is concerned with the needs of others. He has a geographical orientation and is capable of sympathy with those in other lands. He is anxious about his acceptance in the gang, about joining or forming a club, and about his activities after school. Sometimes he is left out of the groups. He still needs the understanding and love of his parents, but they have to be expressed in a way much different from that of his earlier years. Normally he is still sufficiently a part of the family unit to enjoy church affairs with the family.

He has a great sense of justice. He is likely to ask, "Is it fair?" as often as "Is it true?" He is most concerned about the others *being fair to him,* but he accepts the rules of the game when he understands them. The most important rules are those of his peers, and he accepts the rule book of any sport. His conscience is highly developed, and justice is considered far superior to love, especially among boys. He begins to see more clearly the masculine and feminine roles, although tomboys are tolerated provided they can hold their own. By the end of this period, however, puberty has begun for some juniors.

The preadolescent forms several thousand concepts, most of which are based upon personal experience. But he is beginning to build on vicarious experiences, and his reading, radio, and television, and other experiences enable him to form accurate concepts of related meanings. But often the junior will learn concepts that have no relation to reality, because of his inability to go beyond his growing edge. It is hard for him to conceive of life in Palestine unless it is associated with a similar set of conditions in his own experience, but television, picture magazines, comics, and war games give him a geographical perspective. He still needs concrete learning experiences, which is why hobbies that challenge his manual dexterity are so popular, as are sports that demand physical participation and contact (at least among boys). Probably the most important concepts in this period, or shortly before, are those of time and space. Here are the beginnings of a sense of history, indicating that about the sixth grade a junior boy or girl can study a period in history without too much confusion.[10]

The junior hears a good deal of discussion about religion. He likes facts. His new sense of space means that he can appreciate missionary activity, especially among Indians or in the "wild West." He is capable of a great deal of hero worship, but is not likely to derive his hero from religion. He participates in worship but is impatient with adult services. He may stop saying his prayers, or at least insist on privacy.

(6) JUNIOR HIGH (INTERMEDIATE)

With the twelve-year-old, we move into adolescence and the real opening of the "war of independence." No matter how much he is loved and accepted as he is by his parents, he tends to reject them, and he feels strongly the conflict between his own urges and his parents' ways of thinking and acting. He is easily embarrassed by them before friends of his own age. He is striving for leadership in his own age group, or is accepting the leadership of some other person in the group. He normally finds himself at enmity with the opposite sex, although sometimes dating begins during the latter part of this period. His environment now includes some interest in the news of the world, of which he is a part.

He has the masculine and feminine roles clearly in mind. He accepts work in the home, but normally does not show much of a sense of responsibility. He faces the conflict between the moral demands of his background and those of his age group, and sometimes school and church will add to the conflict. He is capable of genuine loyalty, but it has to be won by one group in competition with the others.

His growth is uneven. The girl has matured a year or two ahead of the boy, and this increases the conflict. Girls are less likely to be tomboys. Real skill develops in the use of the body as the awkward stage is passed. From the age of twelve on, many boys and girls are

---

[10] See Robert J. Havighurst, *Developmental Tasks and Education,* 2nd ed. (New York: Longmans, Green Co., 1952), p. 22.

willing to make a genuine decision about Christianity, and confirmation normally takes place during this period, although there is much doubt about their grasp of the intellectual implications of their faith.

They are more likely at this age to have an emotional experience of conversion or decision, and often their feeling for the divine is superior to their understanding. They can be led to see that God's grace is needed, and that it comes through an act of faith; the Lord's Supper, therefore, takes on meaning both as a fellowship and an act of faith for the first time. They can understand the Bible *as history,* and thus the drama of redemption takes on chronological significance, although their theological concepts are still limited to the events by which God has revealed himself. A crucial point may occur when science and religion are seen to conflict, and a wise educational program will anticipate this by constructive interpretation.

(7) SENIOR HIGH

By middle adolescence, the conflict between teen-agers and parents has often reached the stage of undeclared war. Their strong group sense causes them to band together, and they rely on peer relationships for their love and acceptance. Boy-girl relationships are often in the "steady" stage and takes a great deal of their time. Teen-agers need this emotional independence, and at the same time they need parents who are capable of loving them in their most unlovable moments, for a real but hidden understanding of what they are going through provides an almost unrecognized source of genuine security. Their horizon sometimes seems limited to their own egos, but it also stretches to a concern for world affairs and politics.

The moral conflict for the teen-ager comes when popularity demands actions that offend his conscience. Necking, drinking, cheating, and lying to parents are among the standard temptations, and the Christian faith provides help in finding an answer. In some situations, however, the restrictions set up in the name of religion increase the sense of frustration. The teen-ager is developing a sense of values in the midst of his conflicts, and he is using the resources of his past; for he is the product of his earliest and continuing experiences as well as of the present moment. What he learns *now* has significance in terms of what he has experienced through the years, for his basic decisions depend on the total personality pattern that he has developed. He is now seeing himself *as a self* in relation to society, and he is seeking to find out what socially responsible and acceptable behavior is for him.

The biological stresses of adolescence provide additional conflicts. The sexual urges are moving toward maturity in a society that frowns upon sexual expression. He thinks a good deal about sex, and such thoughts may touch upon kissing, bodily contact, and sexual intercourse. Some adolescents are conditioned to refrain from any contact with the opposite sex, many of them enjoy a restrained but healthy contact in games and dancing, others indulge in "selective" necking, others in more advanced petting, and an undetermined number have experiences in intercourse. It is hard to estimate whether such practices are more prevalent in this generation than in previous ones, because of the open attitude toward sex today. The church needs to face up to these conflicts and to provide realistic Christian resources to help the adolescent with this problem.

The adolescent is developing new skills. He is inclined to rethink his religious position. He is capable of a certain amount of abstract analysis, is likely to be skeptical, and is willing to try to think through genuine problems on an intellectual plane. He is looking forward to a vocation or to college at the end of this period and wants to know what the world has in store for him. Often this means anticipation of a tour of duty in the armed forces. Marriage is a live option for seniors in high school, even when college is in the offing. Courses on vocation and marriage are essential for high school seniors.

Religiously he is willing to face up to the decision that Jesus is *his* Christ. Against the background of the work of God in history, he is able to see the meaning of the redemptive act of God in Christ and thus to assimilate the saving grace of God through faith. His self-reliance is thwarted by his real need for a Savior, and he comes to this conclusion when he is provided the opportunity for self-analysis. In this way, doctrine begins to be relevant to his own existence, and he is capable of moving toward maturity in faith. When his needs are met at this level, he stays within the community of the church because it is a means of redemption for him.

This does not mean that he is capable of abstract theological concepts. An experiment with such words as divine, eternal, spirit, providence, infinite, ubiquity, almighty, immutability, omniscient, perfect, and Trinity among boys and girls in Roman Catholic parochial schools showed that at best only about sixty-five per cent could properly define these words after many years of training, and ability to define does not mean ability to comprehend. Furthermore, there was little improvement after the ninth grade.[11] Concepts have value for education only when they are relevant to life's decisions.

(8) OLDER YOUTH AND YOUNG ADULTS

The basic needs of older youth and young adults have not changed since adolescence, but they are expressed in a new way. Older youth have not taken on the responsibilities of adults but are continuing their schooling or are working and living at home. Young adults are the same age, normally about eighteen to twenty-five, but they have taken upon themselves the responsibilities of adults. Both groups are in the process of achieving physical, mental, and spiritual maturity, but they are developing in terms of their opportunities and surroundings within different contexts. Both groups need the resources of the church to help them adjust to their new ways of living.[12]

(9) COUPLES AND PARENTS

The concerns of couples and parents are the establishment of a Christian home and the care of children. Within the Christian community, their fundamental needs are met in the context of their emerging concerns. In many cases the lack of religious resources becomes an acute problem, and those who have drifted from the church return in the hope that they can make up for lost time. Crises in the home, conflicts between husband and wife, concern for the welfare of the children, facing the decision of baptism or dedication of children or the challenge of being a homemaker or provider open up the areas of frustration, failure, insecurity, and sin that influence the outcomes.

(10) MIDDLE ADULTS

Middle adults, whether single or married, become aware of the

---

[11] See John B. McDowell, *The Development of the Idea of God in the Catholic Child* (Washington: Catholic University Press, 1952), p. 77. See also *More than Words* (Greenwich: Seabury Press, 1955).

[12] See below, pp. 309-11.

state of their own souls. This is the age that attends church and Bible classes most regularly. They have reached personal, social, and religious maturity, or have become aware of their shortcomings, failures, and immaturity, and they know that they need the resources of religion for their personal spiritual health. They are adjusting to the independence of their children and to the need to fill this gap meaningfully, or they are dealing with the responsibility of caring for aging parents and relatives, or they are meeting the problems of middle-age with the shift from faster to slower living.

(11) OLDER ADULTS

Older adults are facing retirement, with all of the emotional and financial problems connected with a changing life pattern. Their income is usually reduced, their health is deteriorating, and they face the death of a spouse or their companions. The solace of religion often provides an outlet for their energies as well as meaning for life. The awareness that death is not far off may upset their sense of security, may be a promise of release from pain, or may provide zeal and zest for living out of the remaining days of their lives. The church ministers to them through its activities and organizations as well as through a special program for shut-ins and the sick.[13]

When the church achieves its purpose of being a redemptive community, it is a channel of grace for all its people, children and adults.[14] The sense of belonging and the experience of worship answer the need for love and acceptance, provided the life of the congregation is actually a channel of grace and a fellowship of the Holy Spirit for everyone. The law faces them as essentially moral. Growth for adults is no longer physical, but spiritual and mental development leads to new insights into the meaning of life and death. God's grace continues to be mysterious, and the Holy Spirit offers strength and solace in the continuing experiences of life. The people are seeing the meaning of Jesus' words: "Come unto me, all ye that

---

[13] See Robert J. Havighurst, *Development Tasks and Education* (New York: Longmans, Green & Co., 2nd ed., 1952), pp. 72-98, for a treatment of three periods of adulthood.

[14] See below, Chapter 19, for a discussion of how the church meets the needs of all age groups.

travail and are heavy laden, and I will refresh you" (Matthew 11:28, PB).

EDUCATION AND REVELATION

Christian education is concerned with the wholeness of the personality. It is found in the response of the total person to the divine Person within a community of persons. As the learner makes use of historical knowledge and doctrine within the limitations of his growing edge, and as the church's organization contributes to the effectiveness of techniques and equipment, the learner becomes more acclimatized to the religious life. But important as all these elements are, they are only a preparation for the real thing.

What happens to a person throughout the various stages of his development is of greatest significance, for these experiences and relationships provide the structure of his personality, which is enabled to respond in faith to God's grace. Man's maturity of faith comes from his response to Jesus Christ; and as he is enabled to appreciate the act of God in and through him and to respond freely to God's grace, this is a revelation.[15]

This revelation is normally found through participation in the shared life of the Christian community. That community includes the local congregation, but it also includes the sense of a "cloud of witnesses" who have gone on before. The "communion of saints," past and present, is not only the support of man's faith but also the channel of God's grace.

> Education in church membership is thus in a sense the culmination of all the rest of education in the Christian religion. Yet it often begins simply with habit. Children are associated with a church because their parents are, or because their school is, or because they

---

[15] Archbishop Temple says, "The revelation is not primarily in propositions concerning Christ to which my intellect may assent; it is in Christ Himself, to Whom my whole personality must bow. . . . The revelation is the fact–Jesus Christ Himself. The appeal exercised by this revelation is to the whole Personality. Therefore response to it cannot be reluctant; only where it is willing does it exist at all. . . . The revelation is given in a Person to persons. . . . There is a compulsion upon the soul, but it is exercised through freedom; God puts forth his power upon us, but our servitude is our perfect freedom." *Revelation,* eds. John Baillie and Hugh Martin (New York: The Macmillian Company, 1937), pp. 120-21.

> have friends who go, or because it is the nearest, or because it is a way of getting rid of them for an hour or two on Sundays.[16]

So we have something to work with, no matter what the motives, and when we concern ourselves with the basic needs of persons, within this redemptive community, education into religion takes place. They will learn through satisfying their physiological drives, through their desire for satisfactory emotional experiences, through the guidance of reward and punishment, through association with people they love and whose approval they desire, through the authority of respected leadership, and through reflective thinking. When all of this takes place in "an atmosphere in which grace flourishes," they will be likely to respond through their own freedom to the will of God for them.

---

[16] A. Victor Murray, *Education into Religion* (New York: Harper & Bros., 1954), pp 195-96.

PART TWO

Primary Educational Institutions

CHAPTER 6

RELIGIOUS EDUCATION IN THE HOME

WE TURN now to an evaluation of the forces of Christian education. Our purpose is to discover the resources for teaching religion in the four primary educational institutions: the home, the school, the community, and the church. We are taking them in this order so that we may understand the contributions of those institutions that are not necessarily religious, and then we shall be in a position to see how the church deals with persons who are the products of our American culture.

Religion as a way of life permeates all experience, and every institution contributes in some way to the religious development of each individual. Because the church makes use of the experiences and interpretations of the other institutions, we need to know how these other institutions provide relationships and interpretations before we can see clearly the task of the church.

The way in which the family is unified is the chief factor in the integration of a child's personality. The family initiates motives, manners, prejudices, and ideals. The examples of the parents and other children have various effects on the learner. The general atmosphere of home-life is a determining influence in the development of attitudes. The basic stuff of religious belief and faith is established in early home experiences.

Second only to the home is the school. The school normally is not concerned primarily with religious nurture but with the general improvement of the personality. It teaches in terms of the development of mind and body, of loyalty to country, of adjustment to the mores of the culture, and of understanding of the democratic way of life.

Because it is concerned with character education and spiritual values, it provides an indirect background for religious instruction. To what extent religion or irreligion as such is taught in the public schools is an open question, answered in different ways from school to school and from state to state.

When we see that religion arises from personal relationships and from the adjustment of the individual to community life, and that God is at work in this area of experience whether we know it or not, we understand how religious education is taking place at the school level more easily than do those who identify religious teaching with explicit instruction.

The category of the community as an educational institution is a convenient way of classifying all influences outside of home, school, and church. For the child, it means primarily the impact of the neighborhood and playground on his developing attitudes. For the adolescent and young adult, the community may mean many other forces that help to determine his outlook on life. For the adult at work, his job is as significant as the community forces. By community, we mean a person's play and work, his leisure time activities and his occupation, his concern for the welfare of the larger community and citizenship in town and nation, and all the forces that come into his home or work from the outside. The psychology of modern advertising, as it comes through the printed page or over the air, is part of the impact of the community on one's basic philosophy of life.

The church stands as a community set apart, concerned primarily with the redemption of all mankind. It works with and through the home, school, and community as a fellowship of the Holy Spirit. We place it last in our treatment of educational institutions because it interprets and judges all other experiences. The amount of time spent within the confines of church buildings is too small to be of great significance for the major portion of the population, and yet the church provides meaning for all of life.

The relevance of Christianity for all of life is seen in the church's total educational program, which for some is limited to Sunday morning and for many others extends to church and non-church activities during the week. When the church is a redemptive community, it has power to change one's attitude in his experiences as a member of all kinds of groups in home, school, and community.

CHRISTIAN MARRIAGE

Marriage is part of the natural order of creation. There is nothing specifically Christian about marriage, for it is the result of the fact that God created both male and female with the intention that they should live together and have children. The child and his parents are irrevocably bound together because of their biological relationship, which can be neither denied nor destroyed, even though the family itself may disintegrate. The tendency is toward monogamy, for even in purely sexual love there is the desire for it to be exclusive and permanent. Marriage means "binding," and even in natural religion it is a sacred relationship.

D. S. Bailey writes that genuine sex love *(eros)* seeks a permanent relationship. Natural man seeks mutual companionship *(philia)* as essential to sexual union. Both sexual love and companionship are controlled and enriched by self-giving love *(agape)*. This "trichotomy of love" stands in a balanced relation in marriage, and its significance is made clear when we see how the lack of balance between these three aspects of married love leads so often to disintegration of the marriage relationship.[1]

True marriage as seen from the Christian perspective consists of consent and sexual union whereby the two "become one flesh." It is true that marriages have existed without consent, and only in recent times have women had freedom to choose a mate; yet a degree of consent was present for there to be a genuine marriage. Consent, however, does not make a marriage for it is simply the precondition to marriage.

The true union of marriage in "one flesh" is called *henosis*. Bailey writes that "the true, authentic *henosis* is effected by intercourse following consent between a man and a woman who love one another and who act freely, deliberately, responsibly and with the knowledge and approval of the community, and in so doing (whether they know it or not) conform to the Divine law." [2] Even "common law" marriages, provided they lack nothing but public recognition and legal status, are recognized in Protestantism as genuine marriages that may be blessed in the church.

---

[1] See Derrick Sherwin Bailey, *The Mystery of Love and Marriage* (New York: Harper & Brothers, 1952), pp. 21-22, 24-30.

[2] *Ibid.*, p. 52.

The essence of marriage is found in this coming together in *henosis,* and even the intention to have children is a secondary factor. The consummation of genuine love involves a basic change in the personal relations of man and wife and the acceptance of responsibilities entailed by their relationship.

Christian marriage is conceived as a sacred relationship, because both husband and wife recognize the other as one for whom Christ died. Each recognizes the need of God's grace as a means for making the marriage a successful relationship, and therefore each sees the family as a redemptive cell, as part of the total redemptive community that is the church. Their relationship is more than consent and sexual union, because they ask God's blessing on that union. They have been married in church so that their consenting together in holy wedlock may be recognized as sacred. Marriage is not a sacrament in the technical sense, but it is sacramental in that the ring given and received is a token and pledge of the relationship.

THE CHRISTIAN FAMILY

Christian marriage evolves into the Christian family. There is fellowship between parents and children. They share vital interests together. They are concerned for the growth and development of each individual. The members change, but the family remains. There is what Horace Bushnell calls "the organic unity of the family." This unity is more than influence and involves the power of parents over their children, "not only when they teach, encourage, persuade, and govern, but without any purposed control whatever. The bond is so intimate that they do it unconsciously and undesignedly – they must do it. Their character, feelings, spirit and principles must propagate themselves, whether they will or not." [3] This is *atmosphere,* as opposed to influence, and it reaches the child as naturally as the air he breathes.

Although the family spirit will not be assimilated in equal fashion by the children, the organic unity of the family is the dominating element in the early education of the child. *This is not conscious teaching,* according to Bushnell, but is the natural impact of group

[3] Horace Bushnell, *Christian Nurture* (New Haven: Yale University Press, 1947), p. 76.

life on its members. "Your character," he says, "is a stream, a river, flowing down upon your children, hour by hour." [4] Within this relationship, parents need to admit their own shortcomings and make it clear that they are struggling with their own infirmities. "There are too many Christian families that are only little popedoms," [5] in which parents insist on infallible rules.

Religion in the family is chiefly a matter of personal relationships. These relationships are often broken because of an offense or misunderstanding or unresolved tension. Complex influences from outside the home, as illustrated by cultural pressures, changes in residence, economic reversals or successes, and attitudes of neighbors, may increase the sense of lostness. Individuals within the home reject each other, and this may lead to disruption, disgrace, or divorce.

The power of the Christian faith is illustrated when it is the means for healing broken relationships. When the rejected person seeks forgiveness and reconciliation follows, when forgiveness is freely offered and rectification follows, when self-giving love triumphs over the sense of possessiveness, or when a child says "Please take me back," the power of the Gospel is at work. This power to forgive, to restore the relationship to its previous level, is the ministry of reconciliation, and it rests on the redeeming power of God. The Gospel, then, is re-enacted in Christian homes through the faith of its members. Christ is the Redeemer, and we are recipients of God's grace.

This relationship is described in the second letter to Timothy: "I am reminded of your sincere faith, a faith that dwelt first in your grandmother Lois and your mother Eunice and now, I am sure, dwells in you" (II Tim. 1:5, RSV). Within the home, the devotional life of the family may assist each member to live out the Christian faith. Many families find that saying grace at table, or prayers with the children, or nighttime prayers with the younger children, or special prayers on particularly meaningful days is a help in establishing the right relationships. But the attitudes are what count, and the wrong attitude can make family worship a devastating experience, driving parents and children further apart.

In the home the child learns the answers to his fundamental religious questions by the way he is treated. He learns of the nature of God by the way his fundamental needs are met. *This may be in-*

---

[4] *Ibid.*, p. 98.
[5] *Ibid.*, p. 99.

adequate in every way. If his home is a redemptive cell, he knows that he is loved and accepted as he is, he understands the structure of dependable relations, he is free to grow under guidance, and the mystery of God is a reality in his experience before he can say the word.

MAJOR INFLUENCES WITHIN THE FAMILY

It is perfectly obvious that a Christian home, as we have described it, is a rare experience. Homes are made up of sinners, who are blown about by various influences, who are caught up in their own shortcomings, who are incapable of giving the degree of love necessary to restore relationships, and who are at odds about the way in which children should be brought up. The parents may disagree about the child's activities, and the child soon learns which parent is the "easy mark." Grandparents in the home often interfere with their own brand of religion or their own ethical opinions. Aunts and uncles often feel that they should make suggestions.

Not all families consist of parents and children. Many broken homes have only one parent, or a step-parent and parent. Death, divorce, travel, or military service has separated the child from one parent. These factors are of significance in our grasp of the meaning of a child's home life.

No matter how careful the parents are in dealing with their children, the children will establish their own relationships within the family. One after another will be rejected for one reason or another and then brought back into the orbit again. Sometimes this is a natural and amoral reaction of children as their groups form and re-form, but ostracism of one child may have harmful results.

The surroundings make a difference. The kind of house or apartment lived in, especially in light of the fact that only about twenty per cent of America's families live in one-family detached houses, makes a great difference in the opportunities for children's recreation. Slum areas that lack playgrounds, homes that are overcrowded, parents who work, and contact with other children with similar disadvantages provide the conditions that lead to delinquency. The suburban child, however, is likely to have too many opportunities to exercise his freedom and curiosity, and because of insufficient contact with his parents is equally likely to go astray.

No home operates in isolation from the rest of society. From every angle it is attacked, penetrated, beseiged, and sometimes overcome. But there are agencies in society chiefly interested in supporting the Christian family, and among the home's allies are the school and church. The Christian family does not stand alone. It has resources within itself and among its allies, and because it is grounded in God's natural order of creation, the bond of union between parents becomes the means whereby their attitude toward the children provides much of their Christian nurture.

THE HOME AND CHRISTIAN EDUCATION

The church is concerned about family life. Its educational program may be outlined in terms of the developing needs of young people as they look forward to marriage. Education for family life is essential to any high school course in Christian nurture. The high school senior is looking toward marriage in the foreseeable future, unless he is among the minority who go to college, and today many college students are married. It is close enough so that knowledge of marriage is a genuine concern. The origin of such a course may be pushed back into the period when dating begins, when the concern of our young people is for a Christian attitude toward boy-girl relationships. As an outcome of that situation will come interest in marriage. The approach of such a course will most likely be both sociological and theological. It will involve the deepest meanings of marriage and the predictions of marital success. Young people want to know what to look for in a prospective marriage partner, and relatively reliable information is available.[6] The moral implications of the Kinsey reports are of immediate interest, as they apply both to their future marriage and to their current behavior. The Christian interpretation of *henosis* is a sound guide here.

Some churches will postpone this approach until the young adult stage, and others will reintroduce it at that period. Then anticipation is even keener, and the same subjects may be dealt with more fully. A course on education for marriage may well be a basic element for both young adults and college students.

---

[6] See Ernest W. Burgess and Harvey J. Locke, *The Family* (New York: American Book Co., 1953), pp. 396-442.

PREMARITAL EDUCATION

Premarital instruction is required by some denominations, and this may be approached either through personal counseling or through special classes. Both the theological and sociological elements are involved in the interpretation of Christian marriage. Marriage is seen as "instituted of God, signifying unto us the mystical union that is betwixt Christ and his Church," and is to be entered into "reverently, discreetly, advisedly, soberly, and in the fear of God." [7] The parties are to take each other under any and all conditions until parted by death. When they have "consented together in holy wedlock, and have witnessed the same before God and this company, and thereto have given and pledged their troth, each to the other, and have declared the same by giving and receiving a Ring, and by joining hands," the minister pronounces that "they are Man and Wife." [8] The whole doctrine of Christian marriage is summed up in these remarkable words, and the marriage is consummated as the man and woman become "one flesh" through sexual union.

FACTORS IN SUCCESSFUL MARRIAGE

Young people need to know also the chances of success. Can they measure their love? If we recall Bailey's use of sexual attraction *(eros)*, companionship *(philia)*, and self-giving love *(agape)*, the prediction of marriage success can be made only in terms of companionship. The findings of many researches indicate that success in marriage depends on shared interests. A careful research project on couples about to be married, followed by a classification after five years of marriage into those who had broken up, those who were still married but unhappy about it, and those who were happily married, indicated a direct correlation between interests held in common at the time of marriage and the success of that marriage.[9] This information is of great significance in courses on education for marriage because it provides some norms for selecting persons with

[7] *Book of Common Prayer,* p. 300.

[8] *Book of Common Prayer,* p. 304.

[9] See Ernest W. Burgess and Leonard S. Cottrell, *Predicting Success or Failure in Marriage* (New York: Prentice-Hall, Inc., 1939).

whom courtship might be desirable, and exploring these areas is helpful for the mutual understanding sought through the premarital conference.

Besides premarital counseling and classes in education for Christian marriage, there are other opportunities for the church to work along these lines. Certain Sundays marked for Mother's Day, Father's Day, Family Sunday, and Youth Sunday provide opportunities for sermons on the subject of the Christian Family. Courses of sermons may be offered on money, sex, and recreation. Classes on marriage for high school seniors are essential for adequate training in Christian living. Young people's groups approach the problems of dating, sex, engagement, and marriage in a variety of ways, depending on their particular interests and opportunities. Because successful marriage is based on attitudes developed early in life, some aspects of these subjects should be introduced throughout the educational experience of the children.

PREPARENTAL TRAINING

A new area of training is being explored by obstetricians and others who are concerned with preparental attitudes. Often expectant mothers and fathers will attend a series of lectures to prepare them for becoming parents. They get much sound medical and psychiatric advice, but not often is any help provided for their religious preparation for the arrival of a child.

The churches have so far failed to take advantage of a similar opportunity. Yet, if what we have said about the early religious training of the child in terms of relationships is sound, the potential parents need vital help at exactly this point. If the theological significance of birth and its attendant joys and duties, including the religious meaning of meeting a child's basic needs, were made clear, many more children would begin their lives in a relationship of security and intelligent love at every level of experience.

BAPTISM OR DEDICATION

This leads naturally to the next step in parental education, which is preparation for the responsibilities resulting from infant baptism or dedication. Two aspects of baptism or dedication need to be kept in mind. First, there is what God does, as symbolized by the naming of the child and his acceptance as a child of God. The child is born again, born into a new relationship with God and man. The child having been "received into the congregation of Christ's flock," the second aspect of baptism or dedication is the congregation's responsibility for the promises made in the child's name. The service is a reminder to the congregation, to the minister, to the parents, that this child is to be brought up as a Christian.

The parents are the true ministers of baptism's continuing efficacy. They are accessible, and they provide the primary relationships that will determine the child's capacity to enter into relationships with others and with God. The early determination of attitudes, motives, values, and information is almost solely the responsibility of parents. Psychologically, the parents serve as God to the child, and there is no way for the parents to escape this responsibility. Baptism is the means whereby the church ministers to the child through the parents, and it stands for the meeting of the child's basic needs.

When Jesus says, "Let the children come to me," and when the congregation says, "We receive this child," it stands for the love and acceptance of the child as he is by God and by the congregation. When the parents or godparents promise that the child will learn the Ten Commandments and other Biblical teachings, they are promising that the child will be confronted with the law and structure of society. When the promise is made that the child will ratify and confirm this faith when he is old enough, the service meets the requirements for direction of growth. And underlying the service is faith that God is present and acting on this child through the symbolism of the water that washes one clean, and this is expressed in the life of the congregation as a redemptive and sustaining community of the Holy Spirit.

When parents have this understanding of baptism or dedication, and when it takes place as part of a service of worship with a congregation present, it has an effective power both educationally and evangelically. The error of those who think of baptism as a form of magic is overcome, and the church's ministry to children and adults alike is strengthened.[10]

---

[10] See Reuel L. Howe, *Man's Need and God's Action* (Greenwich: Seabury Press, 1953), pp. 51-61; see my *A Symphony of the Christian Year* (Greenwich: Seabury Press, 1954), pp. 140-52, 207-12.

THE FAMILY IN THE CHURCH

Even if the church has done a proper job with premarital and postmarital education, after baptism or dedication of the infant it still needs to guide the parents in the home during the period before the child comes to church. The relationships during this period are crucial, and much can be done for parents through the right kind of education.

The most important requirement in the church's approach is to work through the family unit. The organic unity of the family becomes an ally of the church at this point, provided the church does not imitate secular society by dividing the family into segregated individuals.

The beginning and center of this approach is family worship in the church. This is most effective when it is a family service, geared to the needs of the children and the concern of the parents for their children, and therefore relevant to all in the family-centered congregation. Often this is a service at 9 or 9:15 A. M., held in the church with a junior choir and conducted by the pastor. It symbolizes the acceptance of the family as a redemptive cell within the larger Christian congregation. Variations of this plan may be developed at the traditional 11 A. M. service by gearing it to family needs for the first half, and then dismissing the children. In some cases the service may be held in the parish house at the same time as the service in the church, but the parents will be with their children.[11]

Worship is here conceived of as part of the educational program, and the educational program is thought of as including worship as the experience-centered curriculum at its best. But congregations should extend their thinking beyond the customary Sunday school to a "school of the church." Wesner Fallaw has put this program into practice by appealing to parents through their concern for their children. A family-based curriculum for all classes leads to family cooperation during the week, and thus to a continuance of the "school of the church" as an interpretation of life during the week. That parents can be converted to such a program is already proved by the fact that so many parishes now have registration by family units.[12]

---

[11] See Chapter 16 on "Methods of Worship."

[12] Wesner Fallaw, *The Modern Parent and the Teaching Church* (New York: The Macmillan Company, 1946), p. 102.

Ernest M. Ligon has developed parent cooperation to a high degree of effectiveness in his Character Education Project.[13] The Presbyterian *Christian Faith and Life Series* of church school lessons, the Congregational-Christian *Pilgrim Series* and the Episcopal *Seabury Series* are among those that provide materials for parents.

After or previous to the family worship, parents attend classes at the same time as their children. In some cases the content is parallel to that of the children, and in others it deals with the major concerns of parents about their children without being tightly geared to the immediate problems being faced by the children. The parents develop their own confession of faith, and understand how this can be relevant to the child's growth in religion. The parents are assisted in their communication of faith to their children, and thus religion in the home becomes a profound reality. To this program is sometimes added coordination between teachers of children and the parents, through home visitations and special interviews, as well as regular reports.

Parish life, when it is family-centered, grows beyond the impact of a Sunday morning program. The usual segregated activities to meet special interests and to minister to those without families are continued, but added to these are the special family-centered recreational and social service programs.

As the family-centered program develops, the parents' class becomes a source for new teachers. The growing practice of having a man and wife teach a class limited to about twelve children has resulted from this family-centered approach. Always there are more parents trained than can be used, and not only do the children learn that their own parents are concerned about religion, but a husband-and-wife team representing the father-mother interest in religion guards against the idea that those who know anything about the church are women.

This same family solidarity is strengthened by the use of public baptism in the family service, for often one or the other parent is baptized along with the children, thus witnessing to the fact that adults need baptism as well as children.

As the religious needs of children change, so their relationships

---

[13] Ernest M. Ligon, *A Greater Generation* (New York: The Macmillan Company, 1948). But Horace Bushnell saw this in 1847, as demonstrated in *Christian Nuture.*

with their parents are altered. The maturity toward which they are moving comes as parents move into the background and youths' conscious relationship with God through the community of the Holy Spirit is mediated through worship and sacrament, through their own group experiences in class, and through their need to make their own decisions in faith. But they *still need their parents!* The church can be of the greatest assistance in making clear the kind of help adolescents need and the kind they reject, the amount of freedom to make mistakes they must have in order to grow up and the kind of safeguards that are possible in order to avoid tragic errors. At this point, a good deal of research has provided available information that is not being used adequately by the churches.

The Christian faith does not result from a good nurturing process. It is not just the unfolding of potentialities of children and youth. But Christian education uses all the potentialities brought out by the right kind of family relationships, along with the resources of school, community, and church. No system, however, can guarantee a response, and it is the response of man's faith to God's grace that is the crucial point. It is during adolescence that such a response normally is made.

A program involving the home and church is essential to a sound educational program in any church and to an effective nurturing process in the home. Although there must always be a place for the children of non-cooperating parents and for adults who do not live in families, the church's program must learn to deal more fully with the family and to meet its needs as a unit. Parents are, in Henri Clavier's words, "religion in action" for their children. The church must assist them at this point so that they can assist the church to be a redemptive and sustaining community.

CHAPTER 7

RELIGIOUS EDUCATION AND THE SCHOOLS

THE SCHOOLS of a nation reflect its political and moral ideals. The changes in communist and fascist nations have involved the educational institutions as part of the process and as part of the continuing influence of these political philosophies. The schools, however, frequently uphold the best ideals of a culture against political pressures. Democracy as lived in the American public schools and universities has had much to do with the strengthening of the American way of life.

Religion has always been a portion of the American pattern of living. It was expressed in the life of the community and in the schools from the earliest days. It was presupposed in the statements concerning democracy by the founding fathers. The moral ideals of the United States of America have been formulated by and supported by the churches. Though Alexander Hamilton objected to prayers as a form of "foreign aid," and though James Madison recognized that "neither moral nor religious motives can be relied upon for adequate control" of factions among legislators, there was general agreement that men were created equal and were endowed by their creator with certain inalienable rights.

The religion reflected in the Declaration of Independence and the Constitution was known as Deism, a semi-secular position not unacceptable to Judaism, Roman Catholicism, and Protestantism, although approaching the full implications of none. It was a kind of natural religion, a forerunner of the secularism that began to influence the schools within two generations after Thomas Jefferson.

The rising secularism of our culture, the increasing concern for vocational and classical subjects, the growing separation of church and state, and the Protestant individualism that led to the proliferating of sectarianism contributed to a system that eliminated religion as a subject from the curriculum of public education. This occurred before Roman Catholicism and Judaism became strong enough to add to the divisiveness.

As tax funds were used to support education, it became clear that no sectarian schools should receive tax money. One state after another passed laws barring the teaching of sectarian or denominational doctrines.[1] The effect was to eliminate religion from the schools, to prohibit religious instruction, and even to promote the use of textbooks written on the assumptions of secularism.

WHAT PUBLIC SCHOOLS TEACH

Either through planned religious activities or through the factual study of religion the public schools still teach some religion, but they are chiefly concerned with the inculcation of democratic values and good citizenship without recourse to religious sanctions or resources. The meaning of freedom and the procedures of democracy are learned through participation in a school life that accepts these precepts. The spiritual values of our culture are studied, normally without reference to the beliefs of any sect. Out of this is expected to come character development, based on a system of values derived from our religious heritage but relying on the sanctions of a democratic and secular culture.

Those who believe most strongly in "a *wall* of separation" between church and state insist that this is all that should be attempted by the public schools and that anything more is unconstitutional. In practice much more is achieved, and it is clear that religious instruction is legal in some states and illegal in others. The most common practice is Bible reading, usually without comment and from the King James version. The most recent tabulation of state laws shows that in twelve states Bible reading is required, in six others it is permitted, in eighteen the law does not cover it and it is permissible, in eight it is

---

[1] A tabulation and discussion of these laws are found in J. Paul Williams, *The New Education and Religion* (New York: Association Press, 1945), pp. 51-55.

forbidden, and in four it is assumed to be banned.[2] There is often a syllabus of passages running from five to twelve verses. In many cases the reading of the Bible is followed by a prayer, often by the Lord's Prayer, and in one case by the last stanza of "America." Pageants and the singing of carols are popular at Christmas time, even in states that forbid Bible reading. It is true that in many schools practices congenial to the community are followed without reference to the interpretations of the laws, but one tendency has been to interpret the laws so that the King James version is a Protestant and sectarian book when compared with the Roman Catholic versions or a Jewish Old Testament.

At best, the schools provide a token recognition of religion. This suits those who are secularists or those who would rather have secularism as a basic philosophy rather than risk having the tenets of any other group than their own taught in the schools. Luther A. Weigle has written that "whenever a group or even an individual has chosen to object, on what are averred to be conscientious grounds, to some religious element in the program or curriculum of the public schools, that element has forthwith been eliminated, and no other religious element has taken its place. The movement has been almost wholly negative." [3] It is almost as if the constitution stands for the establishment of irreligion.

PRESENT STATUS OF RELIGIOUS INSTRUCTION

Except for Bible reading and occasional carols and pageants, there is little to suggest that the public schools are concerned with religion. Individual teachers witness in their own way to their faith – this is of greater significance than may immediately be realized – and many teachers and administrators are aware of their responsibility in the field of religion as well as of the dangers facing them in this controversial area. But little of significance is accomplished through the recognized curriculum, and mention of religion is avoided in many textbooks.

---

[2] Findings prepared by U. S. Office of Education and published in *The Messenger,* April 17, 1941, p. 22.

[3] "Religious Education and the School Administration," in *Educational Progress and School Administration,* ed. Clyde M. Hill (New Haven: Yale University Press, 1936), p. 329.

This means that the chief responsibility in religious education rests on the homes and churches. Most homes have abdicated their responsibility to the churches, although it was shown in the previous chapter that the home is the primary teacher of religion, and there is a strong movement within the churches to enlist the parents in a new endeavor in this direction. For almost a century, however, the Sunday church school has been the primary teacher of religion, limited to its brief hour on Sunday morning, manned by voluntary and often untrained teachers, and provided with educational resources that almost guarantee failure to impart Christian truth in a relevant manner. Yet, in spite of its limitations, millions of children have been nurtured in the faith and have grown into Christian maturity.

VACATION CHURCH SCHOOL

Supplementing the Sunday church school has been the vacation church school. It normally operates during a few weeks in the summer, three hours a day and five days a week, sometimes with professional leadership and with the resources of congregations from several denominations, although more often as a project of the local church. It has been an informal and creative approach to Christian living. In two weeks it has as much time for teaching as the average Sunday church school has in thirty Sundays, and it may run from one to six weeks. It has been highly successful in both urban and rural areas, and in the latter it sometimes appeals to the whole family. The informality of the program allows for play and fun, but when Bible teaching occurs each day there is not as much forgetting between sessions.

Vacation church schools began in 1894, and they have been growing in popularity ever since. They are often both interchurch and community enterprises, thus providing a wider basis for leadership and resources. Some communities have provided a time schedule for the summer, so that athletics, scouting programs, camping periods, and the vacation church school have their alloted times. Libraries and playgrounds cooperate in providing books and equipment. Close home and church cooperation is possible.

Careful planning far in advance will provide leaders who are adequately trained as well as resources for doing the job. Observation and laboratory schools often provide training for those who will teach the following summer. Public school teachers are sometimes available, and ministers with special gifts in dealing with children find this opportunity irresistible.

The value of these vacation church schools has been proved over the years. In 1943, over 3,000,000 pupils were reached through more than 70,000 schools. Sometimes they are an answer to the problem of delinquency, but more often they are a positive response to the need for additional religious education. Bower and Hayward cite the following:

> In a city in Southern California where apartment houses surrounded four of the largest churches, the Y.M.C.A. suggested that all work together on a complete summer program. The association offered to conduct the afternoon and evening programs if the churches would take the mornings. Two of the churches had the vacation church school in July, and the other two had it in August. This proved so successful that it has continued for a number of years.[4]

Many special texts have been prepared through the efforts of the Cooperative Publishing Association working together with the Division of Christian Education of the National Council of Churches, and others, which are usable in cooperative schools,[5] have been produced by denominations.

WEEKDAY CHURCH SCHOOL

The weekday church school, sometimes called the "released time" school, operates on school time but on non-school property, at the written request of parents. It began in 1914 in Gary, Indiana, and today is permissible in almost every state. A series of Supreme Court decisions has finally led to the conclusion that under proper conditions this is not a violation of the separation of church and state.

> The First Amendment within the scope of its coverage (interference with the free exercise of religion and an establishment of religion) permits no exceptions; the prohibition is absolute. The First Amend-

---

[4] William Clayton Bower and Percy Roy Hayward, *Protestantism Faces Its Educational Task Together* (Chicago: National Council of Churches, 1949), p. 174.

[5] See below, pp. 318-23, for discussion of administration.

> ment, however, does not say that in every and all respects there shall be a separation of Church and State. Rather, it studiously defines the manner, the specific ways in which there shall be no concert or union or dependency one on the other. That is the common sense of the matter.

There being no reason why the government should be hostile to religion, "when the state encourages religious instruction by adjusting the schedule of public events to sectarian needs, it follows the best of our traditions. For it then respects the religious nature of our people and accommodates the public service to their spiritual needs." Not only released time for groups, but the right of the pupil for excuse on any religious grounds is indicated by this: "Whether she (the teacher) does it occasionally for a few students, regularly for one, or pursuant to a systematized program designed to further the needs of all the students does not alter the character of the act." The Court also endorsed the practice of parental consent and a report from the priest, rabbi, or minister to the teacher "to make sure the student is not a truant." [6]

Erwin L. Shaver, in commenting on the decision of the Supreme Court, particularly in relation to the New York law that makes it mandatory that a school board grant such a request, said, "It follows that every American child attending a public school now has the privilege of enrolling in a weekday religious education program during school hours and that any religious group in any American community may arrange a program of this character." [7] The doubt about the legality of the program, provided public school property is not used, is now lifted.

A great variety of programs is offered in different locations. All 12 grades are used, but some localities prefer to teach the elementary grades, some junior high grades, and some the high school. Other programs may begin with the third or fourth grade and run through junior high school. Some are limited to one or more schools within the system. The most common selection is grades four through six. In some communities the enrollment runs as high as 90 per cent of available pupils, but the average is close to two-thirds in the elementary schools and one-third in the high schools.

---

[6] Quoted by Erwin L. Shaver, "Weekday Religious Education Secures Its Charter and Faces a Challenge," *Religious Education,* January-February 1953, pp. 38-39.

[7] *Ibid.,* pp. 39-40.

There is a trend toward releasing all the pupils at the same hour, and once in a while the students not electing the courses in religion are dismissed; but the preferred system is a staggered schedule, so that a teacher may be kept busy on a full-time basis throughout the week. Both Roman Catholics and Protestants can make better use of trained teachers on a staggered basis of released time.

In some communities teaching is on a denominational basis, with each child attending his own church or synagogue. More often there is an interfaith committee, which works closely with the board of education in achieving a system that is mutually acceptable, although normally the Jews do not have a program. The details of the time schedule are worked out by the school board, superintendent, various principals, and the religious groups involved, and a cooperative plan is put in action. The Protestants who have joined together often have a general program, with professional teachers and a mutually acceptable curriculum that does not conflict with what is happening on Sundays. This program is sponsored by the local council of churches or ministers in terms of policy and financial support. There is sometimes a minority program conducted by those who cannot conscientiously cooperate with the Protestant council.

The better programs are expensive, involving salaries, equipment, rental, and resources. The yearly cost is about five dollars per pupil for one hour in class a week. The funds are raised through the churches, usually on a quota basis determined by membership and annual budget, with additional appeals to parents and community agencies. Occasionally tuition is charged, but this is not wise in most communities. Some Protestant programs have been conducted on a minimal basis with volunteers, but the quality of such teaching suffers in comparison with that of the schools and the Roman Catholic program. Roman Catholics frequently have the advantage of teachers who are in various orders and do not need to be paid, although they also suffer from a serious shortage of trained teachers.

The teachers need to be specially trained, and there should be a supervisor in the larger systems and a shared supervisor working in several neighboring smaller systems. High standards of teaching are essential to the success of the program. Good materials are available, some prepared by individual systems as in Virginia and New York City, and others available in the Cooperative Series of Weekday Church School Texts, produced by the Cooperative Publishing Association working with the Division of Christian Education of the National Council of Churches.

The most important result of this program is that it brings religion into weekday life and identifies it with the developing attitudes toward life that are the goals of the public school. Home, church, and school cooperate at this level. A second result is the surprising number of unchurched children who attend the weekday classes — in many systems one-third of the pupils have no church connection. The investment in terms of missionary work alone justifies the expense. Third, in over half of the situations, professionally trained teachers and supervisers bring to the learners a proficiency that is absent in many Sunday church schools. Fourth, it provides for unity in terms of church cooperation and racial and economic crossing of lines, for the Protestant class meets at a place near the school and is open to all Protestant children.

In spite of these values, the released time program has serious limitations. It provides for only one hour of class a week, with six days to forget what was taught the previous week. Usually it is restricted to the imparting of information about the Bible or church history, and the class fails to become a community in which faith evolves. The teachers do not get to know the pupils when they teach from twelve to fifteen different classes a week, some of which are large. Often the weekday class seems to be a lone wolf uncorrelated with any other educational activity. The most serious criticism is that it is a stopgap, and even when the calibre of leadership is high, it is jeopardized by competing suggestions for the solution to the problem. Although the vacation church school obviously has permanent value, the weekday church school may degenerate into an amateur attempt to meet a major problem, or it may be replaced by a better solution.[8]

PAROCHIAL SCHOOLS

Since colonial days parochial schools have been another answer to the problem of religious education among both Protestants and Roman Catholics. Except among the Lutherans, Protestant efforts have been on a small scale, but Roman Catholics have reached an

---

[8] See pp. 318-27, for discussion of administration and organization.

high as 48 per cent of their children, although the percentage is not now that high. The values from a sectarian point of view are obvious, for through church control religion can be taught in any way desired and can be combined with worship. The basic value is that religion is integral to all education.

As long as parochial schools are the choice of parents for the education of their children, there is nothing un-American about it, and the Supreme Court has ruled that such a decision is part of our freedom. But is is easy to imagine what would happen if Protestants should support parochial schools with the same effectiveness as Roman Catholics. Each denomination having its own school would divide every neighborhood into factions and aggravate the divisions that already exist. The great achievement of the public schools in their unity across religious and racial boundaries would be undermined. In many communities, where Roman Catholic parochial schools are strong, there is a division between the Roman and non-Roman children. It is conceivable that the parochial schools would be tax-supported and that they would replace many public schools. As Nevin Harner says, "that spells the doom of the American dream and of the ecumenical dream as well." [9]

There are other questions posed by parochial schools. The smaller sects and the communities that have small numbers of the major denominations could not very well support their own schools. In large cities not enough schools could be established to make transportation a simple matter. Costs would rise fantastically because of uneconomic size and locations, and surely the educational standards would drop. Boards of education would be multiplied endlessly, and the shortage of both teachers and administrative personnel would increase.

The chief problem is that of tax support. At one time tax money was used for schools owned and operated by churches, but normally this was cancelled when the public schools offered universal education. In some areas today Catholic parochial schools substitute for public schools and are operated with public money, but these are exceptions to the rule and are probably unconstitutional.

The Roman Catholic Church, which does not share the traditional interpretation of the separation of church and state, has pressed in

[9] Nevin C. Harner, *Religion's Place in General Education* (Richmond: John Knox Press, 1949), p. 58.

recent years for public support. In 1929 a Supreme Court decision made possible the use of tax funds for textbooks, and in 1947 it was ruled that school bus transportation was "welfare" and not education. Most Protestants join with the secularists in objecting even to this much public support, and they are strongly opposed to any additional use of tax funds for church-sponsored education. Federal support for education has been stymied by the Roman Catholic insistence that some federal money be diverted for parochial schools.

PRIVATE SCHOOLS

Although the private schools do not exist for the primary purpose of sponsoring sectarian teaching, many private schools are owned or sponsored by denominations. Both day and boarding schools provide for parents who can afford it a means for their children to escape poor public schools and to have such religious teaching as the school may offer. There is no religious or tax problem involved, and it is an answer open to only a few families, but in areas where private schools are strong the public schools suffer from inadequate support from those parents who are usually best qualified to insist on higher standards. Private colleges, whether sponsored by churches or not, also have this same freedom. The only public support offered these institutions is tax free status.

POSSIBLE SOLUTIONS TO THE PROBLEM

It is an error to believe that the public schools are godless, or that professional educators are opposed to religion, or that religious teaching in the public schools is un-American or impossible. A special interfaith committee of the American Council on Education reported that "public education may not propagate religious dogmas or arbitrate religious differences. But if it does not impel students toward the achievement of a faith and to that end create a sensitive awareness of the religious resources upon which men have learned to rely, it is less than education ought to be." [10]

---

[10] Nevin C. Harner, *Religion's Place in General Education* (Richmond: John Knox Press, 1949), p. 136. The entire report of this committee is the appendix of Harner's book.

Religious freedom does not necessarily mean freedom *from* religion, yet the multiplication of religious sects in America has led many teachers to refuse to teach the religious implications of any subject, and others to feel completely free to attack religion at any time. This is certainly not the intention of the First Amendment, and outside of Russia the United States is the only nation in which such an interpretation has become even partially accepted. "The first obligation of the school with reference to religion is, we believe, to facilitate intelligent contact with it as it has developed in our culture and among our institutions." [11] The schools are not supposed to do the job of our churches, and therefore indoctrination and appeals to decision are beyond the boundaries of this particular problem. But the schools are supposed to guard against illiteracy and ignorance in all fields of human endeavor, including religion.

The peculiarities of American religious culture make it difficult to implement any proposal. But many proposals have been made, and some of them have merit.

(1) DENOMINATIONAL TEACHING

A few religious leaders believe that denominational teaching in the schools is possible, either by having classes for members of each church or by grouping them into Jews, Catholics, and several brands of Protestants. This system has worked in Australia under the church's right of entry, with the teachers being supplied by the churches. Segregated classes would provide sectarian teaching. This proposal is both unconstitutional and unwise.

(2) COMMON CORE

A second proposal is to teach the common core of religious beliefs. Take Protestantism, Catholicism, and Judaism, combine their beliefs held in common, and this is a general religious outlook to which every American would agree! In sufficiently homogenious communities, this approach can and does work, but a least common denominator would be offensive in most cases, and it would not allow for

[11] *Ibid.*, p. 135.

the freedom of the non-church member. It is most often proposed by those who think that religious distinctions do not matter very much, and it is unrealistic in the face of the actual situation. It might lead to a public school religion that would actually be a new sect.

(3) DEMOCRACY AS A WAY OF LIFE

A third proposal is to teach democracy as a way of life. Devotion to democratic ideals, faith in a democratic creed, or democracy as a religion could be taught in terms of both ethical demands and the religious assumptions of the Bill of Rights. The following articles of faith would be included: the individual has surpassing worth, the earth and human culture belong to all men, men can and should rule themselves, the human mind can be trusted, the method of peace is superior to war, minorities should be tolerated, respected, and valued.[12] This kind of education, to result in faith, would arouse joy, elation, wonder, and dedication. It would need adequate and impressive ceremonies. Some schools are achieving loyalty to the democratic way of life, and this is desirable, but the question is whether it has any necessary connection with the Jewish-Christian tradition unless it is grounded in a religious faith. Once this problem is faced, we are back where we started.

(4) PLANNED RELIGIOUS ACTIVITIES

The fourth proposal is to make use of planned religious activities. Under this designation we find devotional periods, with programs including prayers, hymns, religious talks, and Bible reading; special programs celebrating Thanksgiving, Hanukkah, Christmas, and Easter; the saying of grace at meals or of prayers before athletic contests; permitting religious clubs to use school buildings; backing of released time classes; elective courses in the Bible and religion; credit for religious instruction given outside of school.

In many communities these practices are observed with the approval of the majority of citizens, but in some cases they may create

---

[12] *Education of Free Men in American Democracy* (Washington: National Education Association, 1941), chaps. 3 and 5; see J. Paul Williams, *The New Education and Religion* (New York: Association Press, 1945), pp. 180-95.

disturbances. Children may be excused from such observances at the request of their parents.

(5) FACTUAL STUDY OF RELIGION

Many educators are coming to believe that a factual study of religion is a real possibility. Religion has an authentic place in our history and in our culture. This is illustrated in the study of history. Nero without the early Christian martyrs, the sixteenth century without Luther, Calvin, or Cranmer, Jamestown without its Book of Common Prayer, California without Father Juanipero Serra, and the expansion of American influence without the missionaries provide a distorted and inaccurate picture of history. The English Bible and the Book of Common Prayer are as enduring in their influence on the English language as Shakespeare or Milton. In the social sciences, the impact of every agency in the community is to be studied, and the spires on the churches of every New England town make vivid the strategic importance of religious institutions. The study of civics involves the religious beliefs of the founding fathers, and the Christian doctrine of man underlies our faith in democracy. The natural sciences in themselves do not always imply religion, but the questions in the minds of the learners concerning science and religion are perennial.

The special committee of the American Council on Education has pioneered in this approach.[13] They believe that there should be a study of the religious classics, including the Bible, conducted with the same respect and care as are used in the study of literary classics. Each student, for example, could use his own choice of translations of the Bible, and secondary sources could be recommended for the factual study of all religious topics.[14]

---

[13] See Committee on Religion and Education of the American Council on Education, *Religion and Public Education* (Washington: American Council on Education, 1944); *The Relation of Religion to Public Education: Basic Principles* (Washington: American Council on Education, 1947); *The Function of Public Schools in Dealing with Religion* (Washington: American Council of Education, 1953).

[14] Virgil Henry's *The Place of Religion in Public Schools* (New York: Harper & Brothers, 1950), pp. 38-68, contains curriculum proposals and recommended texts meeting these standards.

This proposal does not conflict with the laws of this country or with the curricula of the schools, but it would change the orientation of many teachers and textbooks in the recognition of religion as insuperably bound up with our culture. Also, the courses in the field of religion would increase the demand for trained teachers and new textbooks. The factual study of religion may be explored by the schools of any community seeking for better ways to teach religion as the nucleus of our culture, and when properly handled it need not be offensive to any religious group.[15]

The American Council on Education recognizes that the training of teachers for such an enterprise is a large and exacting task, but its report makes clear that enough teachers are qualified to begin an experiment in this area. The increased interest in religion and religious education in many colleges and universities, both public and private, promises a source of trained teachers in this field. Teachers colleges and schools would have to provide a well-balanced general education with religion as an integral part, plus professional training in dealing with religion in this manner.[16]

All of these possibilities face objections: The first is the widespread secularism, which is jealous of any encroachment of organized religion upon public school time. Those holding this position are either neutral or opposed to religion and do not share the view that religion is associated with culture in any intimate way. The second objection stems from an overemphasized view of the separation of church and state, an insistence that it means *a wall* of separation between religion and education. The third objection comes from minority groups who are afraid that their own positions will be discriminated against. This includes the Jews, various sects holding exclusive views, and sometimes the Roman Catholic Church. The fourth objection is based on the present state of teacher training, which includes no education in how to teach religion in any of the ways described above. The fifth objection comes from the practical administrator who says it will not work.

---

[15] Virgil Henry, in *The Place of Religion in Public Schools* (New York: Harper & Brothers, 1950), outlines a plan for a community approach to this answer to the problem.

[16] See Committee on Religion and Education of the American Council on Education, *The Function of Public Schools in Dealing with Religion* (Washington: American Council on Education, 1953), pp. 74-80.

THE SCHOOL AS A COMMUNITY

As we look at the possible answers to the problem of religion in the schools, we see that some practices take the learners outside the school community. The vacation church school, weekday church school on released or dismissed time, and the parochial and private schools do not solve the problem within the educational matrix of the public school. They avoid the central problem.

The other suggestions, whether acceptable or not on the grounds of church-state relationships and the plausibility of the program in terms of interfaith cooperation, are answers within the school as a community. However these problems are solved, the sense of the school as a community is central. For the school is concerned with the development of the total personalities of its learners within the framework of the school as a community. Of all the groups to which children belong, the school is the most demanding on time, energy, and discipline.

The quality of life within the school is crucial to the construction of religious attitudes no matter what the formal curriculum may be. The experience of being loved and accepted as he is by his teachers and fellows within the community, the sense of order and dependableness that comes from the life of the community and is not imposed as a harsh discipline, the freedom to grow at his own rate of speed with adequate direction, and the sense of the mystery of God which makes possible these relationships are essential to a child's life in the school as much as in the home and church.

This leads beyond the school to the right kind of home-school relations. Because his parents are interested in the school, and because the school is concerned for his parents' cooperation, the child will sense the continuity between these two communities that are the center of his life. Furthermore, parents should take part in school life with their children not only at party and pageant times but to visit when routine learning is going on.[17]

The churches are involved, too, for they have to deal with the children educated in the schools. The churches are concerned with what goes on in the schools, and they are the groups most likely to

---

[17] See James L. Hymes, Jr., *Effective Home-School Relations* (New York: Prentice-Hall, Inc., 1953), especially pp. 156-83.

initiate consideration of programs most likely to succeed in their own communities. As Paul Vieth writes, "Many public school workers would be heartened if they knew that the religious leaders of the community could agree on cooperating with the public school in devising ways and means by which a school might give interpretation of religion and religious institutions which would be given for all the children of the community." [18]

A culture as diffused religiously as ours cannot find an easy answer to the problem of religion in the public schools. But it is certain that the secular answer is not the right one, and the weekday solution is not a real incorporation of religious teaching into the basic educational community that the school should be. Sectarian teaching is undesirable, and yet no nonsectarian religion is possible. But no teacher can avoid the implications of his subject matter, and these implications will either be religious or irreligious. The facts of religion are part of our culture, which means they will appear in the curriculum because of the needs of the students, and to pass them by means that they are unimportant. And when the student's basic needs are not met and his basic questions are not answered, there can be no real community which is essential to any sound education. Knowledge *about* religion as it relates to other subjects and as it relates to the various forms of religion is essential to education.[19]

---

[18] Paul H. Vieth, *The Church and Christian Education* (St. Louis: Bethany Press, 1947), p. 302.

[19] See F. Ernest Johnson, ed., *American Education and Religion* (New York: Harper & Brothers, 1952), pp. 187-203, and especially the quotation on pp. 200-201.

CHAPTER 8

RELIGIOUS EDUCATION AND THE COMMUNITY

"MEN LIVE in community in virtue of the things which they have in common; and communication is the way in which they come to possess things in common." [1] With these words, John Dewey gives a picture of community that is far more meaningful than geographical proximity. There may be no community between a man and his neighbor, and they may not even speak, or, if they speak, they may not understand what the other is saying.

A group that shares aims, beliefs, and aspirations is a true community, and simply by being a member of it a person learns to be loyal to it. We belong to several communities that provide genuine social life and real communication, but that may or may not have any connection with each other. Within that geographical area in which we live, we develop strong loyalties to home, church, and school, which are the major educational institutions; but we also are influenced by other forms of communication and community life within the sphere of our activities.

The problem in this chapter, therefore, is to discover what happens to a person in those areas of experience that are outside the orbit of home, school, or church. We are participating members of many other groups, come under this influence of the mass communication media, take part in organized play or commercial recreation, and absorb many of the secular values of American life. There is a cultural conditioning that results from being a member of a group

[1] John Dewey, *Democracy and Education* (New York: The Macmillan Company, 1916), p. 5.

over a long period of time, for it comes not from verbalizing or from conscious imitation, but from living the way of the group. Ways of behavior and standards of value are the outcome of loyalty to a group in which one is a participating member, and when one belongs to several groups that reflect different standards of action, the result is confusion and dislocation of ideals.

Once we see the power of the community to develop or change the direction of personal development, the connection between theology and community becomes obvious. The story of the Bible, as a drama of redemption, is a record of God's mighty acts in history, and it is also the recounting of one community and its growing relationship to its Lord who is seen to be Lord of the historical process. The coming of Christ is an event that marks a changed relationship between God and the community by means of a new agreement, which fulfills the old one. For the Jew, the old Israel was the nation; for the Christian, the new Israel is the church; and for both, "God is working his purpose out as year succeeds to year." [2]

THE HOLY SPIRIT AND COMMUNITY

The doctrine of the Holy Spirit makes clear that God is concerned with all of life, and that he works through all kinds of groups and individuals.

> The scientist seeking truth, the artist expressing beauty, the statesman striving for justice, the soldier giving his life for his comrade, the mother sacrificing for her children, the businessman working honestly for a living, the carpenter at his workbench, the manual laborer digging a ditch—in every department of human life where men seek to live as men, conformed to the truth as they see it, the good as they know it, the right as they believe it—at every point of experience, there is the working of the Holy Spirit.[3]

This "secular work of the Holy Spirit" is to be found in any community in which redemptive love is at work. It is sometimes pointed out that secular groups practicing the principles of group dynamics

---

[2] *The Hymnal 1940* (New York: Church Hymnal Corp., 1943), No. 538, by Arthur Campbell Ainger (1894).

[3] James A. Pike and W. Norman Pittenger, *The Faith of the Church* (Greenwich: Seabury Press, 1951), p. 121.

have an experience of belonging together that expresses full acceptance of every member of the group by all the rest. It may be described in terms of psychology and sociology, but the evaluation in these terms seems strangely shallow. If the theology of Christian education is adequate to describe the work of the Holy Spirit wherever he may choose to dwell, the Christian is compelled to assume that God is at work in many secular groups, and perhaps in some groups that are consciously antagonistic to the church.

This means that when we begin to examine the working of the groups to which people belong, we must look for resources in them by which the work of Christian education may be strengthened as well as for resistance, which groups offer to the expansion of the Gospel. These groups have partial goals; they serve a single class, or a vested interest, or a stratum of society. They do not operate as religious institutions, but through their influence they have an impact on the religious development of their members.

STANDARDS OF LOYALTY

The Christian, when his loyalty centers in the church as a community of the Holy Spirit or Body of Christ, seeks standards by which he can evaluate these other groups to which he belongs. He relies on the Bible, in so far as he has discovered what the real authority of the Bible is for him. He relies on the teachings of his own parish and denomination. He knows that his own conscience, however it may be trained, is the tool for making his decisions. Above all, he knows that he is a member of a group that has a Gospel. The good news of Jesus Christ, who came into the world to save men from their sins, to reconcile the world to the heavenly Father, and to bring men grace through the church, provides at once a corrective for individual judgment and for corporate evaluations.

Groups may contribute positively to the Christian education of children and adults in our contemporary culture even when they are specifically nonreligious in their major goals.[4] The church should re-

[4] See my article, "The Discovery of Resistance and Resource," in *The Church and Organized Movements,* Volume II in the Interseminary Series, ed. Randolph Crump Miller (New York: Harper & Brothers, 1946), pp. 3-25.

joice to have such cooperation, and should utilize these resources in its own educational program. Most groups, however, fall somewhere in the middle, providing degrees of both resource for and resistance to the aims of the church. And there are some groups that are basically opposed to all that the church stands for, and it is in such groups that our young people are led in the direction of delinquency and disintegration of their personalities.

ORGANIZATIONS IN A COMMUNITY

The most influential organizations for children are those set up by parents and officials of the community. They are usually well supervised and do not lead to crucial problems in behavior. Community nursery schools that are not part of the educational system, various types of play groups, and some of the special organizations such as the Brownies and Cubs for primary children are of this kind.

GANGS AND GROUPS

With juniors and junior high and high school youngsters, the dominating influence is the peer group, usually an unofficial and semi-permanent organization. These casual groupings form their own leadership, establish their own standards, and reflect their own desires in the light of the resources of their neighborhood. These groups form and reform in a myriad ways. Among juniors, they usually reflect the value judgments of other groups, but as adolescence comes on they become a means of making independent judgments, often at the expense of society.

The juvenile delinquents are often those who form in gangs and have no other compelling standards to guide them. Their homes, no matter what strata of society they are in, have not contributed any consistent standards by which they can make judgments. Their experiences in school have caused them to reject any standards to which they have been exposed. Often they have had no church connection, or at best a nominal one. Because the gang is their only opportunity to belong to a group, and because no other agency has contributed to their sense of values, they take out their resentments against all genuine community by becoming anti-social in their judgments and actions.

Where this same gang consciousness is tied in with other loyalties, these same age groups will make their independent judgments in consistency with their other loyalties. Home, school, and church will contribute to the total consciousness of values, and though there will be variations from the norm as young people experiment with their own capacity for freedom, the results will not be shockingly anti-social.

Whether or not a gang contributes to the betterment of the community depends on the particular group. It may be a resource for religious education, or it may provide resistance to religious education and become a bad form of experience. A great deal depends on the quality of life of the neighborhood and of the special groupings within it.

Many young people belong to other youth organizations. The Young Men's Christian Association, the Young Women's Christian Association, and parallel associations among Catholics and Jews (although these two groups often belong to the Christian Associations), provide specifically religious backgrounds for their work. Although the strong Protestant assumptions of the early days of the Christian Associations have been soft-pedaled in recent years, the basic Christian values have been maintained, and the creative approach through games and other activities has provided a strong resource for Christian character education. These organizations have a strong influence among adults as well as among youth, and often their most specific Christian education is through classes for adults. Some of the best pioneering in a dynamic educational program for adults has been accomplished by the Y. M. C. A.[5]

Organized fraternalism reaches down to the high school age, although the strongest influence is among adults. Sometimes these groups become a substitute for the church, and often they are in competition for the time, interests, and loyalty of members. The emphasis on service of many of these organizations, however, leads to activities consistent with the churches' ideals. Fraternalism is a

[5] See Archibald Knowles, *Informal Adult Education* (New York: Association Press, 1950).

mixed blessing as far as the churches are concerned, but a wise use of its idealism can further the program of Christian education.[6]

Many clubs and teams operate under various auspices. Before any evaluation may be made, evidence is needed to discover to what extent boys and girls are being used to further the goals of the sponsor. There is a secularistic idealism in scouting that represents humanism at its best, although sometimes it is claimed that scouting is a sufficient religion in itself. Churches often sponsor scout troops, and a place is made in most scout programs for the worship of the members. Canteens and other activities for teen-agers tend to overcome the destructive forces of anti-social gangs. Secular agencies for social work are often involved in these activities, and the question arises as to what extent organized social work is striving for Christian goals. In many cases the purely humanitarian goals of adjustment to society have no connection with the Christian ideal of love or redemption, but on the other hand there are many social workers inspired primarily by Christian devotion. The danger is that the individual is forgotten in terms of a program, so that personal relations are submerged in the routine of the agency.[7] But this is not necessarily so, and most of these programs are basically sound in building character and preventing delinquency.

RECREATION

Various kinds of play involve boys and girls as they move in and out of organized or unorganized groups. In most neighborhoods, no matter what social caste is represented, there are playgrounds. Some of these are supervised, highly organized, and subject to high morale. In other situations, the play is haphazard, with casual supervision from time to time, and with no real organization. Both types of playgrounds contribute to the development of character, provided the latter type operates in terms of freedom and reasonably high standards. But some playgrounds are dangerous spots because they are dominated by a gang of anti-social boys and girls, or simply because

---

[6] See Dwight C. Smith, "The Church and Organized Fraternalism," in *The Church and Organized Movements,* pp. 131-55.

[7] See Buell G. Gallagher, "Welfare Work: Ally or Alternative?" in *The Church and Organized Movements,* pp. 101-29.

no supervision means that there will be conflict and tension that may become dangerous.

SUMMER CAMPS AND CONFERENCES

Another type of recreation, although not related immediately to the community, should be mentioned at this point. Summer camps and conferences usually provide a combination of supervised recreation and study in line with the churches' purposes for young people and adults. Although they often take boys and girls away from their parents at a time when families might enjoy a vacation together, they offer opportunities for education that are not otherwise available. These camp experiences are becoming available to larger numbers of children from underprivileged sections of cities, who otherwise would have no advantages of this sort.

NEIGHBORHOOD PLAY

Children also learn much from their neighborhood and individual play. Though socialized play is important, the casual relations of boys and girls in the immediate neighborhood is the chief recreation after school and on weekends. Much depends on the leadership of children and parents in the immediate vicinity. Homes that are open to friends of the children contribute much to the sense of belonging. Agreement among parents as to the rules of boundaries and time schedules helps to provide a routine in which children know where they stand.

TRAVEL

Travel is another factor. This enlarges the sense of community. When a man's neighborhood is as large as the area he can cover by plane in twelve hours, he has a vast neighborhood in which to move around. A tour by car across the country, the family as a group seeing the great cities and the National parks, meeting people in all walks of life, and finding schools and churches in all locations, is a broadening experience. When "all the world is God's own field," and the world becomes better known, there are additional resources for Christian education.

COMMERCIALIZED RECREATION

Commercialized recreation provides for much of America's leisure time. There are the sports, which appeal both to the participant and to the onlooker. Healthful afternoons or evenings in the grandstand may not produce many Ty Cobbs, but among boys it may inspire a new DiMaggio. The tendency of American boys to idolize their athletic heroes is likely to be a good thing, for most of them live cleanly and have real integrity. Spectator sports provide many topics of conversation, and serve as hobbies for many adults as well as children.

Although some professional sports draw gamblers and racketeers, and participants in these activities may be more concerned with acting than with athletics, this is true of only a few of them. The trouble becomes serious when a sport is supported primarily by the gambling interests, and when the nonparticipant finds it exciting only when he joins in the gambling process. Commercialized recreation, like secular organizations in the neighborhood, must be judged in terms of whether it provides resources for Christian character or resistance to it.

Fun for pay, as when we enjoy the amusments at a place like Coney Island, or pay to swim or play golf, or go dinner-dancing, is important as recreation. Sometimes the whole family is able to participate as a unit in such activities, or groups of youngsters find fellowship together, or adults belong to a club that finds refreshment in getting away from routine, and this is good. Often it is done in the name of the church to which they belong.

RESOURCES OF A NEIGHBORHOOD

The neighborhood provides resources for becoming a community in all of these ways, even though the sponsorship is primarily secular. The child grows up in such an environment, and these activities are part of his learning process. The adult shares in many of the same activities, and he also continues to learn. On the adult level, there are many other groups in which he participates as he takes part in political, economic, and social action. In each case, an analysis might be made of whether what happens politically or economically is in resistance to what the church stands for or provides resources for the process of redemption.

Though most of these movements in our culture are divorced from religious sanctions, they continue to be led by religious personnel. This takes us back to the home and church, for although statistical evidence is not sufficient on this point, "the conclusion is highly probable that Christian families produce a disproportionately large group of the socially useful members of the community, including many that have no further relation with the churches themselves, and on the other hand, a still more disproportionately small share in the criminals, social parasites, broken homes of the nation. The clearest instances here are the children of the parsonage, who, as every sociologist knows, achieve distinction in all sorts of walks of life far more frequently than any other comparable group." [8] This points back to the previous chapter and suggests that the church works through the home to influence the community, even when the results are humanitarian rather than self-consciously Christian. Christian values emerge in the community because of the leadership of Christians in all of the organizations we have mentioned.

MASS COMMUNICATION MEDIA

Children and adults are being entertained and educated today through the mass communication media – those forms of communication designed to reach men in large groups, even though they reach the individual at the final point. Radio, television, motion pictures, stage drama, printed matter such as comics, circulars, newspapers, magazines, and books are among the media of communication and often they are packaged with advertising appeals designed to reach the same market in order to encourage the purchase of products. Except for books, the stage, and motion pictures, advertising stands behind mass communication, and special advertising techniques reach us through billboards and other stunts.

We have here two questions: first, what comes to us from the mass

---

[8] James H. Nichols, "Secularism in the Church," in *The Challenge of Our Culture,* Vol. I of the Interseminary Series, ed. Clarence Tucker Craig (New York: Harper & Brothers, 1946), p. 186.

communication media in themselves, and, second, what comes to us through the advertising that accompanies most of it?

RADIO

Our main concern is the impact of these media on children. Radio has always had specific programs beamed at children, and usually these are unobjectionable. Fairy tales in traditional form and newly-created modern tales have been presented. Story-telling, children's quiz programs, special music for children, stories from the Bible, science and nature programs, and many others have been presented throughout the years. Teen-age shows are developing more and more popularity as the radio people realize that teen-agers spend money, and some programs provide solid discussions, fashion notes, recent jazz records, and youth participation shows.

Children want action, adventure, chills, and thrills, just as their parents did, and the only new thing about radio is that it is a new means of transmitting the same adventures that a previous generation found in books. Whenever children's programs get too tame, the children will move over into the adult realm, either the soap operas of the early afternoon or the brutal crime stories of later evening.

TELEVISION

Television provides increased vividness of the appeal to the eye. Many of the most popular programs on radio have transferred to television or now appear on both. Children follow their favorite shows and cannot stand to miss them. They also increase in powers of discrimination, discarding a show that fails to satisfy and selecting a new one in its place. Television has more compelling power to hold interest over a longer time span, and it often holds the interest of small children after they have seen the program intended for them. Furthermore, although some students can study with one ear on the radio, they cannot do this with one eye on the television set.

With both radio and television, what programs he should see or hear depends on the individual child. Some children can take a good deal of blood and thunder and it provides an outlet for their emotions.

If the programs especially prepared for them do not provide enough violence, they will insist on seeing and hearing the adult dramas. Other children are disturbed by highly emotional, dramatic presentations, and they need protection. Possibly the most important approach is for parents and children to view programs together often enough to have a basis for mutual evaluation and criticism, but no parent will provide satisfaction if he insists on a milk and water diet.

The connection between crime and any of the mass communication media is still not clear. Although some juveniles may use techniques suggested by the master minds of fiction in one of these media, the basic reason for the delinquency always rests in some maladjustment centering in the home, school, or community, and the exposure to a medium of communication is not the instigator of the act. Practically all of the classics of the last generation's childhood had just as much blood and thunder, and the only difference is the form in which it is offered.

With the arrival of television, young persons' time schedules have been put askew. Normally there is an adjustment to the routine of family and school life, but in some cases boys and girls spend so much time before the television set that sleep and study are sacrificed. This needs to be worked out in family fashion, and preferably before television has entered the home or before the children start school.

Although it is hard to keep very young children from viewing television, it is generally agreed that eight years is young enough to begin attending motion pictures. Many planned programs for children's matinees on Saturdays have been developed, and if enough attention is paid to the need for adventure these may prove very satisfying. Parents can provide a good deal of guidance as to what pre-teen-agers may see, although teen-agers usually go in groups and accept the evaluations of their peers.

More control is possible with the drama and with musical performances. These events are usually sponsored by interested parents and other groups, and therefore are likely to provide high cultural standards. The difficulty is to get the children's interest when they are at the age when it will do them the most good. Children participate in dramatic and musical productions as well as see them, and even when a symphony program is offered, a child guest will often appear on the program.

COMICS

Printed matter comes into the home in great gobs. The most controversial is the comics. A junior-age child goes through comics the way his junior high brother goes through food. They are devoured rather than read, and the degree of concentration is so high that the house could burn down on them without their knowing it. Children's reading parallels their taste in radio and television programs. They want adventure, fantasy and magic, westerns, crime and detective stories, adolescent capers, some humor and even nonsense, and humanized animals. As they grow older, documentaries about real people who are heroes to them, and some history and current events will hold their interest. Children are not the only readers of comics, whether in a newspaper or in a comic magazine, and readers are found in every social class.

Some comics reach a high degree of pictorial art and story telling. Others have a consistent political or moral philosophy, and many of them deal primarily with decent and interesting people. Family life is as important in *Gasoline Alley* as it is in the television program, *Ozzie and Harriet. Terry and the Pirates* illustrates social justice. *Rex Morgan, M.D.,* gives education about medicine. In the crime stories, justice wins out in many cases. There is every reason why both children and adults like comics, and the question is one of guidance and control.

There is a rising concern about the connection between certain comics and juvenile crime. Many of them arouse the emotions to a high pitch, glorify criminals at the expense of law and order, go beyond all bounds in picturing horrible suffering, provide specific instructions on how to inflict pain, use fantastic creatures of the imagination to seduce the minds of impressionable children, and ignore all standards of morality and good taste. Although it cannot be proved that these comics cause crime, the connections between their suggestions and criminal acts are observable by clinical psychologists.[9]

---

[9] See Frederic Wertham, *Seduction of the Innocent* (New York: Rinehart & Co., 1954). His view is much more severe than that of Josette Frank, *Your Child's Reading Today* (New York: Doubleday & Co., Inc., 1954), pp. 245-56. A balanced view of all the mass media of communication may be found in ten articles appearing in *Religious Education,* November-December 1954.

Excessive reading, whether of comics or classics, may be a symptom of a deeper disturbance. Most children grow from the comics to books that meet the same needs, and the popularity of children's books indicates that there is no dropping off of reading. Comics often whet the appetite for the more solid fare of books, provided the books are well written and interesting.

PRINTED MATTER

Other printed matter comes into the home. There are circulars of various kinds, newspapers, and magazines. Some of these are for children and are usually excellent. But the whole world arrives in our mail box, with big headlines and graphic pictures. There is no way to keep children from browsing through the pictures and absorbing the impact of the headlines, and they read avidly the most bloody of the stories. Although control of choice of specific books and magazines is possible, free time for casual reading will inevitably lead to whatever the adults read. Only the comics are traded and therefore kept in uncontrolled circulation, but children will see books and magazines in the homes of other children that carry the stories of the dramatic and tragic happenings of the world.

FAMILY, COMMUNITY, AND CHURCH

Up to the junior high age, the opinions of parents will carry some weight. Guidance is possible in selecting what is worth reading and in evaluating what has been read. But parental choices are often dull and unrewarding to the child, and unless the parent can suggest alternatives that meet the craving for action the suggestions are futile. Parents can try to understand the basic needs of their children, can know what the children are reading, watching, and hearing, can discuss their favorite stories, comics, and programs with them, and can respect their rights and feelings. Then there will be opportunities to assist in the development of critical judgments, to make wise decisions about the use of their time, and to provide alternative activities.

This is not only a family problem. It is a community problem. Just as the difficulties raised by gangs and clubs need attention by agencies of the neighborhood, so the community can cooperate to provide better comics, movies, and radio and television programs. Without resorting to censorship, neighborhood groups can make their wants known, and they can be sure that the distributors will try to please them provided the claims are reasonable.[10]

The churches have most of these mass communication media as a basis of experience that needs to be interpreted and evaluated. These experiences are forms of learning, and much of the curriculum of religious education is the discovery of the relevance of the Gospel to such experiences. Sometimes this may be on the level of using comic strip characters as a basis for character analysis and for Biblical study.[11] Television and radio personalities may be made the basis of stories indicating the relevance of the Bible. Techniques of story telling may make use of these media by imitating a radio program or a magazine layout. The significant factor is that the children discover the relevance of the teaching of the church to their everyday experiences, and this is particularly true in the case of these mass communication media.

ADVERTISING

Most comic magazines and the Sunday comic strips carry advertising in similar comic art form. Most radio and television programs have some kind of sponsorship. Children love to send in box tops to get something that sounds wonderful on the radio or looks fine on television, and when the gift comes up to expectations they are pleased. But, as is so often the case, when the reward that is promised disappoints them, they are disillusioned. The promise that built up the urge to eat a certain cereal leads, when broken, to complete dislike for the cereal.

Much advertising builds up false standards, and children are soon judging their neighbors by the kind of car they drive, or perfume the mother wears, or soap the children use. The snob appeal of advertising often gets through to the children before they learn to relax and talk during the commercials.

People who are worried about the violence of many comics and radio and television programs often accept the advertising without

---

[10] See Josette Frank, *Comics, Radio, Movies—and Children* (New York: Public Affairs Pamphlet No. 148, 1949).

[11] See Raimundo de Ovies, *The Church and the Children* (New York: More house-Gorham Co., 1941), pp. 37-40.

criticism. But though the violent stories usually end with a very moral hero winning, the accompanying advertising frequently inspires false value judgments concerning the material things of life. The children's defense, when they do not succumb, is to become skeptical of all advertising.

How are children to evaluate the advertising on billboards when one minute they see a "man of distinction," and then they see exaggerated claims for gasoline, and later they see a "public service" sign suggesting that they go to church? Powers of discrimination need to be developed in the field of advertising as in the whole realm of the mass communication media.

Robert Bilheimer says:

> Advertising is a means of selling, and almost any device is employed. Sex stimulation, gross exaggeration, unremitting repetition, arresting typography and the pleasing use of color, appeals to ambition, play upon natural fear and sympathy and the desire for security, are all used to impress upon us the absolute necessity of possessing everything from cigarettes to automobiles and old-age pensions. It is not enough that machines make possible the surfeit of our natural desires; these in themselves are stimulated to the end that goods are transformed into the Good.[12]

SECULAR VALUES AND THE COMMUNITY

The secular values of the business world and of our educational systems pervade our culture. Children and adults are subject to the influence of these values, separated from any relationship with God and his moral law, in every neighborhood in the country. The church and the Christian home are the two institutions within the culture which stand for Christian faith and values rooted in the nature of God. The humanitarianism of secularism at its best reflects Christian values, but at its worst secularism leads to materialism, communism, fascism, and finally to the denial of person-to-person relationships. The "I-Thou" relationship of which Martin Buber speaks is hard to discover in a society where the Christian concept of a person has been destroyed.

The Christian concept of vocation is difficult to establish in such

[12] Robert Bilheimer, *What Must the Church Do?* Vol. V of the Interseminary Series (New York: Harper & Brothers 1947), p. 4.

a secular community, for it is in the light of what God did for men in Christ that we "walk worthy of the vocation to which we are called" (Eph. 4:1, KJ). There is a difference between the selection of a job in terms of hours and pay and the acceptance of a vocation in terms of the opportunity for service, and the difference is not in the job as such but in the attitude toward it.

The church itself succumbs to secular assumptions, because the church is made up of people who live in society. In many cases "the churches have ceased to represent real communities. This loss is often obscured by the striking display of conviviality and homeyness in some churches, which is a symptom of the substitution of class and cultural affinities for Christian conceptions and purposes. This is the community of the service club, of the social and business stratum, not of the Church." [13]

Christian education does not exist in a congregation that has lost its Christian fellowship, its participation in the Holy Spirit, its experience of being a member of the Body of Christ. When the church is a redemptive community within the neighborhood, it has the means and the right to stand in judgment on the non-Christian elements in the neighborhood and to work for more resources for Christian judgments and Christian living in all of the activities and experiences of the community. Every organization in the community can be affected by Christians who exert leadership as Christians. The social consciousness of the church, when properly guided and motivated, can be a form of ethical fertility for the entire community. The danger facing the local church is that it may offer withdrawal from the area in which people live and therefore become essentially irrelevant, or it may reflect the demands of the society in which the people live, and therefore provide no ethical or spiritual fertility for remaking society.

As the local parish discovers the areas of resistance to and resource for the gospel in its own environment, its own work is clarified. Christian education involves that nurture and guidance of the individual and the group so that loyalty to Jesus Christ may be expressed through membership in many groups and activities in society. The Christian who has the capacity to see the world from the standpoint of the Gospel is enabled to discover resources for Christian living in every activ-

---

[13] James H. Nichols, "Secularism in the Church," in the *Challenge of Our Culture,* Vol. I of the Interseminary Series, ed. Clarence Tucker Craig (New York: Harper & Brothers, 1946), p. 187.

ity. He will work to make every group a community in the sense of its being subject to the rule of law accepted by each member, or its treating each member as a person who has a part to play, of its providing for some mixture of unlike persons, and of its serving a higher purpose than its own self-interest.[14]

Every experience is educative. Living together enlarges horizons, stimulates imagination, and creates responsibility. But there must be a process of evaluation and decision, and it is at this point that guidance is essential. Whether it be supervision on a playground, selection of reading matter or television programs, or guidance in discussion groups, there must be sound leadership, so that the immature or the unlearned or the uncommitted may be offered a chance to grow into their own decisions concerning their own experiences. All the experiences of community life are communicated, and the job of the church is to use these materials as raw material for interpretation within that redemptive community that teaches through its history of revelation, its factual knowledge, its value judgments, its worship, and the quality of its life in Christian fellowship.

---

[14] See Marjorie Reeves, *Growing Up in a Modern Society* (London: University of London Press, 1946), p. 35.

CHAPTER 9

RELIGIOUS EDUCATION AND THE CHURCH

THE LOCAL church is a group of people, with a minister, a staff, a building, and a plan of action to produce education as one of its goals. Sometimes it is simply an institution, organized to achieve a particular task. Sometimes the institutional aspects are tools for creating a community that is redemptive and sustaining for its members. Within the neighborhood, the local parish is the primary institution for religious education.

The church exists primarily to proclaim the Gospel. The good news to which men respond in faith is given through what the people do together in their worship, study, and activities. The church exists to re-enact the drama of redemption, and to make available to all men the redemption found through faith in Jesus Christ. Christian education takes place whenever men respond in faith to the grace of God channeled through a community of persons, and they are drawn into a community of the Spirit and participate in the fellowship. Their loneliness is overcome, their inadequacy is replaced with stability and power, and their sense of direction is restored. But men in this present age, living in a world that provides satisfactions on a different basis, often do not hear the Gospel or do not realize that God is addressing them. The church is answering questions that men are not asking, for they do not know what their problem really is. They are not fulfilling their potentialities as persons, and they remain slaves to the standards of a secular society. "The great Christian problem of our age, then," says Charles D. Kean, "is to proclaim the Gospel to man in such a way that he can hear it, accept it, respond to it, be transformed and thus discover himself as he was intended by God to be —

a free man who finds life meaningful; a free man who is not at the mercy of any circumstance or force, here or hereafter!" [1]

The local parish operates within a neighborhood in which all kinds of social forces are effectively swaying the personalities of its inhabitants. It is sometimes the only agency through which men are brought to the acceptance of the redeeming power of Christ, and always it is the agency with the chief responsibility. It is a community within a larger community, seeking through its group life to affect the lives of individuals and groups, so that the redemptive work of God will be mediated through its life.

The local congregation is concerned, first of all, with its own life. It is always in need of refreshment, of renewing its sense of dedication, of informing its members both young and old of the truth of the Gospel, of performing its own worship, of deepening its own fellowship, of caring for its own members through pastoral work and counseling, of expanding its own influence, of reaching across all man-made boundaries. For unless the local congregation is a redemptive and sustaining community, it cannot be a true church and cannot bring others to the riches of Christ. But it cannot achieve these goals for itself unless it is concerned with the community that surrounds it, unless it uses the resources of home, school, and community, unless it accepts these resources and distinguishes the resistance to Christ and opposition to the church among the community organizations. But it looks outward and inward at the same time. It faces the specific problem of what to do with its own people, of how to minister to their real needs, of the way in which Christian education can be effective within the confines of its own institution.

The church is a fellowship before it is an institution. Yet the moment it knows itself as an institution it is likely to cease being a fellowship. It can be a truly Christian institution only as long as the togetherness of Christians is its primary goal. Men "are knit together in an organism which includes both equality and difference, the fundamental equality of all and their mutual subordination each to other. The significant mark and essential being of this communion consists in the quality of *agape* – the new ethos of the fellowship and its members." But the church, as it loses this basis of fellowship, seeks security and replaces its creative spirit with "three different forms: the living Word of God

---

[1] Charles D. Kean, *The Christian Gospel and the Parish Church* (Greenwich: Seabury Press, 1953), pp. 29-30.

is secured – and at the same time replaced – by theology and dogma; the fellowship is secured – and replaced – by the institution; faith, which proves its reality by love, is secured – and replaced – by a creed and moral code." [2] The problem of a church as an institution is to keep alive the quality of love by means of the structure of an institution. The tension between the two has existed throughout the history of the Jewish-Christian tradition, between the prophets and priests of Israel, between the reformers and the followers of the status quo in the church, between those who seek to make the church a redemptive community and those who treat it as a social institution today.

There are six functions of the church whereby it seeks to be a redemptive fellowship. Through these functions it expresses its quality of life, and thus it is an educative agency at every point of its life. Through these functions the church meets the needs of individuals and groups within its community, and often reaches beyond the institution to those other agencies that educate all people.

WORSHIP

The first function of the church is its *worship*. It is a worshiping fellowship because this is the primary way of establishing a relationship with God. The worshiper is seeking God, who will pardon his sins and restore him to a right relationship with God and his fellows. God is powerful and holy, and he stands above the worshipers as Lord of creation and of history. When we go to church, we expect to meet God there. We come before the Lord as sinners needing forgiveness, as believers who know that because of Christ our redemption is possible, as listeners to the Word of God, as men of faith who affirm that faith in creeds, as those who express their needs and aspirations in prayer, and as those who receive God's blessing. Through both Word and sacrament, God's grace is channeled to the worshipers.

Worship is an educational experience, whatever else it may be. We learn to worship by worshiping, and not by talking about it. We sense something of the wonder and mystery of worship through participation. Beginning at an early age, we can share the atmosphere long

[2] From *The Misunderstanding of the Church* by Emil Brunner. The Westminster Press, Philadelphia. Copyright by W. L. Jenkins, 1953, p. 53.

before we can articulate our response. Worship is a relationship, as we express our adoration, confession, petition, intercession, and thanksgiving, and therefore come into the presence of God. This act of worship is a reunion of the community. There is truth in the slogan, "The family that prays together stays together." The congregation that knows its highest moments of personal communion in worship finds that this is the great resource for all its other activities. The learner who learns to worship by participation in the worshiping life of the congregation, and who recognizes that his needs are being met and his duties are being presented, is getting first-hand Christian education.

Worship is the heart of the educational program of the local congregation, yet rarely is it so considered. It is not only the means of God's power to lift up individuals and turn them in new directions and restore their relationship to him, but it is also the means whereby families may worship together in the church and thus strengthen the ties of the Christian home. It is the inspiration of all the other activities, and the source of their power to convert individuals and to bring them to a point of decision. Worship pervades every other activity of the church's life, and is not restricted to the formal worship of the congregation at stated services.

FELLOWSHIP

The second function of the church is its *fellowship*. The first name for Christianity was "the way." What convinced and converted many heathen in the days of the primitive church was the love of the brethren. To be "in the apostles' fellowship" was the important thing. The Christian arriving in Rome as a stranger could be sure of a warm welcome from his fellow believers in the catacombs, although secret signs were necessary to avoid exposure by the police.

The "true church" within any congregation or denomination or across all denominational lines is always a redemptive fellowship in which the needs of the members are met and relationships are healed. This is the quality of life that Christ demands, and it is the quality of life that is truly educative. A congregation of sinners needing redemption is also a congregation practicing a ministry of reconciliation.

Every person in the congregation, no matter what his age or status, knows he is a member of a divine community of the Holy Spirit. Every organization within the local parish is to be evaluated in terms of one simple question: Does this group draw everyone it reaches into the fellowship of the redemptive life, meeting the basic needs of love and acceptance, law and dependableness, freedom to grow, and the awareness of the dynamic working of God? When this can be said of the local congregation and of its several organizations, the basis has already been established for a sound program of Christian education.

INSTRUCTION

The third function of the church is its program of *instruction*. This depends primarily on the quality of the first two functions for its effectiveness, because only when the learner can join a congregation on its knees and observe, "Behold how these Christians love one another," is there an atmosphere where communication of Christian truth can take place. Without such an atmosphere, there may be instruction in factual knowledge, but it will not be Christian nurture.

The program of instruction includes preaching, church school classes, study groups, conferences, the church press and books, and many other activities. The teaching church seeks to impart Christian truth. This teaching must be as free from error as is humanly possible, and must be able to give a reason for its truth. The center of its teaching is the Bible, and most churches today could make the Bible understood in terms of the finest recent scholarship so that its relevance for today's living would be made clear to all ages.

The church interprets the will of God for its members, and often for those outside the fold, recognizing that there are no easy answers in a complex and confusing world. The church also sees God at work in the world, sometimes at variance with the wishes of the congregation or the nation, and therefore it teaches that individuals and groups stand under judgment. Finally, the church teaches that Christianity applies to all of life, demanding the allegiance of the total personality in all of his relationships. At this point the church's domain is the whole world, for every aspect of life is under God's providence. The fundamental questions of life are answered by the Gospel, and theology is the attempt to provide the Gospel's answer in accurate and relevant form. Christian education takes place when men's basic questions are answered in terms of the relationships we have with people.

PASTORAL WORK

A fourth function of the church is its *pastoral work.* Throughout its history, the church has been concerned with the needs of its people and has been active in works of mercy, especially among those who are the outcasts of society. Prison work, care for the sick, general deeds of charity, and pastoral oversight have indicated that the parable of the Good Samaritan is among the best known of all Jesus' stories. When Jesus was asked who he was, he answered by saying that "the blind are regaining their sight, the lame can walk, the lepers are being cured and the deaf can hear, the dead are being raised up and good news is being preached to the poor" (Luke 7:22, G).

Although much pastoral work today requires highly specialized techniques restricted to the clergy and others psychologically trained, the church has always insisted that lay people have responsibility in this field. In times of emergency, sickness, tragedy, and death, the congregation ministers through its individual members. This self-giving love of God is channeled by the church's life through individual members far beyond the immediate boundaries of the congregation. Most of the motivation for social welfare in Western culture has come from those trained in Christian ethics, and the church has inspired many kinds of social and political reform, especially during and since the days of the "social gospel."

The pastoral concern of Christian living, moved by love, expresses itself in all the relationships of the Christian. The educational value of this function is most clearly seen in the mission field, through the impact of hospitals, schools, and vocational training, and the results in terms of devotion to Christ among members of the "younger" churches have been amazing.

MISSION TO THE WORLD

The fifth function of the church is its *missionary work.* It is a strange paradox of the effectiveness of the church that its health at home shows a direct correlation to its missionary motive. The good news that God sent Jesus Christ to redeem all of mankind cannot be acquired by anyone who is not willing to share it. If Christianity is worth anything, it is worth giving away. The Gospel cannot be put in a capsule of one's individual faith or parochial activities.

Although it is true that the Christian missionary expansion often was corrupted by various forms of imperialism, and Christian behavior was often confused with Western cultural practices, the churches of the East are proof that Christianity is no more wedded to European or American culture than it was to ancient Palestine. The church has always known this, and expansion has continued from the earliest days. We do not always realize that the greatest period of expansion was the nineteenth century and that we are living on the momentum of the greatest missionary movement in history. The unerring spiritual logic of the church is, "Share the good news or die," and the equally sound business impulse of the church has been, "Spend money on others or your own resources will dry up."

The educational value of this missionary outlook is obvious. Not only in studying the church's history but in understanding the nature of the church as a world-wide Christian fellowship today, this insight is needed in order that the local parish may be an outgoing and redemptive community.

FOR ALL MANKIND

The sixth function of the church is to *transcend all national boundaries*. Institutional churches are normally limited to their own nations, with the exception of the Roman Catholic Church. But the fellowship for which they stand has been able to transcend barriers of race, class, and war, while the conscience they derive from the moral demands of God has enabled them to speak to the nations.

The church's claim to stand above national loyalties is often compromised, but it has been strengthened in recent years by the social gospel, the expansion of the missionary movement, and the ecumenical reformation. Although there were movements toward unity in the nineteenth century, the present thrust began in 1910 with the conference at Edinburgh. Out of a series of great conferences during the next forty years, the World Council of Churches emerged as the great non-Roman fellowship of churches from most of the countries of the world. Archbishop William Temple's words at his enthronement indicate the significance of this new organization:

> As though in preparation for such a time as this, God has been building up a Christian fellowship which now extends to almost every nation, and binds citizens of them all together in true unity

> and mutual love. No human agency has planned this. It is the result of the great missionary enterprise of the last hundred and fifty years. Neither the missionaries nor those who sent them out were aiming at the creation of a world-wide fellowship interpenetrating the nations, bridging the gulf between them, and supplying the promise of a check to their rivalries. The aim for nearly the whole period was to preach the Gospel to as many individuals as could be reached, so that those who were won to discipleship should be put in the way of eternal salvation. Almost incidentally the great world-fellowship has arisen; it is the great new fact of our era; it makes itself apparent from time to time in World Conferences such as . . . have been held in Stockholm, Lausanne, Jerusalem, Oxford, Edinburgh, Madras, Amsterdam.[3]

This "great new fact of our era" reaches the local congregation. A whole list of modern heroes has arisen, including William Temple, Eivind Berggrav, Visser t'Hooft, William Paton, Dietrich Bonhoeffer, and many others. The local parish is a member of the local council of churches; the denomination is a member of the National Council of the Churches of Christ in the United States of America and the World Council of Churches, and often the local parish supports these groups financially. There are mergers taking place, with the union in South India as the most dramatic. The old Protestant isolationism is breaking down, and the tendency toward closer relationships between denominations is increasing. Interdenominational seminaries train ministers for as many as thirty or forty denominations. Individual Christians frequently cross denominational lines in order to find a congregation that seems to meet their needs.

As boys and girls, men and women, begin to grapple with the great problems of our times, they can see in the ecumenical movement resources for united Christian action in an uneasy world. They discover that the local parish has resources far beyond the institution, for it draws on the faith of Christians everywhere in the hope of a new world for tomorrow.[4]

THE PARISH AND COMMUNITY

The local parish in its various functions has relationships with the

[3] William Temple, *The Church Looks Forward* (New York: The Macmillan Company, 1944), p. 2.

[4] See my *What We Can Believe* (New York: Charles Scribner's Sons, 1941), pp. 110-23, for a similar treatment. Also my *You Need the Church* (Cincinnati: Forward Movement, 1953).

community. It belongs to the local council of churches, through which are sponsored various activities, including community worship services. It often sponsors organizations from outside its ranks, including scout troops, fund raising drives for various charities and health organizations, and groups working for civic reform. More often, its members are involved in all kinds of organizations as part of their Christian citizenship. This indirect and personal impact of the church is probably its most important contribution to the welfare of the community.

The local parish cooperates as one agency among others in other activities, joining in those enterprises that commend themselves to the church. It gets involved sometimes in political and police actions when the evidence points to the need for a moral campaign.

The local parish also opposes in one way or another those elements in civic or national life that contradict the express insights of the Gospel. Frequently the preaching of the church is strongest in its power of denunciation of activities that offend the moral sense, although occasionally the church has been concerned with issues that do not present a clearly moral problem, as in its traditional opposition to changing social customs.

The local parish is concerned to discover in the community those groups that provide resources for the expansion of the Gospel and the moral insights that are involved, and to oppose those elements that provide resistance to what the church stands for. At some points, as in the issue about gambling, the churches may disagree among themselves.

The church is involved educationally at two points. One is its concern for the moral climate and spiritual values in a heterogeneous community, in which it cannot expect every citizen to be a member of any church. It therefore asserts its influence both through its power as an institution and through its guidance of individuals to remake the community into a more moral one. It works through the official and unofficial groups, through the informal and impermanent groups, and through the mass communication media to raise the level of living. The second is its interpretation of experience for its own members, for everyone in the church is a member of the larger community and has most of his experiences in this wider field. Therefore, the primary educational concern of the local parish is to interpret daily life in the community in terms of the Gospel. For if the Gospel is heard in church and has no relevance for daily decisions, it is not being accepted or responded to.

The program of Christian education in the local church must be relevant to local conditions. That is why any educational resources that start and end with an era of church history or a Bible story or a biographical sketch, and do not become relevant to the real-life situation where God is faced in the contemporary scene, are like hot-house plants that cannot live when exposed to the climate outside. Christian education must be life-centered, not in terms of what little children feel like talking about or of what teen-agers want to say about yesterday's game or last night's date, but in terms of what their real needs are in the light of the church's concern for their total relationships of life. Perhaps last night's date is the starting point, not in terms of the latest gossip, but in terms of an understanding of boy-girl relationships under the demands of a just and loving God. People live in the community; they find their basic values in the decisions of daily life; they are Christian or not to the degree that they bring the Gospel to bear upon these decisions. The broken relationships that condemn men to hell on earth emerge in the community outside the institution of the church, but the church is the channel whereby God will heal them.

The local parish stands over against the community. As an agency within the community it seeks to raise the life of the community to a higher level, including the lives of those outside the congregation. But the community is where the people live, and therefore the curriculum of Christian education begins with the experiences of daily life that come under the judgment of the Gospel and therefore develop new meanings. Life becomes richer because of a new understanding of Jesus Christ, who came that we might have life, and have it more abundantly (John 10:10).

THE CHURCH AND THE SCHOOL

The relationship of the local parish to the schools in the community has great potentialities for Christian education. (1) First, we need to recognize the values inherent in the public and private schools. The concern for democratic values and Christian character runs throughout the public school system of America, and often these values are connected with their religious roots. This is a primary resource for the local congregation as it seeks to interpret the meaning of experience to its learners.

(2) The churches also often have the opportunity of running a released time program. This is a responsibility of the greatest importance, but it can be worth less than nothing if handled in a haphazard manner without sufficient funds or trained teachers. In most instances, this means a pan-Protestant cooperative program with a common budget rather than individual programs through the local parish.

(3) The churches also have in their membership most of the teachers and administrative officers of the local schools. The presentation of the vocation of teaching as an opportunity for nonsectarian Christian nuture within the limits of interpretation placed by the local community is one of the church's tasks. The understanding of what is involved in religious teaching on the basis of the routine courses is a resource for Christian influence within the schools. This applies at every level of education, from nursery through graduate school.

(4) The public schools are not godless, but the churches need to recognize that some teaching in some schools and colleges is alien or opposed to the truths of religion. When the dominant educational philosophy is purely secular, or when particular teachers choose to attack religion or in a subtle way indicate that it is not intellectually respectable to accept the teachings of any church, the church must object. At this point education becomes a source of resistance to the Gospel, and though the American concept of freedom includes the freedom to be irreligious, the church cannot stand idly by. From the standpoint of American democracy, our school systems should not require religious loyalty or church membership to qualify for teaching, but from the church's point of view, the Christian conscience must oppose non-Christian teaching. Some churches, in the name of academic freedom, would allow the atheist complete freedom to teach his atheism, but other churches would claim that this is license and not freedom. The Christian conviction that truth can win out in any fair battle provides a middle ground, which is that when non-Christian teachings are presented there must be an opportunity for Christian teachings to be offered. The local congregation may have to face the problem that its children are being taught science in a way that is devastating to the children's beliefs, and it must have an answer to this problem.

The local parish, as it finds resistance to the Gospel in the school system, may operate as a pressure group or through the local council of churches in order to clarify and correct the situation. Individual Christians may accept their civic responsibility by serving on the school board and examining the textbooks as well as making clear the responsibilities and limitations of academic freedom.

Within the parish, those who are being educated have most of their experience within the local school system. This is the experience that needs to be interpreted, criticized, and evaluated. This is where the Gospel is relevant. Just as the community provides experiences, so the school provides much learning that is the raw material for Christian interpretation, and our educational resources and materials should be pointed to these ends.

THE CHURCH AND THE HOME

When we are realistic about the homes in which the children dwell, they may be classified as follows: pagan homes that are not really interested in religion but send the children to the church for a variety of reasons; nominally Christian homes that are counted in the church census and think that religion is good for children and that church membership is a sign of respectability; orthodox Christian homes in which all the customs of the church are maintained, in which religion is taken seriously and is talked about, but in which is no sense of a redeeming and sustaining community; homes in which the relationships between members express a self-giving love, in which the church is taken seriously as a source of power, and in which the total outlook results in Christian living in everyday life.

These classifications are an over-simplification, but they indicate that the homes of the local parish offer various degrees of resistance to and resource for the Christian Gospel. In the first two kinds of homes, the children attend church school spasmodically and the parents hardly at all; in the latter two kinds of homes, the church is supported in many of its activities by most of their members, and often by the family as a unit.

Mothers and children spend the greater part of their time at home. The basic experiences of children, which are most influential in determining their present and future character, occur in the home. Neither school nor community has as lasting effect on character, social adjustment, and religious integration as does the home. Most often, experiences of the home are vital for the interpretation of religion to the child. The evaluation of these experiences is crucial to any Christian education.

A program of cooperation between the local parish and the homes of its people is more significant than the relationships of the church to community or school, important as these are. The approach through the family, as suggested in Chapter 6, is essential, and when the family joins as a unit in the church's functions, effective Christian education may take place. Although many homes provide resistance to the Gospel, if the presence of their children at church is permitted there is a point of contact and concern open to the local parish.

The church seeks to foster Christian relationships in the homes of its people, and it seeks the cooperation of the home in carrying out the Christian education that is impossible within the church alone. Both institutions need each other if the education of Christians is to continue effectively. When they are separated, and neither has the resources the other can offer, both agencies become less efficient. The church is always a supplement to home life and never a substitute for it, and yet the church is essential in itself if home life is to be Christian.

THE CHURCH'S ORGANIZATIONS

The church educates through its organizations.[5] The local parish needs a comprehensive plan of education that includes all of its organizations. For example, we do not often think of choir practice as educational, and yet it has possibilities for the remaking of its members through both the ministry of music and the person-to-person relationships of its members. The women's groups that spend most of their time either sewing for missions or cooking for money-raising suppers or planning for a fair or bazaar to help balance the budget may not seem at first glance to be educational organizations, and yet the justification of their existence is in terms of their being a redemptive group within the congregation. A men's social often is a purely secular activity, and if it is no different from a fraternal group it has no real value to the church. Yet the same men's social may use the same activities in order to express a genuine Christian fellowship.

---

[5] See Chapters 17 to 19 for a more complete treatment of administration and organization.

"The atmosphere in which grace flourishes," which may be used to describe any Christian group, is the clue to the matter. When the local parish is truly a fellowship of the Spirit, all of its organizations will be cells in the larger fellowship.

The primary educational activity of the local parish is the church school. Through its worship and classes, it provides a curriculum for the interpretation and evaluation of experience within a group relationship that meets the needs of its members for love and acceptance, law and discipline, freedom to grow, and the awareness of the working of God.

The basic principles guiding the performance of the church school might be listed as follows:

A school of the church is part of the total congregation, experiencing the life of the redemptive community for all of its members.

Worship stands at the center of the church's life, with a service for the entire family as the basic approach.

New educational resources make use of insights into the growth of religion, utilizing the findings of educational psychology within a theological framework.

Adequate leadership must be trained so that the quality of life in the congregation may be shared by the greatest number of members.

Curriculum development is providing many fine resources for all ages. When the problem is seen in radically different terms, avoiding the issue of graded content and interesting methods except as secondary factors, and the emphasis is placed on the relevance of the Gospel for the concerns of the daily living of the individual pupil within the fellowship of the Spirit, a new view of curriculum resources develops. God gives strength and direction for living through the channels of his grace opened by the faith of the church. The teacher is one of these channels, for his ministry is a ministry of reconciliation. This was Paul's approach when he wrote:

> God was in Christ personally reconciling the world to himself—not counting their sins against them—and has commissioned us with the message of reconciliation. We are now Christ's ambassadors, as though God were appealing direct to you through us (II Cor. 5:19-20, P).

Lesson materials are not measured primarily in content assimilated, nor in knowledge properly graded, but in growth in grace. Knowledge of content, development of Christian character, and membership in the church as an institution are important when they are motivated by the underlying appeal of the Gospel itself.

When a local parish operates in these terms, a greater responsibility falls upon the pastor, for he is pastor to the children. The minister cannot evade his duty to all the members, and this includes the youngest as well as the oldest. No matter how ably he delegates administrative responsibility among his assistants and lay people, he cannot avoid the fact that Jesus said, "You must let little children come to me – never stop them" (Mark 10:14, P). The child who comes home radiant because the pastor spoke to him or visited his class or led his worship is in turn a witness to the power of the church in his own home. Pastors will find many ways of ministering to children, and it is important that we recognize the principle.

A second reason why the pastor must be active in the church school is that he is *a man.* Basil Yeaxlee makes clear the need of the male sex and father relationship if we are to teach the deep meaning of the Fatherhood of God. Men should be on the staff at every age level, including the nursery, as a symbol of fatherhood and as excellent teachers. If the idea of two teachers to a class is practical, one should almost always be a man. The pastor always stands as a man, as a shepherd of his flock, as a father to the family of God. This symbolism is theologically significant.[6]

Although the church school is the primary educational organization of the church, we need to recognize that each organization and activity is educational. Through the educational committee and the professional staff, this work should be guided by a consistent and comprehensive educational philosophy applicable to every group and relevant for every member in the local parish. This comprehensiveness and soundness of program reaching into every activity is the only basis on which every member may be guided into Christian truth. In every group, there needs to be proper grading according to capacity and interest, there needs to be sufficient variation to avoid monotony, and there needs to be an over-all unity. No organization is sacred in itself, and simplicity of structure will allow for flexibility to meet real needs. A particular group may go out of existence and not be replaced, provided the need has vanished.

---

[6] See Basil A. Yeaxlee, *Religion and the Growing Mind,* pp. 40, 49, 85, 87, 187, for significant comments.

THE CHURCH EDUCATES

The local parish seeks to become "the church" in the New Testament sense: the life in fellowship of those who have personal loyalty to Jesus Christ. Its educational aims are always evangelistic, for only by an act of decision may one become a disciple of the Lord. As the local parish re-enacts the Gospel story, it is able "to fit his people for the work of service, for building the body of Christ, until we all attain unity in faith, and in the knowledge of the Son of God, and reach mature manhood, and that measure of full development found in Christ" (Eph. 4: 12-13, G).

The over-all objective is "to enable children, young people and adults to find their place in the redemptive fellowship *now*."[7] A. Victor Murray writes that "it is the Church's business to seek to create convinced Christians, to offer training in worship, to give guidance in personal religion, to order and sustain a corporate witness before the world, to care for the ministry of the word and sacraments and to be vitally concerned with the original documents of the faith and with the continuing testimony down the ages."[8] In this redemptive community, we are to find all sorts and conditions of men, and they are to rejoice in their being together, for they will learn to love those who are different from them. That is why there is danger in too much organization, for it separates those who should witness their togetherness.

Christian education depends on loyalty to the local parish, to the denomination, and to the ecumenical church. This involves a genuine discipline of the spirit, for it means that one's loyalty to his group does not imply that another group is false to the Christian revelation. Loyalty to Christ through the church is the goal of both Christian education and evangelism, and it depends in the last analysis on the decision of the individual, a decision that cannot be coerced. It comes by "the means of grace," which is channeled through the quality of life of a particular congregation. Our membership and loyalty are primarily directed to the local congregation; but we are baptized into the community of believers of which Jesus Christ is the head, and therefore we belong to that universal company of believers, which is the historic meaning of the "Catholic" Church.

---

[7] Statement of Department of Christian Education, Protestant Episcopal Church.

[8] *Education into Religion* (New York: Harper & Brothers, 1954), p. 182.

This New Testament view of the church is a "high" view. It applies to all kinds of doctrine and polity, for the emphasis is on the fellowship of the Spirit which is the Body of which Christ is the head. The success of our "education into religion" depends on loyalty to the church in this "high" sense of community and not institution. In many cases, a complete reorientation of the life of the local congregation will be necessary before Christian education can become effective, but often it can start with a small, concerned group willing to do whatever is necessary. This evaluation of parish life is essential to a sound program, giving new life to the redemptive community, and this redemptive power is the essence of the church's life.

PART THREE

Methods in Religious Education

CHAPTER 10

GOOD CLASSROOM PROCEDURE

ERLE STANLEY GARDNER, in speaking of the polygraph or lie-detector, describes its efficiency in terms of the way it is used. As a scientific instrument it shows specific and measurable reactions on the part of the person being interviewed, but the conclusion concerning the truthfulness of the answers depends on the personal insights of the interrogator. His insights concerning the questions to be asked, the way in which he puts them, and his preparation of the subject prior to the test provide relationships which affect the reactions of the subject. The interrogator's skill is much more than that of a technician running a machine, and even when he has the qualifications the results are not infallible.[1]

THE NATURE OF METHOD

Method in teaching is also more than technical proficiency. "Method," says John Dewey, "means that arrangement *of* subject matter which makes it most effective in use. Never is method something outside of the material. . . . It is simply an effective treatment *of* material." [2] Method is the way in which the learner is led to see the relevance of subject matter to the problems of his own life. If his problems and concerns are religious (and according to our definition *any* problem or concern *may be* religious), method is the means

[1] See Erle Stanley Gardner, *The Court of Last Resort* (New York: Pocket Books, 1954), pp. 18-19, 73-74.

[2] John Dewey, *Democracy and Education* (New York: Macmillan Co., 1916), p. 194.

whereby the resources of a religious tradition are made relevant to that problem in everyday experience. The purpose of method is to make a student think, and thinking is facing a real problem with the total resources of one's person, involving, therefore, the resources of the community and whatever comes through these channels from God. The subject matter may come from knowledge of the past, of current ways of solving problems, of lesson materials and resources, and of one's own way of achieving results.

THINKING

John Dewey identifies method with the process of thinking. "The sole direct path to enduring improvement in the methods of instruction and learning consists in centering upon the conditions which exact, promote, and test thinking." [3] He contrasts the formal experiences of the school room with the natural learning of situations outside of school. Thinking begins with experience, but it proceeds to connections involved, inferences, and testing. There is a direct relationship between the problem arising from experience and the subject matter that contributes to the solution of the problem. The reason this process is difficult to establish is that it requires an oversupply of subject matter as resource for solving problems. It is not the lack of techniques but the absence of resources that makes this method of thinking and learning so difficult.

For example, a group of junior high youngsters may be concerned with the actions of a gang who have been systematically "lifting" various items from a neighborhood store. The discussion of the problem, which involves their own schoolmates and perhaps even some of the group, may lead to vital questions concerning rules of behavior, the tendency to break relationships with those who trust us, and lack of loyalty to the community and to God. This genuine concern on the part of the group leads them back to educational resources they do not have, and therefore they need the opportunity to become acquainted with a wide variety of data that may help them understand this problem. Such Biblical passages as the story of Adam hiding from God, or the analysis of sin in Paul's letter to the Romans, or the account of the return of the Prodigal Son, or the idea of reconciliation

---

[3] *Democracy and Education,* pp. 179-180.

in Malachi, or the love of home and church as found in Psalms 68 or 133 may help them to see more deeply into the meaning of the Gospel.

On the other hand, a similar group might be curious about the story of Adam and Eve, and, as the story is retold, tend to identify themselves with the behavior patterns that are described. As this illuminates their own problems and concerns, it leads away from the subject matter; and then more resource material is sought to help them see how they are related to their fellowmen and to God.

In either case, the problem must be real and not artificial. The problems youngsters face must be genuine and relevant, sufficiently within their grasp that they may see the possibility of a solution. The situation must challenge thought and be novel enough to stimulate interest. It is true that one problem, even at this age, is to learn how to face problems that cannot be solved in practice or on a speculative basis; but even in such situations young people can learn how to overcome the obstacles that can be overcome and to accept those facts of experience that cannot be changed.

Of course only a part of learning comes through sense problems, unless the concept of problem is expanded beyond its usual meaning, as Dewey sometimes seems to do. Learning comes also from the response of the pupil in terms of appreciation. In religious education the learner feels this response toward liturgy, music, art, literature, history, and theology as he begins to see their intrinsic rather than instrumental values. A child does not learn good manners by facing problems so much as by the impact of the atmosphere of home life on his behavior. Good taste, discriminating judgment, and ethical distinctions are learned through the subtle influences of community life. The basic needs are met not because they are seen and described and then faced as problems, but because there are redemptive and sustaining influences in home, school, church, and community that provide the atmosphere in which a personality grows.

Where these subtle influences and this redeeming atmosphere do not exist, the conscious facing of problems does not lead to the development of a mature personality. Overambitious stimulation at this point may lead to frustration, and constant striving may build attitudes of insecurity and anxiety, for the learner must be at ease in his community and growth must be permitted to proceed at its own rate.

If method is understood in this comprehensive way, the specific means at our command tend to multiply in terms of the increasing capacities of the students and the creative insights of the teachers. Any honorable technique that presents the subject matter that solves the problem or meets the situation is suitable, provided the situation is faced in terms of what the learner does. Data may be supplied through memory, observation, reading, storytelling, audio-visual aids, and many other forms of communication. Efficiency at this point means using the technique that best provides the data for solving the problem, and avoiding the "cold-storage ideal of knowledge,"[4] which insists that facts be salted away for future use although irrelevant to the situation at hand.

Because every student is solving his own problems, he is a discoverer as he makes learning his own property. The learner does not accumulate ideas. He reaches similar ideas through first-hand wrestling with the problem. He uses the resources provided as the teacher guides him and as he shares in the activities of his group. Curriculum, as has been said before, "is the experience of the learner under guidance."

John Dewey makes a convenient summary:

> The essentials of method are therefore identical with the essentials of reflection. They are first that the pupil have a genuine situation of experience—that there be a continuous activity in which he is interested for its own sake; secondly, that a genuine problem develop within this situation as a stimulus to thought; third, that he possess the information and make the observations needed to deal with it: fourth, that suggested solutions occur to him which he shall be responsible for developing in an orderly way; fifth, that he have an opportunity and occasion to test his ideas by application, to make their meaning clear and to discover for himself their validity.[5]

Dewey does not apply this identification of thinking and method to religion, primarily because of his defective view of religion, but it is clear that the basic relationships by which religion is taught are found in this process of thinking. Theology, which we have defined as truth-about-God-in-relation-to-man, stands behind this process and provides the guidance necessary for the solving of life's problems as subject matter and method are brought together at the learner's level. But when the teacher has an understanding of this organic connection between subject matter and method and has developed the specific skills that are necessary, he cannot simply assume that learn-

---

[4] *Democracy and Education,* p. 186.

[5] *Democracy and Education,* p. 192.

ing will take place. There is still no easy way to learn, and all the motivation and interest aroused by relevant subject matter will not guarantee that this slow and tedious process will be worked out by an individual pupil.

SUBJECT MATTER

Maturity of faith, competency for living, and effective membership in a community demand a mastery of the ideas, traditions, and facts that underlie community life. These ideas, traditions, and facts may be observed, remembered, read and talked about, or presented in many ways. The content of the curriculum is those resources that help the individual to solve his problems and satisfy his needs as a member of various communities. From the standpoint of the learner, these materials are his possibilities; he must grow into an appreciation of them by seeing their relevance for his particular problems. At a certain point, his curiosity may develop to the place where he will seek knowledge for the sake of satisfying his craving for knowledge as such, but this is a high degree of maturity that we do not expect to find except in certain adults and in a few children of genius.

This subject matter, which in time may come into the activities of the learner, must be the resources of the teacher. Mastery of content is a prerequisite of the teacher, so that he may be free to use this content in terms of the aptitudes and interests of his pupils. The primary teacher, for example, just because the content available is so elementary, is freed to spend more time and attention on the needs of the learners. But we do not always see that this same informal feeding of content into the educational process is essential at more advanced levels. In terms of subject matter, the teacher is a resource person and therefore resourceful when subject matter is relevant. To stimulate the pupil to see the interaction of subject matter with his own needs is the primary occupation of the teacher.

The meanings of social living are communicated in terms of relationships. In younger learners, these relationships are primarily physical in their expression, although they involve the total personality. As we pointed out in the chapter on "Growth in Religion," [6] younger children learn primarily through physical activity, and they measure

[6] See pp. 78-81.

their answers to their problems in terms of power to act physically to satisfy their needs. But the power of bodily activity is not limited to the skills of childhood, and many advanced experiments in physics involve manual manipulation of the highest skill. These bodily expressions of relationships operate in both the personal and impersonal spheres, and in the personal sphere they rise to the "I-Thou" of religious meaning. Bodily actions in worship and the use of physical means in the sacraments show that the material aspects of life are essential to education on the highest spiritual level. Gymnastics may be sacramental.

HISTORICAL KNOWLEDGE

We need to know much more than we can react to in terms of physical action, and especially do we need experiences and information from the past if we are to face life's problems today. When the learner makes use of selections from the information of the past as these are relevant to his own concerns, he makes them part of his own accumulated knowledge. The more knowledge he can acquire in this way, the better. He needs a vast storehouse of information in order to deal effectively with his problems. As soon as he can use words, knowledge is communicated in this fashion, but too often the learner, whether he be child or adult, is overcome by irrelevant factual material for which he has no immediate or future use. He can use words to satisfy his teacher, and his immediate problem is solved in terms of verbalisms that make others happy. The memorizing of Bible verses or facts of Biblical history apart from the relevance of God's revelation for one's own faith tends to be merely verbal. Learning involves *relevant* meaning, and this depends on the experience and problems of the learner.

SYSTEMATIZED KNOWLEDGE

Religious knowledge is based primarily on historical events, but it is also systematized in what is known as theology. The abstract concepts of systematized thoughts have grown out of the experiences of the community, and the Bible is the primary record on which Christian theology is based. Mature Christians can work with the abstractions and refinements of theology, and because the basic motivation is the discovery of truth as God has revealed it through the events of history, rational and logical procedures have meaning in that context. Speculative thought is a legitimate procedure, and it carries beyond the immediate concerns into the realms of the nature of being.

Such explorations and exercises in rational systematizing are valid for the purposes of seeking God's revelation in the world of today, but another step must be taken before it becomes relevant for educational purposes except for specialists. Theology must be organized for the purposes of communication, and this immediately brings in the problem of relevance. The abstract concepts of theology illumine present situations and provide the clue to the meaning of existence, and therefore they become the means for meeting basic needs and solving practical problems. Theology, for educational purposes, becomes the-truth-about-God-in-relation-to-man, and therefore it stands behind all kinds of response on the part of the learner to the relationships of life.

ORGANIZATION OF SUBJECT MATTER

Subject matter includes the experience of the race, of the teacher, and of the pupil. It is organized to meet the needs of the community. This means, primarily, that studies are adapted to the needs of the individuals in the church and in their communities outside the church. Subject matter is selected for the purpose of improving the common life within the redemptive community, opening up channels of God's grace so that men may respond in faith to the Gospel. Subject matter is graded in terms of the needs and capacities of individuals, but also in terms of what is primary in the Gospel. Theology determines what is most fundamental, and our knowledge of the group's growth in religion determines how these fundamental truths are related to life situations.

EDUCATION INTO FAITH

When we educate for democratic living in our public schools, we attempt to bring about an appreciation of social living within the context of democratic principles. Education *into* democracy means that one is living the democratic life within the community now, for education is life and not just a means to it. The material results of education are by-products that provide additional opportunities to serve, whereas the expanding realization of meanings within the give-and-take of community life is the major goal.

Education *into* Christian faith is analogous to education into democracy. Within the community, one discovers the meanings of the Gospel as the Christian life is experienced. This quality of life, this "atmosphere in which grace flourishes," is the key to the meaning of the Gospel. It is part of the process, no matter what particular subject matter is relevant to a specific problem or need. Christian behavior does not come from the study of morals but from loyalty to the community in which these aims are part of one's social life.

All the way from block-building in the nursery to block-busting in bombing raids, the same basic relationship between method and subject matter holds good. *Method evolves from the theology of the Christian church, for method is simply the means whereby Christian truth is arranged to make it effective in one's meeting and understanding of life's problems. Life's experiences are interpreted so that the relevance and saving power of Christian truth become evident.*

CLASSROOM RESPONSE

Because Christian education is primarily concerned with the Christian answer to the real needs of the learner, it necessarily starts on a level more personal and less rigid than education treating subject matter as an end in itself.

The right beginning for the Christian teacher in the classroom is to let everyone be himself. In order for the class to become a miniature community in which everyone is accepted as he is, the first task of the teacher is to accept his pupils himself. The teacher should love them as they are, simply because God loves all men as they are, although this love is a gift of grace and cannot be compelled. If God loved mankind enough to let his unique Son be crucified, the teacher by God's grace should love the members of the class. This acceptance of the total person, regardless of his likeableness, is the clue to a right start in Christian teaching. This cannot be achieved by words, and the students are sure to test any protestations of this kind of love by challenging it. In the relationships of the classroom, the teacher who accepts his pupils and thereby becomes acceptable to them is off to a good start.

This mutual relationship of acceptance does not come easily or quickly. Often it is achieved only after much effort and prayer together. But there are techniques that will speed up the process. Knowing pupils' names, discovering their interests and abilities, appreciating their home and school backgrounds, showing a personal concern for each member, keeping track of their responsiveness in class and recording their progress toward becoming the kind of a group in which they can let their hair down without threatening their security, and enlisting the cooperation of their parents are means whereby the teacher's full acceptance of his pupils can be made more obvious. Often an observer can see the evidence the teacher needs in order to determine the degree to which various members have been drawn into the social procedures of learning as a group.

We have already discussed motivation in terms of drive, cue, response, and reinforcement.[7] When interest has been motivated by active response to a stimulus, the process continues toward a desired goal. Ideally one becomes carried away by the object, so that he both loses and finds himself in it. Subject matter, as it engages the activity of the learner, is his interest.[8] Classroom response occurs when the teacher is able to discover those areas of concern that already exist and to enlist interest in other areas of concern that are within the scope of the learners; from this point the class moves as a group toward the resolution of the conflict by achieving desirable goals. These goals must be within the reach of the learners, although the teacher may see long-range values that are beyond their immediate grasp.

As the learner grows and as he becomes an accepted member of the group, he acquires new motives. This is often a highly complicated procedure accompanying the process of maturation. Every increase in relevant knowledge whets his appetite for further practical information. There are changes in his native drives as well as in his environmental situation. Sometimes these changes occur so rapidly that the nature of the entire class will be altered from week to week.[9]

As the class gets under way, the teacher must know how much can be achieved by the class through trial and error and wandering from

---

[7] See pp. 42-43.

[8] See John Dewey, *Democracy and Education,* pp. 148-49.

[9] Mehran K. Thomson lists some of the experimental data that are available, although not conclusive, in this area. See "Motivation in School Learning," in *Educational Psychology,* ed. Charles E. Skinner (New York: Prentice-Hall, Inc., 1951), pp. 306-33.

the pathway, how much through his guidance and the use of factual information, and how much through his keeping quiet. A variety of methods is necessary in order to meet the needs of all of the students, and also to avoid the boredom of routine.

This leads to recognition of the wide differences in ability among learners of the same age and school grade. Social participation by every member of the class depends almost entirely upon the teacher's ability to estimate the potentialities of each pupil and to give him tasks in accord with those abilities that, at the same time, contribute to the ongoing endeavors of the entire class. Let the class as a whole tackle the same problem, and encourage each member to contribute to the solution in terms of his own interests and abilities.

The leadership of the teacher evolves through community action. It is neither the guidance of an autocrat nor a complete lack of direction with all decisions being made by the group. By sharing with his pupils his own maturity and experience, by directing the class in its own endeavors to learn, by seeing the relationship of the subject matter to the total life of each pupil, by having adequate but flexible plans of procedure for each specific session, and by encouraging group action that is responsible, the teacher emerges as a leader whom the pupils accept.

The classroom response depends on a number of tangible elements such as we have mentioned, but above all on the alertness of the teacher to the capacities and needs of the individuals in the group. Mutual acceptance in terms of right attitude is the basis upon which adequate techniques and specific methods can be built.[10]

RESOURCES

Lesson materials in the average Sunday church school vary in quality and educational philosophy from publisher to publisher, and the local church often has a mixture of materials from many sources. How these are chosen and what is available are discussed in a later chapter,[11] but the question here is their use in order to achieve desir-

---

[10] See Harold Spears, *Principles of Teaching* (New York: Prentice-Hall, Inc., 1951), pp. 115-36; Henry P. Smith, *Psychology in Teaching* (New York: Prentice-Hall, Inc., 1954), pp. 240-68; George Betts and Marion O. Hawthorne, *Method in Teaching Religion* (New York: Abingdon Press, 1925), pp. 185-205.

[11] See Chapter 22.

able reactions in the classroom. The emphasis in much of this material is on content, and often the subject matter is relevant and interesting to the learners. The premium, however, is placed upon the mastery of the material as an end in itself rather than on using the subject matter as a help for living as a Christian within today's society. But even when the needs of the learner are considered paramount, the starting point is often not the situations in which the learners find themselves, although occasionally this is approximated by the wise guesses of curriculum writers. The lessons begin with the kind of material learners of a particular age can be expected to master. The use of the Bible is frequently determined in terms of what an age group can verbalize rather than in terms of how God speaks through the Bible to assist the class to be in itself a miniature redemptive community. The goal of mastering the lesson materials supersedes the primary achievement of a faith relationship to God which is expressed in our relationships with our fellows and which should be both the starting point and the goal of any Christian education. There are, of course, many excellent series of materials that use modern approaches to the needs of the learners.

If method is the arrangement of subject matter so that it contributes to the satisfying of basic needs and to the solution of pressing problems, the use that is made of lesson materials will be radically different from what has been customary. The assumption is that *the whole Gospel is relevant to the needs of everyone, and through what we have called "the language of relationships" it is possible for God to work in human community, and especially through the home and church, to alter our lives and help us face our essential problems. Therefore, every session of a class is involved in the understanding of the ultimate meanings of life as these meanings help to overcome the threat to one's existence as a person.*

The significant point is not the teacher's security nor the sanctions of a prearranged lesson plan nor the materials in a book. The important element is the personal relationships within the class and the relationships that are brought before the class for illumination. The starting point is the concerns and problems of the learners, both as they see them and as the wise and sensitive teacher leads them to see them.

Lesson materials are the resources whereby the learners are assisted and guided in appreciating the meanings in their lives. They are materials that must be thoroughly grasped and understood by the leader and that are held in readiness for any situation that may arise. In some cases, this means starting with suggestions brought to the class session by the students; in other cases, the stimulus of the prior worship service is a self-starter for discussion; in still other cases, the loose ends of the previous session provide a starting point, although this is true only with boys and girls who can recall a discussion held several days or a week previously. Often the subject matter the teacher has planned to present is relevant and interesting and leads into the genuine concerns of the pupils.

This kind of an approach does not lend itself easily to those lesson materials that map out each session in advance throughout the year. It does not fit uniform lessons in which the same Bible passage is studied by the entire church school. It does not adapt itself to those educational philosophies that emphasize the covering of a certain amount of material no matter what the capacities of the pupils may be. But the point is that even these materials may be used in a relevant manner if the straitjacket is removed from their external demands. They are to be thought of as resources, and they are to be related to life.

Such an approach as is suggested here may not get through the material, but it gets through *to* the learner. The course of lesson materials becomes a storehouse of subject matter that is to be arranged to suit the needs of the learner, and a vast amount of additional material needs to be added. To find answers to their questions and means to solve their problems, the learners are carried beyond the limits of the lesson materials and the confines of the classroom. They go beyond the required Bible reading, seeking answers in books that are suited to their needs and often requesting additional assistance not only from the teacher but from resource persons. There are many religious books for younger readers, some of which have been developed as home readers for family use in connection with regular courses (as in the case of the Presbyterian Christian Faith and Life Series), and these should be available in parish libraries.

In order to improve classroom response, suitable equipment is helpful.[12] In many local parishes there is inadequate space. Classes meet in improperly lighted and equipped rooms, or several classes meet in the same room, and some have to talk over the backs of pews in

---

[12] See pp. 292-93.

the nave of the church. Adequate equipment means comfortable chairs with space for writing, blackboards, notebooks, pencils, reference books, opportunity to use visual aids, and freedom from distractions. Although exceptional teachers work with inadequate equipment and achieve remarkable results, it is too much to hope that the normal teacher can do so. Clever improvising, the use of nearby homes, and weekday classes may lessen the difficulty.

DIAGNOSING THE PROBLEMS

Some teachers can diagnose the problems of classroom response, but often they need assistance. This is achieved in two ways. An observer is placed in the class for a period of time, taking notes and checking on both the pupils and the teacher, evaluating the relevance of the curriculum materials, observing the use of equipment, and estimating the work of this class in relation to the standards of the congregation. Frequently the observer also can relate conditions in the homes, schools, and community to what is going on in the classroom. A second approach is similar, involving a trained supervisor who meets with the teacher, visits the class, and makes a similar type of evaluation.[13]

Although a specific class may be the source of trouble in some parishes, it is more likely that the chief difficulty lies in the quality of life in the congregation itself. Where adults are not really concerned with the basic needs of the younger members, or where they have no real understanding of what Christian education is, or where the life of the parish is not primarily seen as a redemptive community in action, it is difficult for any teacher to achieve the *rapport* that makes for good classroom procedure.

Sometimes, however, one class that really catches a vision of the Christian faith becomes a redemptive cell within the congregation, and soon the life of the parish begins to change. There are specific methods that may be used to evaluate the spiritual values in the life of the congregation, such as the parish life weekend,[14] a parish workshop,[15] or special types of leadership training.[16] These procedures

---

[13] See pp. 343-45.
[14] See pp. 339-41.
[15] See pp. 339-41.
[16] See pp. 336-45.

are used to achieve specific goals, of which the following are of particular significance in helping the teacher in the classroom:

(1) Develop the educational concerns of the local congregation so that members will see the significance for Christian education of every activity of parish life.

(2) Involve parents in the program through home cooperation and a parents' class.

(3) Enlist teachers in terms of their devotion as Christians and provide the necessary skills by means of a thoroughgoing leadership training program. Techniques are important, but they are always secondary to the capacity of the teacher to love the pupils as they are because of his awareness of God's love for all mankind. The teachers must have the capacity to master the subject matter as resources for life's situations, to understand enough psychology to know both his pupils and his methods, and to work hard at a demanding task.

(4) Evaluate the lesson materials and additional resources in terms of the demands of the Gospel, the capacity of the learners, and the relevance of theology for Christian living in today's world. This may mean rejecting materials that are irrelevant, inadequate, and unsound on grounds of theology, history, psychology, sociology, or teaching methods.[17]

(5) Develop the program so that there is a correlation between the worship service and the classroom. In many instances this will mean a family worship service for everyone, followed by class discussions that begin with what happened in worship. Departmentalized worship may be used in the same manner but not so effectively.[18]

(6) Make the best possible use of existing space and equipment, and purchase what is necessary for effective teaching.[19] Sometimes this means merely appropriating equipment and space held by adults for the use of younger members, but it may mean rearranging the day's schedule or providing additional space and equipment.

---

[17] See pp. 351-55.
[18] See pp. 246-50.
[19] See pp. 292-93.

CHAPTER II

TYPES AND SELECTION OF METHOD

A FAMILIAR distinction is that between content-centered and life-centered teaching. In the former, the emphasis is on the content to be mastered for its own sake. In the latter, the emphasis is on the mastery and use of content for the solving of problems. The emphasis on material often leads to aims centering in the material *alone,* without consideration of the needs or capacities or interests of the students. The emphasis on problems often leads to an unguided program in which the students wallow in their own ignorance. But both of these extremes fail to do justice to the insights of each general type of method.

MATERIAL-CENTERED TEACHING

In the field of religion, material-centered teaching makes use of the Bible, the church, or doctrine as the main emphasis. The goal is the mastery of a given set of beliefs, facts, and meanings as interpreted by the local congregation or by the denomination to which it belongs.

BIBLE-CENTERED

Bible-centered teaching in many courses of lesson materials is concerned with the mastery of the content of Scripture. By reading, memorizing, and recitation, the student learns what is in the Bible. Passages are selected in terms of his capacity to understand, or at least to read and recite. The goal is knowledge for its own sake. His reward is the mastery of the material, a grade, a prize, or praise.

This approach has certain obvious values. When it is successful, it provides a storehouse of facts, quotations, stories, and history that may satisfy his curiosity and answer certain intellectual questions. It serves as a basis for beliefs about God, man, and society, and may provide guidance for the development of his character. When used in conjunction with other methods, it is an essential part of Christian education.

A Bible-centered method has many dangers, however, when it stands by itself. It is often a mechanical approach, with little adaptation to the capacities or needs of the age groups, and often the material is introduced before the child can grasp its meaning. It is unrelated to life's problems, and the great drama of redemption is reduced to some strangely dressed historical figures who talked in a language quite different from that of today. There is no structure that permits God to speak to the pupil's needs through the drama of his mighty acts in history. There is little or no attention to the developments of Biblical scholarship, whereby we place the Biblical narratives in the life situations by which God reveals himself, and thus the total picture is inadequate for theological purposes even when the material is mastered. The Bible becomes an end in itself, and there is danger of a Bibliolatry that stands in the way of a right relationship with God.

CHURCH-CENTERED

Church-centered teaching is open to some of the same criticisms, although it also has value when properly conceived. Loyalty to the local congregation, and through it to the denomination and to the whole body of Christ's church, is one of the significant goals of Christian education. But this loyalty develops when the individual is incorporated into the life of a redemptive community, which turns on life-centered principles. Understanding of the church's ways, so that one knows why he is a member of a particular parish and denomination, is important. This involves acquaintance with the history of the church, with the specific teachings that mark off one denomination from another, with the ways of worship, the demands of behavior, and the ideals of stewardship and missionary activity held by the church.

But loyalty to the church can become idolatry. The local parish may become the sole center of loyalty. The denomination may become the only means of salvation. The exclusiveness of the church may become a barrier to fellowship among Christians. At the sectarian extreme, this may lead to a denial of religious freedom for all religious bodies except the "true church to which I belong." The Gospel is paraphrased to read: "In the beginning was the church, and the church was with God, and the church was God."

DOCTRINE-CENTERED

Doctrine-centered teaching places the emphasis on beliefs to be learned. When properly understood in its relationship to life's problems, nothing is more important than the understanding of truth. Wrong beliefs may be as efficient as right beliefs, but the results are demonic. Wrong beliefs provide a narrowing of perspective, a distortion of the sense of value, and integration on a low level. There is room for freedom of belief and even for wrong ideas about nonessentials, but the essential teachings of the Christian faith, which have emerged from God's revelation of himself through the events recorded in the Bible, are our guides to action. The beliefs with which we are concerned are those that provide direction for action, and therefore it is terribly important that we seek the right things, the right values, and the right God. Beliefs become faith when they direct our loyalties.[1]

When indoctrination becomes an end in itself, however, real dangers are faced. The great doctrine of justification by faith, which involves man's decision to respond to God's grace, is reduced to its caricature, justification by right belief. The verbal recitation of ideas, as in a creed, may satisfy the teacher, but it has no necessary relationship to one's behavior. That Christians merely assert certain beliefs on Sunday and live by another creed during the week is the standard criticism of hypocritical Christians by those outside the church, and it is the result, all too often, of this kind of teaching.

TEACHING CONTENT

Many lesson materials place such an emphasis on content that it is considered an end in itself. Yet mastering content is valid only when

---

[1] See my *What We Can Believe* (New York: Charles Scribner's Sons, 1941), pp. 10-11.

the real problem is that of satisfying the intellect. The task of Christian education is much greater than this, for it must enlist the total personality in loyalty to God, transforming him by God's grace, through the ministry of persons within the redemptive community. Mastery of the content of the Bible, of the church's ways, and of doctrine is essential to Christian education, but content must never get in the way of the true goal, which is one's relationship to the God of Jesus Christ.

The classical way of beginning with content and relating it to life is the method attributed to Johann Friedrich Herbart. This has been modified in the light of recent educational developments, but still places content at the center.

(1) *Preparation* is the way in which the pupil is motivated. The goals are made attractive in terms of the pupil's real needs. A reading assignment may become an exciting adventure when the child knows why he is reading it. The promise of clarification of a problem, of guidance for living, or of getting along with one's parents or peers will enlist his cooperation.

(2) *Presentation* may follow a number of methods. Different tasks may be assigned in the light of individual capacities and problems. Books, lectures, audio-visual aids, field trips, and discussion are among the many easily available resources. Class committees, research teams, or the use of resource persons adds zest to the program.

(3) *Association* is the manner in which the new material is related to the old. The pupil moves from the known to the unknown, from the local situation to a broader view, from people he knows to people he comes to know. A child living in the Imperial Valley of California, with its date trees and dead sea, has little trouble understanding the geography and climate of Palestine, whereas a child in New England has a more difficult time making the association. Unless this association is achieved, there is the danger of verbalisms that satisfy the teacher but do not lead to significant learning.

(4) *Systematization or organization* is the process of putting new and old facts together. This tendency to generalize emerges at an early age as a means of seeing the similarity of various facts and experiences. Often guidance is needed from the teacher at this point, but it should be limited to suggestions and the teacher should refrain from providing easy answers. Discussion, experiment, and further reading often assist the process.

(5) *Application* is the use of knowledge in a concrete situation.

If a new principle of behavior or of relationships has been discovered, such as Buber's "I-Thou" relationship, it will be applied to such real problems as relationships with parents, public school classroom or playground experiences, dating, or working at a job. When application provides satisfaction, the pupil comes into a new or closer relationship with the teacher who was the source of the motivation in the first step of *presentation,* and therefore will face the next problem with greater eagerness.[2]

Although the main emphasis is on content, many of the principles of life-centered teaching are followed in using these steps. At any point in the process the teacher must be willing to improvise, to allow for the introduction of information from members of the class, and to accept contributions that may seem wide of the mark.

LIFE-CENTERED METHOD

The emphasis in life-centered teaching, as contrasted with material-centered teaching, is on the development of the pupil rather than the mastery of content. We learn to live by living.

The classroom is never as natural a place to learn as out-of-school experiences.[3] But the classroom can deal with genuine experiences and crucial problems. In general, there are three types of problems: (1) the need to act, (2) the need to know, and (3) the need to trust. In facing human and divine relationships, these three are combined. The child needs to understand his relationship with his mother, to do something about it, and to trust her. A girl needs to understand why boys act as they do, what to do about a particular boy, and to what extent she can trust them. A child needs to learn how to pray, to understand what prayer is for, and to commit himself to his heavenly Father. A boy needs to understand how God acted to reconcile the world to himself, what to do about it in terms of forgiving a friend who has broken his fountain pen, and how this act of forgiveness is an expression of his faith in God.

The steps in this approach have been developed by John Dewey.[4]

---

[2] See Henry P. Smith, *Psychology in Teaching* (New York: Prentice-Hall, Inc., 1954), pp. 258-63.

[3] See my *A Guide for Church School Teachers,* p. 39.

[4] See John Dewey, *How We Think* (Boston: D. C. Heath & Co., 1933), pp. 106-15; also, *Democracy and Education,* p. 192.

(1) *One must become aware of a problem.* Problems arise from the aims and purposes of the individuals in the class, and the wider the experiences of the members the more problems there are. A slum-bred child knows little of the problems of farming, just as a child in a strictly white and Protestant community knows little of the prejudices against Jews, Negroes, and Roman Catholics. A problem exists when the road to a desired end is blocked by one or more obstacles.

(2) *The problem must be clarified.* The objective must be clearly perceived. The facts and conditions involved must be discovered. The way to the desired end must be pursued. For example, a high school class faces the problem of a Christian vocation. Secular and Christian factors are clarified in terms of the individual's capacity, opportunities for education, openings in the field, and the meaning of vocation in Christian terms. Irrelevant questions are discarded, and steps are taken toward an answer that can be acted upon. Subject matter, which may be highly technical and detailed, comes into the picture, and because it is relevant it is mastered. The significant data are discovered, and the data that are not involved are discarded.

(3) *Proposed solutions* are then dealt with as hypotheses. The clarification of the problem may lead to immediate action, and all the intermediate steps may be omitted or telescoped. The more complex the problem is, especially as it involves the free response of other human beings, the more data are required for proposing and evaluating hypotheses. The pooled experience of all the individuals in the class is the first source of information. The wider the experience, the more information will be at hand to help provide an answer. In the use of the Bible, for example, both the information already held and the wise use of a concordance as a means of gaining additional information are of great assistance in suggesting and evaluating hypotheses.

As children grow older, they gain in maturity and judgment and, therefore, handle the material more effectively. With younger children, the teacher may have to control the amount of data presented so as to avoid confusion and at the same time to permit intelligent decisions to be made at that age level. In the face of a problem that the group cannot solve within its own framework, another framework or a similar problem already solved may be substituted. In a discussion of cheating in examinations, which sometimes cannot be solved in terms of a high school situation, the problem takes on new light when it is applied to a student in medical school cheating in an examination on how to remove a gall bladder.

(4) *Selection of the best hypothesis is the next step.* Sometimes the first hypothesis is so obviously the answer that no further analysis is needed, but when the problem is new, unique, or complex, a number of hypotheses will be considered. Quick rejections or acceptances involve some evaluation, but considered evaluation means reviewing the previous steps, looking at solutions offered in the experience of the class and in the resources available, and analyses of the most likely suggestions that emerge. The class may come to an agreement as to the manner in which their relationships should be handled, and this points to specific steps to improve their relationships. It might be a study of the relation of freedom and authority among teen-agers in their homes and at school, or the attempt to understand how Christ is central in religious thinking and behavior, or the best resolution of boy-girl relationships within a peer group.

(5) *Testing the hypothesis in experience* is the final step. Each member of the class who shares in the selection of a workable hypothesis attempts to live in that manner in various situations. This experiment brings to light new data, which may necessitate re-evaluating the first decision. Perhaps young people are working on their relationships with parents. Parents react as expected to a situation, and therefore the answer seems to be right; or perhaps they react in quite a different manner, and therefore the whole process has to be repeated. The satisfactions promised in a special worship service do not work out, or it has results far beyond the expectations of the more skeptical members of the group. New relationships are discovered and the agreed upon activities have deeper meanings for daily living.

THE IMPORTANCE OF THE GROUP

Although individuals have problems that are solved in terms of their own basic resources and decisions, they also have many others that are more effectively solved within the context of a group. Furthermore, many of the problems are those of the group as a whole and cannot be solved by the individual apart from his social context.

Many personal problems are solved when the class becomes a group, for the individual discovers that he is accepted for what he is, is subject to the same laws as the others, is free to grow in terms of his own capacity, and is energized by the grace of God as he works through the group. In the security of this kind of group experience, he knows that he can speak clearly of his own problems without being censured, and he can be himself as the group works at its problems.

Over and above these advantages are the resources a group provides. There are wider experience, more suggestions for dealing with the situation, diversity of viewpoints, reconciliation of conflicting goals, more criticisms of proposals, stimulation of new ideas within the group, interpersonal relations leading to more dynamic procedures, and acceptance of freedom of the individual to act contrary to the answers preferred by others.[5]

As the group becomes a redemptive cell within the life of the local congregation, it has resources for Christian living that make the members do two things: (1) They seek to become more and more the kind of a group in which Christian living is significant in daily life. (2) They become concerned with the subject matter of the Gospel as it relates to both their immediate problems and to their theological understanding of the nature of Christianity. This awareness leads to the recognition of the real nature of the human situation and to problems of which they were previously unaware. Experience in the sharing of problems widens the horizon, and experience of being a group increases their skill in communication. They become adept at discussion and at clarifying the problems that face them. This increase in skills of group procedures is accompanied by the development of ability to dig up new facts and deeper meanings in their lives. The insights that come from this procedure sometimes carry people beyond their depth, but more often they stimulate the development of Christian maturity.

THE LESSON PLAN

The lesson plan for any given session should evolve from the previous class period. There are four basic elements in every lesson plan: definition of aim, selection of materials, procedure, and conclusion. Some teachers, as they evaluate the previous session or recall their experience with the pupils, may provide two or three lesson plans, and then be ready to improvise if necessary.

(1) *Definition of aim* includes the evaluation of the previous session, which provides a clue for the present session. A stray question may suggest a genuine need that should be followed up, or the loose

[5] For this whole discussion of life-centered method, see Robert L. Thorndike, "How Children Learn the Principles and Techniques of Problem-Solving," *Learning and Instruction,* Forty-Ninth Yearbook, Pt. I., of National Society for the Study of Education (Chicago: University of Chicago Press, 1950), pp. 192-215.

ends of the previous discussion may need to be brought together, or certain subject matter may seem to be relevant at this point in the development of the class. The teacher selects his aim on the basis of this background as he takes into account the over-all objective of the course, the pupils' status in relation to that objective, and the possibilities at this point in their development. His goal may be in terms of subject matter to be mastered, attitudes and interests to be developed, or results to be achieved in daily living. How these are combined depends on the specific situation.

(2) *Selection of resources* is the next step. The teacher may have to do reading far beyond the limits of the teacher's manual, selecting Bible passages, other stories, poems, pictures or other visual aids, materials for creative activities, and whatever else he may conceivably need in order that the pupils may achieve a worthwhile goal. He needs to select also the resources for the pupils' own research, so that they will do their own seeking as a background for their decisions.

(3) The big decision for the teacher comes when he selects his *procedure*. First, he must have a *starting point* that reflects the concerns of the class and stimulates them to respond within the area of the goal for the day. There are many such points for getting the class under way. One of the best is the sharing of experiences of the past week; this may be on any subject of interest to the pupil or may be within certain agreed upon limitations. These experiences may have occurred at home or school, on the playground or on a trip. This approach can be widened by including reports on reading, television or radio, or other activities of this kind. The family worship service may have started a train of thought. An experience the class had together may be worth recalling. Questions by the teacher may enlist the immediate interest of the entire group. A story from the Bible, lesson materials, or other sources may set up a problem worth solving. The teacher might recite a personal experience, either from his past or present. The group may be at such a stage in a project that a progress report is the proper starting point. An audio-visual experience can open up the discussion. These few suggestions indicate that a teacher rich in imagination should have no trouble getting the class started.

Once the session is under way, the subject matter determines the method. The procedure now is to arrange the resources so that they are effective in the lives of the pupils. Normally a combination of methods is desirable in the course of the class session – showing, telling, exchanging ideas, group planning and activity.[6] These may be used in any order and mixture, depending on the goal to be achieved. A picture on a blackboard may start a discussion or summarize it. A story may lead to role-playing or to a project. Group planning may lead to a field trip or to a verse choir. The concern of one class for a social problem may lead to a special family worship service or to a parents' committee to meet the problem in the community.

Many teachers' manuals do not allow for this kind of variety, but that is no excuse for not working in this direction. The task of the teacher is to teach the pupils and this means using all the resources of method that evolve from the nature of the subject matter as it relates to the needs of the learners. Workbooks, for example, impose a strict method upon the pupil, but there is no reason why the subject matter of the workbook cannot be used freely to stimulate discussion, role playing, Bible reading, or field trips. It is the job of the church not to teach either penmanship or spelling, but to lead pupils into an understanding of their relationships with Christ and their fellows. Fixed topics for each Sunday also place a straitjacket upon the class, but there is no reason why the teacher cannot use these lessons creatively as resources for helping pupils solve their problems.

(4) *The conclusion* of a class session must be defined in terms of the process. Having started with a relevant goal, it is desirable that the conclusions express that goal in terms of new knowledge, deeper understanding, development of attitudes, and a challenge to the student's daily life. The conclusions that are reached, however, should be those of the class. A neat package wrapped up by the teacher and delivered at the close of the class is not likely to have value, unless the class is ready for that answer in the light of its own conclusions.

Houston Peterson wrote that when some lecturers finished a lecture, the conclusions were there, neatly measured and packaged to taste, and everyone was satisfied. But no one was anxious to return to the subject again. He compared such teachers with those who struggled with genuine problems and were not too systematic; when they concluded their lectures, there were a lot of loose ends, but they were live ends and someone could do something with them.[7]

---

[6] See Chapters 12, 13, 14, 15.

[7] *Great Teachers* (New Brunswick: Rutgers University Press, 1946), pp. 346-47.

A few live ends at the conclusion of a class provide something to pick up to start the next session, as well as something to think about and work with during the week.[8]

STUDY AND ASSIGNMENTS

The tendency in most church schools is to avoid any assignments. They add a burden to those who are used to homework and they are forgotten by those who never have done any.

Some lesson materials, written in a fashion that holds young people's interest, have been collected into student readers, and these are being read at home. Assignments for special research by individuals who are to report back to class are successful when the motivation is right. Other materials have suggestions for special assignments for individuals and committees who make reports at the start of the new session. Holding interviews, writing letters for information, and visits to museums may provide desirable activities.

It takes time to make assignments properly. They must be clearly defined, with adequate guidance about what to look for and where, and with the purpose understood and accepted by the class. Volunteers often accept special assignments in their own fields of interest.

In church schools with long class sessions, there is time for a brief study period. A five- or ten-minute reading period, when introduced in terms of its function, often gets a discussion off to a good start. Sometimes, when the class gets bogged down in its own ignorance, the use of a reading period in the middle of the session may prove helpful. It is often wise to assign different portions, so that each student is solely responsible for what he has read.

UNITS OF WORK

Teaching by units has become increasingly popular. A unit centers subject matter around a unifying principle. It carries over a topic, a center of concern, a project, or any significant item for a period of time. Units of work may be centered in subject matter or in experience, and often the difference is one of emphasis rather than of con-

---

[8] See George Herbert Betts and Marion O. Hawthorne, *Method in Teaching Religion* (New York: Abingdon Press, 1925), pp. 285-92.

tent to be mastered. Both types of units use both subject matter and experience.[9]

This process is of obvious value in the understanding of relationships in the field of religion. When the emphasis is on the needs of the pupil, when the unit is developed cooperatively, and when it leads to direct experiences of the "I-Thou" relationship, the results in understanding the religious situation are significant. Because the pupils are members of the church, which seeks to be a redemptive and redeeming community, they are sustained by God's grace in their attempts to meet the needs of others. Within the class, the group activity as such meets their need for fellowship at the level of cooperative endeavor, and this is an achievement in Christian terms.

The outgoing nature of a project developed on the unit system leads to activities outside the classroom that are part of their response to the Gospel. The emphasis on the interaction with other persons, with the community, and with life itself, leads to those relationships that are described in the Gospel. The failure to overcome barriers of personal relationships, which leads to frustration and loneliness, is seen as due to disloyalty to the fellowship of the Holy Spirit, which is the church.

A unit of work, like the lesson plan for a single session, involves the use of all possible methods that are relevant. The purpose of the session, the needs of the learners, and the subject matter that provides the clue to the answer must be considered in the selection of the combination of methods to be used.

CONCLUSION

The Christian Gospel provides meanings that make sense of life. The teachings of the Christian church are the subject matter of Christian education. Method, in Christian education, is the arrangement of the Gospel that makes it effective in daily living. Method may emphasize either the subject matter or the experiences of the learners, but it never really comes alive until the two are brought together. Good

[9] See William H. Burton, "Implications for Organization of Instruction and Instructional Adjuncts," *Learning and Instruction,* Forty-ninth Yearbook, Pt I, of the National Society for the Study of Education (Chicago: University of Chicago Press, 1950), chap. 9, pp. 242-43. See my *A Guide for Church School Teachers,* pp. 52-58.

material-centered teaching must always be relevant to life or it will not be learned in an effective way. Good life-centered teaching must always use subject matter, for that is where the meaning lies. The task of the teacher is to use whatever methods serve the purpose at a particular moment, provided the aims are clear and the understanding of the pupils is accurate. Both the practical and the intellectual problems of the pupils may be faced through single lesson plans and through units of work, provided the teacher's plans are always flexible enough to meet the emerging needs of the pupils and to point to the answers found in the Gospel, answers which each student must discover for himself.

CHAPTER 12

TELLING

METHODS, we have said, are lines of action that take their cue from what there is to be done. Most of the specific techniques can be listed under the categories of (1) telling, (2) showing, (3) exchanging ideas, and (4) group planning and activity. Behind these techniques lie the requirements of proper motivation, clear goals, and adequate use of what is learned. No matter how important the content may be, it will be forgotten if it has no significance for the learner, if it is presented in a confused and vague manner, and if there is no opportunity to put it into practice.

CONE OF EXPERIENCE

Edgar Dale's "cone of experience" is helpful in pointing out the elements in the learning process. The most concrete way of learning is through direct experience. Less concrete is observation of one kind or another. Finally there is the process of symbolizing in terms of visual and verbal symbols. The degrees of abstractness are correlated with the distance from concreteness in the learning process. This does not mean that the most desirable learning is concrete, but it makes clear how we learn from sensory experience. A child who can read and write is using verbal symbols and is learning from written and spoken words. These abstractions and symbols are essential, but they cannot be understood until there is at least a small element of concrete experience involved. Some college students learn more from a laboratory experiment, others from an examination, and others from a research project or term paper. They respond to different levels in the "cone of experience." This is one reason why a variety of methods must be used.

Dale subdivides the "cone of experience" into three major groups:

(1) Direct experiences (2) Contrived experiences (3) Dramatic participation	involve DOING in order of decreasing effectiveness
(4) Demonstrations (5) Field trips (6) Exhibits (7) Motion pictures (8) Radio, Recordings, Still pictures	involve OBSERVING in order of decreasing effectiveness
(9) Visual symbols (10) Verbal symbols	involve SYMBOLIZING in order of increasing abstractness [1]

With any specific subject matter, we can find the place on the "cone" where the students are most likely to respond. A child who can read or write a single word is already at the pinnacle of the cone, even though there is a great deal of difference between the word, *book,* and the goals of *beauty, goodness,* and *truth.* Storytelling may be a means whereby the listener identifies himself with a character and thus becomes more than an observer although he is not a responsible participant. When we are telling or showing, our learners are observers. When we are exchanging ideas or planning activities, our learners are participants. But in order for meaning to evolve from observation or participation, there must be symbolizing.

STORY METHOD

When the cave man wanted to teach, he used three methods: he drew a picture on the wall of his cave, he told a story or recorded it on stone or papyrus, and he worked it into his ritual. Stories were recounted around the fireside as the nomadic people gathered together, or they were told as part of the worship of the tribe through words, dances, and other ceremonials, or they were recited as secret rites of initiation into the manhood of the tribe. In such ways, our great Old Testament stories were handed down from generation to generation before they were reduced to writing.

[1] Edgar Dale, *Audio-Visual Methods in Teaching* (New York: The Dryden Press, Inc., 1946), p. 52; see pp. 37-52.

Religious teachers have always told stories. The parables of Jesus show that he was a master storyteller, taking the most profound and abstract truths and reducing them to vivid and concrete terms that appeal to child and adult alike. The earliest account of the Gospel is Peter's sermon in Acts, which is a simple recounting of the events in the life of Jesus. The canonical Gospels arose from the stories about Jesus, which were an essential part of the worship of the early church. The tendency to expand these stories is shown in the apocryphal gospels, which went far beyond the historical evidence. The legends of the saints, especially in Roman Catholic literature, show how storytelling appeals to the common people. Great teaching and preaching today is possible only when storytelling is an essential part of the art of communication.

A good story is *interesting*. It needs no other justification than this. We are much more successful with older learners if we are as careful in using stories for them as we are for children. One reason the sermonette in the family service is influential is that it is full of stories geared for the younger children, which become a means of communication for young people and parents!

An interesting story draws people together and thus a *fellowship* is formed. Because the family service should develop a sense of belonging to a redemptive community, the use of the story is essential as a means of establishing the feeling of mutual acceptance. In the classroom, a story breaks down barriers and overcomes shyness. The universal appeal of the pictorial language of a story is almost irresistible.

Above all, a story is a *teaching* device. The listeners tend to identify themselves with the characters and therefore to share in their experiences and decisions. At this point, the story operates in the area between observation and participation. The listeners become involved in the plot, and make decisions for the characters in the story. They share their temptations and sufferings, and rejoice in their triumphs. No matter how abstract the question may be, the story offers a vivid and concrete statement of the problem and its solution.

Often the story stands by itself. It carries the listeners through the entire problem, and then leaves it to them to make their own application and decision. This is especially true of stories used in worship, which may end with Jesus' admonition, "Go and do thou likewise."

The story may be a vivid presentation of content to be learned.

There are various devices that may be used to put in story form large chunks of relevant material. Historical subject matter is often more palatable when presented in biographical form, and this is often done with children who have not reached the age of accurate historical thinking. Historical episodes of the long ago introduce children to the wonders of the Old Testament or to the stature of a Martin Luther or a Dwight L. Moody. Jesus' parables are retold in modern dress and retain much of their original power, and they gain in relevance when the central problem of the parable is put in terms of the children's own situations.

Although there are many kinds of illustrations, the short story is among the most effective. Combined with sermon, lecture, discussion, or almost any other approach, an illustration that makes the point without obscuring or overshadowing it increases the vividness and appeal of the presentation.

Especially when a story is cut off at the climax, with the problem fully and vividly presented, can it serve as a discussion starter. The effect may be like the old serial motion picture, which leaves the audience wondering how the hero can escape. Stories of rejection, temptation, adventure, and challenge can be presented without endangering the security and "face" of individuals in the group, and yet they identify themselves with both the problem and the possible solutions.

Sometimes the teacher may tell the story at the end of the search for an answer, either picking up and ending the partly told story that served as a starter or supplying a new story as a vivid conclusion to a question. Jesus often told his parables as answers to direct questions.[2]

ELEMENTS IN A STORY

(1) A story must have a *plot*. This holds together the various incidents and gives credibility to the characters. A well-ordered plot is the skeleton of the story on which are built the elaboration, color, and conversation that make the story come alive. The good plot is unified and relevant both in its essential structure and in its detail. It is a likely tale from the point of view of the listeners. It is interesting and sufficiently concrete to reach the particular age group. It

[2] See Paul H. Vieth, *How to Teach in the Church School* (Philadelphia: Westminster Press, 1935), pp. 123-25.

builds to a genuine climax. In some cases, the story may stop at this point to provide for discussion, role-playing, or dramatization.

(2) The *characters* in the story must be genuine. Often they are colorless or potential prigs. It helps to have a group of readily identifiable characters who reappear in many stories. These characters have to be reasonably consistent from story to story, but their age and locale may change. If they have unusual names that mark them off, they are easier to use. In rare cases, a science-fiction device may carry them to other centuries. For example, a group of three children named Raimundo, Rosita, and Esmeralda have appeared in many stories through the years and instant attention is gained in the family service simply by beginning a story with the word, "Raimundo." Many true stories are available in which the characters are well-known persons.

(3) *Conversation* is essential to a good story, for it takes the listener inside the minds of the characters. Thus suspense is built up, temptations are shared, frustrations are understood, and suffering is sympathized with. Conversation often is either stilted or vulgar, but the good storyteller, by the proper use of his voice and gestures can arouse the feeling of reality without spoiling the literary quality. The monolog at this point may reflect what is going on in the thinking of a character who faces a decision.

(4) *Description* is effective for establishing the mood of the story, but minute descriptions of unfamiliar surroundings impede its progress. The skillful use of description often swells the climax and makes even more effective the identification of the listener with the characters involved, but it is easy to overdo it.

The basic outline of a story is as follows: (1) A good story has a *brief introduction* that is clear and to the point. One sentence sometimes is enough, especially if the character is a familiar one. The time, place, and setting of the story, along with an introduction of the characters, are all that is necessary.

(2) The *body of the story* should maintain the interest established at the beginning. As the series of incidents and conversations are related, the plot must become increasingly clear. Action, emotion, and suspense must build toward the climax.

(3) The *climax* must stand out clearly. It may have a surprise twist, or it may build up the tension and suspense, or it may evolve out of the situation as the learners hope. It should never be incongruous or unreal, and nothing should be introduced at the last moment

that has been hidden from the listener. (The rule of a good detective story holds here.) Anti-climaxes and details that obscure the main point should be avoided.

(4) The *conclusion* should be as brief and clear as the introduction. If the story is well told no moralizing will be necessary, and if it is badly told no moralizing will do any good. "Sermonizing" after the story ends is as ineffective as a television commercial.

A good reader may be quite successful *reading stories* that are written for the age group, but in most cases the original story needs adaptation to the needs of the learners and to the personality of the teacher. The secret of successful story telling is *thorough preparation.* You begin with a study of the story itself, becoming familiar with the people in it, the things they do and talk about, the climax and conclusion. Then you adapt it to the purposes of the class. You live with the story but do not memorize it. The secret is to remember how you *felt* at the age of your listeners, not simply how you thought.

The good storyteller never needs to strive for attention – he gets it automatically. Before he begins, he may anticipate some of the difficult elements, such as strange words or surroundings, and any questions that might interrupt the story.

Good stories are hard to find, and yet there are many available. They should meet the following requirements: (1) be worth telling; (2) be suited to the age group; (3) have a built-in moral; (4) have sound literary standards. Sometimes the story will be found in the lesson materials, but other sources include books, magazine articles, newspaper stories, and stories of the teacher's own childhood. The stories may come from the great amount of traditional material, from history, from modern life, from nature, and from the Bible. Many times a book of stories provides only a few the teacher can use.[3]

A good story bears *retelling.* This is true with most age groups. The storyteller finds himself being requested to repeat his listeners' favorite stories, and they may be used wherever the decision at the climax is relevant to the problems of the class.

Besides the vividness and interest element in good stories, much can

---

[3] See George H. Betts and Marion O. Hawthorne, *Method in Teaching Religion,* pp. 324-50; Paul H. Vieth, *How to Teach in the Church School,* pp. 123-30; and my *A Guide for Church School Teachers,* pp. 43-44. Books suitable for various ages, which may be sources for stories, are suggested in Dora P. Chaplin, *Children and Religion* (New York: Charles Scribner's Sons, 1948), pp. 118-19, 179-87; Josette Frank, *Your Child's Reading Today* (New York: Doubleday & Co., Inc., 1954), pp. 210-14, 217-23.

be done with humor. The right use of humor in stories with a religious bearing can do much to take the stuffiness out of religion. There is no contradiction between humor and faith, and through humor, approaches may be made to problems that otherwise would threaten the security of the listeners. The humor should be kind and relevant to the plot, and should be in terms the listeners can grasp.[4]

STORIES FROM THE BIBLE

The Bible is "the greatest story ever told," and it is also the heart of the material of Christian education. The Bible as a whole is the record of the mighty acts of God in history, the drama of redemption, the story of what God has done and will do for mankind. The Word of God comes to us in story form.

As we look at the Bible, we discover that God is both the author and the chief actor. This is the perspective from which we begin. The Jew never says "Washington crossed the Delaware" or "Caesar crossed the Rubicon," but "By a prophet the Lord brought Israel up from Egypt" (Hos. 12:13, RSV). God is not an idea, but a living being who is Lord of history.[5]

The focal point of the Bible story is the life, death, and resurrection of Jesus Christ. "In this the love of God was made manifest among us, that God sent his only Son into the world, so that we might live through him" (I John 4:9, RSV). The life of Jesus is the climax of the story. We share in this story because we are members of the fellowship of the Spirit, the Body of Christ. Stories about Jesus are from this perspective, and they lose their point when they are not placed in the proper framework.

The people in the story of the Bible are real. They have the same problems, frustrations, temptations, sins, sufferings, victories, and joys as the rest of us. Their meaning as people centers in their faith in the God who acts to save us from our sins. Their significance for us is their relationship to Yahweh and to the Father of Jesus Christ.

The particular stories that make up the drama of redemption are

---

[4] See Raimundo de Ovies, *The Church and the Children* (New York: Morehouse-Gorham Co., 1941), pp. 94-102, for a magnificent treatment of humor in Christian education.

[5] See my *Religion Makes Sense* (Greenwich: Seabury Press, 1950), pp. 252-265, for a treatment of "God as Idea and as Living."

life-centered. The task of the teller of Bible stories is to make the characters contemporaneous. Every story is related to a problem of life, to the condition of the nation, to the condition of the soul, to an ethical or social situation. Bible stories are not simply strange tales about people in long robes who talked in outlandish English. They are historical events by which God made himself known to his chosen people, and they are events by which God is revealed to us.

The teacher must master this approach to the Bible if he is to be an able teller of Bible stories. Within this framework, all Bible stories have relevance to life. The story then comes alive in the minds of the hearer, for he sees vividly the story in its own setting and he sees the relevance of the story for his own life. The Bible is the church's book, containing the lore and tradition of the community to which the learner belongs as well as the story of God's acts in history. The recounting of Bible events is for the purpose of letting God speak to the one who reads or hears.

Sometimes this can be accomplished by telling the Bible story and then by recounting a modern tale of the peer group that has exactly the same plot. Such obvious examples as the lost sheep or the lost coin or the widow's mite can be adapted to the modern conditions of almost any age group. Characters who are already established and whom the children recognize as their favorites may have experiences that parallel those of people in the Bible, and thus the relevance of the Bible for the contemporary scene is made vivid.

Bible paraphrases are essential with small children and are effective with almost any age group. The telling of a familiar story with a different vocabulary and with an interpretation that brings out its deeper meaning will often send the listeners to the Bible for more information.

Today many translations are readily available. Not only is the Revised Standard Version becoming the authorized version for many educational programs, but the private translations of Goodspeed, Moffatt, Weymouth, Phillips, Knox, and others are written in an accurate vernacular that the people can understand. The teacher should make wide use of all of these resources.

The danger of misinterpreting the Bible always haunts the untrained teacher. An adequate perspective on the Bible as a drama of redemption, when supplemented by the findings of Biblical scholars, is the most important element at this point. Many books have been written in recent years for the guidance of lay people, and out of the confusing details of professional scholarship have come findings that are reliable.

With this kind of background, the teacher can use Bible stories as the main resource of his lesson materials. He can choose the stories that have meaning for his age group and that are theologically suitable in the light of the total framework of the Biblical drama of redemption. He will know the background of the stories and therefore give them a relevance they would otherwise fail to have.

Furthermore, he will know how to go to the Bible for answers to the problems of daily living that perplex his students. Whether he starts with the story or with the problem, his teaching of the Bible will be life-centered, and his listeners will see God as the great actor in the unfolding drama of redemption that gives meaning to all of life. As this becomes apparent within the scope of their daily lives, the Gospel is made relevant and God is seen as an actor in nature, in history, in society, and in the individual. Not every story can achieve these objectives, but a story is justified in terms of Christian education when it points in these directions.

THE LECTURE

The lecture is still the most popular of all educational methods. The tendency today is to deprecate it, but under the right conditions there is no more economical way to provide information. Good lecturing makes use of stories, life situations, and the enthusiasm of the lecturer. It provides a basis for authority when the lecturer is an expert in his field. It often takes account of the needs, interests, and feelings of the individual students. Furthermore, people like to listen to lectures and often will prefer a lecture when given the option of several methods.

The lecture is frequently used without reliance on supplemental methods, but it may be a basis for a question and answer period, for group discussion, for an introduction to a project, a motion picture, or a dramatization. It may be broken up into a panel of speakers, a debate, or a forum. Good lecturing almost always includes stories and illustrations. Informal lecturing is interrupted by questions or objections.

Some lectures may be only a minute in length, as in giving instructions for a class session. Brief lectures may be used to recite the relevant facts for a discussion. Others may take up the entire class time.

The usual rules hold good. The speaker must be able to catch the interest of the learners. He must be able to lead them from their "growing edge" into new fields. He must be able to refer to situations that are familiar to them or that are not beyond the scope of their imaginations. His material should be well organized, with ideas progressing from the simple to the complex in a logical or psychological sequence. Illustrations should be introduced to give concrete significance to all generalizations. Humor should be introduced wherever it is helpful. He should relate the present to both the past and the future. Wherever necessary, he should review what has been said, and there should be a brief summing up before the conclusion. Often the lecturer is guilty of overestimating the listeners' information and underrating their intelligence. But when the information is inserted, if new words are explained and generalizations are illustrated, the average audience can follow the logical and psychological developments to the proper conclusion. This involves thinking on the part of the listeners, and as they say "Yes" or "No" to the lecturer they are participating in a process of learning just as much as if the method were a panel or a group discussion. The difficulty is not with the lecture method as such, but with the many abuses to which this method is subject.[6]

Although lectures are particularly effective with young people and adults, the brief use of this method is possible with younger children.

AUDIO AIDS

The advent of the long-playing record (33⅓ revolutions per minute) has made available new ways of telling. Although many uses of records and radio should be listed under "Showing," [7] we need to recognize that recordings of stories, lectures, poetry, drama, and music are among the resources for telling.

A three-speed player uses records with speeds of 78, 45, and 33⅓ r.p.m., with sizes of 7, 10, and 12 inches. For big auditoriums, a large speaker is necessary. A portable player is suitable for a small classroom.

---

[6] See Malcolm S. Knowles, *Informal Adult Education* (New York: Association Press, 1950), pp. 39-41; my *A Guide for Church School Teachers,* pp. 49-50.

[7] See p. 205.

Recordings have several real advantages. They can be stopped at any time for discussion, they can be repeated, they can be fitted to the time schedule, they can be previewed during the preparation for an adequate lesson plan, and they can be made by a teacher or a class.

Whenever aids are used that require mechanical skills, it is important that someone know how to run the machine. It should be tested to make sure it is working. There should be careful preparation of the students so that they will be ready for the experience. The teacher should anticipate the ways in which the experience can be related to daily life.[8]

Tape recorders offer another form of audio aid. They can be used to capture recordings, radio programs, the sound tracks of television programs, visiting lecturers, and the class session. They can be edited, spliced together, and made doubly effective by being aimed directly at the need of the class. Some teachers automatically "tape" every class session as a basis for planning the next class. Others use sections from the previous class as a playback to introduce the new session. A simulated newscast of Bible events might introduce a Bible story. The possibilities are limited only by the imagination of the teacher.

CONCLUSION

The method of telling is the oldest of all oral means of communication and education. Foremost is the story. It can be used effectively with any age, and as it reflects the relationships of the learner with man and God it may lead him into new insights, deeper meanings, and closer relationships within the community.

The Bible is the great story that includes many stories about God's relationships with men. The same principles apply to the telling of Bible stories as to any other kind, and parallel stories, paraphrases, edited Bibles, and the various translations of the Bible may be used.

The lecture is more often a recounting of facts, but because the information has meaning relevant to the situation in which the learner finds himself, it also may lead him to use this information as a means for solving his own problems in daily living.

Both story and lecture may be put on recordings or tapes and be used to introduce a unit, illustrate facts and concepts, provide a dramatic conclusion to a unit of study, or evaluate the previous session.

[8] See Edgar Dale, *Audio-Visual Methods in Teaching,* pp. 250-66.

CHAPTER 13

SHOWING

PICTURES were probably the earliest form of written communication. The cave man drew pictures on the wall before he made symbols on stone. Even after written language had developed, pictures remained a universal form of discourse. They carry the viewer beyond the limits of his direct experience and offer a challenge to his previous ways of seeing and thinking. They are more adequate than words for providing knowledge of the concrete, although they cannot reflect certain abstract concepts that are essential to learning.

In Edgar Dale's "cone of experience," [1] there are three major categories involving doing, observing, and symbolizing. The method of showing deals with all the techniques of observing, appealing mostly to the eye but also to the ear. We have discussed the techniques that appeal primarily to the ear under the method of telling, and now we turn to those that appeal primarily to the eye. These are known as *visual* and *audio-visual* aids to instruction. They help to make clear facts, skills, attitudes, knowledge, understanding, and appreciation. But they are *aids* to instruction and do not work automatically. They will do the job only when they are properly used, and this involves all that we have said about the nature of method and classroom procedure. Both visual and audio-visual aids may be misused, and when they are used as entertainment, as time-killers, or as ends in themselves, they may actually hinder the processes of thought that are education.

Showing is normally the beginning of the educational process. It provides means for making concrete the body of experience, which is

[1] See pp. 186-87.

the basis for thought. Observation is a way of gaining additional data for thinking. The concrete leads to the abstract. The specific leads to the general. Education takes place when we generalize on the basis of experience. Any means we have of making vivid the concrete experiences of life will lead to more accurate concepts. But too often we get lost in the trees and cannot find out what the forest is like, which is just as bad as having a general idea of the forest without ever having seen a tree. We must deal more than we do with the concrete experiences and relationships of daily life before we can have any general idea of what God is like. Abstract definitions of God are of no use without the concrete data of the events whereby he has made himself known, but concrete events do not provide the meaning of God without proper interpretation through the development of concepts.

RELIGION AND VISUAL AIDS

Christianity has a great tradition of visual aids. The architecture of the cathedrals and churches has expressed the faith with their spires, their cruciform design, the altar toward the east, the raised pulpit, the great stained glass windows and murals, the statues, the symbols, and the vestments. These and many other features tell a story that appeals to the eye. To the modern eye, some traditional pictorial references are confusing, but with a little imagination and acquaintance with the assumptions of the period in which the art forms were developed, the story is concrete and clear. When we remember that the early Christians visiting Rome were in danger of execution as subversives we understand how the surreptitious making of the sign of the cross in the dirt became an appeal to the eye upon which one's life depended. Architects today are seeking new art forms by which they can tell the old story, and some new churches include appeals to the eye that show what the Gospel means in modern life.

THE BLACKBOARD

The blackboard has been part of the schoolroom for many years. Either a wall or a portable board may be found in most church school classrooms. The blackboard is unequaled as a means for driving home the main point or points. It is essential for listing the outline for group discussions. On it may be placed drawings, sketches, maps, graphs, diagrams, technical words, and many other visual aids to learning.

The material should be brief and simple. Colored chalks help, especially chrome yellow and green. Unrelated material should be erased. Underlining helps to focus attention on important points. The teacher should stand to one side and use a pointer. Advance planning and checking will help make a class go more smoothly.

Imaginative teachers will find many uses for the blackboard. It can be used for chalk talks, as a tracing screen, and for many kinds of diagrams.[2]

THE BULLETIN BOARD

Two types of bulletin boards are helpful in Christian education: one is for announcements and various kinds of follow through by the instructor, the other is for the display of student work. Careful control is necessary so that the boards will not be cluttered, and frequent changes of display are necessary if the board is to maintain the interest of the students.

The teacher will do well to accumulate a file of material that can be placed on the board and removed at the proper time. Contemporary materials, such as announcements, newspaper clippings, cartoons, and personal news can be placed on the board briefly and then be destroyed.

The student board may be used to list decisions made by the class, to summarize a unit of study, to display cartoons and drawings illustrating the work of the class, or to tell a story.

PICTURES AND DIAGRAMS IN BOOKS

Many books are well illustrated. Some new readers for church schools, for example, have art work that is both pleasing and accurate. Good color, accurate painting, fine photographs, and clear charts and diagrams make the reading of the books a delight. These same illustrations may be used with an opaque projector for class discussions.

---

[2] See Kenneth B. Haas and Harry Q. Packer, *Preparation and Use of Audio-Visual Aids* (New York: Prentice-Hall, Inc., 1950), pp. 133-38.

The use of the comic book technique may be equally effective. There are some comic books with fine art, good grammar in the blurbs, and fine stories. Most of these are secular, and there are few if any, good religious comics today. Ethical decisions made vivid by "comic" art may provide a basis for discussion.

PICTURES AND PHOTOGRAPHS

There is an unlimited supply of good pictures that can be obtained easily and cheaply. Although much religious "art" is sentimental and in bad taste, Bible pictures by Elsie Anna Wood and other first-rate artists are available. Some of the best pictures available are those of the contemporary scene, of the peer group of the learner, of modern conditions, and of modern advertising.

There are pictures everywhere. Into the home of every teacher come magazines such as *Life, Look, Sports Illustrated, Parents' Magazine,* and the *National Geographic,* plus a number of religious magazines that contain excellent pictures. Most religious publishing houses sell good and bad religious pictures.

Pictures may be mounted, provided with captions, and labeled for filing, if they are worth keeping. If you make your own photographs, they should be enlarged to show the central theme and mounted. They may be held up before the class, passed around for individual inspection, placed on the bulletin board, projected, or placed in a picture stand for display. The picture may be shown as many times as necessary.

Pictures do not teach automatically. They need to be explained, discussed, evaluated, and applied. The visual aid works through other processes in order for the student to learn.[3]

POSTERS

Posters tell a story quickly and vividly by means of a picture or a drawing. We see them everywhere and in all sizes from billboards to postage stamps. They are widely used in advertising and in promoting everything from a special Easter service to the every-member canvass.

---

[3] See Haas and Packer, *Preparation and Use of Audio-Visual Aids,* pp. 111-31.

Posters are used in the classroom to teach specific subject matter, to create attitudes, and to communicate more general ideas on the basis of specific instances. Posters are based on a simplified idea and stress a central point.

There are many sources of posters. Advertising firms, travel agencies, museums, and many other groups will provide attractive ones. They are especially valuable for church school classes studying foreign lands, but also may be used to make vivid the problems the class needs to solve. Students may make posters in a variety of ways. A stencil alphabet and some glue for pasting pictures from magazines will do the job. Silhouettes and tracings are popular. A pantograph [4] may be used to make scaled-down or scaled-up copies of original drawings. They may be displayed on the bulletin board or on special easels, or held up in front of the class.

A poster does not teach by itself. It is a visual aid that becomes part of the process of learning. Proper preparation and relevant application in the follow-up are essential.

FLASH CARDS

Flash cards are a special form of the poster technique. They are normally 10 by 12 inches and are used to present key words and ideas by showing them briefly before the class. They are lettered so that the words can be read quickly, and sometimes they contain simple diagrams. Usually the teacher makes his own, although in some situations large numbers of sets are prepared by commercial printers. A pile of cards may be used, or they may be placed on an easel for easy turning as with "flip sheets."

The flash cards may provide the outline of a lecture, the questions to be discussed, sentences with blanks to be filled in orally (with the answer on the reverse side to be flashed at the proper time), or review.

OBJECTS, SPECIMENS, AND EXHIBITS

To see and feel anything is much better than to talk about it. A collection of objects, specimens, and models has the advantage of appealing to all the senses. Stories and sermonettes gain interest when objects are used as illustrations. A specimen page from an old Bible

[4] See Edgar Dale, *Audio-Visual Methods in Teaching,* pp. 276-77, for picture and use of pantography.

or Prayer Book makes vivid the conditions in the early days of printing. Models of Biblical cities or of first-century synagogues or of a Succoth booth help in the appreciation of interfaith relations.

An exhibit is simply a way of bringing a number of objects, specimens, and models together under a single theme. Both the creation and viewing of exhibits may have significant meaning. An exhibit is placed where it can be seen, with labels that are short, uniform, and simple. It symbolizes some kind of motion or progress or historical development. If it is well lighted and has color, it is more effective.

Exhibits of permanent value are found in museums, and field trips have the additional value of providing an element of adventure. In some smaller cities, exhibits prepared in other churches may be worth visiting, and an occasional field trip to a large city museum is often possible. No youngster ever forgets a trip to the Palestine Institute of the Pacific School of Religion, where he can learn more about the arts and crafts of Bible times in a few minutes than he can by reading through many books on the subject. Visits to museums of natural history or to planetaria are memorable occasions.

Objects and specimens may also be the subject of demonstrations. They are valuable for making missionary work more vivid. Much is done in liturgical churches with demonstrations of the use of vestments and the preparing of the altar. Various translations of the Bible and their uses may be demonstrated through careful selections from an exhibit. Student participation in the demonstration is especially significant, for they can learn through trial and success. Edgar Dale suggests that a demonstration should be carefully planned, rehearsed in advance, outlined on a blackboard, kept simple and free from digressions, checked for understanding as the procedure develops, seen by all, never hurried or dragged out, summarized from time to time, accompanied by written materials, repeated as often as necessary, and evaluated.[5]

MAPS, CHARTS, AND DIAGRAMS

Maps have been part of Christian education from the earliest days. Most "study" Bibles have maps in the back. Maps of Bible lands still appear in many church school classrooms. They are essential for an understanding of the Bible, church history, and missions.

---

[5] See Edgar Dale, *Audio-Visual Methods in Teaching,* pp. 121-30.

The teacher who cannot afford large wall maps can make them from the smaller ones either by copying on a large scale of measurement, or by means of an opaque projector. The teacher should make clear why he is using various colors, and he should use many maps of the same area if he is demonstrating events, crops, governments, or eras of history by visual symbols. No map should have too much detail. It is always helpful to have a globe at hand so that perspective may be gained.

Charts are a means of comparing and contrasting subject matter. They are of particular value in presenting history, statistics, growth and development, organization, and the Bible. The Old Testament, in particular, is susceptible to greater understanding if an accurate chart portrays the great kings and prophets in relation to secular history. The class may study charts or make them as part of a unit of study.

Graphs are closely related to charts. They present in visual form various data. Their statistics may be presented as bars, which are easily seen, as lines showing development, as divisions of a pie, or in pictorial form. When they are simple and easy to read, they tell their story with a minimum of text. They may be used from about the fifth grade up.

A diagram, in its technical meaning for visual aids, is made up of lines and geometrical forms without pictures. Geometry is always taught by means of diagrams, but they may be used for almost any purpose. They are more abstract than other visual aids, but they may serve as guides for constructing a toy automobile or a miniature altar. Biblical history may be diagrammed to show how short is the period since the coming of Jesus Christ in relation both to Biblical events and to natural history. Stage directions for a drama or pageant should be diagrammed.

Maps, charts, graphs and diagrams have many uses, but they are no better than the techniques used to prepare the students, to present the materials, to apply the information, and to find out if the information has been made relevant to the students' needs.

OPAQUE PROJECTOR

We turn now to materials to be projected on a screen, so that all members of the class may share the experience at the same time. The most flexible and usable of projectors is the one that reflects any nontransparent flat picture on the screen, known as the opaque projector. It projects anything that is flat, including coins, leaves, pictures, photographs, cartoons, a textbook page, or a small object. When these materials are mounted, they may be classified, stored easily, and located rapidly. But much of the material is gathered for a particular session and then discarded.

Good opaque projectors are now available that work well under almost all conditions. The material to be projected must have adequate clarity. A blower is essential if unmounted material is not to curl.

With all projected material, the lighting, wiring, and projector should be tested before the class begins, and everything should be ready for action. An extra lamp should always be on hand.

There are several other machines that project flat objects. The visual cast projector can project the same items as the opaque projector, but they must first be converted to transparencies. The instructor may write on the transparencies or use the blank transparency for designs and writing with a chemically prepared pencil. The pencil markings may be removed with a cloth. The stereograph and Viewmaster provide pictures and designs in the third dimension, but may be used by only one student at a time, although Viewmaster pictures may be projected in two dimensions with a special projector.

SLIDES

The use of slides has been popular for many years. A single slide may provide a center for worship; another may be the clincher for a discussion; a few slides may summarize a class session. Most parishes have a library of such slides.

The most popular slide is the 2-by-2 color transparency. These are often homemade, although they are readily available through many supply houses throughout the country for both rental and purchase. The class may make its own color slides as a special project.

Slides of 3¼ by 4 inches are still available, although they have lost their previous popularity. Hand-made slides of etched glass, clear glass, cellophane, and special transparencies are produced for many uses.[6]

Various kinds of projectors are available for interchangeable use of both sizes of slides, and the most practical ones may be used for

[6] See Edgar Dale, *Audio-Visual Methods in Teaching,* pp. 240-45.

either 2-by-2 inch slides or filmstrips. Some projectors are now equipped with built-in record pickup and loud speaker synchronized with the filmstrip or slides.

FILMSTRIPS

Filmstrips are uncut frames of 35-mm. film. They often have captions or include either a narrative script or a recording. Normally they contain from 10 to 100 pictures, and they may be used in many ways. The teacher may prefer to use many pictures with only quick glances by the class, skip frames that are irrelevant, use only a portion of the filmstrip, or cut off the showing for a full discussion before showing the conclusion of the film. This flexibility is sacrificed when the narrative is on records. Slides, of course, offer greater flexibility than any filmstrip.

Filmstrips are available on many subjects pertaining to religion. Some of them are selected frames from motion pictures and serve as an aid in recalling a motion picture previously viewed. Others tell their own story. Those who have real skill may make a filmstrip with a 35-mm. camera, or select pictures and have them processed into a filmstrip edited by the teacher. A running commentary may be written or recorded.

Careful preparation, including previewing and checking all equipment, is essential for use of a filmstrip. The students must be prepared and their interest developed, so that they will know what to look for and why. Often the filmstrip presents a problem to be discussed, possibly with several answers as distinct possibilities. In other cases, a purely informational filmstrip may be shown, which may be stopped at any time for questions and discussion. But in most cases, the filmstrip is shown in its entirety, after which there is discussion, evaluation, and application.

MOTION PICTURES

Motion pictures can capture an audience and present material in a manner that marks them off from all other audio-visual aids. The distinctive element is the motion. We can observe the process as it takes place, whether it be a doctor in surgery, a missionary in Africa, or a Martin Luther defying the Pope. We see history in the making, young people making their decisions, and Jesus Christ living among the people of Palestine. The speed of the motion can be controlled, so that special skills can be observed in slow motion. The size of an object can be made large or small. The interesting and satisfying experiences captured by motion pictures lead to new understandings of relationships between God, people, and things.

There is no doubt of the power of motion pictures to provide information and to change attitudes. Feature films as well as educational and documentary films have a profound effect on the viewers even when not accompanied by proper educational introductions and evaluations. Stereotypes in Biblical films, as well as in the presentation of racial characteristics or vocational groups in feature films, tend to build prejudices. Value judgments of characters in motion pictures tend to be reproduced in life. The cumulative effect of a series of pictures with the same value judgments in the most sympathetic characters is often very great.

There are certain danger points in the use of motion pictures. Because of the cost, many church boards consider it economical to show a motion picture to the whole church school. This eliminates the primary educational concern, which is to use an appropriate film at the proper juncture in the development of a unit within a class. It ignores age-level characteristics, the purpose of the curriculum, and the needs of the specific class session. Often it causes the loss of an entire session for an irrelevant purpose. Poor mechanics of use can destroy the movie's value. The expense of motion picture rental must be considered, and often a filmstrip may serve the same purpose more effectively; but the false economics of numbers seeing the film must be discarded.

There are motion pictures that the whole congregation or church school should see. Some are suitable for the worship service, for family night programs, and in connection with the great festivals of the Christian year all class sessions might be eliminated for the purpose of seeing a suitable film.

Certain errors emerge from seeing motion pictures. Children frequently get the wrong time sequence from historical pictures. They see time telescoped as the script jumps two or three centuries, or they fail to grasp the period in history when the events took place, or they think that events are causally related because they occurred in sequence. The size of objects is often misunderstood unless some object of familiar size is related to the novel object appearing for the first time. Inaccuracies appear in the best motion pictures and historical events are frequently distorted in commercially produced films, but the viewer accepts the camera record unless the error is a glaring one.

The technique of using motion pictures is simple, but it must be worked out carefully. The preparation of the student is essential. He needs to know what to look for, what questions are likely to emerge, how he will be tested, and how he will benefit from it. Most educational films are accompanied by guides that will help the teacher after he has previewed the film. After the film has been shown to the class, the problems should be discussed and possible solutions should be evaluated. A filmstrip based on the motion picture may help with review, or special quizzes may be prepared if they are not suggested in the guide.

With the close time schedule in most church school classes or assemblies, there is no excuse for delays. The projectionist (usually the teacher) must have everything ready, the projector tested, the electric outlet checked with lights out, the seating and ventilation checked, the film inserted, and the image focused on the screen. A spare lamp should be on hand, and the projectionist should know how to make a replacement quickly. A brief introduction should be followed by the showing of the film. If the film is of 20-minute duration, there will normally be 15 to 25 minutes for discussion and application.

Commercially made religious films are available in abundance, although they are limited mostly to Biblical subjects. Many documentaries, especially for youth, have been prepared by secular agencies; these set up problems that need Christian answers. The film does not need to be obviously religious, provided the subject matter of the film is related to the religious situation of the viewers. Some classes may enjoy making their own movies.[7]

COMMERCIAL FILMS

Occasional feature films are reduced to 16-mm. size for educational use, and some churches are equipped with 35-mm. cameras for showing standard features. The most obvious example has been the showing of *The King of Kings* for three decades in both sizes.

---

[7] See *How to Make Good Movies* (Rochester, N. Y.: Eastman Kodak Co.).

Specifically religious stories appear in commercial motion pictures, on television, and on radio. In most cases the advice of religious leaders has been obtained, and on the whole such stories are satisfactory. In one case, a denomination sponsored the production and distribution of a feature picture of *Martin Luther* that was a great commercial success. Commercial firms have presented Bible stories or religious figures on both television and radio, obtaining a wide audience with their excellent programs.

Television and radio programs sponsored by the Protestant Radio Commission and by Roman Catholic and Jewish groups have maintained a high standard, but there are many other groups whose programs offend many listeners and sometimes do more harm than good. As in the case of commercially produced programs, there are good and bad programs sponsored by religious groups.

Because all feature movies and programs on television and radio live by their public support, the churches can do much on the positive side to encourage a large audience for whatever is good. In some cases, the indirect advertising among church people has saved a commercially sponsored religious program and built it to proportions where it is reasonably secure. All good programs, whether specifically religious or not, deserve this kind of support.

THE WHOLE SYSTEM OF SHOWING

The church that wishes to use all the resources of showing needs a director or secretary to take care of the visual and audio-visual aids listed in this chapter. The educational budget of the local church should be adequate for the purchase and maintenance of equipment and for the purchase and rental of material. Assistance should be provided so that teachers can improve their skills and know what is available and suitable for their classes. A system of allocating materials and equipment for use on specific dates should be worked out so that all ages may benefit.

A large congregation normally owns an opaque projector, a lantern slide projector, a slide and filmstrip projector, and a 16-mm. sound projector. Smaller congregations may purchase only one of these, and others may be borrowed from members of the congregation or from other agencies in the area. Smaller congregations find that motion picture rentals for small groups are a great strain on the budget, but homemade movies, filmstrips, slides, and material for an opaque projector cost practically nothing and may be used from year to year. The investment in blackboards and bulletin boards is a necessity for every congregation, and pictures, photographs, posters, manuals, flash cards, maps, charts, graphs, and diagrams can be made at little or no cost.

The methods of showing have value when they are integrated into the over-all educational philosophy and program of the local parish. They justify themselves when they act as channels for the redemptive and sustaining grace of God within the community of the Holy Spirit. There is no magic in the ways of showing or in any other method, although the attractiveness and interest-getting power of the appeal to the eye and to the eye and ear together often make this method seem to be worthwhile in itself. Congregations have gone off the deep end in the use of motion pictures, and then have found that their problems of Christian education have not been solved. The relationships between persons and between man and God are at the heart of Christian education whatever method is used.

We need to check our ways of showing by asking some questions: Do these materials help our students to think more clearly about their Christian faith? Do they give a true picture of our human predicament and especially of the specific problems facing the individuals in the class? Do they add to the meaning of life? Are they suitable to the age group? Do they justify the expense?

CONCLUSION

The appeal to the eye is one of the most effective ways of teaching, and this is especially true when the eye and ear are reached simultaneously. Pictures and diagrams can overcome limitations of vocabulary and barriers of language. They can present experiences that are otherwise beyond the reach of the learner. The method of showing can be used with any age. The blackboard, the bulletin board, pictures and diagrams (whether in or out of books), photographs, posters, flash cards; objects, specimens, and exhibits, maps, charts and diagrams; the opaque projector, slides, filmstrips, and motion pictures can be tools of learning.

The special content of religion, including the Bible, church history, and contemporary life, can be made more vivid and can be presented more interestingly with the assistance of the ways of showing.

CHAPTER 14

EXCHANGING IDEAS

WHEN A GROUP exchanges ideas, minds are stimulated by suggestions, criticisms, opposing statements, and supplementary information. Group procedures by which ideas are exchanged include discussion, questions and answers, various types of quiz sessions, buzz sessions, and role-playing.

If ideas are to be exchanged with freedom and sincerity, the teacher must work from the beginning to help the pupils express their genuine concerns with the confidence that they will not be rebuffed. This cannot be achieved by words or direct action, but only by an atmosphere of encouragement. Many pupils have had no experience in the exchange of ideas, and they lack a sense of security and confidence when they attempt to say what they really mean. In home, school, and church, most pupils have had their own ideas rebuffed and they have been encouraged to say whatever pleases the adult in authority. Therefore, they are not ready to speak or to hear what other students say.

When they discover that they are free to speak their minds, they are likely to react in one of two ways: They will either attempt to take over the class and present utterly inconsequential material even from their own point of view, or they will seek to please the teacher by using the right verbalisms when they have no sense of the relationship of these words to the reality of their situation.

If young persons or adults are to be free to speak, the teacher must help them by constructive listening. There is no real freedom until the teacher accepts them as they are. Because they know that they may express themselves without condemnation, they will move into deeper meanings and make evaluations of both themselves and others.

Slowly but surely the problems that bother them at the depths of their existence will become more and more evident as the group becomes a genuine community of persons.

The teacher cannot guarantee that this will happen, for the redemptive work of God is what knits a community together. Some classes never achieve this goal even with expert guidance and others seem to become this kind of a community very quickly because of the personal relations into which the teacher leads them. There is no magic here, but there is mystery.

The teacher's task in the exchange of ideas is to assist in the clarification of the issues being discussed. The class needs to be free to wander, but often the teacher needs to bring them back to the main track. There will be many concrete instances and experiences that seem only vaguely related to the main subject, but the impact of all these observations will lead to sound generalizations in time. It is hard to get very far away from the central themes of the Gospel, and the problem is to discover the sources of the Gospel in daily experience. Therefore, everything that happens is relevant, and the problem is to see that whatever happens to a person is related to God's concern for his salvation.

RELEVANCE OF THE GOSPEL

The teacher must never lose sight of the relevance of the Gospel to any and all problems that may be discussed. Experiences by themselves may be discussed within the framework of secular humanism. "All we ever discuss is last night's dates," said one girl. Such a discussion may deal entirely with the problem of how to explore a boy's pocketbook at a drive-in, but it also might serve as the basis for understanding Christian relationships in the boy-girl area. A class may spend an entire year studying the Old Testament; and although literary values, history, and geography may be grasped, no personal faith results unless the student finds himself being described and therefore discovers where he stands within the drama of redemption.

The group that exchanges ideas is more likely to become a fellowship of the Holy Spirit if it worships together. If the members take part wholeheartedly in a family service and if there is genuine worship in the classroom or assembly, this will help to build an active fellowship. When the fundamental needs of the pupils are met, and they know that they are loved and accepted as they are by the rest of the group, that there are rules and regulations that guide their actions, that there is guidance for their growth, and that the mysterious power of God knits them together in fellowship, the exchange of ideas will be mutually helpful.

The teacher must meet certain basic requirements if the exchange of ideas is to lead to spiritual growth. It is easy for the teacher to dominate and therefore to short-circuit the process. It is easy to be satisfied with traditional answers when the students do not realize what the words mean. It is easy to blunt searching minds by the wrong kind of comments. It is easy to let the exchange of ideas wander into irrelevancies, the mutual interchange of ignorance, or simply into confused thinking based on improper use of facts.

The teacher needs the capacity (1) to love every member of the class, to accept his foibles, negligences, and ignorances, and to remember that if God loved enough to let Christ die on the cross there is no sacrifice too great for a teacher to make.

(2) To listen deeply means to be sympathetic and understanding, to see beneath the words to the person and his problems, and to be shockproof and encouraging.

(3) Comments must be handled with skill. Once the teacher accepts what is said, he can acknowledge it without breaking the train of thought by a nod or look or grunt. When the subject seems to run dry, a period of silence may help. Shy pupils need time to screw up their courage. The deeper the problem, the more time is necessary for wrestling with the issues. A comment reflecting what has been said will encourage further participation. The use of encouragement, the question "Why?" and getting ideas phrased by more than one member of the group will help. Each student must share in a discovery before an idea can be exchanged.

(4) At various times, the teacher needs to pull all the loose ends together. He may organize what has been said as a summary point for further discussion, or he may want to aim toward a conclusion. Sometimes guiding questions may steer the class toward the logical implications of much that has been said, and the class draws its own conclusions with this help. At the end of a session, someone needs to reorient the class so that they can see what progress has been made and what needs to be thought about before the next session. A brief lecture, a presentation of factual information, a vote on how members of the class feel at this point, or the introduction of the

ways of showing or telling may help at this point. Loose ends are not to be feared however, for usually they are live ends for future reference. When the teacher organizes the subject matter, he must be careful not to wrap it in too neat a package, for then it loses its appeal and dynamic power.

THE DISCUSSION

The most successful method with all who have enough intellectual background to participate is the discussion method. It works best with junior high, high school, young adults, and adults, but in simplified form it is used with the youngest children. It demands expert and resourceful leadership in order to be distinguished from "bull sessions" in which ignorance is passed from one to the other. It is not an argument or a debate. In a discussion, each participant contributes something from his experience or knowledge that aids in solving a common and clearly defined problem.

The discussion method helps to make the group a genuine fellowship. The process of discussion tends to draw the whole class into the facing of a problem, and as the process goes on, the members become more secure in their relations to each other. Each member has a share in the over-all task and therefore feels that he belongs. When real problems are faced, there is a development in clear thinking, honesty, persistence, and the marshalling of evidence. Any statement may be challenged by another member of the class, which helps to overcome prejudice and statements not based on facts, but it also develops the ability to withstand criticism without losing the sense of fellowship. The members of the class may agree to disagree, and this leads to a constructive tolerance that distinguishes between acceptance of a person and rejection of his opinions. As the class works toward a solution, the members learn what it means to compromise for the good of the whole. Subject matter is introduced when it is relevant, and if the teacher is a good resource person opportunities to master subject matter will not be overlooked.[1]

Group discussion is usually the best method when the purpose is to plan for action, to reach decisions based on commonly shared knowledge, to influence value judgments, to relate knowledge to experience, and to develop religious, social, and personal attitudes.

---

[1] See Paul H. Vieth, *How to Teach in the Church School,* pp. 114-15.

Although discussions are notably unpredictable if the leader is willing to let the real issues come up, a class session may have these divisions.

(1) The problem should be launched in such a way that the students will desire to participate. The problem must seem significant to the members of the class. The problem may be launched in a number of ways: a carefully prepared question, a story, a lecture, a series of flash cards, a filmstrip, a motion picture, a roleplay, or a dramatization by a few members of the class. For example, a discussion of the relationship of freedom and authority might be launched by having members of the class play the parts of an irate father and a daughter who has come home an hour after an agreed-upon deadline. Or a motion picture might show a girl who runs with a crowd that emphasizes drinking or petting and who wants to be in the group without conforming at these points.

(2) Everyone should come to a clear understanding of the problem. On the surface this is not a difficult achievement, but the underlying problem reflects the religious situation in which the members find themselves. Beginning with the problem as the members see it, the major purpose is to get underneath the surface and to see the predicament of man in relation to God and to his fellows. This takes genuine Christian insight as well as skills in leading discussion on the part of the leader. The right kind of questions leads to a redefining of the problem on the religious level without losing sight of the immediate symptoms that need to be treated.

(3) Group participation may be obtained at any point. Sometimes it comes with the launching of the problem. Always it must be present in the process of defining the problem as the pupils see it and then redefining it on a deeper level. A genuine discussion soon moves from the teacher-pupil relationship to participation across all lines, as students address one another and as the problem absorbs the interest of the group. The task of the leader is to keep certain pupils from monopolizing the discussion, to make sure that everyone participates, to decide when seeming digressions are worth following through, to provide factual information when it is relevant, and to make summaries from time to time so that the group will keep its primary orientation.

(4) Some discussions will come to clear decisions and the group will follow through with a plan of action. Even when no unanimous

decision is reached, if a plan of action is necessary, the class may want to make certain compromises in order that the proper actions may be taken. The process of discussion is educative in itself, and some students will gain understanding of the deeper aspects of the problem, whereas others will fail to see the fundamental issues and will be satisfied with a surface solution. Often the discussion will end with a recognition that the problem cannot be solved without additional information, and new data will be brought to the next session.

But there are problems that cannot be solved within the framework of discussion, and such problems need to be rephrased in terms of how to live with our unanswered problems. The problem of evil may be overwhelming on the junior high and high school level, and all the theoretical solutions may fail to satisfy the person who is facing death, tragedy, or suffering. The religious recognition that this is God's world and that God's ways are not man's ways demands a maturity that teen-agers rarely achieve, and it takes more than discussion to achieve it.

Careful planning is essential for a good discussion. A lesson plan should include the purpose of the session, several possible starting points, adequate resource material, pump-priming and continuation questions, and possible conclusions. The plan may have to be rejected within five minutes, and some teachers may have two or three lesson plans ready. The starting point will depend on the previous session, on what the teacher knows about his pupils, and on the over-all purpose of the course. Some teachers have a committee from the class, which meets and suggests the major problems to be discussed in the next session. Other teachers have a tape recording of the discussion, and they listen to it before working out their new lesson plan. Others follow the textbook more closely, and proceed to whatever is suggested for the next session.

There is some difference of opinion concerning the conclusion of a discussion. Some believe that the discussion should be free to roam and that the conclusions should depend on the participants. The validity of this approach depends to a great extent on the knowledge and maturity of the class. Others believe that the teacher should determine the conclusion and should do everything possible to achieve it. The teacher normally has both accurate knowledge and strong opinions, and his expertness is one of his qualifications for his job; therefore some combination of these two approaches is desirable. The right kind of leadership, the proper use of questions, the insertion of relevant material, and the ability to see the implications of the contributions of the members of the class will do much to guide the class to the conclusion that the teacher feels is right. But because religion deals primarily with attitudes and value judgments, only the genuine acceptance of conclusions by members of the class has significance at this point.

The type of classroom has much to do with the ease of conducting a discussion. A separate room is almost mandatory for a group of more than eight and is desirable for any group. The arrangement of chairs around a table or in a circle helps the students to feel that they belong and avoids the authoritarian location of the teacher. It is best for the teacher to have a position no more prominent than the participants. A good discussion takes time, and 50 minutes to an hour and a half is preferable for junior highs and those older, with 30 minutes as an absolute minimum.

There are several variations of the discussion method. Most of these are ways of starting a discussion. The *lecture-forum* begins with a lecture by a qualified person and is followed by a question and discussion period. The danger is that the expert will dominate the question period and there will be no genuine discussion, and if the lecture is too long the listeners will be too passive to participate.

The *symposium* begins with three or more persons expressing different points of view, and this is followed by questions and discussions. The problem here is to get three people of equal ability and genuinely different viewpoints.

The *panel discussion* is similar to the symposium but includes briefer presentations and conversation among the panel members before the discussion is opened.

The *forum dialog* is a public conversation between two people, followed by discussion.

The *movie forum* begins with one or more movies that raise issues for discussion.

The *group interview* has an interviewer who asks questions of several people, and this is followed by discussion. The pertinence of the questions will keep those who answer on the subjects in which the group is interested. Although these variations are suitable to larger groups, they also may be used effectively in the classroom.[2]

[2] See Malcolm S. Knowles, *Informal Adult Education* (New York: Association Press, 1950), pp. 43-44.

QUESTION AND ANSWER

The question and answer is often the best way into a discussion. It is a means of ascertaining the experiences of the previous week that may be relevant to the discussion. It is a way of understanding attitudes and evaluations of experiences. It is a means of finding out what factual knowledge the class already has before plunging into a subject. It helps to correct misinformation and misunderstanding. It orients both the teacher and the pupils so that they know where they stand in relation to one another.

Once a discussion is under way, the right kind of questioning causes associations in the pupils' minds that they never saw clearly before. Often they have knowledge of the Bible or of theology that has seemed irrelevant to them, and by the use of leading questions the teacher may bring out a previously unrecognized connection.

The process of group reasoning can be led by questioning. An inductive process starts with agreed-upon concrete elements in experience, and questioning helps to connect these concrete elements with one another and with generalizations. Education is always a process of thinking, and as the group proceeds from question to question and from answer to answer it will discover new connections and new values. It is out of such a process that the relevance of the Gospel for daily life will be discovered.

This creative type of questioning is informal and nonthreatening. It is a group procedure in which any and all answers are accepted at their face value. It may lead at any point into a full-fledged discussion, and then revert back to further questions and answers. Members of the class may challenge the answers that others give, and thus new insights, evaluations, and factual information may be provided for further discussion.

A variation of the question and answer method is known as the guide and cue method. The teacher asks questions in such a way that hints are given for the source of the answer, guiding the pupils into directed reading or some other kind of research by giving them helpful clues or hints. The questions arouse their curiosity, and they know what to look for as they delve into a passage of Scripture, a paragraph in a book, a story, a dictionary, or a reference book. They are guided by these clues as to what they should look for, and therefore they have a purpose for their search.

The question and answer method may also be strictly factual. The teacher uses questions to discover what the members of the class actually know. This approach may be used to check on reading, on general information, on research projects, or on their memory of the previous session. It may be oral or written, informal or formal, addressed to specific pupils or to the class in general.

The principles of good questioning are applicable to all age groups.

(1) The teacher must ask questions without being enslaved to the printed page. The questions should be phrased in terms of the needs and capacities of the pupils. Except where memory work is the basis of the questioning, the answers should be in the vocabulary natural to the pupils. Strange words may appear, but the question is seeking for the communication of meaning and not the parroting of words. The danger of verbalisms is very great with this method, and its avoidance can be assured by making the pupil put the answer in his own words.

(2) The questions should be relevant to the subject matter in the text and to details brought out in the discussion. The teacher whose questions seem to come out of the empty air will not impress his pupils with the significance and relevance of what is being studied.

(3) A series of questions should have logical and temporal coherence. The class should be able to construct its answers to a series of questions so that the pupils will gain an over-all picture of the subject matter.

(4) Questions must be clear, so that any informed pupil can instantly see the meaning of the question and move to the associations in his own mind that are essential to his answer. The danger with catechetical questions is that they contain words and phrases which are beyond the scope of the pupils and which do not imply the answer provided unless the pupil knows both question and answer verbatim. Questions should never be so general that many answers are possible. "What happens when we sing a hymn?" suggests a number of answers, and unless the purpose is to elicit an exhaustive discussion of hymn-singing, the question is unsuitable.

(5) Questions should be asked in such a manner that the security of the members of the class is not threatened. This means using a conversational style and having an attitude of helpfulness, avoiding belittling and sarcasm. It is wise to ask the question in such a way that the whole class has a chance to consider the answer, even when the question is to be pointed to an individual.

It is hard to adapt the catechetical method to these requirements. Normally, the catechetical approach depends on fixed questions and answers. It becomes mechanical and unthinking, although it may have limited value as a means of indoctrination. However, it is possible to use a catechism creatively. The basic problem is to discover the meaning of the words that are used and to translate them into language that makes sense to the pupils. They need to learn technical terms in order to be intelligent pupils, and a great deal of study of the catechism is in terms of mastering the great words of the Christian tradition.

It is possible for twelve-year-olds to understand the classic definition of a sacrament as "an outward and visible sign of an inward and spiritual grace," but the definition as it stands is likely to be a pure verbalism. It is possible to come to an understanding of the Apostles' and Nicene Creeds, so that they will have meaning when used in worship, but only after a complete breakdown of the various phrases in terms of their own factual information and vocabulary. Juniors and junior highs might well write their own "translation" of the catechism and creeds, and such a project is essential in those denominations that emphasize them, but this means using these great traditional confessions in such a way that the students will see their relevance.[3]

QUIZZES

The love of quizzes is evidenced by the popularity of radio and television programs. From the days of the spelling bee, any kind of competition between individuals or teams has been enjoyed by the participants and the observers.

Written quizzes to establish estimates of information and attitudes help both the teacher and the pupils to know where they stand. Inventories of interests are helpful in outlining a series of programs for a youth group. Various kinds of tests show gaps in the students' knowledge that need to be filled.

Many church schools have discovered that quizzes modeled after radio and television programs are popular. A "What's My Name?" program, an imitation of the "Double or Nothing" or the "Dr. IQ"

[3] See Chad Walsh, *Knock and Enter* (New York: Morehouse-Gorham Co., 1953), as an example of a story approach to the catechism.

program, or an adaptation of the "Quiz Kids" may prove popular. Usually the best means is to divide into teams, and to let each team have three chances at a question, so that the information will be drawn from the students. The purpose is to learn, and not to show up the ignorance of those who do not know. These programs may be used in assemblies or classes, and some churches find them suitable in the family worship sermonette period.

The adaptation of "Quiz Kids" involves the entire student body by classes. The teachers submit questions based on the previous class session, and the questions are asked of the particular class, with the first hand to be raised having first chance. Each question is scored according to the adequacy of the answer, and at the end of a period of from six to ten sessions the winning scores are announced. A high degree of interest and accuracy is obtained. It offers a check on both the pupils and the teachers. Everyone participates, and if no one in a given class can answer the question it is thrown open to the whole group. The questions relate to the subject matter of the various courses, but through comments on the answers the relation to daily experience is brought out. Questions may be simple and direct for primary children, completion or multiple choice or with three or four parts for juniors and older.

The element of competition enters these quizzes, and this involves the motives for learning. There are educators who argue that any kind of reward or prize for competitive activity hinders the learning process, and that even grades or classing students in terms of their achievements is harmful. There are others who say that life is competitive, and that any educational system that does not take account of the love of competition is avoiding one of the most effective of all motives for learning. A third position recognizes the element of competition and tries to make a distinction between bribery to do what is unpleasant and rewards for achieving what is worthwhile on its own. This latter position would use prizes for achievement and would give grades where necessary, but it would avoid such promises as "Be good during the lesson, and I will tell you a story, or buy you an ice cream cone." Attendance awards are probably closer to bribery than to an award for merit, but the presentation of a Bible for having met the requirements for confirmation might well be a reward for a task well done.

GROUP PROCEDURES

When the group is thought of as a living organism that develops along the lines of the pattern of individual growth, a new concept of group leadership emerges. A new group needs a strong guiding hand and seeks the approval of its leader, for there is not much coordination between the members and its movements are awkward as it faces problems. It is not clear about its goals and tends to wander about. As it gains more confidence, like an adolescent it may become impatient with its leadership and seek to cast it off, and yet it is not secure in its conclusions and will disintegrate unless leadership is provided. Finally, the group becomes mature enough to rely on its own inner resources, and leadership emerges from the group. The group acts as a whole because it is concerned with problems to which the entire group addresses itself. The individuals within the group come to feel that they have no personal prestige at stake when their ideas are discussed, evaluated, and possibly rejected.[4]

No group stays constantly at any of these stages. A group may need the strong hand of authority one day, a more permissive type of leadership at another session, and leadership identified entirely with the group process at another time. Discussions have to be steered, especially when the subject matter is new or difficult. Once the group is established, however, the leader's job is a democratic one.

Malcolm Knowles lists his tasks as follows: He should know the literature of the subject well enough to determine the major points that might be discussed and to see the religious implications of the topic. He should know a good deal about the members of the group. The subject should be introduced by the leader as he indicates what agreements already exist, as he opens up conflicts, as he asks key questions, or as he provides a case study. The group will tend to establish its own agreed-upon goals, and the leader will tactfully bring the members back to the main points. His chief task is to ask questions that will open up new channels, make them re-evaluate their conclusions, bring out different points of view, or cover up dead spots when the discussion comes to a dead end. He must help the shy ones

---

[4] See Malcolm S. Knowles, *Informal Adult Education,* pp. 55-56.

to speak and keep the bolder ones from speaking too much. Skillful interruptions of long and boring speeches by members are essential to group leadership. Often the leader uses questions to relate generalizations to specific instances. He provides occasional reviews and summaries, and there is a general summary of the main points at the end.

This approach can be misused. The leader, seemingly democratic, may really be a manipulator. By the use of the loaded question, by pulling what he wants to hear out of the comments that are made, by listing on the blackboard what he wants the person to have said, by eliminating all contributions to the discussion that contradict the conclusions desired, and by the subtle use of propaganda techniques, the leader may be as authoritarian as if he had given a lecture.[5]

GROUP DYNAMICS

Leadership may become entirely group-centered. This is the discovery that usually is called *group dynamics*. The wide research in this field in recent years has led to experiments among many church groups, especially with adults, which have shown the effectivness of this approach. Within a group are individuals who seek to satisfy their own urges. They have their own concepts of themselves and their needs, and they tend to reject any threat to their own security. But if they are within a group that accepts them as they are, they tend to accept other persons within the group. This change that comes from mutual acceptance within the group breaks down the barriers to communication, and the concerns of the group become the concerns of the individual. The reversal of the normal process of self-centeredness into group-centeredness makes possible group-centered leadership.

This achievement of becoming a group is in itself a Christian experience when seen in its deeper significance. Although much of the evidence for the working of group dynamics is on a secular plane, the elements of acceptance and of breaking down barriers between persons is a secular parallel of the Christian experience of redemption. The healing of relationships and the bringing of those who are lost into the redemptive community are elements in the Christian experience of forgiveness. The formation of a group in which the individuals have

[5] See Malcolm S. Knowles, *Informal Adult Education*, pp. 57-60.

learned to understand and accept themselves, and in turn to become more understanding and accepting of others, lies at the heart of the Christian religion. The church, then, needs to understand clearly the processes of group dynamics and to use the insights of the secular experiments in this field for increasing its own effectiveness.

As the group develops, it needs less leadership from any one individual. A small cell of three or four within the group, who have some insight into the nature of the process, may soon take over and divide the leadership activities among them. This leadership team may rotate its responsibilities, and also may bring others in as individuals withdraw. As the initial leadership establishes the atmosphere of relationships, it begins to relinquish its responsibilities to the group as a whole. The group as a whole begins to define its objectives and get organized for its purposes. As it moves toward decisions, the group as a whole accepts responsibility for them. As it becomes more mature, it evaluates its processes and seeks for greater efficiency.

The chief means of increasing effectiveness is by the use of an observer. His function is to see what is going on, to check on the participation of members and the interplay between them, to work closely with the chairman in keeping the discussion on the right track, to call for authoritative information, to check the group and to ask for specific illustrations when generalizations become hazy, and to make notes on the progress of the discussion. He needs to be a person who is accepted by the group, so that his comments will not jeopardize anyone's sense of belonging. Only as the group is sensitive to the feelings of its members does it achieve its major purpose, for feelings are just as significant as ideas in the group process. Occasionally, the group calls in a resource person to ply him with questions; he is not to be a guest lecturer. From time to time the group needs to test its ideas and to see if its thinking is straight.

Experiments with church groups show that this method is remarkably successful. It may be used with boys and girls in the junior department and up, and it is spectacularly successful with young adults, parents' classes, and adult groups. It takes time for it to work properly, but it will work within the structure of the church school. With teacher training groups, adults, boards of trustees, and others, it may be used over a two-day period or even longer. There is no better way to start the fall term of church school than by using this approach for the preparation of the staff.

BUZZ GROUPS

Small clusters of people from a larger number are often assigned a topic for discussion for a brief period of from five to fifteen minutes. These buzz groups are divided in various ways, such as counting, tables, rows, or sections of a room, and each group chooses its own chairman and secretary. The groups discuss the problem and then report briefly to the larger group.

The buzz group is an excellent device for defining a problem, outlining a course or a lecture or a discussion, developing goals for a course, refining ideas, or listing possible solutions to a problem. At any point in the process of group procedures, the larger group may divide into buzz groups for a specific purpose.

When used with a group that is not yet well integrated, they provide an initial opportunity for each individual to speak within a smaller and more informal group. When the members come back into the larger group, they have had the experience of speaking that overcomes their initial shyness. The use of buzz groups produces results, and when the reports of all the groups are combined, the possibilities have been pretty well exhausted.

Sometimes buzz groups are used with smaller numbers. A class of eight might divide into two groups, and then come together again. Or one group might discuss the problem while the other observes, and then the observations are given and the roles reversed with the same or another problem. Many variations will occur to imaginative leaders.

Buzz groups have been used with very large crowds. A dinner group of a thousand people may be divided by tables to discuss what has been heard in a panel discussion. A church supper may be followed by a lecture and buzz groups with brief reports being given by several groups afterwards. Many high school organizations use buzz groups to discuss a series of problems, which are then presented to the entire group for a general discussion. A large group of juniors may discuss eight different problems for five minutes in buzz groups, and then the conclusions may be discussed by the whole department or fellowship.

Normally, buzz groups arouse enthusiasm and participation, but they involve work on the part of the participants. Adults, especially, sometimes become tired of having to think and work out problems, and they stay away from a program that challenges them. As the novelty wears off, the overdoing of this approach leads to negative results. But when rightly used as part of a group procedure and not as a crutch to keep people occupied, it is an effective means of education.

ROLE-PLAYING

Role-playing is one of the most effective ways of coming to an understanding of the problems of others. Without rehearsal or memorizing anything, the members of the group are asked to act out a situation. This is to be distinguished from play-acting or dramatizing a story. This is the imaginative seeing of a situation and acting out the situation without a script.

People are never cast in their own roles in role-playing. Psychodrama, in which people play themselves, is a technique for experts in psychotherapy and not for teachers. The participants in role-playing are trying on another person's thoughts, feelings, and ways of behaving. In their imagination, as they act out the part, they become more understanding of the other person. The members of the class who observe the episode find that their own ideas are stimulated.

When the brief performance is over, each member of the cast needs to interpret what he has done. He must clear his own emotions so that he does not identify what has happened to him in the role-play as part of the class's reaction to his real self. In the discussion that follows, the role-player should be referred to by the name used in the performance and not by his real name.

Sometimes deep animosities and resentments are revealed, along with feelings of frustration and loneliness. The expression of such attitudes may prove quite explosive, but it is good to get them out in the open where they can be looked at objectively. Strong feelings against teachers and parents need to be analyzed. If a member of the class loses his temper while role-playing, it opens the whole question of how to control one's temper as well as how to seek forgiveness and to heal the broken relationship after one has exploded. Problems and attitudes become evident that were previously unsuspected, or that the young people were too shy to tell about in regular conversation or discussion.

Role-playing takes some planning, clear objectives, and specific directions. If the problem to be acted out involves parent-child relations, the leader must make clear the nature of a concrete problem and characterize those taking part. When everyone understands his role, a definite starting signal should be given, such as "Action; camera." When the scene has run long enough, the leader may call, "Cut." It should continue as long as it illuminates the problem and the possible solutions, and should be stopped as soon as the point is clearly made and before the actors begin to flounder. The discussion should begin with the feelings of the participants. The rest of the class may then contribute their comments. If there is an observer, he may be able to say something from an objective point of view.

Some classes will flounder in their first attempt. Someone will want to clown his part. Someone else will become too shy to speak at all. But as individuals come to appreciate its values, role-playing may be introduced at any point in the session, sometimes to resolve a conflict within the class.

Although role-playing works with those under the junior high age, they usually lack facility to use their imagination and vocabularies to project themselves into a scene before they are twelve or thirteen. With younger children, puppets may serve the same purpose, for the sense of identification is not as close.

CONCLUSION

Education begins when a process of thinking occurs. The ways of telling and showing are effective in stimulating the processes of thought, but the exchange of ideas provides a mutual stimulation and therefore a corrective within the process of thought. Furthermore, when an exchange of ideas takes place within a group, the change in one's personality affects not only his thoughts but also his emotions and will. The total personality is more likely to be guided through group procedures than through any external stimulus.

Storytelling and the showing of visual aids may well operate within a group process, and therefore they may assist in the development of the total personality. On the other hand, there are arid discussions that lead nowhere, there are quizzes that build enmity between the teacher and the group, and there are buzz sessions that bore people to death. A John Wesley may mold a crowd or mob into a group more integrated than another crowd guided by democratic processes.

When we see the importance of the group theologically, and especially when we see the church as a redemptive and sustaining community in which the grace of God is at work, we begin to understand the significance of the exchange of ideas for Christian education. This is not a secular procedure that has been baptized by borrowing. The basic concept of the church as the fellowship of the Holy Spirit has always included the ideas of acceptance, law, and growth for its members. If we are to be justified by faith within the community of faithful people, we must have the opportunity to live according to the ethics of the Gospel.

Techniques that are used by the experts in the exchange of ideas – the discussion method, question and answer, quizzes, group procedures, buzz groups, and role-playing – may be borrowed, but they are then placed within the framework of the church and therefore they serve a Christian purpose. The exchange of ideas as a means of communicating the Gospel and sharing the Gospel fellowship becomes an experience of the Gospel. Education is not for the future; it is the present experience, the sharing of fellowship, assimilation of facts, interpretation of meanings, and decisions to act in terms of the situation in which a person finds himself.

CHAPTER 15

GROUP PLANNING AND ACTIVITY

WHEN JESUS finished telling the story of the Good Samaritan, he said, "Go and do so yourself!" (Luke 10:37, G). When an angel appeared to Philip, he said, "Get up and go south, by the road that runs from Jerusalem to Gaza" (Acts, 8:26, G). In the letter of James, we read, "My brothers, what is the good of a man's saying he has faith, if he has no good deeds to show? . . . So faith by itself, if it has no good deeds to show, is dead. . . . Do you believe in one God? Very well! So do the demons, and they shudder" (James 2: 14, 17, 19, G).

If the educational process meets the basic needs of acceptance, structure for living, freedom to grow, and a sense of the mystery of life, the results show in changed attitudes, new knowledge of facts about the nature of the world in which we live, an opportunity to meet the obstacles and challenges of life by doing something about them, and worshipping the one in whom we live and move and have our being. All education does not lead to overt action, but all education is the response to a stimulus, and when the stimulus should result in overt action the educational process is thwarted unless something is done about it. We learn through doing when we use our minds, listen to something that is told, look at something that is shown, share in the ideas of others, become a member of a group, or take some kind of action as an individual or as a group.

Group planning and activity is one of the four important ways of education, along with telling, showing, and exchanging ideas. This method is based upon a series of activities resulting from the experiences and concerns of the learners. These activities are planned and carried through to a purposeful end by the group, either as a problem to be solved or as a project to be achieved. They cannot be imposed from the outside but must come naturally from a life situation. They may be worked out in terms of physical or social activity, aesthetic enjoyment, research, field trips, library excursions, directed reading, or dramatic activity. They may be for the purpose of solving intellectual problems of belief or of history, of gaining new ethical insights, of understanding how people live, of developing certain skills, of taking a stand on the moral implications of social and political issues, of participating in social action, or of improving human relationships at any and every level of experience.

PROJECTS

A project is the way a class carries out activities related to its abilities and interests. The members seek for information, discover facts and relationships, come to solutions or decisions, and carry the enterprise through to completion.[1]

Betts and Hawthorne list some of the values of the project method. Because its subject matter arises from life situations, it is related to the concrete religious problems of the pupils. Working on a problem as a team is the most natural way of learning, stimulating the members to use all of their resources for mastering the problem. There is a certain amount of continuity as the same project is worked on over a period of time. The problem challenges the total personalities of the students, develops their interests and their capacities to participate in group action, and brings out the qualities of leadership among the members. Because they are dealing with a genuine concern, they will be more likely to engage in serious and sustained thinking and to take the time to do whatever is necessary for the good of the group in working out a solution. They become a more responsible group as their self-reliance and self-control develop.

Of course this is not the only way that people learn. The project is not suitable when the same subject matter may be mastered in more efficient ways. The project tends to take a large block of time, and sometimes the purpose is out of line with the time required. A solution to a problem may easily be isolated from other kinds of knowledge, and other methods are needed to systematize the students' information.

Wherever activity is required for achieving essential information, or changes in conditions are desirable, or direct experience is part of

---

[1] See George Herbert Betts and Marion O. Hawthorne, *Method in Teaching Religion,* p. 215.

the learning process, or certain skills need to be developed, or an intellectual dilemma needs to be resolved, or better relationships need to be achieved, the project method is more likely to be successful than the other ways of teaching.[2] After a project has been concluded, parents are likely to say, "I don't know what has gotten into Johnny, but he shows a new feeling for cooperation." The changes that take place are more than intellectual, for they involve the whole personality and the relationships of members within and outside the group.[3]

KINDS OF PROJECTS

Projects may be classified into several kinds. (1) Making or doing something is one of the most popular activities. It may be a Succoth booth in connection with the Thanksgiving festival, or a relief map of Palestine in relation to understanding more fully the ways Jesus travelled, or pictures to illustrate a story. It may be "handwork" in a creative sense, either as a brief portion of a session or as a unit of work.

This emphasis on doing something with the hands often degenerates into "busy work." The coloring process at the end of class usually serves no purpose except to let the children enjoy the development of a physical skill. Even the making of a model church or a map may have no value other than the enjoyment of physical activity unless it is related to an over-all religious purpose.

Doing something as a group may involve a number of possible activities. The problems faced by a new boy's coming into the class, by a Negro boy in a Scout troop that is otherwise white, by a teen-age canteen into which some boys bring liquor, by a parent who includes the church among the places his boy or girl cannot go on Sunday nights, or by a group raising money to send some members to a summer church conference may be among those about which a group can do something.

(2) A project may be for the purpose of enjoyment. Many field trips are enjoyable occasions, and even what is seen and heard is primarily in terms of having a good time. Class parties, dances, picnics,

---

[2] Betts and Hawthorne, *op. cit.,* pp. 218-19, 304-5.

[3] See Mildred Moody Eakin and Frank Eakin, *The Church School Teacher's Job* (New York: The Macmillan Company, 1949), pp. 43-63 for examples of projects and activities.

sports, and a booth at the bazaar arranged by the class are enjoyable projects in which fellowship and fun are primary goals.

(3) Solving a problem is another variation in the project method. These problems may be intellectual ones, and the group works out a plan whereby facts are gathered and arranged, discussions are held, and conclusions may be reached. The Bible presents many problems at all ages, and they are significant enough to be allotted time for solving them. Junior high students come up against the problems of science and religion, the Bible and how it was written, ethical concerns and the Christian answer, and other such difficulties. The parent-adolescent conflict needs more than discussion in order to understand or relieve it, and a project toward that end is worthwhile especially with high school students. An understanding of who Jesus was and of how accurate the Gospels are as historical documents might involve a research project of some magnitude.

(4) A project might also be used for specific learning situations. The class might arrange for a special drill, review, examination, or study program by means of which they memorize certain significant Bible passages, grasp specific facts related to an over-all purpose, or enter into a program whereby the gaps in their present knowledge might be tested. Many of the quiz techniques mentioned earlier [4] might be introduced as a class project.

Out of all these variations in the project method may come the decision that some kind of social action is necessary. Young people and adults become frustrated if they find that the best they can do is to pass a resolution. Sometimes only a portion of the group is interested in following through with specific action, and they form themselves into a sub-group for this purpose. The selection of social goals is important. Often they are too large, too closely associated with the vested interests of the church officers, too abstract, or simply beyond the powers of the group to achieve a desirable outcome. Before any action is taken on a selected project, the facts must be obtained. Interviews, examinations of public records, guest speakers, and other research approaches may be made. As a strategy develops, it is usually wise to tell the larger group how the activities are being mapped out.

When it is clear what the facts are and what *ought* to be done about them, stock must be taken of what *can* be done. The social action

[4] See pp. 217-20.

comes when the group is able to influence those who are in a position to do something about the situation. This may be done through resolutions, if the group is assured that those involved will listen to their resolutions. Letters to newspapers and magazines as well as to influential individuals help to build up public opinion. Conferences sponsored by the group, to which the responsible officials are invited as participants, frequently change the atmosphere and therefore increase the chances of a desirable outcome. Delegations may be sent to council meetings and other gatherings where policy is made. Some groups go as far as non-violent picketing if the situation warrants it. More often, if officials will not listen to a church group, the originator of the action may combine with other groups in the community such as the Parent-Teacher Association, merchants' group, labor union, or Rotary to bring social pressure to bear on those responsible. Through influencing the votes of citizens, the group may go as far as to "throw the rascals out" and place in power men who will follow through on the project.[5]

STEPS IN A PROJECT

The steps in a project have been implied in the foregoing comments.

(1) The teacher must be adequately prepared to lead the class into the unit by providing background and evoking interest.

(2) The members as a group locate and define the problem, purpose, or project in their own terms.

(3) They outline a plan for getting the facts, interpreting them, and reaching conclusions.

(4) They carry out the plan with variations on their previous expectations as they learn new facts and change their interpretations. The leader is a resource person at this point, providing stories, illustrations, factual data, and assistance in interpretation without dominating the group.

(5) The evaluation of the results, conclusions, or goals reached is made by the pupils. This process should be a critical one, as they re-examine the way in which they reached their decisions as well as the conclusions reached. In some cases they come out where the teacher expected, and in even fewer cases they come out where individual members of the class expected. More often, they come into the possession of information and become acquainted with situations

---

[5] See Malcolm S. Knowles, *Informal Adult Education,* pp. 131-33.

that change their outlooks and in some cases their personalities. Especially in projects that deal with human relations across class, monetary, and color lines, they are likely to reach new appreciations of their fellow men.

The actual testing of such activities is difficult, for the criteria cannot be discovered in a factual examination. The real test is whether the students have come closer together in their own Christian relationships, whether they have seen the relevance of the Gospel to the situations in which they have found themselves, whether they have changed in the direction of more Christian attitudes in their daily lives, whether they have learned to think more clearly and realistically about the significance of the profound religious problems that underlie the solving of the surface problems. In such terms as these, a project may be evaluated, but on the whole the testing will be subjective. Concerning the achievement of an agreed-upon goal, however, whether it be the purchase of a new rug for the church or the changing of membership requirements of a teen-age canteen or the accumulation of new knowledge about the Bible as an unfolding drama of redemption, there can be agreement among the members who shared in the project.

The conclusion of a project often opens up new problems. The gathering of data, the observations of life, the research into the history of the church, the new insights into the Bible, or whatever else may have occurred in the course of achieving a specific goal are likely to suggest a new project going in some other direction. The relating of the two previous projects often may serve as a third project.

As one aspect of guiding group planning and activity, the project takes an important place. Because it is applicable to so many varieties of subject matter when the concern is the relevance of subject matter to life, this method may be used with every age group and with many kinds of problems. It has its limitations, it can become mechanical and unimaginative, and it is wasteful of time in some instances, but it stands as an important contribution of the study of method to the learning process within the Christian community.[6]

DRAMATIZATION METHOD

From the earliest days in the history of religion, drama has been one of its essential elements. Drama probably had its origin in

---

[6] See Betts and Hawthorne, *Method in Teaching Religion,* pp. 304-21.

religion, even though at times religion has condemned drama as the work of Satan. The Biblical story may be seen most clearly as an unfolding drama of redemption, told upon the stage of history, as God has acted within his creation for the salvation of mankind. The symbolism and sacraments of the church, the festivals of the Christian year, the postures and vestments of worship, the use of music in hymns, oratorios, and masses, and many types of preaching involve dramatic principles.

Education occurs when one participates in or observes a drama. The simplest play-acting of children as well as the observation of a great play such as *Green Pastures* may have profound religious significance. The basic urges to interpret, to imitate, to create, to act, and to enjoy are satisfied imaginatively and vicariously by the dramatic method. The group planning and activity essential to all dramatic situations except the monolog contribute extensively to their attractiveness. The moral, social, and religious values that are acted out or observed are likely to affect the imitation of value-judgments as boys and girls and men and women assimilate the ways of responding of the group to which they belong.

Little children will imitate anything real or make-believe, human or nonhuman. A child is just as happy being a house or a tree, a cat or a dog, a parent or a grandparent, as he is being a child. As he grows older, his world includes all of fairyland, angels and ghosts, mermaids and nymphs, and heroes of the past, as well as contemporary figures. He is ready for dramatic situations demanding moral decisions as the Christian virtues become part of his experience. By the time he is a junior, he wants realism, vigor, and adventure, with nonspeculative concrete situations to challenge him. He is reading comic books and watching television, and he is ready for the hard-boiled school of acting. By the time he reaches adolescence, the emphasis is more on the peer group, sex consciousness, and romantic idealism.[7]

The use of dramatic methods depends on the capacities of the learners, the goals to be achieved, and the time available. Whether the use of dramatics be simple or complex, certain requirements should be met. The story must have dramatic possibilities, action, and interest. Generalizations or abstract ideas are difficult to dramatize, although when these are translated into concrete situations they may have

[7] See Chapter 5 for more complete treatment of age group characteristics.

dramatic possibilities. The demands of the dramatic episode must be adapted to the understanding and capacities of those taking part. There must be an educational purpose, so that moral and religious insights will develop from participation or observation. The material must be selected to fit the kind of dramatic action desired.

The sources of dramatic material are as rich as life itself. Daily experiences are possibilities for every age, for children and adults can act out any kind of story that relates to their own lives. All sorts of conflicts and problems may be acted out spontaneously in this manner. School and playground experiences, home situations, church relationships, economic problems, community interests, international and worldwide and missionary activities, and any situations demanding moral or religious decisions are suitable. The world of nature offers many opportunities, especially for younger children. The ways of showing, including drawings, pictures, filmstrips, slides, and motion pictures, may suggest an episode that should be acted. Literature, both religious and secular, provides source material that may be dramatized in a number of ways. History provides episodes that can be highlighted by imaginative and dramatic treatment. The church with its history and world-wide activities presents many possibilities. The primary source is the Bible, which provides many stories and episodes. Both the Old and New Testaments offer suggestions for the creative and imaginative mind.

INFORMAL DRAMATICS

Informal dramatics offer the greatest educational opportunities in the classroom. The spontaneous acting out of stories from the sources mentioned above catches the imagination of the class. With younger children, the teacher may retell the story as the children act it out in pantomime. A simple tableau may be formed by the children to symbolize an historical episode, imitate a picture, or illustrate a decision that needs to be made.

The use of specific dramatic forms may be informal. An ad libbed radio or television show provides the framework with which the actors are familiar, and often they will want to add the commercials. Such props as are available in the classroom may be used for an informal play. Role-playing, already referred to in a previous chapter,[8]

[8] See pp. 225-26.

may provide a group outlet for getting a problem before the class, but in this case the story is not completed but is left open for discussion. Cast-reading, using a prepared script, also may be done informally in the class.

Spontaneous dramatics may take the form of writing an informal play. The pupils may have studied a hymn, listened to a recording, seen a picture, heard a story, or conducted a discussion and reached a tentative conclusion. The class decides to put the problem and its solution in dramatic form. They work as a group to decide on the episodes, write the dialog, create the characters, and use whatever resources they have for stage-setting, scenery, and costumes. This unit may take a number of sessions, or it may be a brief project of only a few lines of one scene. Whether the drama is acted or not, preparing the drama demands group participation, critical analysis of the characters and the problem, development of vocabulary and writing skills, and a deeper understanding of the religious principles. In some cases, the results are evident in terms of the relationships between the players, decisions of the group about the problems involved, or even some kind of a project to implement the drama in working out a problem. When an informal play is outstanding, it often is turned into a production before a larger audience, but this is a secondary result and does not lie in the original purpose.

FORMAL DRAMATICS

Formal or prepared plays, pageants, and tableaux have many of the same values as informal drama. The difference is that the creative and imaginative work that has educational value comes at a different point and that the effect on the audience is at least as important as the impact on the actors. Some of the same problems remain: the play must be studied, the characters interpreted, and the setting provided. But the plot and the lines and the stage directions are part of the given, and the educational value is in the interpretation and the acting, and in the message that the play carries.

Particularly suited to churches is the sanctuary play. This is held in the church, with the altar, pulpit, lectern, choir, and aisle between the stalls as the setting. Stage effects are produced primarily by lighting. In some cases, the congregation is considered part of the cast from time to time and participates in familiar responses or sings hymns. *Murder in the Cathedral* is an elaborate example of the sanctuary play, but simple one-act plays for the sanctuary are being written and produced.

Pageants include tableaux, pantomimes, rhythmic movements, plays, and music. They offer a means of incorporating a large number of people in a dramatic activity. They are used to tell Bible stories, to make clear moral, social, and religious values, to stimulate the Christian idea of community, and to give significant places to their participants and technical assistants. Frequently they are connected with the Christian year, and churches have pageants during Advent, at Christmas, during Lent, on Good Friday, at Easter, or at Pentecost. Puppet shows put on by the children and those conducted for the children have dramatic value. Musical dramatics, as in the great oratorios, are important. On a less ambitious scale, dramatics that combine the spoken word and music may prove influential.

PREPARATION FOR DRAMATICS

The prepared play or pageant, unlike the informal drama, depends for its effectiveness upon the competence of production, direction, and acting. This involves from the beginning an understanding of the capacities of those participating, the equipment and setting available, and the time that can be spent in getting ready. Often the material needs to be cut and adapted before being used.

Certain preliminary steps are necessary. The selection of a play or pageant needs to be made carefully, and normally this should be a group procedure. Perhaps the producer or director has found three plays or pageants that he thinks are suitable. By means of storytelling and with some spot cast-reading, a selection is made. This is followed by a detailed plot and character analysis, and the group has an opportunity to become acquainted with the text. There needs to be some research in order to understand the psychology of the times, the kind of stage setting that is most effective, and the costumes of the period. At this point, there should be some discussion of the meaning of the play or pageant for the present day.

Then should come the try-outs. A public performance normally depends on the most capable actors, but consideration needs to be taken of those in the group who are not as competent. This always provides a dilemma for the director who needs support in order to provide a polished performance. In some churches, the opportunity to have leading roles is rotated from play to play regardless of ability; in others, the standards of production tend to keep the best actors in the leading roles. Some directors are willing to train several casts for the same play, so that each cast has one performance, or so that one cast is selected after the final rehearsal for the single performance.

No way of selecting the cast makes everyone happy, but the best players do not always need to be selected for the large parts, for frequently a good player can hold a play together while playing a minor role. With younger actors, especially, care must be taken not to cast the same boys or girls in the villain's part too often. There is also a problem concerning the character of those who portray Jesus or Mary or Judas, for here there may be strong contradictions between their personal characters and the parts they are asked to play; and a bad boy should never play the part of Judas.

Every director has his own way of conducting rehearsals. The important thing is to have enough rehearsals to provide competence on the part of the players, and to have the technical crew well trained. With some plays, rehearsals may be by groups until time to work out the play as a whole. With pageants, tableaux, and pantomimes, there are usually many scenes that can be rehearsed independently until the last few rehearsals. Some players need individual coaching.

Costumes, stage setting, and equipment are always a problem. When a group has been working together on a play or pageant as a project, the cast and the technical crew together can work out the requirements for costumes and setting. If a play or pageant demands an all-male cast, the girls may be the stage crew and the makers of costumes. If the cast is a mixed group, the others can do the technical work. Lighting frequently captures the imagination of a boy or man interested in its technical aspects, and as a result he will make effective use of both foot and flood lights to provide the proper shading and color for each scene. In both pageants and plays, the combination of color and lighting helps to produce the desired effect. Even with poor equipment, a little ingenuity will go a long way.[9]

The tradition of the stage that the director has absolute authority cannot always be combined with the more democratic procedures of

[9] See Betts and Hawthorne, *Method in Teaching Religion,* pp. 353-73.

the group. Professional competence in producing dramatics for public consumption is desirable, but in the church this competence should never be obtained at the sacrifice of the educational values of putting on a production. It is not easy to reach such a goal, but the educational values are primary, and decisions need to be made with this in mind. The play must be good enough to draw a crowd and to put over its message, and yet the cast must operate as a group in putting it on. Compromises will frequently be necessary in order to reach such a goal.

Many pageants are very simple and do not need such competent direction as a play. A popular pageant for Epiphany is *The Feast of Lights,* which emphasizes the coming of the wise men and the significance of Jesus Christ as the light of the world. It takes place within the church, and can be put on by a church school class within the setting of a worship service. The text has variations in it, so that it may be made more complex or more simple, depending upon the members of the cast and the size of the church. In such a production, democratic procedures are more easily followed that in meeting the high standards of a professional play.

Ritual is a form of pageantry, and many pageants make use of the traditional church ritual. Worship services may make use of many dramatic insights, but the danger is that the drama may point to itself rather than to the ongoing process of worship. Sound liturgical insights serve as a background here. The class may well study the historical elements in the development of worship, the meaning of the vestments and ecclesiastical appointments, and the proper use of them according to their religious meaning. Then they will use the ritual in the proper order and the ceremonial will be consistent with the theological assumptions. This applies to nonliturgical and liturgical churches alike, for they both have a rationale for whatever ritual they use.

SOME IMPLICATIONS OF GROUP PLANNING

The group processes that we have been discussing in the chapter on exchanging ideas and in the section on project and dramatization methods point to the social factors in learning. We have assumed that one of the most important ways of learning is through participation in a group. In school and church, on the playground and in the community, the learner is always a member of one or more groups. The learner solves his problems within the context of a culture, and he tends to take on the ways of the groups within the culture to which he belongs.

However, we must never forget that it is the *individual who learns.* The group does not learn. The group develops and reinforces the learning process in the individual. Without being a member of the group, there are many things that the individual would never learn. The emotional, social, and personal interdependence is controlled by the teacher and by the members of the group. The participation of the individual in the group tests his assumptions, mastery of facts, generalizations, and decisions. The individual is under group pressure at all times.

An adequate group process never sets conformity as an ideal. The individual in the group tends to accept the findings of the group as to what thinking and behavior are socially, morally, and religiously desirable, and he comes to see what it means to be a Christian citizen. Within this wide boundary, he is free to think and behave as he pleases. What he learns outside of school and church is equally important, but the church seeks to become the controlling group assisting him in his value judgments in his daily life. Such a process demands much from both the teacher and the pupil. They both must be willing to accept confusion and doubt as part of the educational process. Frustration is accepted as inevitable. The student is required to develop the ability to direct his own efforts, to be objective about his own and others' ideas, and to be willing to work at problems.

ROLES OF THE TEACHER

Within the group, the teacher has six different roles that Herbert A. Thelen and Ralph W. Tyler have identified as follows: (1) He is a person with certain ideas and biases. He belongs to the church and has deeply Christian convictions. He is a member of a particular substructure of society, and he feels free to express his own personal feelings and opinions.

(2) However, as a teacher, he needs to be enough of a social analyst to see his own subculture against the broad background of American culture. He needs to see his own theological position against

the background of the possible positions within his own denomination and to deal objectively with the opinions of his students.

(3) Because he is a subject-matter expert with the authority of a teacher, he must know where his expertness stops and his ignorance begins, so that he will not pose as an expert on issues on which he lacks competence. He must be willing to bring in experts when necessary.

(4) He must be able to see the problems of the group as having priority over his own needs and to use his expertness as judiciously as possible. He must be sensitive to the class problems and insights and must help the class test its own hypotheses.

(5) He must have enough of the qualities of a personal counselor to handle anxiety and tension in such a way that the individuals in the class will know that they are accepted by him even when their behavior does not warrant it.

(6) He must realize that as a teacher he will be seen in a different light by different individuals. Children, youth, and adults will seek relations with him that reflect their own needs. A little child may desire a father-child relationship; older children will see him as a representative of the opposite sex; students may express antipathy to him as an outlet for their attitude toward other adults; or he may provide the freedom in which they can speak freely of all their antipathies and anxieties.[10]

CONCLUSION

The basic ways of education are telling, showing, exchanging ideas, and group planning and activity. From the Christian point of view, one of the most important achievements of the educational process is individuals becoming a group in which the basic needs are met. Although this is achieved to some extent through the ways of telling and showing, the group consciousness develops most fully through participation that demands the exchange of ideas and the cooperative activity of all the members of the group. This is not automatic, however, for techniques need to be supplemented by attitudes in an atmosphere in which God's grace prevails. A project might well lead

[10] See "Improving Instruction in High School," in *Learning and Instruction,* Forty-ninth Yearbook, Pt. I, of the National Society for the Study of Education (Chicago: University of Chicago Press, 1950), pp. 329-30.

to the kind of competition that builds up barriers in the group. An exchange of ideas might well lead to an argument involving comments about personalities. A drama might cause the explosion of artistic temperaments all over the parish.

On the other hand, only the group can achieve the kind of community in which Christian faith may be assimilated. The Body of Christ is a fellowship *(koinonia)* of believers and not a gathering of like-minded individuals. Within this fellowship is the greatest of diversity, for Christ died for the redemption of *all mankind!* The church, ideally, is a community of uncongenial minds who are resolved to become congenial persons within the fellowship.

Group processes, therefore, are essential to Christian education. Baptism is becoming a member of the congregation of Christ's flock. Holy Communion may be celebrated whenever two or three are gathered together in Christ's name, and not by individuals. Christians have been known by the words of the old observer of the early church who said, "Behold how these Christians love one another!"

Method evolves from the theology of the Christian church. The belief that the church is a community leads inevitably to the acceptance of methods of group procedure as essential to Christian education. Each group within the church is bound to accept its members as they are, to provide a structure of law and order by which the group may operate, to make possible the conditions whereby each member may grow in wisdom and in favor with God and man, and to open up all the channels that, by human devotion, can bring the grace of God into the group.

CHAPTER 16

METHODS OF WORSHIP

THE CHURCH is a worshiping fellowship. Even when every other function of the church has been curtailed by hostile governments, its worship has kept it alive. Worship in the fields at night, worship in the catacombs, worship in houses with the shades drawn, worship under the rigid tyranny of kings and of modern totalitarianism, and worship in heathen countries by little groups of converts – in such ways the church has kept faith with its Lord.

If children and all of us are to learn the way of Christian living, we must be captured by the Holy Spirit through worship. The church school has an unequaled opportunity to expose pupils of all ages to the best atmosphere of Christian worship, and as the individual grows as a member of the worshiping community he learns that through participation in congregational worship he is made strong to live as a disciple of Jesus Christ.

Church schools have failed on the whole to take advantage of this opportunity. The worst form of worship has been defiled by the name of "opening exercises," something to be gotten out of the way so that the serious business of learning the Bible can take place. Usually held in the parish house, often in a poorly equipped room and sometimes in the basement, the "opening exercise" starts with someone shouting for order or ringing a bell. Then come a few hymns chosen at random and often having the quality of religious jazz. Because there has to be a responsive reading, one is chosen quickly from the back of the hymnal or a psalm is picked out. There may be a Bible reading at this point, with no introduction to make clear why it is being used. A prayer or a series of prayers follow, closing with the Lord's Prayer.

Announcements are then given, and the boys and girls march out to a rousing hymn. Such an occasion might be fun, but it hardly qualifies as worship.

Another point of view is that only a brief assembly is necessary because everyone goes to church. But there is serious question that a service geared for adults meets all the needs of children for genuine worship, and if the service is adapted to the children there will be adults who will object.

Even when worship is taken seriously, most leaders do not know what do about it. What we need are experts in children's or family worship, and this takes insights and experience that many superintendents and pastors lack. Services are on mimeographed sheets, which are hard to read and distracting because of the noise they make. Worship is held in the parish house and not in the church. It is not geared to the genuine needs of the congregation. There is too little student participation in the act of worship. The service is too short or too long. The story or sermonette is too dull, too long, or wanting in opportunity for the children to do anything about it.

ELEMENTS IN WORSHIP

The basic attitudes of worship apply to all age groups, although they may be expressed in many different ways as the sense of the relationship to God and one's fellows develops. First, we praise and adore God for his majesty and his glory. Then we express our sense of separation from God and our fellows as our self-will sets up a barrier to true fellowship, and this is our confession of sin. There is the discovery of God's will for us as we listen to the Scriptures and sermon. We confess our common faith in the God of Jesus Christ, state our deepest needs and desires for ourselves and others, and thank God for all our blessings. We offer ourselves and our possessions to God. Worship closes with the assurance that God will continue to bless us in all our doings.

These attitudes are expressed in the common worship of our churches, through prayers, litanies, and hymns, through informal services and the Lord's Supper, through listening to God's Word as it is mediated through Scripture and sermon, through the simplicities of nonliturgical worship and the intricacies of the most involved liturgical worship.

The task of the educator is to know how these attitudes are to be brought out for the various age groups, to know how a service for all ages will express the sense of community and become a fellowship of the Holy Spirit, to know how to lead the congregation to a deeper understanding of the nature of worship, and to know how the impulse to worship may be made specifically Christian. As a leader of worship, he needs to know how to create the atmosphere of worship through the proper use of his voice, the sense of timing, and the organization of the service. The most important quality of leadership is to achieve sufficient expertness to be able to worship sincerely himself as he leads others.

EXPERIENCE-CENTERED WORSHIP

The only way to learn to worship is through worshiping. Like learning to play baseball or tennis or bridge, reading books and talking about worship are helpful only if one is practicing. Worship, whether it takes place in a family service, departmental assembly, or classroom, is experience-centered education, for the worshiper learns by doing.

It is important, therefore, that meaningful participation be possible. The most significant participation is as responding members of the congregation. Leadership and assistance in the service is secondary. Saying the Lord's Prayer together is a way of experiencing corporateness even before all the phrases are understood. The worshipers affirm the fact that they belong to a community of believers when they join in the creed. They sing the hymns not because the music has a pleasant jingle but because the words and music combine to arouse in them a sense of the presence of Almighty God. They are active participants when they listen to the Bible reading and the story or sermonette. They respond to the responsive reading. They offer themselves through their gifts of money. They make their own silent prayers and join in the corporate prayers, and they say "Amen" ("so be it") in many churches at the close of each prayer.

Underlying their participation is the *ethos* of worship. Every legitimate help is needed to create the atmosphere of worship. This lack of atmosphere is what destroys most services in assembly rooms and annihilates "opening exercises." The use of the church with its architecture suited to worship is preferable to a special chapel.

Atmosphere is created by the music before the service begins, by the orderliness of a carefully planned service, by the way in which the choir and ushers behave, and chiefly by the expectations of the leader who is sincere in his own faith and is able to communicate his own devotion to the congregation. The danger comes from pious overtones that are unnatural, the wrong use of esthetic devices such as the appeals to purely subjective emotions through vestments and candles and pictures that are liturgically out of place (although these are liturgically proper in many churches when used correctly), and from the use of children as leaders in such a way that it is play-acting rather than worship.

Children's worship should lead to an appreciation of adult worship. When a child has had experience in the worship of the church school, he should be at home in the major services of his own tradition. In the liturgical churches, for example, the order of service and the traditional responses should be identical in both the church school worship and the adult worship. *The Book of Common Prayer* has much in it that children cannot understand, but exposure to the worship of the Prayer Book gives one the vocabulary of worship, the rhythm of prayer, the sense of awesomeness, fellowship with the religious yearning of the ages, and the basic attitudes of worship. But most of the prayers are too abstract, too theological, and too technical for young minds, and therefore a brief selection of prayers from the Prayer Book and from other sources that are suited to children should be used. In the nonliturgical churches, the same principles hold. Whatever occurs at the main service of the day in terms of order of service, psychology of worship, and use of ritual should be adapted to the needs and requirements of the children so that they will feel at home when they attend the main service or when they grow beyond the Sunday School age.

FAMILY WORSHIP

The family is an essential unit of the congregation. The cooperation of parents is necessary in order that what is learned in church school may be applied in daily life. Most children learn the fundamentals of prayer from their parents, and in some cases the family has worshiped together.

A program of Christian education, in order to meet the needs of the family as a unit, must offer it a chance to worship together. Normally, the usual church service cannot meet this need because it is geared to the requirements of adults and ignores the needs of the children. Although some congregations have successfully appealed to families at the major service, in most cases the younger members refuse to participate or attend under pressure.

The family service, often held at 9 or 9:15 A.M., may be held every Sunday, with a class for parents following, or it may be held only once or twice a month. It is specifically tailored to the congregation of young and old. It is based on the assumption that parents are primarily concerned with the religious development and worship of their children, and that parents will be reached through what is said to the children. From the standpoint of the psychology of worship and of the traditions of the denomination, it is a full-fledged service. Modeled after the later service, it contains the same variations, with Holy Communion, Baptism, Litanies, and other services occurring from time to time. On special festivals such as Thanksgiving, the junior and senior choirs are combined, and the service is adapted to appeal to all who are present. On Easter morning, parents and children attend a special service of their own that is just as beautiful and musical as the other services on that day.

The greatest difference in the family service is the sermonette or story. Here is the opportunity for the pastor or leader to communicate with the congregation on a family basis, informally, dynamically, and with the children primarily in mind. He needs to know the techniques of the ways of telling and showing, and he can make use of devices that would be frowned upon in the main service of the day.[1] The use of a junior choir, vestments, assistants to read lessons or help at the altar, and other practices should be the same in the family service as at the main service.

The one problem with a family service, lasting probably 25 to 30 minutes, and never more than 45 minutes, is the restlessness of those below the first grade. They definitely should be present! One solution is that they see the choir come in, know at least one stanza of the opening hymn, have an opportunity to share in the Lord's Prayer, and then leave at an appropriate place in the service. The nursery and

---

[1] Raimundo de Ovies, *The Church and the Children* (New York: Morehouse-Gorham Co., 1941), contains the best collection.

kindergarten children therefore have almost a half-hour longer class, during which they have a departmental service or opportunities for spontaneous worship on their own level. The importance of their presence is that they experience the fellowship of the worshiping community and know that they are accepted in the "big church." In churches using infant baptism in the family service, nursery and kindergarten children should be permitted to remain and be placed where they can see the baptism take place. On Sundays when it is customary to have Holy Communion, there should be an appropriate time for younger children to leave; some churches have everyone leave except those who receive communion, or those within one year of being qualified to receive.

There are variations on these practices, depending on the equipment available, the need for a unified plan in some downtown or rural churches, the customs and practices of a particular denomination, or the size of the staff. But the principle of a family service is sound, for it incorporates the family as a unit into the worshiping fellowship and into the educational program of the church.

DEPARTMENTAL WORSHIP

The obvious value of departmental worship is that it can be graded within a three-year span. The portions of the service are selected with the needs of a specific group in mind. The children are more likely to understand what is happening and will participate in their own way.

Nursery and kindergarten children have their own worship even when they have participated briefly in the family service. In some cases they have altars or worship centers in their class or assembly rooms, although others believe that altars and worship centers belong only in chapels or the church. When altars are in rooms associated with any other purpose, they are likely to be treated with irreverence or indifference; so the church should be made available if an altar is thought necessary.

The materials of worship must be within the comprehension of the age group, which limits leaders of younger children to the simplest of concepts. Simple Bible stories may be retold, but reading from the Bible itself is likely to be beyond their comprehension. Hymns and prayers are extremely simple, although the younger children should know the hymns they sing in the family service and should know the

Lord's Prayer in order to express their sense of belonging together in the church. Repetition is popular with this age, and the ritual should be routine. They like the familiar, and novelty should be introduced within a familiar framework.

Primary worship should be informal, and the children are still not ready to read anything unfamiliar until the third grade. Sometimes, in larger church schools, the first- and second-graders worship together, and the third- and fourth-graders become a separate group. The same principles apply as in the nursery and kindergarten departments, but the concepts and materials are more advanced. The children become familiar with more of the standard hymns and prayers, can listen to a small selection of brief stories read from the Bible, and are able to participate more fully in responses. They are able to come together for the purpose of worship and are enthusiastic when a chapel or room is available for their worship. In a few cases, a primary choir can be trained to help with the singing and to sing a brief anthem. Occasionally this age group may wish to imitate an adult or family service.

Junior department worship is sometimes combined with the remainder of the church school in a "junior church." From the fourth grade up, a service in the church similar to our description of the family service is of immense meaning and value. It lacks the sense of family participation, but in congregations not ready for the family service it is the next best.

Junior department worship in their own assembly or chapel is a next step beyond primary worship. Its value lies in the close grading of hymns, prayers, Bible selections, and sermonette, although frequently this service is kept very short and all the formal teaching is done in the classroom. The service may include a choir and the leader may be vested as a minister.

Junior high and senior high worship is often held together, either because the senior department is small or because of lack of space for both groups to worship separately. At this age level, the pupils normally are confirmed or have joined the church, and they have the right to receive Holy Communion. The service should be sufficiently similar to the main service so that they will feel at home in both. They still feel that they are a separate group, however, and some congregations provide youth hymnals for their morning and evening youth groups.

Many church schools have classes for young adults, parents, and adults. When the family service is used, these age groups are included and feel that they have a definite part. Sometimes they are considered as a separate department and have their own service. More often they meet as a class for a portion of the church school time and then attend the main service of the day.

A variation of the departmentalized service is the organization according to "class units." Fairly large classes are group-graded (two- or three- or four-year span in each group), and they meet under one teacher for both worship and instruction. In this way, the worship theme may be tied in closely with the subject matter of the class session. Informal worship may occur at any point in the total session, depending on its suitability.

WORSHIP IN CLASS

The class period provides an opportunity for worship. Teachers worry about culminating experiences for a day's work or for their units or for the conclusion of the year's course. A group studying the New Testament compiled a list of the prayers discovered there, and worked out a service using those prayers. Another group created their own prayers using a new translation of Scripture. Prayer normally should follow the successful conclusion of a project, the facing of a serious problem by the group, or thanksgiving for escape from danger.

If the class has really become a group, it will seem natural for them to pray together. The pupils themselves have resources on which to draw. They may suggest different kinds of prayer, or may desire to go to the chancel for a service they have prepared, or may work out a series of prayers to be used at home.

Not only in the class, but in every organization throughout the church there should be opportunity for lay leadership in worship. The family service, the main service of the day, and some departmentalized services should have leadership by the clergy, but in young people's groups, couples' clubs, the women's groups, the men's groups, and other organizations, worship should be in charge of the lay people. These are the proper places for creative and imaginative experiences as the aspirations of the group are expressed through devoted lay people. They need help from the clergy, but they should not seek to become carbon copies of the pastor.

EDUCATION IN WORSHIP

Most important in education for worship is that the teacher assume that God is at work in every aspect of life. This has no correlation with a pious tone or a holier-than-thou attitude, which defeats the purpose. To be able to speak of God in a natural and reverent way, to be able to discuss religious experiences without embarrassment, to be able to open and close the class with prayer, and to let the pupils express their mood in hymn, prayer, or silence are part of the work of the teacher.

Training in the meaning of worship is essential. Often the children will come from their worship full of questions. These questions are relevant and contemporaneous, and they should be discussed immediately, no matter what the lesson plan may demand. The family service or a church festival will be apt to produce more questions. In the case of a six-year-old who was to be baptized, the first-grade class in one church school spent two weeks in preparation, attended the baptism at the family service, and then talked more about what had happened to Nancy. There are units on worship in many courses, and they need to be related to the pupils' experiences outside of church, so that they will begin to see the interrelationships between dynamic worship and social and ethical decisions.

Most important is the guidance in worship that they receive while they are worshiping. This will come partly from the teacher before and after the service, but chiefly from the example of the teacher during worship, and the basic guidance from the pastor or other leader during the service. The leader who is alert to the atmosphere of the congregation will provide guidance in a subtle and sensitive way as the service proceeds. He will use the sermonette period from time to time to explain what the service means and how the congregation should respond. Chiefly, the children need to feel at home in church, to know that they are accepted, to understand how things are done decently and in order, and to have the opportunity to grow in their communion with God. This is accomplished more by the quality of life of the total congregation than by any kind of instruction.

When a special service is coming on the following Sunday, the teacher can do much to prepare the pupils for what to expect. After any service, the teacher may deal with points that the children missed or misunderstood. He can observe the point in the service at which the leader lost the attention of the congregation. He should teach the children prayers to say after they come into the church and before the service begins, and at the close of the service before they leave. During the service, the teacher may assist the pupils nearby to find their places in hymnals or prayer books or on the leaflets (although pupils may sit with parents, teachers or by themselves). Above all, *the teacher must be on time for the worship service, setting an example of promptness, devotion, and participation that will impress and inspire his pupils.*

THE PASTOR AND WORSHIP

Most congregations have only one minister. He is the pastor of the entire group, including those in the church school. As their pastor, one of his responsibilities is to be their leader in worship. He needs to know how and why children worship, to speak to them religiously at their level, to lead them in their devotions, and to be in a pastoral relationship to them. He should be one who loves and understands children.

When the main service of the church school is the family service, there is no great difficulty in having the pastor conduct the service. To do so adequately, he must have planned the selections for worship just as carefully as he has worked out the main service. In many churches, as far as numbers is concerned, the family service is the chief service.

When departmentalized services are used, the pastor can only attend or lead one or two of them on a given Sunday. In some cases, he will choose to be the permanent leader of one department or of a combination of departments worshiping together. In other situations, he may prefer to go from one department to another each Sunday, telling the story and perhaps taking the prayer each time. Or departments may take turns coming into the church; so the pastor may conduct a service for one department at 9:15 and another at 10, with the other departments worshiping in their assemblies with their lay superintendents.

If it is taken for granted that the pastor will lead his children in worship, he must work closely with the department superintendents and teachers to know what is happening in the departments and classes. When a class has been working on a unit on worship, he may wish to incorporate some of their findings into the worship service on the following Sunday. He will want to know what Bible portions are being studied, so that his story or sermonette will have relevance. In these and many other ways he will be able to correlate the worship with what goes on in the classes. He will also work closely with the various choir directors so that the music and hymns will have coherence.

In larger parishes having more than one minister it is possible to divide the responsibility; but the current practice of assigning the church school worship to the least experienced member of the staff is dangerous. Usually, younger assistants do not stay long, so all the children get is inexperienced leadership and a lack of continuity. No matter how many ministers are on the staff and how the work is divided, the chief minister is chief pastor to the children. There is no escape from this responsibility unless the pastor is incapable of leading children in worship, and then there is a question about his competence to lead anyone. When there is a director of Christian education, he or she may help the pastor and his assistants to gain the insights they need for this important task.

There are some parishes with a long tradition of lay leadership in the church school. This has the advantage of placing devoted people in key positions over a long period of time, and this leadership is important. The question raised here is whether children will have a greater sense of belonging to the redemptive community and of being ministered to by their pastor if a division of labor is arranged so that the pastor rather than the lay superintendent or assistant minister will have responsibility for the family or church school or department worship. The lay people are not displaced, but are freed to do the things that the minister cannot do; at the same time the minister is challenged to be a pastor to the children.

"FITLY FRAMED TOGETHER"

George Hedley, in his book on *Christian Worship,*[2] entitles one of his chapters, "Fitly Framed Together." The construction of a worship

[2] New York: The Macmillan Company, 1953, pp. 89-101.

service is a work of art. The hymns, canticles, responsive readings, Bible lessons, prayers, music by the choir, and sermon should fit together in harmony.

Before the service begins, there is normally a prelude on the organ or piano. It should be selected to create the atmosphere of worship, to inspire quiet and meditation, and to focus on the main theme of the service. At the close of the service, the postlude should reflect all that has gone on before, and though it may be quite lively, it should not be a march to class. In some church schools there is no music at the close of the service; the congregation rises from silent prayer and goes quietly to the classes.

HYMNS

The selection of hymns should be in the hands of the minister or worked out in collaboration with the choir director or organist. Most hymnals today have a large proportion of excellent hymns, and it is possible to escape religious jazz and banal theology. The fundamental factor in the choice of hymns is the *words*. The words express theological meanings, and they have great value as a teaching device. They should be within the scope of the pupils' understanding, and they should express teaching consistent with the theology of the local congregation. Many of the great hymns of the church are profoundly simple. Children do not need a soft diet of sentimental love songs. Perhaps there should be a balance between good hymns written for children and the great hymns that they should come to know.

The *tunes* of the hymns should be good music. The increased use of folk melodies and chorales plus the new twentieth-century tunes is freeing us from reliance on sentimental and jazz-type tunes. In most hymnals, it is easy to switch tunes if the words are desirable and the tune is unsingable or unsuitable.

A large repertoire of hymns is undesirable. Children like to repeat their favorites, and a careful selection of about sixty to eighty hymns is enough for a family worship service. Smaller children will have fewer hymns in their repertoire, but except for the few hymns limited to their age and unsuited to the older children, most of their hymns should be those in the over-all repertoire of the church school.

There is a question about special hymnals for children. Most denominational hymnals now have a children's section, and there are usually enough specialized hymns. Many hymns written originally for children now appear among the general hymns or among those for special days of the church year. Many congregations, especially those in which the children worship in the church, prefer to have them use the regular hymnal, and if one gets torn now and then because it is heavy, no one is going to mind.

Hymns in the repertoire are selected for specific Sundays. The theme of the service, the period of the church year, and the needs of the congregation should be taken into account in selecting the hymns. In the family service, for example, one system is to use every hymn for three or four consecutive Sundays, rotating one hymn each week into the series of three or four selections. The processional hymn remains the same for three or four Sundays, and therefore even the littlest children have a chance to learn at least the first stanza and feel that they are participating in the service. The nursery and kindergarten teachers are alerted several Sundays in advance and teach the hymn to the children. The big breaks in the rotation come with Thanksgiving, Advent, Christmas, Epiphany, Lent, Easter, and Pentecost. The hymn being rotated into the system is often the sermon hymn, thus providing the background in words and music for the minister's story or sermonette. In departmentalized worship, a similar system can be worked out.

Introducing new hymns to the repertoire should be an educational experience. The meaning and pronunciation of the words should be made clear, so that children will not sing about "Gladly, the cross-eyed bear" or "Eat carrots for me" (for "Gladly the cross I'd bear" and "He careth for me"). The approach with small children is through the meanings they can see, and pictures of the objects mentioned in the hymn are helpful. With older children, the words should be in front of them; and the approach may be through the story of how the hymn was written, who the author is, and what the words mean. They might read it as a verse choir before trying to sing it, or the choir might sing the first stanza to acquaint them with the tune. New hymns should be repeated in at least two cycles of three or four Sundays each during the year.[3]

---

[3] Many parishes have their lists of favorite hymns, and there are also traditional hymns for Advent, Christmas, Lent, Easter, Holy Communion and evening services. The hymns listed on the following page are suggested for services of family worship, seeking for a balance between hymns for children and their parents which reflect a sound theology and good singing. Those with an asterisk (*) are especially suitable for children.

Chants, canticles, offertory and prayer responses, and amens are usually sung to a few fixed tunes by the adult congregation. These should be introduced wherever suitable in the children's services and become fixed in the order of the ritual.

"A mighty fortress is our God"
"All creatures of our God and King"
"All people that on earth do dwell"
"All things bright and beautiful"
"Be thou my Vision, O Lord of my heart"
"Christ is the world's true Light"
"Come, labor on, who dares stand idle on the harvest plain?"
*"Day by day, dear Lord, of thee three things I pray"
"Dear Lord and Father of mankind"
*"Eternal God, whose power upholds both flower and flaming star"
*"Fairest Lord Jesus"
*"Father of mercy, lover of all children"
*"God be in my head and in my understanding"
*"God my Father, loving me"
"God of grace and God of glory"
*"God of our fathers, whose almighty hand"
*"God who made the earth, the air, the sky, the sea"
"He who would valiant be"
"Holy, holy, holy, Lord God almighty"
"How firm a foundation"
*"I sing a song of the saints of God"
*"I think when I read that sweet story of old"
*"In Christ there is no East or West"
*"Let us with a gladsome mind, praise the Lord for he is kind"
"Lord Christ, when first thou cam'st to men"
*"Lord of all hopefulness, Lord of all joy"
"Now thank we all our God"
*"O God, beneath thy guiding hand"
"O God, our help in ages past"
"O Son of man, our hero strong and tender"
"Onward, Christian soldiers"
*"Our Father, by whose Name all fatherhood is known"
"Our Father, thy dear Name doth show the greatness of thy love"
"Praise to the Lord, the Almighty, the King of creation"
*"Remember all the people who live in far off lands"
"Rise up, O men of God!"
*"Savior, like a shepherd lead us"
"The church's one foundation"
*"The King of love my Shepherd is"
*"The Lord is my Shepherd, no want shall I know"
*"We gather together to ask the Lord's blessing"
*"We plow the fields and scatter"
"When Jesus left his Father's throne"
*"When morning gilds the skies"

RESPONSIVE READINGS

Responsive readings and psalms should be brief and within the scope of the congregation's understanding. The selections in the back of hymnals may have to be cut in half, and long psalms should be cut to about 12 verses. But there are many short psalms that have great value, including 1, 8, 15, 19:1-6, 23, 24, 67, 100, 121, 150, and others. They may be repeated quite often, so that a small selection is sufficient.

BIBLE READING

Bible readings in the family or departmentalized services offer three major difficulties. First, there is the problem of a passage that has meaning and religious value for the particular group that is listening. Second, there is the choice of a translation that will communicate. Third, there is the difficulty of capturing the interest of the listeners.

Careful study has led to the conclusion that very few passages are suitable under primary age, a number of stories can be used with primary children, juniors can grasp the historical sequence, and junior high and senior high boys and girls can grasp most passages that are intelligible to adults.[4] The popular reception of the Revised Standard Version provides a translation that speaks the language of the people, although some will prefer the more vivid usages of Goodspeed, Phillips, or Moffatt.[5] For a few passages, such as the Twenty-third Psalm, the King James Version may still be preferable. The main point in reading Scripture is to communicate the Word of God, and not to speak in Elizabethan English.

A few words of introduction usually serve to capture the interest of the congregation. The leader tells them what to look for, or relates the selected passage to the hymns or prayers or sermonette, or

[4] See Ethel Smither, *The Use of the Bible with Children* (Nashville: Abingdon-Cokesbury Press, 1937).

[5] *The Complete Bible: An American Translation,* by Edgar J. Goodspeed and J. M. Powis Smith (Chicago: University of Chicago Press, 1939); *The Four Gospels* and *Letters to Young Churches,* by J. B. Phillips (New York: The Macmillan Company, 1952 and 1947); *The Bible: A New Translation,* by James Moffatt (New York: Harper & Brothers, 1935, 1950).

promises that he will re-read the story with some mistakes during the story period and that the congregation will have a chance to correct him, or announces that a quiz on this passage will occur during the story period or at the opening of the class session. Once the habit of listening is established, if the selections continue to have relevance, only a bit of orientation will be necessary.

PRAYERS

Prayers should be composed, selected, or extemporized with the specific needs of the congregation in mind. There are now available many good prayers that speak the needs of children and youth, and a series of three to five brief collects is sufficient. Pastoral prayers should be limited to one to two minutes and should be subject to the same requirements of relevance. Children will be reverent during the prayer period once they understand what is expected of them, provided they are not expected to be quiet for too long. Prayers in which they may join are especially helpful. They love such great prayers as those attributed to Francis of Assisi and Ignatius Loyola.

ANTHEM

Somewhere in more formal services there may be an anthem by the junior choir. Usually it is given during the collection of the offering. This provides an opportunity to introduce tunes and hymns that later will be used by the congregation, and there are many simple anthems with excellent words and music that a children's choir can easily learn. Close cooperation between the pastor and the choir director is necessary if the anthem is to be fitted into the service.

STORY OR SERMONETTE

The sermonette or story is crucial in the success of the service. Its purpose in relation to the children and parents is the same as the sermon in a regular service: to inform, strengthen, direct, and inspire, and to bring them more consciously into the presence and under the direction of the God and Father of Jesus Christ. The informal situation makes possible the use of chalk talks, cartoons, object lessons, and other devices provided the method does not overshadow the message. Too often all that remains is the vivid imagery and the lesson is forgotten. Participation on the part of the students as they analyze the situation illustrated by these means can be directed toward daily decisions. For example, the students might analyze the character of the cartoon dog, "Napoleon," and then relate his character to those in the Bible or to their own lives. This involves more than rhetorical questions, and the leader must expect a vocal response from his hearers.

Question-and-answer sessions may be used within the structure of the worship service. Many of the techniques mentioned earlier,[6] including "Quiz Kids," may be used with good effect. Questions based on the reading from the Bible and graded for the various classes might be used.

The most effective approach is the story. With older children and adults, stories may appear within the structure of a sermonette, but with all children and youth the story itself is the best means of proclaiming the Gospel. The story deals with people who are real to the listeners, with concrete problems that enlist the active interest and decisions of the congregation, and with the relevance of the Gospel in daily living. It ties in with the hymns, responsive reading, Bible selection, and prayers of the service, so that the whole worship service is "fitly framed together." In departmentalized worship, the story will take about three minutes in nursery or kindergarten, about five minutes in the primary grades, about seven minutes in the junior department, and about ten minutes with the older boys and girls. In the family service, seven to ten minutes is about right.

Stories are found everywhere. Worship guides, lesson materials, and story books have some suitable stories in them. The chief source is the Bible. A Bible story may be retold. The plot of a Bible story may be adapted to the modern situation and the story constructed in terms of real boys and girls and men and women of today, with no reference to the source. At the conclusion of the story, which carries its own moral, the teller may ask if anyone knows of a Bible parallel, or he may simply say, "That's the story of Ruth in modern dress." Most adults have had a few of their own childhood experiences that can be made into stories. Many books provide stories that are adaptable, and the leader should accumulate a large number of such books as

---

[6] See p. 220.

resource material. Stories about contemporary children, historical episodes, and various hero stories are particularly suitable. In many cases, the story will lead up to a point of decision; several live options are present. Then the teller might stop and say, "What would you do? Think about this for a minute and reach your own decision." After a period of silence, he may either ask for solutions or proceed to the solution in the story as his listeners contrast it with the decision they have reached.

ANNOUNCEMENTS

The question of announcements during the service needs to be met. If there is a closing assembly, announcements may be made at that time. However, where the opening service is a complete one, the classes will be dismissed with a closing prayer in the classroom, and the only opportunity for announcements comes during the service. Let them come at the same point as in the main service, possibly before the sermon hymn and after the prayers. Give them clearly and with a light touch, and when the time and date are important ask the congregation to repeat them. When there is a family service, a bulletin is usually available for both services and most of the announcements will be printed, but the most important news still must be given orally as well.

SOME SAMPLE SERVICES

The following service outline might be used with a junior church group or at a family service in a nonliturgical parish.

PRELUDE on piano or organ
CALL TO WORSHIP
RESPONSE from a hymn, chant, or unison prayer
HYMN
SCRIPTURE, responsive reading, or memory passage
OFFERING, prayer, and response
HYMN
STORY, talk or dramatization
LEADER'S PRAYER
CLOSING HYMN
UNISON BENEDICTION
POSTLUDE [7]

[7] See Betts and Hawthorne, *Method in Teaching Religion,* p. 483.

Another form of service, for more liturgical churches, might be as follows:

PRELUDE
PROCESSIONAL HYMN
Choir marches in
OPENING SENTENCES OR CALL TO WORSHIP
LORD'S PRAYER
VERSICLES
VENITE
Children in nursery and kindergarten leave.
PSALM or responsive reading
LESSON FROM THE BIBLE
HYMN
PRAYERS
Some congregations will say the Creed before this series of brief prayers.
ANNOUNCEMENTS
HYMN
STORY or sermonette
BIRTHDAY OFFERING—OFFERING—DOXOLOGY
An anthem might be sung by choir at this point.
CLOSING PRAYERS AND BENEDICTION
RECESSIONAL HYMN
POSTLUDE [8]

These are two standard outlines suitable to many parishes. The task, as we have said, is to make real and meaningful to the younger members of the congregation their own worship of God in terms that will make the adult service familiar and a means of grace. The local parish may want to adapt its communion service for occasional use in the family service or in the departments in which the children are qualified to receive communion. Services of baptism will be used in the family service or in all of the department services from time to time. Special services may be put together by the children in a given class or on a special committee for the purpose.

CONCLUSION

Worship is an essential part of Christian education. It is the framework in which Christian education takes place, for in worship the believing community is in communion with God, who provides the

[8] See my *A Guide for Church School Teachers,* pp. 68-70.

redemption that the community needs. Without the means of grace vouchsafed through worship, education is likely to founder on the rocks of factual knowledge, moralism, and loyalty to the church as an idolatrous end in itself.

The teacher's responsibility in guiding the pupils in the ways of worship is very great, both in the classroom and in the church. The pastor has his own unique responsibility, as he leads the children and their parents in family or departmentalized worship. Worship is the heart of Christian living. From it comes the power and the glory of increased faith in Jesus Christ as Lord and Savior. If we are to lead our children into the deepest riches of life in Christ, we must induct them into the mysteries of worship, so that they will never desire to forego the services and sacraments of the church in the days to come. But the main purpose of worship is to be in communion with God now, and when a child goes to church he should be sure that he will meet God there. The quality of life in the worshiping congregation that says, "Let the little children come," will bring the children into the presence of God, and they will be strengthened in their faith, guided in their decisions, and upheld by God's grace.

PART FOUR

Administration of Religious Education

CHAPTER 17

A COMPREHENSIVE PROGRAM OF RELIGIOUS EDUCATION

THE QUALITY of life in the local congregation is the chief educative factor among its members and among those touched by its outreach. The nature of the Christian fellowship is such that every activity of its members is influential in the forming of attitudes, the making of value judgments, the decisions of the will, and assimilation of factual knowledge. The local church is a part of a worldwide brotherhood that we call the Body of Christ or the fellowship of the Holy Spirit.

Our problem is to look at the local congregation from the standpoint of organization and administration. The local church is an institution working to achieve and to maintain a community life in which its members are sustained by the grace of God. The local church is a unified body, organized and administered to educate it members in Christian living. Good organization is essential if every member of the congregation is to know that he is accepted and loved as he is, that all human beings are equal in the sight of God, and that the resources of the Gospel are for all mankind.

The program of Christian education involves the total congregation. As the members experience the redemptive and sustaining love of Christ through the relationships of the congregation, Christian education is taking place. The concern of each member of the congregation becomes the concern of all. The congregation is a community of believers, a communion of saints in the New Testament meaning of "saint," a fellowship of children and adults.

Organization and administration will not turn a group of people into such a community automatically, but it will provide the opportunities for individuals to become such a fellowship. A properly organized congregation, administered in terms of objectives that are clearly formulated, is more likely to achieve that quality of life whereby Christian education will be the experience of every member, than will a congregation organized for the tastes of a few individuals, or for the adults only, or for children only. Such organization takes skill and tact as well as Christian conviction.

Such a congregation is organized for the purpose of ministering to all. Each member thinks of himself as a servant of other men, women, and children. Although the preaching of the Word will always be an exalted task of the pastor, the congregation will not think of itself as a pulpit-centered institution. Although worship and fellowship together will always be the key meaning of the church, the horizon of its worship and fellowship will be God and all mankind.

This concern for the needs of every individual works in two directions. It means that the congregation will be unified as it seeks to be a fellowship. When a little child knows that he is an accepted member of the entire group and therefore feels as secure in the activities of the congregation as his grandmother, a step has been taken in the right direction. But such an atmosphere is achieved only when good administration is correlated with the quality of life of the members of the congregation. The other direction of administration is indicated when the same child and his grandmother have specialized activities that meet their particular needs. Within a small group, every person finds others with whom he can communicate on the deeper levels of the basic needs of life, and the Gospel therefore comes alive in terms of his own situation. This specialized grouping takes on meaning in relation to the sense of the unity of the whole group.

BEYOND THE LOCAL PARISH

The local congregation is not alone in its problems of administration and organization. Behind it stands the denomination, with its traditions, its agencies, and its publications. The work being done by the national departments of Christian education is of particular importance. They have suggestions for improving the administrative set-up of the local program of Christian education, for making worship more meaningful, for enlisting and training teachers and staff members, for new curriculum materials and resources, and for helping parents in their task of Christian education in the home. Some of them provide help for those setting up weekday and vacation church schools. Most of them have a special division devoted to youth and adult work.

They produce vast quantities of literature designed to meet the specific needs of the local churches, and they take into account the actual conditions and handicaps under which many local parishes must operate.

Behind the local congregation also stand the many interdenominational agencies. Some large cities have a department of Christian education within the council of churches, which operates leadership training institutes, weekday and vacation church schools, filmstrip and motion picture libraries, and curriculum displays. States or portions of states have councils of churches, and their departments perform similar functions to help congregations in smaller towns and to work with the state denominational headquarters in various ways. This ecumenical endeavor at the grass roots level not only increases cooperation across denominational lines but also adds greatly to the resources of the local congregation.

The most significant interdenominational effort is the Division of Christian Education of the National Council of the Churches of Christ in the United States of America, formerly the International Council of Religious Education. Much of the research that has made religious education more effective was carried through by this group in close cooperation with the national denominational agencies. Every educator in charge of a program in the local church should be acquainted with the literature published by this group, and especially with *The International Journal of Religious Education*. Committees work on uniform lessons, graded lessons, children's work, youth work, adult work, administration and leadership, weekday religious education, audio-visual and radio education, religion and public education, and from time to time special committees may work on such problems as objectives, religious drama, or camps and conferences. Work also has been done on newspaper lesson syndicates, community Christian education, laboratory schools, and education in emergency areas. There are four committees on missionary education. Other agencies also stand ready to be helpful in various ways.[1]

FUNCTIONS OF THE LOCAL CHURCH

At a congregational meeting, a list of parish activities having educational implications was placed on the blackboard. The congregation discovered that *every* parish activity was educationally valuable or

---

[1] See pp. 13-15.

detrimental. Either it increased appreciation of the meaning of Christian faith or it decreased it.

How a child is greeted as he crosses the church lawn on his way to church school may be more significant than a verse from the Bible that he recites as part of his worship. How a woman is welcomed to the women's group may be more important than the opening devotions. What happens at choir practice may be crucial in the religious development of a member. The words of a hymn may cause revulsion to the crucifixion, or the treatment of the sexton by a prominent member may be witnessed by a newcomer and cause the stranger to leave.

Although we think of instruction in the classroom as the chief agent of Christian education, we need to be aware that worship, fellowship, pastoral care, missionary activity, and world wide Christian service are educational experiences. A boy may come to a new appreciation of worship because he is asked to participate in the service by reading the Scripture, carrying the processional cross, or assisting at the Lord's table. A pastoral visit at the hospital may meet a real need. The coffee hour after church may provide the fellowship a young service man or woman or any stranger is hungry for. A project by the young people's group or the ladies' society may bring new leadership to the fore. A talk about missionary work or the ecumenical movement may occur at the time a person is thinking of his vocation.

The basic functions of the church cross all organizational lines. Worship may occur in connection with the parish bazaar or fair, fellowship is essential to choir rehearsal, instruction is connected with marriages, pastoral care before and after a funeral is a great opportunity for the bereaved to come to a new appreciation of the Christian view of death, the missionary responsibility of the church appears in youth groups and men's clubs, and the cooperation of the local congregation with other churches is a possibility at every level of organization, as youth groups, young adults, parents, and older adults find fellowship across denominational lines a way of sharing their problems and solutions.

The traditional marks of the church were given by John Calvin: "For wherever we find the word of God purely preached and heard, and the sacraments administered according to the institution of Christ, there, it is not to be doubted is a Church of God." [2] Preaching and the

---

[2] *Institutes,* IV, i, 9.

sacraments of Baptism and the Lord's Supper carry within them means of communication that have many educational possibilities. The Gospel is proclaimed through preaching, and this should be true of sermonettes and stories for children or for the family as well as of sermons at the traditional service. The Holy Scriptures stand behind both preaching and sacraments, and the educational problem is to make sure that the listeners hear the Word of God through faith when they listen to the reading of the Bible. Preaching, Bible reading, and the sacraments "derive their meaning as the Word of God only so far as they testify to God's revelation of Himself in Jesus Christ. He is the Word, who is only served by the preacher and the book. And their service to Him in every generation of the Church is actualized by the power of the Holy Spirit, who interprets the record of events in the history of Jesus Christ and makes them to be revelation." [3]

Both preaching and the sacraments may become so institutionalized that the form is considered sufficient without faith, and Martin Luther is supposed to have said that the devil himself could preach and administer the sacraments in proper form.[4] This is both a theological and an educational problem, and when right doctrine and right method come together the problem can be solved. Faith is a prerequisite to hearing the Word of God and to receiving the Body and Blood of Christ, and faith is strengthened when we come into the presence of God.

Although preaching and the sacraments are the major activities of every church, the other organized activities of parish life are equally educational. Every way in which these groups serve the parish has educational value, and the problem is to organize them in such a manner that the education will be in terms of the Gospel. Personal counseling and pastoral work provide more intimate opportunities for Christian education. Study groups, not only in church school classes but throughout the parish organizations, are the most effective of all for concentrated and continuous educational work. Good organization and administration will make it possible for every member of the parish to share in all types of activities.

---

[3] J. Robert Nelson, *The Realm of Redemption* (Greenwich: Seabury Press, 1951), p. 112.

[4] See *ibid.*, p. 137.

PRINCIPLES OF ORGANIZATION

Behind all organization and administration for Christian education are certain assumptions.

(1) The purpose of the church is to create an atmosphere in which concern for the welfare of individuals and society in relation to the Gospel is paramount.

(2) Every aspect of parish life has educational significance in meeting the basic needs of individuals and groups.

(3) Organization and administration are part of the curriculum of Christian education. To share in this process is educational in itself.

(4) Organization and administration are never ends in themselves. They are justified in terms of how they contribute to the health of the redemptive community.[5]

This leads into the consideration of four basic principles of organization. (1) The organization should be as *simple* as possible in the light of the objectives to be achieved. Clear relationships should be established between the various activities within the parish in order to avoid overlapping and confusion. *Unity* of organization avoids duplications and omissions in the program and provides a sense of community. There may be many or few activities, depending on the needs of the members of the parish and of the community they serve. Occasionally this unity is achieved through an over-all parish project of service to the community. Often it comes through the family worship service or a special family night program. The church school is seen as part of the total educational program of the parish, and its members are as much members of the congregation as any others. If the relationships and functions are clearly perceived, the parish will operate as a single unit.

(2) The organization should be *flexible*. Local congregations and their denominations have traditional forms of organization, and it is inconceivable that either the church school or the ladies' missionary society should be abolished, but even these may be transformed to meet the needs of the people. The difficulty arises when specific or-

---

[5] See *Principles and Objectives of Religious Education* (Chicago: International Council of Religious Education, 1932 and 1935), p. 66.

ganizations attain positions of privilege and vested interest and refuse to give them up after their usefulness has been lost. Organization needs constantly to be modified through imaginative leadership in order to provide a varied program that meets the emerging needs of the congregation and to avoid the monotony of routine without purpose.

(3) The organization should be *graded*. Grading should be in terms of the needs of the groups making up the congregation and of the numbers in each group. In larger parishes, close grading in terms of intellectual and social achievement is desirable, whereas in small parishes this type of grading must be modified in order to have enough people in the group. However, in the small church school it is better to have a large number of small classes, especially if a single room is used, for any teacher can handle a small group even when there are distractions. Parents are sometimes graded according to their children's standing in large churches, but even smaller churches should maintain a separate parents' group if they believe in the family unit as a basis for Christian education. Other adults are classified according to their needs. This grading is effective only when it does not sacrifice the unity of parish life, and this involves careful organization.

(4) The organization should be *democratic*. The degree of democratic leadership depends to some extent upon the polity of the denomination, but primarily it is due to the people in positions of leadership. The pastor, over a period of time, may introduce means whereby the congregation takes more responsibility. So-called "indispensable" lay people may be educated to see that more effective leadership will evolve from shared responsibility. Delegation of responsibility and democratic procedures in this development of policy are essential not only to efficient procedures, but also to providing the climate in which grace flourishes. The whole problem of each member's feeling that he is accepted as he is turns on the possibility of his assuming responsibility for the spiritual health of the parish. The techniques of democratic procedures may have evolved from our political history and from experiments in educational groups, but theologically they are rooted in the Gospel. The Christian parish is concerned with discovering the aptitudes of its members, bringing out in them the power to witness to their faith in Christ, and inspiring them to behave as loyal members of the community of faithful people.[6]

[6] See *The Organization and Administration of Christian Education in the Local Church* (Chicago: International Council of Religious Education, 1935, 1940), pp. 27-28.

These principles are particularly important in relation to the church school. In many parishes there is a gap between the church school and the church. In some cases the church school achieves such significance that it is the tail that wags the dog. In other cases the church looks on the church school as a poor relation. In a few cases there is an undeclared civil war going on. Rivalry and jealousy may develop when the family service outdraws the main service of the day. Good organization and administration, which bring all activities of the parish together under one over-all planning group, are essential if the barriers are to be overcome.

SPECIAL DAYS AND SEASONS

Many of the goals listed above are more easily attained if attention is given to the special days and seasons in the church's life. They are the means by which the Christian education of the parish may be carried forward, providing both variety and unity for all. The Christian year provides many opportunities for a variety of emphases, and when it is supplemented by many nontraditional observances, most of the facets of the Gospel will be realized.

The rhythm of the church year as it brings out the facets of the life of Christ makes for a well-rounded emphasis. The major feasts of Christmas, Easter, and Whitsunday provide opportunities for special worship services, pageants, festivals, and class sessions. Special days, such as Family Sunday, Religious Education Week, Race Relations Sunday, Youth Sunday, and Rally Day, give attention to the special interests of groups within the congregation.[7] These services create interest and increase attendance, but such goals should remain secondary. The only valid reason for such observances is that they make more effective the Christian education program of the parish.

Good planning is essential to making these days educational. Preparation should begin in plenty of time. Normally the days are spotted throughout the year, and an over-all plan can be combined with specific planning after one celebration is concluded. Leaders need to be informed of the meaning of the celebration and of their responsibility, and it is wise to have their assistance in the planning. Attention should

[7] See my *A Symphony of the Christian Year* (Greenwich: Seabury Press, 1954), especially pp. 3-11.

be centered on the educational values to be achieved. The preparation of those participating in the special day should carry a portion of the educational goal.

This emphasis on educational values will often meet opposition from those who want "old-time" religious celebrations, and time must be spent in overcoming prejudices. Special care must be taken that the by-products of the celebration are equally desirable from an educational point of view. With imaginative leadership, the true meaning of these days may be understood by all members of the parish. Careful group planning and the infusion of new blood into the leadership of specific occasions are essential.[8]

PROMOTING CHRISTIAN EDUCATION

The place to begin promoting Christian education is with the staff, teachers, and pupils. Good morale within the church school is the most important single element in promoting the educational program. Clear objectives that are understood and accepted by teachers and pupils provide a sense of things being done decently and in order. Inspiring leadership is essential, for if the Christian faith does not provide radiance in the leaders, we cannot expect it in the learners. Genuine fellowship both within and outside the sessions of church school provides the sense of acceptance. Worship that is reverent and relevant is considered by some educators as the most important single element. A challenging program that corresponds to the needs and interests of all members is sure to arouse enthusiasm.

Much of the promoting of the educational program comes from person-to-person contact. Nothing is more contagious than the enthusiasm of an excited participant who has become a recruiting officer for a church school, a study group, or some other activity in the church. Church school and young people's memberships often change with great rapidity from one church to another because of such enthusiastic salesmanship. When the morale is good, this enthusiasm is automatically produced, and good administration will guide it into constructive channels. It may be used to recapture old members who

---

[8] See Paul H. Vieth, *Improving Your Sunday School* (Philadelphia: Westminster Press, 1930), pp. 137-47; John Leslie Lobingier, *The Better Church School* (Boston: Pilgrim Press, 1952), pp. 105-21.

have dropped aside, to enlist new members who are otherwise unchurched, or to convince other members of the congregation of the significance of a particular educational activity.

Some church schools are overcrowded and have limited enrollments, but most congregations are willing to increase their numbers even if it means placing the church school on a double or triple shift. Many churches built for large numbers are partially empty because of failure to capture new members from the immediate neighborhood. Proper organization will provide activities for all who might come, which means grading the church school from nursery to adults. Prospects will be discovered among lapsed members and among the non-church members in the neighborhood of the church. In some cases, transportation will be provided. Although some big campaigns may be successful, the most important recruiting is the day-by-day contacts made by members of the congregation.

Some kind of permanent committee on membership should be available each Sunday to take care of newcomers and to make sure they are made to feel at home. They should be quickly absorbed into the educational processes that are going on, so that the merits of Christian worship and fellowship, rather than some artificial device of promotion, will capture their interest and make them desire to return. Contests and mass appeals may work for one occasion, but trained recruiters and the enthusiasm of the individual members are the only means of genuine Christian appeal.[9]

All kinds of publicity are available to assist in promoting Christian education. When there is enough variety in the program to be newsworthy, newspapers, radio and television stations, and even magazines will be glad to present the news. The wise use of paid advertising will help. The parish bulletin or newsletter is likely to be read by all the members when it carries interesting information. Direct mail to members of the parish helps to promote almost any event. A member of the congregation trained as a newspaper reporter or an advertiser may be found to undertake this work.[10] Much may be done by the pastor through his oral announcements at services and meetings, so that the congregation will be informed of what is happening.

---

[9] See Ralph D. Heim, *Leading a Sunday Church School* (Philadelphia: Muhlenberg Press, 1950), pp. 297-309.

[10] See Willard A. Pleuthner, *Building Up Your Congregation* (Greenwich: Seabury Press, 1950, 1951), pp. 73-113, and *More Power for Your Church* (New York: Farrar, Strauss & Young, 1952) pp. 306-16.

A COMPREHENSIVE PROGRAM

A comprehensive program is a unified one. A director of Christian education often finds himself in charge of the church school, but with no responsibility in relation to the educational activities of the men's club, women's groups, young adult groups, couples' clubs, the choirs, or the Scouts. There is no over-all planning of Christian education for all groups, no coming together of the officers responsible for Christian education, and no mergers of overlapping groups.

The structure of organization of the local parish may be tested in at least four ways. (1) What is the proportion of participating members to the total group available for this series of activities? Numbers are not always the answer, but they indicate at least the extent to which the parish is alive to some of the needs of its members, although these will not always be the needs the Gospel aspires to meet. In some cases, of course, the Gospel may be preached with such contradiction to the mores of the congregation that they prefer not to face the challenge.

(2) Why do the people claim they participate? Although lay people are not articulate about their reasons for participation in church life, if they cannot get somewhere near to the heart of the Gospels' proclamation of new life there is something wrong with the quality of life in the parish.

(3) What happens to those who take seriously their activities in the church? It is notorious that non-church members frequently hold to higher ethical standards than churchgoers, and it is often true that people attend church for the wrong reasons. The test comes when we observe how people behave in the face of bereavement, economic loss or unemployment, long illness, broken relationships in the family, or sacrifices for their country.

(4) What is the impact of the parish upon the community? The local congregation has more influence in the community than it knows, and the question is the quality of its impact. It may be dealing with the liquor problem, teen-age canteens, the local school board, or a welfare program. Even when the parish as a group does not espouse such a program, leaders' and members' participation reflects the parish's concern for the needs of its community.[11]

---

[11] See Charles D. Kean, *The Christian Gospel and the Parish Church* (Greenwich: Seabury Press, 1953), pp. 57-69.

Good organization and administration are means for achieving such ends through a unified parish program of Christian education, but they do not guarantee it. Only when we discover the kind of Gospel that is proclaimed in actual practice, and not just in theory, do we know what quality of life exists within the congregation. Relationships within the governing boards, the committees delegated to special tasks, the groups of men, women, couples, young adults, boys and girls, and children, determine what is happening in the parish. The purposes of these groups cannot be at cross-purposes, and good administration is necessary if all groups are to be brought under the governing theory of Christian education. A comprehensive program, based on a sound and relevant theology, will bring about the achievement of these goals.

CHAPTER 18

THE CHURCH ORGANIZED FOR RELIGIOUS EDUCATION

ORGANIZATION is a problem that involves the Sunday church school and other educational agencies of the congregation. Good organization at this level is important. But if what we have said about a *comprehensive* program of Christian education in the parish is accepted, the entire congregation must be organized with Christian education as one of the chief vital elements. Unity of organization and administration involves all the officers and members of the congregation.

Any structure of organization will be altered in the light of denominational practices and local conditions, but the basic structure should be such that integration of educational programing is achievable. In most Protestant churches the congregation has final authority. The congregation elects its pastor and his assistants, the official board or parish council, the board of deacons or its equivalent, and the board of trustees or vestry. The congregation's authority is normally delegated to its elected officers, although in some cases major decisions must be referred to a congregational meeting.

This overhead administration needs to be unified. The official board, made up of the boards of deacons and trustees plus members at large, with the pastor as chairman, may be the general policy-making body of the congregation. In other denominations, this church or parish council may operate with membership drawn from the vestry, the lay elders, and representatives of men's, women's, and children's groups in the congregation. The important element in this organization is to have a clearing house for planning so that members can come to a common understanding about the nature and function of the church.

Christian education is one item among others, which include evangelism, missionary activities, money raising functions, and all other parish activities. Through this board or council, every other group in the church is organically and functionally related to the entire congregation. The programs of all subsidiary units are reviewed by this board or council. Except for the work specifically delegated to the deacons or trustees by the polity of the denomination, the over-all planning is done by a single, representative, and responsible agency. Christian education is an integral part of the over-all strategy of the parish.

THE BOARD OF CHRISTIAN EDUCATION

Once the overhead administration is integrated so that it operates in the name of the entire congregation, the next step toward a unified educational program is the board or committee of Christian education. Ideally it should consist of members from the board of trustees, elders or deacons, educational officers of the major groups in the church, and representatives of the church school faculty and staff. It should be large enough to be a committee of the congregation and small enough to function effectively. It may be elected at a congregational meeting, or representatives on the board may be elected by the respective groups, or members may be appointed by responsible officers of the congregation. The pastor and director of Christian education, and possibly the general superintendent, should be members *ex officio*. Members should be rotated, none serving over three years.

This is not a committee for the church school. It is responsible to the congregation for the educational policies of the entire parish. If the congregation is not willing to go this far in unifying its Christian education, the representation should be cut down so that the board will be effective for the tasks delegated to it. No matter how small or how large the parish, such a committee can function effectively. It should have enough competent educators on it to provide leadership in self-study, but primarily the members should be concerned for the increasing effectiveness of the educational policies and practices of the church.

The first job of such a board of Christian education is to become acquainted with what is going on in the field. This involves acquiring knowledge of what the denominational department of Christian education is doing and recommending, of what other denominations are seeking to do, and of what the Division of Christian Education of the National Council of Churches is achieving.

It must become acquainted with what is going on in the congregation in the name of Christian education. An evaluation by means of such a standard as that prepared by the Division of Christian Education of the National Council of Churches or one prepared by the denominational department may bring to light many of the shortcomings, areas of neglect, deficiencies in teaching or curriculum, failures in worship, and lack of fellowship.

Against the background of its knowledge of what Christian education is about and of what the facts are in the parish, the board of Christian education is ready to determine policies. It may prepare a statement of what the parish stands for in Christian education, and then prepare the steps that should achieve these goals. This may be a long process as conditions are faced in finances, curriculum, leadership training, housing and equipment, and other areas. Much information and many of the suggestions will come from the staff and teachers, who in their meetings are concerned with the same problems, or from the educational secretaries of the various groups. The board will then be ready to plan a program to meet the needs of all members of the congregation.

At every point the congregation needs to be informed and persuaded. Although a competent committee is greatly to be desired, the whole congregation needs to go forward with them, to share their insights, and ultimately to approve of their policies. Reports to the congregation may be made through sermons, announcements, articles in the church bulletin, tracts, presentations to various organizations, and in many other ways.

The organization of the parish for education is sometimes a responsibility of the board of Christian education. The church school, the vacation church school, Bible classes, special study groups, and confirmation classes are normally organized and integrated by the board. They coordinate the educational programs of the men's and women's groups, although usually the actual organizing is done within the group. The specific organization of the church school continues under the direction of the staff.

The board has power in the election of officers and teachers. Sometimes the superintendent is elected by the congregation, and then the board should have the right to nominate. In some cases, the pastor or director of Christian education nominates officers and teachers, and the board elects them. All elections should be for a one-year term, including that of the general superintendent. When the responsibility rests with the board, ineffective members may be shifted or removed from office with less hard feeling.

The board has charge of supervision and training of the staff and teachers. It may provide for intensive training at the beginning of the fall term, pay the tuition for attendance at institutes during the term, and require attendance at regular staff meetings. Under ideal circumstances, it provides for adequate supervision of the teaching process and of working conditions. Additions to the library and the purchase of educational resources should be part of its responsibility.

Although the upkeep of housing and equipment normally is the responsibility of the trustees or vestry, the policy of providing adequate equipment is the responsibility of the board. Through study and planning, within the limitations of the budget and the capacity of the trustees to make capital expenses, the equipment may be made more adequate.

The board of Christian education may take on any other tasks that seem wise. They may work on a policy of parent cooperation; they may set up a program for scholarships for summer church camps and conferences; they may work on a policy of weekday education; they may cooperate with denominational and interdenominational bodies of Christian education; they may set up a program of measurement and testing; they may be subdivided into committees on children's, youth, and adult work, and leadership training, with new members being added to the subcommittees.

If a parish has never had a board of Christian education, getting it started may be a major task. Usually a new pastor's ideas are heard and accepted, although this concept may be too radical for many congregations. A subcommittee on Christian education may be formed within the trustees or vestry, or the staff of the church school may fulfill some of the functions, or the addition of a director of Christian education may provide an opportunity to alter the old organization. Unless the pastor is convinced that it is worth the effort, nothing is likely to happen even if the committee or board is formed.[1]

---

[1] The best descriptions of a board of Christian education are found in Paul H. Vieth, *Improving Your Sunday School* (Philadelphia: Westminster Press, 1930), pp. 23-37; Ralph D. Heim, *Leading a Sunday Church School* (Philadelphia: Muhlenberg Press, 1950), pp. 75-77; John Leslie Lobingier, *The Better Church School* (Boston: Pilgrim Press, 1952), pp. 134-39.

ACTIVITIES OF THE OFFICERS

The size of a congregation has much to do with the number of officers on the educational staff. The smallest congregation, however, has the same functions as the largest, and in order to get the work done the offices may be combined in a smaller number of people. The pastor of a large parish needs to delegate more responsibility than does the minister of a small church, although the pastor of a string of rural missions may have to delegate most of his educational authority to lay people.

THE PASTOR

The key person in the program of Christian education is the pastor. This is true of his responsibility even in a large parish in which authority and responsibility may be delegated. The Methodist discipline, as one example, states clearly that the minister is the responsible officer, that the church school is a vital part of his work, and that he should work with the superintendent in carrying out the program.

There are reasons why many ministers are not pastors to the children. The pressure of their other work makes it easy for them to neglect the educational side of their vocation. Many of them lack the training to do the job properly. If they want to be "promoted," they need to build the financial and statistical structure of the parish. Yet, in the ordination service of the Protestant Episcopal Church there is this question: "And are you determined, out of the said Scriptures to instruct the people committed to your charge. . .?" This emphasis on the minister as an educator runs throughout the traditions of many denominations, and yet it is often ignored completely.

In most parishes the enrollment in the Sunday church school is less than one hundred. There is no director of Christian education, and the superintendent is likely to be devoted but uninformed. The minister has no choice but to be his own director of Christian education. Though he may have a board of Christian education to back him up, he is responsible for interpreting the program and meaning of Christian education to his congregation, he is the only one who can organize a program of Christian education so that the entire membership will be reached, he needs to inspire and encourage the educational activities already going on, he has to find and train the leaders, he must teach a communicants' class, and he is the leader of the church school worship.[2] In many cases he will double as a superintendent and supervisor, and not infrequently he will be one of the regular teachers of a class.

Many of these functions will be fulfilled by the pastor even in a larger parish, which may have a competent general superintendent or a director of Christian education. The pastor is the executive officer and under him are the various members of the staff. He may delegate certain tasks to others, with certain exceptions. He cannot forego his responsibilities to be present at the Sunday church school, to take an active part in the worship or to take some part in the departmental services from Sunday to Sunday, and to be a final authority in situations within his scope. If the pastor dodges these tasks, he is failing to be a pastor to the children and young people. He may transfer authority in the selection of lesson materials, enlistment of teachers, and teaching of the communicants' class. Either the pastor or the director of Christian education should be *ex officio* chairman of the board of Christian education, although in some cases it has an elected chairman; at all events he should be present at meetings of the board.

The sermonette or story during the family worship service or the departmental service is often the minister's responsibility. What has been said about storytelling applies here. Raimundo de Ovies, who taught a class of 85 juniors when he was dean of the cathedral in Atlanta, gives some good advice. Love the children, or at least be interested in them. Know their names and as much about them as possible. Know the characteristics of the age groups in the congregation. Be interested in the story as well as in the children. Get up early enough to be alert. Be natural. Never give any indication of being annoyed. Be willing to be interrupted and listen carefully to what is contributed; if it is off the subject, either the child's mind has made an interesting association or the sermonette has missed its point. Give the pupils something to do. Let the teaching become action.[3]

The pastor's educational responsibilities do not stop with the church

[2] See Nevin C. Harner, "The Educational Ministry of the Church," in *Orientation in Religious Education,* ed. Philip H. Lotz, pp. 381-84.

[3] See Raimundo de Ovies, *The Church and the Children* (New York: Morehouse-Gorham Co., 1941), pp. 22-24.

school or with his relationships with the board of Christian education. He is *an educator in every task.* Whether he is addressing a Rotary club, conducting a premarital conference, sipping tea with one of his members, or playing golf, he never ceases to be a Christian educator.

As the executive of the educational program of the local church, he is the head of a team and not a dictator. He needs to work out a clear and concise working relationship with his director of Christian education and general superintendent. He needs to be clear about the delegation of responsibility and authority, respecting the professional training of the director of Christian education and the insights and previous service of the superintendent.

Over a period of years, the program of Christian education will reflect the interest and concern of the pastor. He may start with a poor program and an inadequate staff. As times goes on, he may recruit those who are more competent; improved organization and administration, as well as constant education of the whole congregation, may result in a more efficient educational program. The chances of this happening without the active participation of the pastor are slight. Therefore, he needs all the training he can get in the seminary, and he needs to keep reading and attending conferences after he enters the ministry.

THE DIRECTOR OF CHRISTIAN EDUCATION

The title of Director of Christian Education or Minister of Education should be given to a man or woman who is professionally trained in the field. Otherwise, the title should be Assistant in Christian Education or Assistant Minister. Many young ministers and women without graduate training now serve in this capacity.[4]

The trained director has had from one to three years of graduate training in a theological seminary, specializing in Christian education. Often he has expert knowledge surpassing that of the pastor. He is ready to do a specific task. He serves as the executive secretary and resource person on the policy-making board of Christian education. He has the information needed for making intelligent decisions, and he is influential in determining policy. In many cases he replaces the general superintendent, and in others a division of labor and respon-

[4] See John Leslie Lobingier, *The Better Church School,* p. 143.

sibility is worked out. The director does much background work, carrying out the policies of the board, making contacts with those who will do the necessary jobs, keeping and checking records, and outlining plans of procedure. He is responsible for teacher training meetings and staff discussions. Frequently he is in charge of the evening youth groups and of the educational programs of many midweek meetings of groups of all ages. He does a great amount of calling on parents and children, his chief concern being the relationships between the church and the family unit; he locates candidates for baptism and confirmation, or for dedication and adult baptism; he is always a recruiting officer for the various educational activities in the congregation; he is looking for potential teachers and staff members.

The director's relationship to the pastor and other members of the staff depends on the structure of organization and on the personalities involved. Some ministers think that a director is a combination errand boy and secretary, and that by having such a person the minister is absolved of any educational responsibility. If the director is professionally trained and fulfills the functions we have listed, he has no time for general parish calling, running a mimeograph machine, or routine office work. The director should share some of the minister's responsibility and assist him in interpreting the policies of Christian education to the congregation, in organizing and vitalizing the educational program, in procuring and training leaders, and in participating in group meetings and the church school sessions. In some cases the director will assume most of the responsibility for the worship services, especially if the minister is incompetent to talk to younger Christians. He may take over parish surveys in order to promote membership.

A special task of the director is to help teachers, in any of a number of ways. In large church schools supervisors and assistant teachers observe the teaching process and discuss it with the teacher. This is followed by a personal conference with the director. In some parishes the director is his own supervisor and follows through with a personal meeting. Even when no supervision is necessary, teachers wish to talk over their problems with a competent counselor. The director provides guidance, books, and resource materials to assist them. The regular staff and faculty meetings, under the leadership of the director, are primarily training sessions, with business items postponed to the end of the meeting or handled by subcommittees. The director encourages the teachers to attend various denominational and interdenominational institutes. Frequently a special group of high school students may be selected for teacher training, so that they will be prepared to teach when they become mature enough.

THE GENERAL SUPERINTENDENT

Most parishes do not have a director of Christian education. The key person in the organization, administration, and supervision of Christian education is the general superintendent. He should be a sound administrator, a competent educator, and a devoted Christian. He is a volunteer and an amateur, and yet many of the responsibilities of a director of Christian education fall on him.

The superintendent is the executive secretary of the board of Christian education, responsible for putting into action the policies formulated by the board. Because he heads the staff of the church school, his personal relationships are essential to a successful operation of the entire enterprise. These include relationships with the congregation as a unit, the minister, the board of Christian education, the officers and teachers on the staff, the parents, and the pupils. As an administrator he works primarily in the background, and his success depends on the way he can get other people to do their jobs.

There is plenty to keep the superintendent busy during the week as well as on Sundays. He, along with the pastor, makes recommendations to the board of Christian education for the appointment of teachers; he is responsible for an ongoing program of supervision and teacher training; he checks on educational resources and supplies, proper record-keeping, the condition of equipment, the enrollment of new pupils, and the supervision of late-comers; he is responsible for notifying substitutes or setting up a program so that no class is ever without a teacher, for organizing plans for increased enrollment, for seeing that absences are followed up by postcards, phone calls, or personal calls by the teachers, and that extended absences or sicknesses are checked by the pastor; he sets up programs for closer home cooperation, and he is on the job every Sunday overseeing the total program.

It is just as well that the general superintendent in many parishes is not responsible for leading the worship. Where family worship is the norm the minister is in charge, although the superintendent and some pupils may assist in the service. Where departmentalized worship is customary, the department superintendents have chief responsibility, with the minister taking part as may be arranged.

A large church school may have one or more associate superintendents. Because the superintendent cannot be everywhere at once on a Sunday morning, his staff divides some of his functions among themselves.

DEPARTMENT SUPERINTENDENTS

In schools large enough to be divided into departments for purposes of worship, assembly, and groupings of teachers, superintendents are needed. On a limited scale, the department superintendent does for his department what the general superintendent does for the whole school. He has special knowledge of the characteristics of the age group in his department. When worship is arranged on a departmental basis, he normally is the leader.

Nursery and kindergarten superintendents need special skills in order to take care of the needs of younger children. Sometimes the chief teacher in the nursery or kindergarten is also the superintendent, and his staff consists of the assistant teachers under his direction.

SECRETARY AND STAFF

The work of the secretary is primarily to enroll new pupils, to keep attendance records, to handle correspondence, to send out cards to absentees, to take minutes at staff meetings, and to prepare reports to the superintendent, faculty, and board of Christian education. However, there is much more to be done when full records are kept or surveys are made. Often church schools keep many types of records, including records of absence and attendance, achievements, class data, curriculum materials, leaders, personality profiles, prospects, reports to parents, and withdrawals. These may be taken care of by the paid secretarial staff in larger churches, but they are the responsibility of the church school secretary in many cases.

SUPPLY SECRETARY

The supply secretary has charge of all kinds of material that may be used at a given session. He sees that adequate supplies are on hand.

Sometimes his tasks are combined with those of the audio-visual secretary, who takes care of orders for filmstrips and slides and makes arrangements for the use of projectors.

THE TREASURER

Two goals need to be achieved in the financial affairs of the church: First, the practice of giving should be an educational experience. Second, the total educational program should be the responsibility of the entire parish. This suggests that everyone should give to the total work of the parish and to its outside projects, and that giving should always be within the context of worship. A single treasury for the parish, with the comprehensive educational program accounted for in the budget, is becoming the most effective form of administration of the financial side.

All members of the church school should have the opportunity to give regularly and consistently, using the same form of pledge and envelopes as the rest of the congregation. They should know what their gifts are for and how they are spent. The offering should be made at a service of worship and not in the classroom. Beyond this, the members should have the opportunity to contribute to special offerings, including those made through the denominational program for children and those to which the local parish is committed.

An adequate budget for the church school, young people's groups, and other educational activities should be worked out by the board of Christian education. This budget in itself is of educational value when discussed by the trustees or vestry and by the congregation. The church school should not be expected to be self-supporting. With an adequate budget, the means of dispersal is secondary. It is often convenient in a large church to have a separate bank account and treasurer for the paying of church school expenses, although the money comes originally from the unified treasury. All accounts are audited in the usual way.

The treasurer should be able to see the relationship between the educational and financial purposes of the church school. He supervises the financial system, helps with stewardship education, keeps track of all offerings, works with the parish treasurer concerning deposits and withdrawals, keeps careful records, pays all approved bills promptly, watches the budget in relation to expenses, and makes reports.

THE LIBRARIAN

Even if a church has only a tract rack, a librarian is needed to keep track of literature. Many smaller parishes now have libraries, sometimes consisting of a few books for lay people borrowed from the public library or from the minister; and as educational resources are purchased they are used by teachers and pupils alike. Books vanish if no records are kept, and some kind of a list of available books and borrowers is essential if the literature is to circulate. Sometimes the supply secretary may serve in this capacity, but in larger parishes it may take one person's available time.

CHOIRS AND MUSIC

If the music is to reach the standards we have suggested,[5] there must be close cooperation between the pastor and the choir director. A mutual understanding of the religious purpose of music in worship is essential. In most denominations the minister has control and authority in this field, although he often delegates much of it to the director of music. If worship is to be "fitly framed together," the words of the hymns must fit the theme of the service, and this means that the minister normally chooses the hymns. Whoever leads departmental worship has this same privilege.

Some churches have one junior choir. Others may have a number of graded choirs. Both the rehearsal and participation in worship should be an educational experience. The opportunity to understand the background and the meaning of the hymns, canticles, and anthems and to see their relationships to present-day living is offered at every rehearsal. Much may be done with tape recorders to improve the quality of singing. Reasonable rules, preferably set up by the members themselves, should be enforced as to rehearsals, discipline, and punctuality.

Some churches have a minister of music who oversees all the choirs and musical activities. Others have separate directors for the senior and junior choirs. Whatever arrangement is customary in the local parish, close cooperation is essential in order that the music may be suitable.

---

[5] See above, pp. 254-56.

JUNIOR PARISH COUNCIL

One of the most effective groups in the successful administration of the educational program among younger members is the junior parish council or junior official board. Its members usually represent classes from the third grade up through the young people's group. Often one of its members sits on the board of Christian education.

This group is in a position to suggest changes in policy, to make suggestions concerning the budget, to help determine pupils' needs, to deal with pupils' complaints, to assist in maintaining discipline, to welcome newcomers, to provide ushers at services, to organize school projects, to assist in counting the offering, and to interpret the program to the members of the church school.

THE SUPERVISORS

The techniques of supervising are discussed in Chapter 21. The supervisor may be the minister, the superintendent, or the assistant teacher in the class. Often he is a trained educator who works closely with the teachers. He visits their classes and discusses improvements in their teaching procedures. He may make recommendations to the board of Christian education concerning changes in conditions or personnel, and he is a resource person at training sessions for the teachers. His task may be expanded so that he is a specialist in charge of all teacher training. Some larger schools have a supervisor for each department.

THE TEACHERS

The teacher is an administrative officer as well. Organization of the class is important. Although nursery children do not elect class presidents, their class periods have to be carefully organized and mapped out in advance. Organization is a means of promoting morale, the sense of security and belonging, and the feeling of accomplishment. With younger children this may be part of the teaching technique, but it involves proper organization and administration of the class period, with allowance for greeting and welcoming new pupils, taking special pains with bashful and backward children, and leading them to achievements they can comprehend and appreciate. With juniors, a highly organized class structure with officers and special duties will do more to promote morale and efficiency than expert teaching, although both are necessary. Good administration utilizes the resources of the class members for the achievement of desirable ends.

Promotion of membership is part of the teacher's task. He has intimate relationships with the pupils, who are the chief missionaries. A good teacher draws new pupils by winning the ones he already has. When the pupils say, "We worship and we study hard, but it's fun," they will hunt other children to join them.

Checking on sick and absent members is part of the teacher's duty. In a well-organized school a card signed by the pastor or superintendent automatically goes to the absentee, but that is never enough. The personal interest of the teacher is what counts. He may phone the pupil, or call on him at home, or see him at the hospital, and thus build an outside-church relationship that is essential to good teaching. If the absence is not due to illness, the teacher has an opportunity to find out the real reason. This also partially fulfills the teacher's responsibility for promoting membership; for the main issue is making the student want to attend, and this arises from good personal relations.

Making contact with the home is another duty of the teacher. There are at least three reasons for this. First, through knowledge of home conditions the teacher is better prepared to meet the pupil's real needs at his "growing edge." The teacher may know the general conditions of the school and community, but he knows the unique condition of each pupil only by entering his home as a friend. He then can handle disciplinary problems constructively, can comprehend the reasons for lack of interest, can use discretion in promoting special offerings, and can adjust the curriculum to meet the real needs of the pupil.

Second, parental cooperation is essential for more effective teaching. Here is the opportunity to enlist the parents in the family worship and parents' class, if such are available. The best modern lesson materials have readers to be taken home, so that parents may read to younger children and supervise the reading of older ones. The main point is that the parents understand what is happening and cooperate with their children in the facing of the basic problems of life.

Third, religion in the home is the best background for teaching. The wise and tactful teacher may drop hints, leave literature, and give invitations that make religion more vital in the home. A campaign to introduce "grace" at meals, bedtime prayers, reading religious stories, or family prayers may prove a useful innovation.[6]

The teacher as a member of the faculty has certain administrative responsibilities. He helps by keeping the records of his own class and making reports to the secretary. He assists in interpreting stewardship and obtaining pledges. As a member of the faculty, he joins in recommendations to the board of Christian education.

In many church schools, there are assistant teachers. They act primarily as observers, taking notes or running a tape recorder, joining in the discussion when they see a point of student concern that the teacher has missed, discussing the class session with the teacher afterwards, and acting as a substitute when the teacher is absent. Many husband-and-wife teams work together in this way, and the combination of a man and a woman is often desirable from many angles. This is true particularly with the younger children, who are not always aware that men are concerned with religion, and it has profound psychological effects in teaching the Fatherhood of God.[7]

EDUCATIONAL SECRETARIES

The educational secretaries of the various organizations in the parish are often isolated. They may follow the instructions from denominational headquarters for their own group, but they are not integrated into the ongoing program of Christian education in the local church. They do not have access to the total resources of the parish.

When there is a board of Christian education, this handicap is partially overcome; for the educational secretaries are represented on the board and cooperate in developing the educational policies of the parish. In larger parishes, there will be a number of subcommittees concerned with children's work, young people's work, leadership training, and adult work. The adult subcommittee should include the educational secretaries from the women's organizations, men's club, couples' club, parents' class, young adults, missionary societies, choir,

[6] See my *A Guide for Church School Teachers*, pp. 74-77.

[7] See Basil A. Yeaxlee, *Religion and the Growing Mind* (Greenwich: Seabury Press, 1952), pp. 85, 87, 187.

and any other group primarily for adults. Through this subcommittee an over-all strategy for adult education may be developed and submitted for action to the board of Christian education.

Within his own group the educational secretary is responsible for an ongoing program. He may have an educational committee or he may work alone in the development of programs. He should be acquainted with the best methods of adult education, and be ready to experiment with new ways of group procedure. He also has the responsibility of explaining the over-all educational policy to his own group.

HOUSING AND EQUIPMENT

Planning and policies of the board of Christian education must be realistic in terms of personnel, finances, housing, and equipment. Personnel can be trained and finances are not too hard to handle when there is a high level of enthusiasm. But old buildings and equipment are difficult to alter, and sometimes their limitations present hurdles that are impossible to jump.

Once a new program is accepted, it is surprising how much can be accomplished. The ingenuity of the congregation finds ways of achieving miracles. Creative imagination, when applied with vigor, may make dreams come true. There are certain steps to take.

Make the best use of what is available. There are spaces that are unused, or are used unwisely. If there is a large hall in which three classes have to meet, and these classes are so large that no one can hear, cut down the size of the classes to six or eight and six of them will be able to meet in the same hall without too much interference.

Give the younger members a break. They should have the most comfortable rooms, the equipment suited to their needs, and the resources for the job to be done. Remember that the youngest ones cannot protest. If you have some money to spend, buy nursery chairs. More money will be found soon for adult chairs. But if you buy the adult chairs first, the nursery children will continue to sit on the cold floor.

As far as possible provide separate rooms for each group. Perhaps a big room that is not used to capacity can be partitioned to hold several classes.

Multiple use of rooms is essential. No group has a vested interest in any room, even if they did buy the curtains. Rooms should be budgeted throughout the week. Even on Sundays, the worship and class times may be staggered to use the rooms at least twice.

Every room should be as attractive as possible. Proper lighting, a good paint job, floor coverings, curtains, and draperies will not bankrupt any treasury if volunteer labor is offered.

When new equipment is purchased, buy for permanence. There are no bargains in equipment, and buying a little good equipment each year eliminates the need to replace cheap and tasteless furnishings.[8]

Plans for remodeling or for new buildings should be in terms of the total program of the parish and of the expectations of future growth. As far as education is concerned, one of the consultants should be a competent educator, so that the ideals of church architecture and educational functions may be properly combined.

Classroom furnishings should be in good taste and should meet educational standards. This means that the pictures should have educational and artistic value and should be properly graded. The furniture must be chosen for the comfort of the age group, with chairs and tables the right size. Older boys and girls use table-arm chairs. The seating arrangement should be such that the pupils do not look into the light. There should be a cabinet for supplies, a blackboard and display board, and in the rooms for younger children perhaps a piano.

If the worship service is not held in the church, attractive chapels should be available. An assembly hall, through the proper use of curtains, lights, and furnishings, may serve as a chapel. In more fortunate situations, a special children's chapel may be available either in the educational building or in the transept of the church.

THE SUNDAY CHURCH SCHOOL

Large Sunday church schools are usually divided by departments, and the students are closely graded according to their secular grades.

Department	*Ages*	*Grades*
Nursery	1, 2, 3	—
Kindergarten	4, 5	—
Primary	6, 7, 8	1, 2, 3
Junior	9, 10, 11	4, 5, 6

[8] See *The Organization and Administration of the Local Church* (Chicago: International Council of Religious Education, 1940), pp. 57-58.

Department	*Ages*	*Grades*
Junior High (or Intermediate)	12, 13, 14	7, 8, 9
Senior	15, 16, 17	10, 11, 12
Older Youth—Young Adults	18–24	
Parents		
Adults	from 25 up	
Older Adults	from 65 up	

Small church schools, numbering from 25 to 50 members, might have a class for each department. Schools of 75 to 125 may work out their classes according to the physical conditions and available personnel; smaller classes and closer grading is normally desirable, especially when only one room is available.

Through the junior age, it is sometimes wiser to divide classes on a two-year span, as follows:

Department	*Age*	*Grade*
Nursery	2, 3	—
Kindergarten	4, 5	—
Primary	6, 7	1, 2
Lower Junior	8, 9	3, 4
Upper Junior	10, 11	5, 6

The Congregational-Christian and the Evangelical and Reformed Churches have prepared their lesson materials on this basis, although they are also suitable for closely graded schools. The Christian Faith and Life Series of the Presbyterian Church, U.S.A., is prepared on a three-year cycle, although it also is used in closely graded schools. The Seabury Series is closely graded, but the two-year span is kept in mind in the elementary grades.

The chief problem in many Sunday church schools is irregularity in attendance. There are many causes for irregularity, some of which are outside the control of the church school. The point of attack on this problem lies in the quality of life of the congregation, especially as it reflects in the attractiveness of the church school program. If the church school is a continuous and joyous fellowship of those who know Christ, attendance will pick up. "It takes a long time to grow a Christian. . . . Joyousness is the secret of this needed continuity." [9] How many of our pupils can say, "I was glad when they said unto me, We will go into the house of the Lord"? (Psalm 122:1, PB.) Chil-

[9] Philip Cowell Jones, *The Church School Superintendent* (New York: Abingdon Press, 1939), p. 25.

dren respond to the radiance of the Gospel, and dullness is a form of malignancy that eats away a budding faith.

Real concern for the pupils is a second factor in maintaining attendance. A careful check on absentees, interest in the real problems of the students in their worship and in their classes, genuine friendship and fellowship not only in the church school but in all parochial relationships, and recognition of achievement in the light of ability, all contribute to the morale of the entire school.

Enrollment of families by units engages the interest of all. This breaks down the indifference when only a few in a family normally attend, avoids distractions on Sunday mornings, and permits the whole family to worship together and to study at the same hour. Bad weather, Sunday spectacles, and other excuses do not affect family attendance as badly as individual attendance. The parents' class never slumps as badly as the remainder of the church school. Cooperation between home and church school in curriculum activities, family nights, and other activities in the church strengthens the bond and increases attendance.

Punctuality is another serious problem. If the staff is on time and if the service or session begins on time *every* Sunday, punctuality will improve. Late-comers may be made to wait until a proper break in the service. But many parishioners and their children simply do not know any better, and only constant education will improve the conditions. An earlier or a later starting time seems to have no effect on punctuality. In spite of the claims of some parents concerning getting up early on Sunday morning, a school that opens at 9 A.M. is as likely to have as punctual a crowd as one that starts at 11 A.M.

Disorder is almost a disease in some church schools. It arises from tradition, from poor equipment, from inadequate planning, from lack of morale, from tardy arrivals of teachers, from irrelevant lesson materials, from poor teaching, and from home conditions.

Although occasionally an individual student may need disciplining, the general confusion of most church schools can be straightened out by good administration. As the causes just mentioned are eliminated and as the program begins to be clear and interesting to the pupils, disorder seems to vanish. Noise will continue, but noise is evidence of active interest and only needs direction. Noise should, however, be eliminated from a reverent service of worship.

Much depends on the standards of the school. A reasonable expectation of good behavior in terms of what children can achieve, when it is made clear to them, will inspire them to behave. High expectations, knowledge of the facts of the case, regulations that are clearly understood and accepted, responsibility placed on the students and their student council, and an interesting curriculum will normally result in a lively response that is positive and constructive.

An adequate time schedule will strengthen the educational impact of the church school. A one-hour schedule with 20 minutes for worship, 10 minutes for announcements and other business details, 25 minutes for class, and 5 minutes for a closing assembly almost guarantees defeat. Although no schedule is completely satisfactory, there are certain requirements that should be met. The class session should run about 50 minutes; the worship service should last from 25 to 35 minutes; therefore, an hour and a quarter to an hour and a half is the minimum time for an adequate program. This may be achieved in a number of ways.

Some church schools open at 9 or 9:15 A.M. with a family worship service or the departmental services, and after 30 to 35 minutes the students go to their classes; they are dismissed at 10:45 with a brief class prayer. Another schedule opens the classes at 10 A.M., and those from the third grade up attend the 11 A.M. service. A variation on this is to have a worship service at 10:15 for those below the ninth grade, who then have a full hour or more of class at 11 A.M., whereas the high school and parents' classes meet from 10:15 to 11, and then attend church. In all of these schedules, younger children have a shorter worship service and a longer class session, even if they participate in the family service. Some parishes have expanded-time sessions, which run as long as two or three hours.

RECORDS AND REPORTS

Records are important. One can get lost in a mess of useless cards that have no meaning, but the proper use of records gives an adequate picture of what is happening. The superintendent should know the status of attendance. The gross attendance figures are not enough, for what is meaningful is the percentage of those present out of the possible number. The average attendance is obtained by checking the actual attendance against those on the active membership list, and if the percentage is below 70 per cent something is wrong with either the morale of the school, the weather, or the follow-up on absentees.

A record of those who have become inactive or have withdrawn should be checked and an investigation made of those who are still in the community. Lapsed church school members are often won back to the church by a little attention.

The pupil's permanent record should be detailed enough to give an accurate picture of his situation. It should provide such obvious facts as his name, birth date, grade in school, and family situation. It should record his status of church membership, his church school class, curriculum, and teachers, and his record of progress.

The teacher may want to build on this information until he has a profile sheet, with much information about the pupil's background, attitudes, interests, and activities in the class. A class attendance book is the simplest way of checking attendance.

The importance of records is that they give a picture of what is happening. They are the basis for reports to the board of Christian education and to the congregation concerning attendance, achievements, curriculum materials, leadership, finances, and new plans for the future. They have enough information about the pupils so that intelligent reports may be sent home.

Attempts are being made to formulate reports that will give parents an accurate picture of the progress being made by their children. Besides the usual information concerning attendance and payments on his pledge, the pupil's progress in learning facts, meaning, memory work, and passing tests is judged in terms of "usually, frequently, and seldom." But equally important is the pupil's development in the group, and this is reported in terms of participation in class discussion, sharing in group activities, getting along with other pupils, and showing reverence in worship.[10] Other forms give room for comments by the teacher but lack such specific categories.

CONCLUSION

Administration is the functioning of an individual or of a group for the purpose of achieving specific goals. Organization provides the forms or channels by which administration proceeds. It combines unification and diversification in such a manner that all members of the

---

[10] See John Leslie Lobingier, *The Better Church School,* p. 4.

group see and accept responsibility for the fulfilling of the tasks delegated to them. Because the parish is a single community and not a federation of autonomous groups, a comprehensive program of Christian education includes all parish activities. Yet, because people must be grouped according to age groups, interests, and free time, organizations must have a semi-autonomous quality.

Too often, in the past, the congregation of Christ's flock has been fragmented. The church school, the women's group, the young people, the choir, the missionary society, and other groups have become in themselves centers of loyalty at the expense of the community of faithful people. The true fellowship of Christian believers has not operated as a single unit, has not shared a common aim in Christian education or in its other functions, and has not been the redemptive and sustaining community in which every member knows himself to be accepted by all the other members because Christ died for all mankind.

Administration and organization cannot solve this problem. Only the Holy Spirit can bind men together in unity. But poor administration and under- or over-organization may be barriers to the unity that, by God's grace, is possible. When the vision of unity is captured on the level of the local congregation, it may be shared with the denomination and ultimately with that ecumenical fellowship of Christians throughout the world.

CHAPTER 19

CHILDREN, YOUTHS, AND ADULTS

THE PRINCIPLES of unity and diversification must be combined in a good organization. The Christian fellowship draws all ages of men into its fold, and yet each group needs its own program and fellowship. Because the total congregation is concerned with the needs of every individual, its organization is arranged to provide those groupings that are most congenial. Only through strong groups and departments can the over-all educational strategy of the local parish be effectively administered.

The number of groups is determined by the size of the church, the total in each bracket or age group, the time schedule of activities, and the physical facilities. A church school may be so small that nursery and kindergarten may be combined; a parish may be so large that there will be 20 neighborhood groups of the women's society.

The organization for education is identical with the organization of the total parish. In what follows, the *structure and functions* are significant, whereas the specific groupings may always be telescoped in order to avoid overorganization. The needs to be met are similar in every parish and the objectives of Christian education are identical, even though they may be implemented by different means.

In Chapter 5, we dealt with the different age groups in terms of their basic needs of love and acceptance, of a structure of law and order, of their freedom to grow, and of their hunger for the grace of God. The problem of organization is to meet these needs with all the resources of the congregation in the most effective way.

The central theological demands are clear. Each individual shall know himself as

> a child of God and an inheritor of the kingdom of heaven
> separated from God and his fellows and under the promise of redemption through faith in Christ

experiencing the healing of those broken relationships with his fellow men and with God through the power of God's grace
sustained in his faith and obedient to God's will as he understands it
knowing the power of God through the proclaiming of the Word in preaching, the power of the sacraments, the fellowship of the Holy Spirit, prayer and worship, learning God's truth and the promises of Holy Scripture, pastoral care that he gives and receives, missionary and evangelistic activities, acceptance of the ethical demands of the Gospel in social and personal relations, stewardship, and membership in the total Body of Christ through the ecumenical movement.

This is learned through the relationships of everyday living, through the relationships experienced in church, and through the interpretation of these relationships in the light of the teachings of the Gospel. Our task is to organize and administer a program of Christian education so that each individual, in the light of his needs and capacities, may grow into these experiences and see their meaning for his life now.

CHILDREN

Christianity begins with love, and love is the first experience of a new-born baby. With all his limitations, the infant's experiences with his parents are the beginnings of religion. He has no equipment for grasping the idea of God, but his emotional attitudes toward his mother and father are similar to those that mature believers have toward God. Says Basil Yeaxlee:

> By his experience of such qualities in his parents as real, and as answering his vital needs, the tiny child is prepared for a true understanding of the existence and nature of God when later his mental development enables him to grasp these intellectually—though even his earliest states are not for him devoid of an element of meaning. Furthermore, it becomes evident that in these most elemental and natural early relationships the parents . . . are actually interpreting or misinterpreting God to the child in the only medium possible, though often the parents have not the faintest notion that religion enters into the matter at all, whether they account themselves religious or not.[1]

[1] Basil A. Yeaxlee, *Religion and the Growing Mind* (Greenwich: Seabury Press, 1952), pp. 44-45.

The problem of administration is to help parents realize and implement this insight. We need a program for reaching parents, for our access to the infant is through those on whom he depends. We need to realize that the resources of religion lie in the parent-infant relationships. We need to bring parents to the recognition that the language of relationships is the only means of communication with the infant, and that only those who are close to the infant may have a lasting influence.

The traditional cradle roll approach, through keeping the child on the list, remembrance of his birthday, and occasional pious leaflets for the parents, cannot accomplish the task, and yet the organizational idea is correct. The cradle roll leader, through contact with the home, is the most important person in the organization. This is the point of contact with the church for the parents, and therefore the cradle roll leader has the opportunity of bringing into the home the guidance and information the parents need.

Once it is recognized that the parents are the chief ministers to their infants, many churches will organize a class for prospective and recent parents. This may be a group within a single parents' class in smaller congregations, and in larger churches parents may be divided into several classes according to their interests. From this point of view, the parents' class exists for the good of their children, and the nurturing of the parents in their own faith is a secondary motive, although as they become concerned about the Christian nurture of their children their own faith will deepen.

Many churches are experiencing a deepening concern about infant baptism and dedication. The grace of baptism or dedication is seen to depend to some extent on the ministry of parents. Instruction of parents and sponsors is a prerequisite to public baptism or dedication in many parishes of all denominations. Private counseling by the minister, classes for parents prior to traditional days for public baptism or dedication, and a pastoral follow-up by the minister and cradle roll leader have become normal procedure. In some cases lay people have been trained as leaders in this program, doing the home counseling, teaching the parents' classes, and following up during the next several years.[2]

---

[2] See Reuel L. Howe, "The Need for a Ministry to the Pre-School Child," *Religious Education* (May-June 1950), pp. 148-50. Reprinted as a pamphlet by Seabury Press.

Adequate materials for this procedure have not been developed, but books for the leaders are available. By the time the child is two, he may still be at home and under the exclusive care of his parents, or he may be coming to church and joining the nursery class. The cradle roll responsibility should provide a connection with the church school whenever this takes place.

THREE YEARS OLD

Sometime before he reaches four, and perhaps as young as two, the child will begin attending church school. He may accompany his parents, attend the family service very briefly, and then go to his class. He may arrive with his parents and go directly to his own room, meeting them again at the close of the session. His parents may see that he gets to the church or send him with friends.

How and when the parents leave the child is crucial at the beginning of the church school year. He has been looking forward to a new adventure and to the beginning of his independence, but he is scared. He may be so paralyzed with fear that he cannot speak or act, or he may become hysterical, or he may withdraw. He needs all the security that his parents can offer through preparation, accompanying him to the church and to the class, staying long enough to be sure he can accept his new responsibility, and achieving that balance between coddling and granting of freedom that the particular child needs. The impact of this first experience in church may be a lasting one, and the parents can do more than the church.

Previous relationships between the family and the church are significant. If the pre-nursery ministry to the family and the child has been adequate, they will know the cradle-roll visitor and she will be in the nursery on the first few Sundays of the fall term. The guidance of the church for a ministry to the pre-school child will have provided secure relationships that can be carried over to the church and nursery experience. Now the next step must be made in a different environment.

The main emphasis in administration is to provide the means whereby the child is made secure and at ease. Equipment for hanging up his coat, seats the right size, a room with color, books with pictures, and procedures that are casual and informal are essential to the nursery class. The staff should be large enough to provide guidance to small groups and to give individual attention to those who need it. Toilet facilities should be immediately available. A large and sunny first-floor room is desirable.

The program in the class should be varied and informal. Most teachers' guides have excellent suggestions for proper procedures. The relaxed and friendly atmosphere is more important than content at this level, for the teaching is almost entirely through relationships. Worship should be spontaneous and natural, although nursery children are impressed for a brief period by the more formal ritual in the family service.

Some schools grade their nursery for those two and three, others for two, three, and four, and others for three and four. In areas having public kindergartens for those who are five, the nursery should contain all under kindergarten age; but often the lesson materials are prepared with a two-year cycle of two- and three-year-olds for the nursery and four- and five-year-olds for kindergarten. These can be adapted to any plan that seems wise in the local situation.

FOUR AND FIVE

As with the nursery child, adequate physical facilities are essential for the four- or five-year-old. He learns through activity, and the equipment should provide concrete ways of learning. A visit to a public school kindergarten will show what furnishings, toys, and other items are essential.

Kindergarten is an experience in group living. Children gather in groups that interest them, wander from one group to another, change their tasks frequently, and keep learning. They learn through play, imitation, repetition, handling things, making motions with their songs and verses, and through being secure within both the small and large groupings of the class.

The administration of the kindergarten is identical with the teaching procedures. The teacher is also the superintendent, and the assistant teachers serve as secretary, nurse maid, or whatever else is required. The worship, stories, study of pictures, singing, play, and other activities occur spontaneously or whenever the leader senses the need. Kindergarten children like field trips and learn much from them. When they attend family worship, they are reverent and appreciative, and like to have explanations of what has happened.

THE ELEMENTARY GROUPS

The traditional division of the first six grades has been into primary and junior departments, but more careful study of age group characteristics has led to the conclusion that two-year groups are more suitable. In larger church schools with adequate space, there is no difficulty in having a primary (first two grades), lower junior (grades three and four), and upper junior (grades five and six). A smaller school might prefer to keep all six grades in one department, and have classes divided on the two-year span, for a division into primary and junior departments on the three-year system would separate third and fourth graders.[3]

Whether the elementary group is divided into two or three departments, in the larger churches each department has a superintendent. When worship is departmentalized, the superintendent has charge. Grading follows the secular schools, with boys and girls together. When classes become too large, they can be separated on a mixed basis. The ideal is about twelve to a class, with a teacher and an observer for each. Classroom space may be as little as 10 to 15 square feet per pupil. There should be equipment for such creative activities as sand-table work, informal dramatics, drawing, and modeling. A blackboard is essential. It should be possible to darken the room for the use of visual aids, or a visual aid room should be available. Normally motion pictures are not advisable below the age of ten or twelve, although there are some exceptional ones prepared for the younger ages.

Above the third grade it may be wise to organize the classes, with officers to conduct business, to take the attendance, and to hear reports from the student council. Each class has a representative on the student council.

JUNIOR HIGH

The seventh, eighth, and ninth grades make a natural unit in themselves. In the flush of early adolescence, children of these grades share pretty much the same problems. In communities that have junior

[3] See John Leslie Lobingier, *The Better Church School,* pp. 20-21.

high schools, such a department fits into the scheme of things. But some communities still operate on older or unique systems, and it may be advisable to follow the secular system.

No matter how the ages are divided, this is the crucial age period for most church schools. During this time the boys and girls normally make a confession of faith, accept believers' baptism, or are confirmed; they become communicants of the church. But it is also the time when parental discipline begins to lag, indifference to religion may begin, and drop-outs are common. The instability of a youngster during this period has something to do with it: he tends to follow the peer group formed outside the church. Often the group in the church is not his natural neighborhood or school group, and therefore he has no interests in common with it.

A separate department, organized in terms of the needs of this age group and enlisting their full participation, is the administrative answer. They may retain their interest in a family worship service, but in churches without this unity of devotion they should have a separate service of their own. Fortunate is the school that has a high school department to which they may look forward, for custom has much to do with their decision to remain.

Chiefly, however, the solution is found in the calibre of leadership and the nature of the curriculum. Their interests center in themselves, and yet they are not fully vocal when it comes to expressing their real concerns. They still are dealing with concrete problems and are not at home with either abstract ideas or events that do not concern them directly. The church has many tasks boys and girls of this age can do, and good administration, with a little guidance and much patience, will point them in the right direction. Classes should be organized, projects should be planned that will capture their interests between Sundays, and they should be given tasks in the worship service.

This age group often has its own Sunday evening fellowship. It should supplement the church school activities and not replace them. It serves to provide additional activities, to form the group into a more enduring fellowship (especially if they attend different schools during the week), and gives them the opportunity for a fuller exploration of their problems. Summer camps and conferences are open to junior high boys and girls, and increased loyalty to the whole church of Christ as well as to the local parish is usually the result. The financial problem of attending these camps and conferences can often be solved by activities sponsored by the young people themselves.

Chiefly, this group needs to believe that they are fully accepted in the church. The way instruction for church membership is handled helps to achieve the feeling of belonging, but the problem is deeper than that. Unless the members of the congregation accept these boys and girls as they are and include them within the community, they will fall by the wayside no matter how well they are organized.

SENIOR HIGH

In most communities this is the tenth, eleventh, and twelfth grades, but sometimes it concludes the ninth and in rare instances the eighth. John Leslie Lobingier reports a survey that shows 50 per cent of the churches planning for this age group and holding them, although some churches do not count it when the boys and girls shift to the young people's program in the evening.[4] In some instances, the evening program is as well-rounded as the morning one, and in overcrowded church schools this is one solution to the problem of space; but more often the evening fellowship is not of the same value in terms of the sense of belonging to the total congregation, which is something youth needs.

Granted the desirability of a high school class in the church school and the presence of such a class in half of the churches, we face the problems of organization and administration. Boys and girls of this age need a responsible separateness from other boys and girls and a sense of full membership in the church. They need to do much of their own planning, and yet they want someone to fall back on as a resource person.

A small group may constitute only one class. Larger congregations may have a number of classes divided by grades. In a few cases boys and girls have been separated successfully, but normally at this age they want to be together. The department should be organized on the same pattern as the younger ones. Excellent curriculum materials are available for this age, and often it is possible to provide elective courses. In some cases, classes are made up in terms of interests rather than grades. One of the most successful means of holding high school students' interest is a teacher training course during the last year or two, and in some instances this has continued for a year beyond high

[4] See *The Better Church School*, p. 24.

school. This provides a constant stream of trained young people who can begin to teach when they become sufficiently mature. (By all means, high school students should never teach a class!)

The main problem of the church is to understand the needs of the high school age. They like to make their own decisions, but they lack the resources and imagination to see what might be accomplished. The initial group already in the church is the starting point. They may be in the church school, in a youth group, in the choir, or in the regular congregation. We begin where they are, and as they find their purpose within the total community their activities lead to the groups they need.

No two parishes are alike. Some groups meet on weekday evenings in order to have at least two hours for discussion. Others would not miss the family worship service or the regular morning service, and they plan their class sessions accordingly. Others set up a full-fledged school in combination with their Sunday evening activities, meeting for three hours at a time.

In any youth group, the principles of organization are clear. They should have as much freedom to direct themselves as possible, combined with the resources of adult guidance. They should know what the adult rules and limitations are at the very beginning, and they should know the reasons for them. The purpose of the group should be clearly known and be acceptable to the members. They should be represented on the church school council and possibly on the official board or board of Christian education. They should have some choice in the selection of their meeting place and of the times it is available.

In a large group consisting of several classes, a youth council should have over-all control within the agreed-upon limits. They should be helped to work out a well-rounded program that includes recreation. Where they have their own departmentalized worship and in the worship at their evening meetings, their own worship committee should plan and conduct the service, although if they wish it, the pastor and others might be invited to participate.[5]

If these essentials are adhered to in the organization and administration of a youth department, the boys and girls will know that they are accepted in the congregation. But what is more important, they will see that religion as their church represents it involves the whole of their lives and not just an adult-dominated Sunday morning program.

---

[5] See Dorothy M. Roberts, *Leadership of Teen-Age Groups* (New York: Association Press, 1950), pp. 42-45, 61-64.

YOUTH GROUPS

Youth fellowships are often set up for both junior high and senior high boys and girls. The basic principles of organization for their classes in church school apply also to the youth groups, although in the latter there is a larger place for self-government and a wider program of recreation along with study, worship, and service.

The best youth groups combine the greatest amount of self-government with the most painstaking supervision. The basic principle for the adult leader is to be a resource person who is fully trusted by the young people. They need help when they ask for it, and yet they resent advice and imposed planning by adults.

Advance planning by the executive committee is essential. Good programs do not just happen but are the result of careful consideration of interests, goals, and procedures. In some cases, the executive committee and the advisors have a one- or two-day meeting before the beginning of the fall season, and at the first meeting they have a general plan for the year ready to submit for the approval of the entire membership. Many of the suggestions may have come from the advisors, but by the time they reach the constituency they belong to the executive committee. Most denominations prepare manuals to guide their young people, and these can be the starting point for specific plans.

Subcommittees on worship, study, service, and recreation plan the specific details of each meeting and take responsibility for carrying out their part of the program. They also take the same responsibility in relation to any weekday activities of the group.

The young people need to participate not only in the planning and leadership but also in the actual procedures. What we have said about group procedures, buzz groups, and full participation in discussions is extremely effective with high school young people, and often works well with junior high boys and girls after they learn how to enter into the more dynamic procedures of learning.[6]

If the numbers are large enough, the fellowships might be divided into three: seventh and eighth grades, ninth and tenth grades, eleventh and twelfth grades. When tenth graders or those younger are included in a single fellowship of high school age, the eleventh and twelfth

[6] See above, pp. 221-26.

graders tend to drop out. Smaller churches have a serious problem at this point, for when a group drops below a membership of six or eight it is likely to vanish, and yet there is little in common between the fourteen-year-old and the seventeen-year-old. One answer is to combine the youth groups of three smaller churches, with each parish taking one of the three divisions of the junior and senior high ages; but this has the drawback of failing to incorporate the youth into the life of a single parish.

The youth groups in the local parish reach out in various directions. Their program may expand to meet needs in the community, especially if the community as a whole has failed to provide an outlet for their energy. They are often tied in closely with other youth projects in the community, and they expect the parish to back them up in this co-operation. Often an active youth division of the local council of churches enlists their interest. They are drawn into state and national offices in the youth movements of their own denomination; they attend church summer camps and conferences; they are tied in with the United Christian Youth Movement; they have attended sections of the World Council of Churches. The Methodist Youth Caravans have trained thousands of youngsters for special service to the church during the summer. Work camps have become popular.

When all possible activities of youth are brought under a single pattern within the congregation, centered in a subcommittee on youth work made up mostly of young people and related directly to the board of Christian education, the two-fold goal will be within the realm of possibility: the young people will feel that they are full-fledged members of the redemptive community in the local parish, and they will be free to be themselves within the structure of specific groups and activities that are theirs.

OLDER YOUNG PEOPLE AND YOUNG ADULTS

From the standpoint of age, older young people and young adults are the group out of high school and under 25. Psychologically, they are quite different groups.

Older young people are those who have not taken on the responsibilities of adulthood; they may still be in school but are living within the radius of the parish; they may be working but are still living at home.

Young adults are those who are self-supporting, living away from their parents, married and without children, or, in some parishes, young parents.

The older young people are usually those who have grown up in the parish. The young adults include old parishioners and those who have moved to a new locality. The interests of these two groups are quite different. Older young people sometimes like to hang on in the high school fellowship or class, whereas young adults have found a new orientation.

There is no reason why both groups should not be in the church school, with regular classes, or why there should not be fellowship groups for them. Except in the smallest churches, no attempt should be made to mix them. Individuals who are not clearly in one group or the other will gravitate to the one of their choice.

Although both groups are capable of serious study and discussion, their interests are sufficiently different to require separate lesson materials and different weekday activities. Both should be organized on the fellowship basis, with their own officers and planning committees, and both need resources provided by the leadership of the parish. Once they have been helped with their planning and programing, and have developed leadership for handling their discussions and activities, little supervision is needed. But good leadership does not always emerge in such groups, or older leadership hangs on too long. Rules for rotation of officers and for retirement from the group at a certain age help. Inclusion in the leadership training program and on the board of Christian education helps even more, for it is in sharing the educational philosophy and methods of the parish that the group finds its way to becoming effective in meeting the needs of its members.

College young people pose a special problem. They normally leave home to attend college and during the school year are lost to the church except for vacation periods. On the other hand, many parishes are in towns where junior colleges, colleges, and universities are located and, therefore, have a number of college students in the congregation.

The program for college students who have left home is a simple one. The church should notify the college pastor, should keep in touch with its members away at college, and should have some kind of celebration for them during the holidays. The students normally affiliate with the Wesley Foundation, Westminster Foundation, Canterbury Club, or other group of their choice on the campus or at a nearby church.

College students in the congregation may be incorporated in the program for older young people, or if the numbers justify it, they may become a separate class in the church school and fellowship in the church. Parishes close to a campus without a college chaplain of their own denomination are often affiliated with the national department of college work and have their own special organization.

COUPLES AND PARENTS

The interests of unmarried young adults and young couples are often so different that their combination is not successful. Young couples have an orientation of their own, and they do not always find that the church speaks to their needs. They are potential or actual parents, and they have responsibilities and needs that stand out as unique in their experience. They need fellowship with others in their own situation within the framework of the church. Above all, they need the resources of the Christian faith in reference to their own problems.

There should be a fellowship group for young couples, where there is similarity of age, length of marriage, age of children, and intellectual and cultural outlooks. They should pursue guidance to meet their fundamental problems. The curriculum should emerge from these problems and should not be imposed by fixed lessons on any subject. Dynamic principles of teaching under the leadership of members of their own group should be used.[7]

When family worship is the custom, a parents' class or several of them may be held at the same time as the children's classes. Parents and children worship together and then proceed to their own discussions. The couples' groups may also have a weekly or monthly evening meeting based on their mutual fellowship and interests with a program much wider than the Sunday morning discussions.

Out of such classes come informed parents who are willing to accept assignments as officers and teachers in the church school. Sometimes a young couples' group will accept certain responsibilities for the

[7] See George Gleason, *Church Activities for Young Couples* (New York: Association Press, 1949), p. 85.

nursery or kindergarten, and a class of older parents will work with the teachers and children in the departments ministering to their children. Many couples will take over a class as a husband-and-wife team.

Smaller churches may have only one parents' class and corresponding couples' club. Larger churches may provide classes for parents on various bases. Some use the combined ages of husband and wife, with the youngest couples' group being those whose combined ages total less than 50, the next less than 70, the next less than 90. Others do it by the age of the youngest child, but gives the parents the option of choosing a group or class according to the age of any of their children. There will always be some overlapping. In one church, the married couples were divided as follows: Young Couples, age 20–28; Home Builders, age 25–35; Fidelis Class, age 30–48; Wesleyans, age 40–60.

Each had been organized as a young couples' group and had kept together through the years. There was a place for everyone concerned primarily with marriage and children.

Wesner Fallaw provides a warning at this point. Many parents' groups duplicate what can be provided through secular agencies in child guidance and parental education. This is not the purpose of church groups for parents. The church should be free to help parents face the serious and difficult problems of Christian education guidance, making use of the best findings of child psychology, of child-adult relationships, and of barriers in child development within the perspective of Christian faith. The point of concern is the Christian nurture of children, and anything that contributes to this is a valid topic of study.[8] One approach that has provided help is to attack a problem of Christian living from the parents' perspective and, after they see the relevance of this aspect of the Christian faith, to attack the same problem from the perspective of their children.

James D. Smart writes:

> One of the significant discoveries where parents have been awakened to their educational responsibilities is that they become keenly aware of their own inadequacies and begin to make more use of their opportunities for gaining a better understanding of their faith. It is when a person undertakes to teach that he learns how little he himself knows, and many things that he has taken for granted must be care-

[8] Wesner Fallaw, *The Modern Parent and the Teaching Church* (New York: The Macmillan Company, 1946), pp. 67-72.

fully re-examined. Thus, a recovery of the true Christian order of the home is likely to have as one result the sparking of an adult education movement that could reach very large proportions.[9]

A democratic organization, with elected officers, helps the couples' clubs and classes to operate smoothly. Often the leadership is provided by a couple who have a particularly rich background. George Gleason lists the occupations of 389 teachers of couples' groups, and 169 of them represented professions or trades in which teaching was not an element.[10] The church's leadership training program helps at this point. These groups should be represented on the board of Christian education, and their interests should be specifically considered in a subcommittee on adult education or, in cases where the organization is more complex, in a subcommittee on couples' and parents' groups.

ADULTS

In thousands of parishes the largest and most consistently attended church school class is for adults. In most cases these are Bible classes, taught by a lay person who knows the contents of the Bible and who lectures in an interesting manner for the full session. In some cases, these classes are so popular that they are broadcast. The numbers attending rival that of the morning congregation, and in many cases they are the same people. A large parish may have from 5 to 20 such classes meeting during Sunday school. The curriculum is derived from the International Bible Lessons (uniform series), special adult forum materials, and elective courses.

These Bible classes have an inherent value, for they have been the means whereby the content of the Bible has been made relevant to life. Their continuing popularity indicates that a need is being met and that this is more than simply an absorbing of content. In some cases, however, they have been the occasion of disputation, with arguments over Biblical scholarship, or they have been irrelevant to life's problems. Christian decisions do not follow automatically from knowledge of the content of the Scriptures.

---

[9] From *The Teaching Ministry of the Church,* by James D. Smart, The Westminster Press, Philadelphia. Copyright by W. L. Jenkins, 1954, p. 185. See also Paul H. Vieth, *The Church and Christian Education* (St. Louis: Bethany Press, 1947), pp. 188-89.

[10] *Church Activities for Young Couples,* pp. 47-49.

Adults need knowledge of the Bible, but they need it in the context of their own situations. Malcolm S. Knowles suggests that they need to acquire a mature understanding of themselves, an attitude of love and acceptance toward others, a dynamic attitude toward life, ability to react to the causes rather than the symptoms of behavior, skills to achieve the potentialities of their personalities, knowledge of the values inherent in the past, and understanding of their society and the changes needed to improve it.[11] The Bible is relevant to all of this as men come to a deeper understanding of the Gospel.

Part of the educational value of the adult group comes from its organization and administration. The adult group should be incorporated into the educational philosophy of the board of Christian education. The subcommittee on adult work should include representatives from the adult classes and study groups, plus those from the women's, men's, missionary, and other organizations. A planning committee of the adult division of the church school should work on a program to meet the needs of the adults attending classes.

Although smaller churches have one or two adult classes, and larger churches have many more, the members of the adult division should have final choice of areas of study. In some churches, there is a preference for separate men's and women's classes, or for classes according to age, or for classes according to courses elected. Some groups prefer to remain stable in membership, following their own selections within the scope of the educational policies of the parish, and new groups are formed as the need arises. In other situations, groups re-form after an agreed-upon period and divide according to the electives they have chosen.

The fixed groups usually prefer to keep their teacher on a permanent basis, although officers change each year. When groups are flexible, new leadership needs to be discovered for each series of courses, although frequently it is discovered within the group when group procedures are used for attacking the problems.[12]

The adult classes appeal both to the couples and parents and to adults acting as individuals. In every church there are individuals who have no family ties, members of families who attend alone, and

---

[11] See Malcolm S. Knowles, *Informal Adult Education* (New York: Association Press, 1950), pp. 9-10.

[12] See *How to Teach Adults* (Greenwich: Seabury Press, 1951), for an excellent pamphlet on group procedures and leadership.

husbands and wives who prefer separated classes. These people, who are no longer young adults and are not interested in the couples' and parents' groups, make up the adult division. In some parishes all adults will be grouped together, but in others the concern for the ministry of parenthood will require a separate division and a special subcommittee of the board of Christian education for parents as a special kind of adults. The important administrative problem is to make sure that all adults are ministered to.

Some churches have evening forums and midweek services that are a form of adult education. All parishes have women's groups, and many have men's groups. In each of these is to be found an educational program. They need to be brought into the over-all unity of the comprehensive educational program of the congregation.

OLDER ADULTS

It is estimated that there will be twenty million adults over the age of 65 in the United States by 1970. The churches are beginning to see the importance of a special program for this age group. They often come to church, and they may belong to one of the midweek groups that has grown older through the years, but a policy of administration and organization is usually lacking.

The program for older adults should be different from that of other age-groups. Many of them are retired and in good health. They need activities and interests to help them understand their particular situation. They need to handle their own organization and to be represented on the subcommittee on adult work.

Some of them enjoy the elective system by which they may join any group to work on a problem of their own choice. Others like to stay with their own group and continue the traditional Bible class pattern. Others prefer their own group, but like to explore new patterns of education. In larger churches all of these options may be provided. In smaller churches one adult class includes all ages, or at best there is one group under 65 and another group over that age.

Some kind of transportation pool is often advisable for churches located some distance from their constituency, and some older adults need transportation for short distances.

An activities program for older adults provides what they need most: knowledge that they can be useful. They have been known to write to those facing difficulties, to keep track of newspaper stories about the church and to write the editors about them, to attend meetings relating to civic welfare, to act as baby-sitters for young parents, to call on the shut-ins, to become "foster grandparents" to children in the congregation, to check the quality of magazines, comics, and paper-back books on the newsstands, and to promote their own group in the church.[13]

THE HANDICAPPED AND SHUT-INS

Many parishes have a special home department to carry the program of Christian education to those who are unable to attend church or church school regularly. Besides the handicapped and shut-ins, this occasionally includes those who have occupations that demand Sunday work. The staff includes a superintendent, secretary, and home visitors or teachers. Each teacher is assigned to not more than ten pupils, to whom he takes magazines, lesson materials, and other educational resources. In the case of an invalid child, he may teach a lesson or leave the material for the parents to teach. Most of the shut-ins are adults, and monthly or quarterly calls are made. Sometimes tape-recorded services are taken to their homes.

Although shut-ins cannot get to the normal church services, many of them can get to a special meeting at a convenient time. Those who are sensitive about their wheel chairs and crutches do not mind if others in the same situation are present, and the elderly people come together for a special service just for them. They are helped to church by relatives and volunteers, and often this trip is their only outing for that period of time.

FOR ALL AGES

What of the small church school? Throughout the land are isolated churches with only a few members. If 25 children and adults show up on Sunday, they think it must be Easter! In some denominations, over two thirds of the church schools have enrollments of under 100.

Certain principles of organization stand out. Small classes are best, and they are the easiest to teach even if they meet in a single assembly

---

[13] See Willard A. Pleuthner, *More Power for Your Church* (New York: Farrar, Straus & Young, 1952), pp. 125-138.

room. Five classes of from four to seven students each, classified into groups as close together in school grade as possible, work with an enrollment of 25. With 50 pupils, ten classes provide fairly accurate grading. With 80 pupils, school grades can be followed through the junior high, with one class for senior high, and one for adults or parents. Departmental superintendents are not necessary until an enrollment of about 100 is reached.

No matter how small or how large the enrollment in educational activities may be, there is need for a unified philosophy of education as developed by a responsible board of Christian education and functioning through the administration to meet the needs of all the members. How the boards and committees are telescoped in smaller churches is a matter of indifference, provided the functioning is efficient.

Most churches today will find themselves large enough to administer a full program if they put it in action, for the number of lapsed children, indifferent or untouched parents, and potential students among the adults is great enough to increase substantially the number of students.

The really large parishes, with their staff of ministers and director of Christian education, need to multiply the number of committees, classes, and teachers in order to meet adequately the needs of those already in their program.

But numbers, large or small, are not the important element. Each individual is significant because he is a child of God, and he is to be drawn into the congregation of faithful people who by their quality of life will be channels of God's grace. Administration exists only to make more effective the proclaiming of the Gospel and to make clear its relevance in the relationships of everyday living, providing the hope of redemption and salvation as we are justified by faith through grace.

CHAPTER 20

VACATION AND WEEKDAY CHURCH SCHOOLS; CAMPS AND CONFERENCES

THE VACATION church school program has grown rapidly since it began sometime around the turn of the century.[1] But in too many cases it has been isolated from the over-all educational program of the church. It is a vacation *church* school, and like the Sunday *church* school or the weekday *church* school it is part of the program of the parish to meet the needs of its people.

The vacation church school is the church in action, teaching boys and girls to know the love of Christ in their everyday lives. The experience of fellowship in the church during vacation time is geared specifically to the needs and activities of the children, showing them in unmistakable ways how they are members of the redemptive community.

The chief asset of the vacation church school is that if it runs for three hours a day for two five-day weeks, it provides 30 hours of instruction, as much as a whole year of Sunday school. It may run for a longer period of time, and the build-up and carry-over of consecutive sessions have great educational value. The three-hour sessions customary in most schools make possible types of activity not available to the short classes on Sundays, and the flexibility of the program provides as much time as necessary for a particular activity. Because the vacation church school is not bound by traditions, it may make experiments in Christian education that are frowned upon in Sunday church school. It may make use of professional leadership from the

[1] See Paul H. Vieth, *The Church and Christian Education* (St. Louis: Bethany Press, 1947), p. 34.

public schools. The pastor is more free to cooperate than in the wintertime educational activities. Above all, it has great evangelistic value, bringing in the unchurched children and introducing them to a vital and interesting series of Christian activities.

Some people see the value of the vacation church school as the answer to juvenile delinquency. During the summer months, the abundance of leisure time opens up possibilities for all kinds of random activities by bored children and young people, and many of these are destructive. The vacation church school provides a live alternative in terms of developing hobbies, crafts, participation in music and art and nature study, and learning through discussion.

Parents send their children for a variety of reasons. Parents who are church members see the value of the program and desire the good things it offers their children. Parents who are afraid of the Sunday sessions because of the requirements of good clothes and a certain "Protestant respectability" are willing for their children to attend weekday sessions in play clothes. Parents who are desperate to find something for their children to do send them in order to get rid of them. Children often come of their own accord and are incorporated into the life of the church in spite of their parents' indifference.

ORGANIZATION

There are four types of vacation church schools.

Type 1 is run by a local parish. It serves its own constituency and its own neighborhood. Its board of Christian education sets the policy, personnel, and curriculum, and arranges the financial details.

Type 2 is run by two or more parishes of the same denomination. The boards of Christian education of the cooperating parishes work together to supervise the program, which may be carried on in a single church or be divided by departments among the several churches.

Type 3 is run by two or more parishes of different denominations, and is often sponsored by an interdenominational board. Various churches throughout the city are used as the need arises. The budget is raised on a pro rata basis, and the board supervises the personnel, curriculum, and maintenance of the program.

Type 4 is unrelated to the churches, and ministers to various unchurched areas, rural districts, urban centers, and housing areas. Its motivation is primarily missionary, and it seeks unchurched children.

In some cases such groups work under the jurisdiction of the local council of churches, but in others they are independent groups.[2]

Each of these groups has its values. In larger cities all four types may be going on during the summer, and correlation is essential to avoid overlapping and duplication. Other organizations in the community working with children and youth need to be consulted so that the whole summer program of all agencies will most effectively serve the community. The vacation church school, when it is oriented to the needs of the community, makes use of the experiences provided by all other agencies as a basis for its own program.

Paul H. Vieth suggests the conditions that must be fulfilled:

> 1. The curriculum should fit in with the total church program in Christian education as part of a long-term policy.
> 2. It must last long enough to do the job. A five- or six-week period is more effective than a one- or two-week term.
> 3. A competent staff of workers should be in charge. They should be paid for their work.
> 4. The budget for the vacation church school should be part of the parish budget of Christian education.
> 5. The pastor should be involved in the program. This is one of his greatest opportunities to minister to the children.
> 6. When the program is interdenominational in nature, the students should have an opportunity to become acquainted with all the parishes involved.[3]

The principles of grading depend on the enrollment. Large schools may be divided into departments, with the grades based on school grades. The children will like it better if they are in the grade they will enter the following autumn. Smaller schools may have two-year or three-year spans in their classes. Some schools are limited to elementary grades, whereas others include junior and senior high and even adults.

The program should include worship, fellowship and play, creative activities, and study. Close cooperation between departments is often necessary in order to plan for specific activities. For instance, a motion picture planned for two departments of older children may require the use of the larger room normally occupied by the primary department or kindergarten. Breaks for use of the rest rooms should be stag-

---

[2] See *How to Plan and Conduct a Vacation Church School* (Chicago: International Council of Religious Education, 1947), p. 8.

[3] *The Church and Christian Education,* pp. 117-18.

gered. Groups may take turns using the gymnasium or church yard for play periods. The kindergarten should provide a snack period in the middle of the morning. Some schools begin with worship for the whole school; others have worship by groups at whatever time seems advisable. The main point is to have a flexible program, so that the routine from day to day will change with the needs and interests of the children. The continuity is provided by the day-to-day sessions, and the excellent units prepared especially for vacation church schools provide a unity of structure and a basis for achievement.

The closing program has special value. Drawing the parents together to see what has happened, the closing session may be a sample of what happens each day, an exhibit of handwork, a dramatization of the unit of study, a family supper and group demonstrations, or whatever emerges from the term's work and play together that the children prefer. Exploitation of the children and spotlighting of individuals should be avoided.[4]

Vacation church schools need good administration. A subcommittee of the board of Christian education, whether it is the subcommittee on children's work or a special group chosen for the task, should have the responsibility for organizing, promoting, financing, and supervising the program. Assisting them should be a group of parents, who are concerned not only with the total program but also with the ways in which parents can cooperate.

Adequate publicity within the parish, coming early enough to influence summer plans of families, is possible through the bulletin, announcements, parents' class, and student parish council. Posters, stories in the newspaper, and letters to parents of prospective students from the neighborhood should appear about a month before the opening.

Unless there is a competing school in the community, as in the type 1 organization, a neighborhood canvass is important for finding the unchurched children. Canvassers should be trained, although children may be instructed to seek out their friends.

Adequate leadership should be enlisted far enough in advance to guarantee adequate preparation and any special training that is needed. Normally a school needs a supervisor or director, preferably a trained educator. A public school teacher or official is often available during

---

[4] See *How to Plan and Conduct a Vacation Church School,* pp. 16-31 for suggestions for program, and pp. 33-35 for a list of resource materials.

the summer months. Larger schools need department superintendents. Enough teachers to provide a teacher and an assistant for each eight or ten children in the kindergarten, for each ten or twelve primary children, and for each twelve to fifteen juniors make up the teaching staff. There is need for an adequate secretarial and library staff. Especially when the staff is paid, it is not hard to find teachers among public school teachers, college and seminary students, church school teachers, and parents. There should be time for several staff meetings and for a leadership training program during the last month or two before the session begins.

The ideal way of financing the vacation church school is to place it in the parish budget. Sometimes the parish underwrites the entire cost, and at other times they begin by accepting partial responsibility. Other groups within the parish may desire to contribute to the school as part of their service to the community. Secular organizations in the community are likely to help support interdenominational schools. Some schools charge tuition, but this depends upon the financial status of the parents. Scholarships are sometimes provided for those in the community who otherwise could not attend tuition-supported schools. Some schools charge for materials, but the cost of salaries and maintenance is covered by other means. A free-will offering at the closing session sometimes defrays some of the expenses, but there is no guarantee that such an offering will underwrite the budget.[5]

Because of the community nature of the vacation church school, its size does not contribute to its effectiveness. Small churches and meetings in farmhouses with a few children can follow the same basic principles laid down here. After adaptations are made for the limitations of space, much can be accomplished with a two-department school meeting in a one-room parish house.

In rural areas, vacation church school schedules must be correlated with the harvesting of crops. One approach is to have a mobile staff that spends the summer in a rural area, planning vacation church schools for times when the children are not needed on the farms. A centrally located farmhouse or church is used for the children in one area for as long a period as possible, and then the team moves with its equipment to another location. With careful planning, a whole area may be covered during the summer. A similar system may be used in a group of small towns that lack their own resources. Such a plan

---

[5] See *How to Plan and Conduct a Vacation Church School,* p. 12.

may be worked out for a denomination or on an interdenominational basis.

Vacation church schools tend to become permanent. They may start with a two-week experiment, but the schools become popular and demand for a longer session appears. The same children return summer after summer. Therefore, it is essential that plans be on a long-term basis, be tied in with the curriculum of the Sunday church school, and be worked out in terms of the needs of the community. Permanent records should be kept on all students, and reports should be made to the boards of Christian education of the cooperating parishes and to parents.

THE WEEKDAY CHURCH SCHOOL

A solution to the problem of religion in the schools has been sought in weekday released-time religious education. The program, as it works out in most states, calls for voluntary classes based on enrollment by parents. It uses no public school buildings or funds, but requires a minimum of cooperation and coordination in order to make it work effectively. There have been many variations in the plan, some providing courses for credit and using public school buildings and others being more independent of the public schools. Attempts have been made to use dismissed time (all children are dismissed and those who wish go to religious classes) and free time (after school hours), but normally some form of released time (with other children remaining in school) has been most widespread.

Sometimes these programs are set up on a denominational basis, with each church taking its own children, but this has limitations of transportation and personnel and often develops into an interfaith program. This latter is the most widely used approach. Roman Catholics, Jews, and Protestants combine to form an interfaith committee. They work with each other, with the school board, and with the principals of the schools to develop a mutually satisfactory program. The Protestant organization works together to provide curriculum, personnel, buildings and equipment, promotion and publicity, and adequate financing. A great deal of preparatory work is necessary, and normally it takes a year or more before the machinery is running smoothly enough to make a start on sound principles.

In some instances the Protestants are divided into two or more groups who feel that they cannot cooperate for theological reasons.

Unless these difficulties are overcome, it may be necessary to have two competing Protestant systems. Occasionally one denomination will insist on having its private classes on the same basis as the Protestant program. This needs to be worked out in the Protestant committee and then with the school board and principals.

Classes are held in nearby churches or homes. Location is a serious matter because of the schedule, and pupils should be able to walk to classes in not more than five minutes, although in the case of large campuses ten minutes may be necessary. Large rumpus rooms in homes are often as well lighted and equipped as parish house rooms.

The staff should be selected with care. A director or supervisor of the program should be competent in administration, education, and the Christian faith. The teachers should be equal in competence and training to the public school teachers. The salaries should be sufficient to entice teachers of high quality and devotion. It should be noted that some systems have met these standards, but that others have sought to get by with amateurs, seminarians, church school teachers, and others who will work for low or no pay. The greatest percentage of failures has come from the unwise selection of personnel and low budget figures.

In *The Church and Christian Education,* Paul H. Vieth writes, "We may predict that if the Protestant church is not willing to furnish an adequately trained and adequately paid teaching force for weekday schools of religion, it will lose this great opportunity through neglect and inefficiency. We venture to suggest that if we could give more assurance at the point of salary and security we might recruit an increasing number of trained and experienced public school teachers for work in the weekday school. With a minimum of training and with skillful supervision, these teachers would prove to be most effective." [6] This is also true of ex-school teachers who have been freed of the responsibility of their small children and wish to return to their vocation in the service of the church. Because so few women are being trained in theological seminaries, there will be a shortage of competent weekday teachers of religion unless imaginative recruiting is combined with adequate pay and security.

The economical use of teachers depends on the time pupils are released. When all pupils are excused at the same hour, a large staff

---

[6] Paul H. Vieth, *The Church and Christian Education* (St. Louis: Bethany Press, 1947), pp. 202-3.

is required for one hour of teaching, and therefore no salaried full-time teachers are possible. When students are released at different hours in the various schools (the staggered schedule), teachers on a full-time basis go from school to school. A few teachers may still be needed on a "spot" basis, but the main impact falls on the full-time staff.

Curriculum poses difficult problems. The pupils come from all churches, each one of which has its own emphasis for different years, and the first problem is to discover how to avoid duplication. Many of these youngsters are active and alert and well educated in the Christian faith, and they need supplementary materials. Others have attended church school only spasmodically, and they need to have the gaps in their learning filled in. As many as one third have had no church connection and must start from the beginning.

The weekday church schools do not always reflect an awareness of these varying needs. Some systems have adopted the best materials of the Methodists, Pilgrim Series, Scripture Press Series, Cloister Series, or some other Sunday publication and therefore duplicate the material of one denomination. Other systems have their own curriculum, sometimes developed by the state council of churches as in New York or Virginia. Others use the Cooperative Series of Weekday Church School Texts, which are the development of many cooperating denominations.

Enrollment is promoted through the usual publicity channels. Because it is an interfaith operation (although the Jews usually do not hold classes), newspaper publicity helps at the beginning of each school term. Churches make appeals to their own constituencies. The parents of unchurched children are reached through letters and phone crews. As the program grows, enrollment often hits as high as 90 per cent of the children in the grades affected.

Weekday church schools are an expensive proposition. If they pay adequate salaries, provide for pensions, cover transportation for teachers and sometimes a bus system for pupils, buy good texts, cover the costs of buildings, heating, lighting, and janitorial service, and keep classes down to an efficient size, the cost per pupil may run as high as ten or twelve dollars per year, although some systems run for about a dollar per pupil per year. If good standards are maintained and paid for, the cost will be at least five dollars per pupil per year.[7]

---

[7] See Erwin L. Shaver, "The Weekday Church School," in *Orientation in Religious Education,* ed. Philip Henry Lotz, p. 276.

In communities with many children and struggling churches, this cost is almost prohibitive; but unless the budget can be underwritten it is dangerous to make a false start. The most widely recommended procedure is for the churches to accept quotas on the basis of their over-all or local-church expense budgets. A community-wide campaign may supplement this, and an appeal to parents may add to the total, but the chief responsibility lies with the cooperating churches. Charging for tuition or texts is usually not wise.

Although weekday religious instruction does not solve the problem of teaching religion in the public schools, it is a valuable instrument. It brings religion into close psychological relationship with secular instruction, and therefore the student may understand that religion is part of his daily living and not just a Sunday activity. It increases the effectiveness of Sunday school teaching by providing more time during the week and by releasing the Sunday school to teach the denominational aspects of the faith. The educational standards are normally higher than in many church schools in terms of teaching standards, texts, and equipment. This, in turn, stimulates many church schools to reach such standards. It has great missionary value, which to many churches is in itself worth the relatively high cost of operation, and it draws many of its unchurched pupils into the church. The church that holds the class has an advantage at this point. It symbolizes for the parents some aspects of their responsibility for the Christian education of their children. The Protestant cooperation in most systems provides a taste of the ecumenical movement at the grass roots level, and the fact that a curriculum acceptable to all the cooperating churches is in operation emphasizes our common Biblical heritage. The interfaith aspect of cooperation does not often reach down to the pupils, although they are aware that the other pupils have classes at the same time.[8]

The legal question is generally agreed to have been solved. Objections are in terms of discrimination, especially against Jews or atheists, or in terms of an extreme theory of the separation of church and state. The first objection is met in many systems by an adequate interpretation of interfaith relations and a study of interfaith customs of worship and practice, thus using the existing segregation as a means of relevant teaching. The second objection was answered by the Supreme

[8] See Paul H. Vieth, *The Church and Christian Education,* pp. 38-40.

Court decision that when the proper conditions are met, weekday released time religious instruction is part of the American way of life.[9]

CAMPS AND CONFERENCES

There are many types of camps and conferences held during the summer or at other periods throughout the year. They are for all ages, reach many different groups, have a variety of programs, and all make an impact on the parishes from which the people come.

A camp may be distinguished from a conference as follows: the camp utilizes an outdoor setting, with tents and cabins, and makes the experience of group living in this setting the primary curriculum. A conference may use an outdoor setting, a conference center, a college, or a hotel, and the primary emphasis is on the enrichment of life through classes and living together. It is obvious that the two programs overlap, and that many camps are more like conferences, institutes, or assemblies. Training, enrichment, and fellowship are the goals of both movements.

Church camping is relatively recent and developed primarily from the effort to provide a suitable summer program for early adolescents. The most important contribution of the churches to the camping movement was their experience in coeducational camps for junior high students. It became in many denominations the most important single means of utilizing the capacities of the early teen-age groups. Successful camps have been held for juniors as well.

Although many of these camps are held for a period of days or weeks at camp sites some distance from the local church, often supported by the denomination in that area or by a group of parishes, many other kinds of camps have become popular, such as family camps, work camps, weekend camps, trip camps, and day camps. Camp sites are being provided ample space at many conference centers.

Summer meetings known as conferences, institutes, and assemblies have been held since Lake Chautauqua days. The emphasis has been on the training of young people and adults for leadership in the church. The central goal has been the imparting of information and skills

---

[9] See Erwin L. Shaver, "Weekday Religious Education Secures Its Charter and Faces a Challenge," *Religious Education* (January-February 1953), pp. 38-43; "Three Years after the Campaign Case," *Religious Education* (January-February 1951), pp. 33-38.

rather than group living as such, although most conferences are successful in terms of the latter as well. The programs have been expanded to include recreational facilities and organized games, with opportunities for democratic decisions and learning from each other. Many of the developments of the church camping movement occurred first as part of the conference movement, so that there has been a mutual influence between the two movements.

What happens to a local congregation when a large number of its people attend summer camps and conferences that are well conceived often approaches a miracle. Experiences in group living, dynamic discussion groups, courses on the content of the faith, leadership training, and worship lead to reborn people. Those who attend the camps and conferences are more devoted and more capable, and they frequently become the nucleus for new experiments and advances in the life of the congregation.

The local parish should consider the camping and conference program as an extension of its own educational program. Through the board of Christian education three major items are of importance: recruiting the right people to attend camps and conferences, providing personnel and financial help in the leadership of camps and conferences, utilizing the new enthusiasm, knowledge, skills, and devotion with which the people return from their camp and conference experiences.

A subcommittee on camping and conferences may be organized, or the responsibility may be turned over to some other subcommittee such as the one on leadership training. This group should be acquainted with all the opportunities open to its members, and should make these opportunities widely known throughout the congregation. It should work on recruiting of those who show potentialities for leadership, who need special help, or who will benefit the parish through the experience. It should provide scholarship help for those who need it, and in some cases it may set up special programs of assigning scholarships. Members of the subcommittee should be available to work on the boards of directors of the camping and conference program of the community, diocese, synod, state, or whatever the unit of organization may be. Outstanding leaders in the parish may be made known to the board of directors so that they may be recruited for the camp and conference program. Whenever it is required, the parish budget may include a special quota to assist financially in the operation of the program. All of this cooperation has no particular value for the local congregation unless the subcommittee on camps and conferences takes pains to incorporate the findings and experiences of those attending into the life of the parish. A program should be administered to guarantee that the new insights will be made available to the rest of the congregation, that new leaders will emerge, and that the spirit of the parish will be affected. Some parishes have been able to set up their own parish programs and purchase their own property for the purpose.[10]

CONCLUSION

No congregation ever has time enough for Christian education. Often it misses some of the best opportunities, such as those offered by the vacation church school, the weekday released time church school, and the camp and conference program. These should be seen as extensions of the parish program, and therefore they should be incorporated into the educational policies and structure of the congregation. They are not extras, but are essential parts of the over-all program.

---

[10] See Clarice M. Bowman, *Spiritual Values of Camping* (New York: Association Press, 1954), for one of the best books on the entire subject.

CHAPTER 21

RECRUITING AND TRAINING LEADERS

When Jesus talked about leadership, he said:

> You know that those who are supposed to rule the heathen lord it over them, and their great men tyrannize over them; but it is not to be so among you. Whoever wants to be great among you must be your servant, and whoever wants to hold first place among you must be everybody's slave. For the Son of Man himself has not come to be waited on, but to wait on other people, and to give his life to free many others (Mark 10:42-45, G).

Leaders in the church are called to greater service than others, and their responsibility is in terms of their aptitudes for meeting the needs of others. Not everyone is called to be a leader or a teacher in the church. It is a task that requires special qualifications, including the ability to communicate the Gospel by words and actions, to share the riches of Christian living through relationships, to acquire certain skills and techniques by which the group is stimulated to respond to the challenge of the Gospel, and to be the kind of a person through whom God's grace may be channeled to those for whom he is responsible. The leader or teacher is in the service of the Master and of those committed to his charge. He is not to "lord it" or "tyrannize" over them.

TEACHING TO CREATE FAITH

To teach is to communicate feelings, insights, attitudes, facts, and meanings. To have faith is to trust, to commit one's self, to decide, to be assured of things hoped for and to have convictions about the unseen. Teaching to create faith means sharing in a fellowship in which the members find it possible to trust each other and to join together in mutual trust in God.

Faith arises out of specific educational conditions, although it cannot be compelled by anything that we do. One has faith in his parents because they are trustworthy. Some homes provide an atmosphere in which grace flourishes, and faith comes naturally in such an environment. But there are no ideal social conditions, in home, church, school, or community, and many experiences thwart the development of faith or destroy it altogether. Relationships are broken and need to be healed through acts of forgiveness. The basic symbolism of the Christian faith turns on the "lost and found" motif of the Prodigal Son, or the "dead and alive again" theme of the Cross and Resurrection, or the "dead to sin and alive to righteousness" rhythm of Paul's letters. "Do not be conformed to this world," said Paul, "but be transformed by the renewal of your mind, that you may prove what is the will of God, what is good and acceptable and perfect" (Romans 12: 2, RSV).

The Christian home and the church are the two institutions seeking to make faith in the God of Jesus Christ a real possibility. Although the church ideally is a fellowship of the Spirit, in everyday experience it is a congregation of sinners whose relationships have been shattered by human selfishness. The church is a redemptive and sustaining community, in which the members stand in need of redemption through faith in Jesus Christ and seek at the same time to be channels of God's love through their ministry of reconciliation.

What has all of this to do with leadership in the church? The answer is, *everything*. Faith is created by God's grace as men respond to God's love within the fellowship of the Holy Spirit. All that men can do is to provide the atmosphere in which grace flourishes, using every technique and tool at their command, but realizing that though Paul and Apollos may do the planting and watering, it is always God who provides the increase. Growth in grace is never an educational procedure but is always due to the mysterious providence of Almighty God. Integration of personality in the maturity of Christian faith is never an achievement of teaching or leadership techniques, but is always the result of a personal relationship with God within the community of the faithful.

The teacher's religious task within the class is to seek to be a channel of God's grace, whereby the children find that they are loved and accepted as they are (not as some adult thinks they ought to be), they are within a structure of law, order, and discipline that is within their understanding and is somewhere near their growing edge, they are guided in growth at their own rate, and they are exposed to worship that is meaningful to them and that indicates that they are members of the total Christian community. Methods and lesson materials are simply tools by which these needs are answered, and they assist the teacher in his ministry of reconciliation.

The teacher's task within the church is to work for the children, so that the people will let the children come unto them. A congregation finds it hard to love childish and teen-age sinners, who combine their sinfulness with the pure cussedness of going through "stages." Yet if the life of the congregation fails to be a redemptive experience for its younger members, we can never teach to create faith within the class. All that we have said about family worship, parents' classes, preparation for the public baptism of infants, and the incorporation of young people into parish life witnesses to the fact that all ages are one in Christ.

The teacher's task in the home is to make meaningful the parents' cooperation. The child's developing faith depends primarily on his relationships in home and church, and his loyalty to these two fellowships is the crux of the matter if he is to live in terms of Christian faith among the manifold experiences of daily life. Because the home is the fellowship that commands most of his time, the young child is ministered to through his parents.

Teachers and other leaders need to understand the basic nature of Christian leadership operating within the faith-grace relationship. This means, as A. Victor Murray wrote, that "there is something to know, something to feel, something to choose, something to do, and something to belong to." [1] Because Christianity is historical, the facts of Biblical and Christian history and doctrine are essential to a full faith, but they have meaning only when they are lived within a congregation. The basic element in religion is its ability to capture the total personality, so that he knows, feels, worships, decides, joins, and acts. This historical covenant between God and man is found within the community of the covenant, based on the fact that "God so loved the world that he gave his only Son, that whoever believes on him should not perish but have eternal life" (John 3:16,RSV).

---

[1] A. Victor Murray, *Education into Religion* (New York: Harper & Brothers, 1954), p. 14.

There are no shortcuts to teaching to create faith. It is the total task of the entire congregation. Teachers and leaders alone are helpless to overcome the inertia and barriers of many congregations; pastors can do little unless there is at least a small group at work; but a little leaven may raise the whole lump. Christian education takes place when the quality of life is such that "the unsearchable riches of Christ" are mediated through the living faith of its members, and little children as well as adults find that they are being ministered to through a ministry of reconciliation that centers in Jesus Christ who is our Redeemer.[2]

THE NATURE OF LEADERSHIP

Because the development of faith is a shared experience, teachers and leaders need to be competent. This means that those who lead others must have an adequate grasp of the Bible, church history, and doctrine in terms of content and of its relevance for daily living. Even a kindergarten teacher who can communicate the faith only in simple words and actions must have an adult faith that is adequate for daily living. Every teacher is impressing a theology of some kind on his students, and therefore theological ignorance is inexcusable. This does not mean that he teaches doctrine as such, but that the implications of every interpretation of life have doctrinal significance.

The teacher or leader must hold intelligent Christian beliefs. Every teacher assumes that *his* beliefs are intelligent, but this must be judged by others whose competence is agreed upon. Many church school teachers do teach error; they are misinformed; they answer questions when they lack knowledge; they have been ignorant of the content of the Bible and the scholarship concerning it.

The teacher or leader must be capable of leadership. This involves the nature of his personality, his power to attract others to him, his clear insight into the nature of the problems of his students, his love of others, and his techniques and skills. Just as he can learn intelligent beliefs, so he can learn most of the techniques of good leadership. The potentiality must be present if he is to develop into a useful servant through his leadership of others.

The teacher must be worthy of admiration. As far as the response of children is concerned, this often involves trifles of dress, voice, mannerisms, and physical appearance. The fundamental elements of

---

[2] See "Teaching to Create Faith," *Baptist Leader* (October 1954), pp. 5, 16.

character are decisive. When he is honestly interested in his pupils, when he is so interested in the subject matter that they share his enthusiasm, when they know they can trust him, and when he teaches because he really wants to, they will respond to almost any suggestion. Sometimes this approaches hero worship, which at certain ages is a perfectly healthy reaction.

The teacher must be committed to the God of Jesus Christ. In his humility, he knows he is not worthy and yet he knows that he must serve. He may not want to spend so much time in preparation and to be present on time every Sunday, and yet he responds to this call to duty. He may have evaded this responsibility for years, and then someone responsibile for recruiting leaders has faced him with this vocation and he cannot turn away.

If there be a priesthood of the laity, the chief ministers, next to parents, are the church school teachers. Upon them lies the responsibility for bringing God to the children and the children to God through the church. The future well-being of Christianity depends upon what happens to the younger generation now. That is chiefly in the hands of the church school teacher.[3]

All leadership in the church fits this same pattern we have applied to the church school teacher. Whenever a man or woman accepts a position of leadership in the congregation, he is called to *serve*. Those who seek to tyrannize over their fellows have not caught the vision of Christian leadership. There is authority in leadership that is a combination of law, mercy, and love as men walk humbly with God, but this does not justify coercion for selfish ends.

RECRUITING TEACHERS AND LEADERS

The recruiting of teachers and leaders involves two basic tasks: *finding* those who are qualified, and *enrolling* them for a specific task.

Most congregations include a number of people with aptitudes for teaching and leading people. The subcommittee on personnel of the board of Christian education should have a list of those who are potential teachers and leaders. These names might be listed in reference to the various jobs that are open, or they might be kept in reserve for future reference for jobs that are now filled. Teachers,

[3] See my *A Guide for Church School Teachers* (Greenwich: Seabury Press, 1947), pp. 96-101.

assistant teachers, supervisors, superintendents, secretaries, treasurers, cradle roll leaders, educational secretaries of organizations, and many other such positions are involved. If the positions are elective, as in the case of superintendents and educational secretaries of organizations in some parishes, nominations might be made by the subcommittee on personnel.

When the time comes to make actual selections, care must be taken to know the time schedule of busy persons. Some people who have family or work responsibilities on Sundays may be available to help on weekdays; some who can come only once in a while on Sundays might be placed on the list of substitute teachers.

If working in the church school is considered an honor, because the work is difficult and the morale is high, the first hurdle has been jumped.

The actual process of recruiting works best if certain conditions are met. Offer a specific task, with the duties clearly outlined. Make it clear that the requirements are set on a high level: on-time attendance every Sunday, adequate preparation, time for reading suggested resources, attendance at workers' conferences, enrolling in an interchurch institute, calling in the homes, keeping required records. Sometimes it is helpful if a definite limit is set to the term of service, which is a protection both to the parish and to the leader. Some parishes send out invitations each year, and rotate all teachers and leaders out of office on a staggered basis every three to five years. Recognition for service, especially through services dramatizing their work and through a dedication service, is helpful. The teachers and leaders operate as a team, and their fellowship adds to the morale of the educational program; such opportunities should be made clear. Necessary help for teachers and leaders should be provided through a program of supervision, observation, assistant teachers, and conferences. Adequate resource material should be purchased as needed. In most cases, unless there are good private reasons, capable Christians will respond to such an offer, and normally there is a waiting list of teachers-to-be. The training program for high school seniors and parents provides a backlog of potential teachers and leaders who will move in as needed.

Such a program will not work efficiently in a parish with low standards and poor morale. It takes time to develop the kind of atmosphere that provides enthusiasm and willingness to sacrifice. Volunteers are not asked for, but teachers and leaders are drafted for their jobs by a competent committee. The proof that this kind of approach works is seen in parishes that have small classes of ten or twelve students taught by a team of teacher and assistant teacher, with a backlog of those ready to teach when called.

TRAINING OF TEACHERS AND LEADERS

Teacher training has been going on for a long time. Herman J. Sweet traces it back to the early part of the nineteenth century. The American Sunday School Union published *The Teacher Taught* in 1839. Dr. John H. Vincent was making his own experiments with fellow Methodists by 1860. When the uniform lessons were published in 1873, teacher training received a big boost. The emphasis during these years was on the organization of content, and in many cases the level of teaching was above that of the public schools.

STANDARD LEADERSHIP CURRICULUM

In recent years, the International Council of Religious Education has had a Standard Curriculum of Leadership Education. Individual denominations have had their own systems. Groups of fundamentalist churches have had their Evangelical Leadership Training Association. The churches have become more aware of the needs of their teachers, they have raised their standards, and they have insisted on a more adequate training program for a greater number of teachers.[4]

The important possibilities for teacher and leadership training are workers' conferences, study groups, institutes, camps and conferences, laboratory schools, workshops, reading, and church related colleges.

WORKERS' CONFERENCES

Workers' conferences or teachers' meetings are the most frequently held training sessions. Often they are simply business meetings with little or no reference to training. But many parishes have introduced a two-hour session, with an hour and a half of training and a half hour

[4] See Herman J. Sweet, "The Education of Leaders," in *Orientation in Religious Education,* ed. Philip Henry Lotz, pp. 392-402.

of business. Other groups have separated their business meetings from their training meetings, which provide an hour on the content of the faith and a second hour of departmental meetings on the age group and lesson content problems. The lesson preview has become popular especially in churches using group-graded lessons, or series with the same general topic each week. Held on either a monthly or weekly basis, lesson previews deal with the general plan of the coming lessons, provide needed resources for the teacher, and give help with the forthcoming lesson plans. Sometimes a role-playing class session is held, with the teachers acting as pupils and the department superintendent as the teacher. Sometimes a number of churches using the same lessons combine in previewing the next few sessions. Workers' conferences also make use of the Standard Leadership Education Curriculum published by the Division of Christian Education of the National Council of Churches, although these series are more popular in institutes.

STUDY GROUPS

Study groups and classes offer opportunity for leadership training. Sometimes the last two years of high school are used for this purpose. Parents' classes, dealing with the same problems as the teachers, are always working in this general area. New teachers, already selected for the following year, may attend a study group the previous term.

INSTITUTES

Institutes are made up of a series of meetings for the study of teacher problems. They may come on the same week night for from four to ten weeks, they may be every night for a week, or they may be a two-day group meeting or conference. These meetings are based on lectures, seminars, group procedures, visual aids, reports, demonstrations, and other techniques. Institutes are of three kinds.

(1) Local parish institutes are effective in large parishes or in communities where outside leaders are available. These are sometimes one-man meetings, with lectures followed by discussion. They meet for an hour or an hour and a half for a series of evenings. The concerns are primarily with the specific problems of the parish, and the results are usually satisfactory. Such institutes often use conference or workshop approaches to their problems.

(2) Denominational institutes bring together teachers and leaders from a number of parishes of the same denomination. This provides a cohesiveness of interest and a concern for similar curriculum patterns. When such institutes have expert promotion, organization, and leaders, they are excellent, but in many cases they are run by untrained leaders who give rather dull lectures specializing in content. The hesitation of some groups to call in experts from other denominations limits the number of good leaders available. Sometimes the Standard Leadership Training Courses are used, with excellent results.

(3) The widest scope in leadership training is offered by the interdenominational institute. Sponsored usually by the local federation of churches, it draws on the best leaders and has the combined resources of the cooperating parishes. Secular school leaders, outstanding citizens, and experts from outside the community may be invited to lead various sessions, and an adequate budget is provided.

The actual class sessions are normally based on the Standard Leadership Training Courses, and many teachers take them for credit. Accredited interdenominational and denominational schools are held throughout the country every year. There are specific requirements for standards, administration, faculty, courses of study, and textbooks. The courses deal with content, personal religion, age groups and their problems, teaching methods, administration of educational programs in local churches, and certain other subjects listed as "experimental courses." There are three series. Certificates are given to those who meet certain requirements.[5]

SUMMER CONFERENCES

Summer conferences usually include many classes and activities that contribute to teacher training. Such subjects as the Bible, church history, doctrine, social ethics, and the nature of the family are among the courses offered. Courses on techniques and theory of Christian education, sometimes backed by laboratory schools, help the teachers to find more effective ways of teaching.

[5] See Paul H. Vieth, *The Church and Christian Education*, pp. 217-19; Herman J. Sweet, in *Orientation in Religious Education*, ed. Philip Henry Lotz, pp. 396-97; Bulletins 501 and 502, *The Standard Leadership Curriculum*, Series 1 and 2 (Chicago: Division of Christian Education, National Council of Churches).

Attending a summer conference is one of the surest ways to become a part of the church's social fellowship. A week or two of study, worship, and fellowship enriches and deepens the spiritual life. It widens the experience of the quality of life of the redemptive community, so that the church is no longer simply the local parish but includes the experience of a wider fellowship.

LABORATORY SCHOOLS

Laboratory schools are those in which teachers work with students under the guidance of experienced leaders. "Perhaps the best single tribute to the laboratory school is the fact that so many older and experienced teachers point to their first laboratory-school experience as a turning point in their lives, both in personal religious growth and in educational insight and practice," writes Herman J. Sweet.[6] Most of these schools have high standards, and their popularity is spreading. In some cases they have been tied in with summer conferences. The instructors must be capable of teaching both the adults and the children who participate in the program, careful selection of children and practice teachers is essential, democratic planning and spiritual motivation must be present, and the whole process must be taken seriously. The discussion following the laboratory class is most important.

A variation of the laboratory school is the demonstration school, in which a trained teacher works with students in the presence of observers. There are pre-class and follow-up sessions with the observers, so that they come to an accurate evaluation of what they have observed.

Another variation is the role-playing of class situations, in which a group of teachers act out a lesson plan, taking the parts of typical children of the age group being demonstrated. This has the particular value of forcing the participants to see the world through the eyes of their students.

WORKSHOPS

The workshop has been adapted, sometimes rather loosely, to the training of church school leaders and teachers. It is concerned with

[6] "The Education of Leaders," in *Orientation in Religious Education,* ed. Philip Henry Lotz, p. 398.

both the theory of teaching and the practical problems facing the teachers. Although it provides resources in terms of trained leaders as well as books, visual aids, and other helps, it works primarily through the group. It makes use of small discussion groups, provides time for individual conferences, puts its stress on fellowship and recreation, and normally is held at a location away from distractions.

To distinguish a workshop from other ways of leadership training, Earl C. Kelley suggests the following:

> We think that there must be a *planning session* where all are involved at the beginning.
>
> There must be a considerable time for *work sessions* where all have an opportunity to work with others on the problems most significant to them.
>
> There must be a *summarizing and evaluating session* at the close.
>
> In order to accomplish all this, giving enough time to working groups to get something done, the workshop must be a minimum of two days in duration.[7]

The best time for such a workshop is before the opening of the fall term. The whole staff is brought together at a camp or conference center or at a hotel in a remote location, and after dinner on the first evening there is time for introductions. Perhaps the opening gambit might be to list on the blackboard all of the educational activities of the parish or of the church school. The key question might then be posed by the leader: "How do any of these activities bring our pupils into the redemptive community and guide them in facing the dilemmas of everyday decisions?" This question might be discussed in buzz groups, and then brief reports might be received before the end of the evening.

After breakfast and worship the next morning, the group might continue the discussion of the previous evening. This might turn to the problem of whether the key question is a valid one. Other key questions might better bring out the basic purpose of the educational program. About half-way through the morning, the problem may be acute enough for a small group to role-play a class situation in which the redemption of one child is the crucial problem.

After lunch and a reception period, the group may begin to consider the lesson materials on hand for the forthcoming year. Presumably they have been cursorily examined before the workshop

[7] Earl C. Kelley, *The Workshop Way of Learning* (New York: Harper & Brothers, 1951), p. 137.

began. Now is the time to look at them again and see whether they contain resources for achieving the aims and purposes of Christian education as these goals have evolved in the workshop. The leader must judge when the group is ready for this step.

The materials will suggest both the areas of concern for the teaching during the coming year and the information the teachers need to lead the pupils into an understanding of the relevance of the Gospel for their own lives. This discussion may work best if the staff breaks up in departmental groups or in terms of the topical arrangement of the materials.

By the evening meal, or perhaps after breakfast on the next day if the conference lasts that long, the group may be ready for their own decisions: "What do we do about all this when we come to our own classes?" They have begun to see the magnitude of their task and they may be overwhelmed by it. They have begun to see much more clearly the real needs of their pupils and the relevance of the Gospel to their lives. They need to make clear in their own minds what they can do about it.

The resource persons, including the leader and the more experienced members of the staff, may have to provide some suggestions at this point, because the group is now *able to hear* what they are saying. But until the group can formulate these suggestions in terms of their own teaching situations there is no real learning. This is the point at which the workshop must be judged for its practical effect on the health of parish life.

READING

One of the most consistent and satisfying ways of leadership training is through reading. A church school library should always be available. Churches with adequate financial resources should have an item for books and magazines in their annual budget. Other churches may have to use the public library and the books and magazines of the minister. Many teachers prefer to buy their own books, and parishes may have bookshelves with books for sale. The chief reason for lack of reading is failure of encouragement, opportunity, and guidance. Not only teachers but most lay people will read good, nontechnical religious books. The important thing is to see that they are available.

A basic book list for teachers should be prepared and made available. This list should be revised and kept up to date by the librarian, the director of Christian education, or the superintendent. Some parish libraries might well join one of the religious book clubs. *The International Journal of Religious Education* might be subscribed to for everyone on the staff, and most denominations publish one or more magazines that are helpful for guidance and resources. *Children's Religion, The Baptist Leader, The Church School Worker, The Christian Home, Child Study,* and *Religious Education* are some magazines that should be considered.

CHURCH-RELATED COLLEGES

Many church-related colleges are now offering courses in Bible, religion, and Christian education. The graduates of these colleges often have the training necessary for good teaching. This is one of the age groups often missing from the church's leadership, and yet it consists of young men and women sufficiently mature and adequately trained for church school teaching. If we could guide our young people to take the proper courses in the field of religion, they would become a reservoir of strength in the educational program of the local church.

RESULTS

It is obvious that the results of leadership training have been unsatisfactory. Only a small percentage of teachers are reached through these means. Others continue in the same routine year after year. After they are trained, the turnover in church school teachers (which has been estimated to be as high as one-third of all church school staff leaving each year) is sufficient to require continual repetition of primary training, leaving little or no time to deal with the problems of the veteran teachers.

The board of Christian education of every parish, through its subcommittee on leadership training, needs to give special attention to this problem. Its concern is not with leadership training in general but with the specific needs of its particular teachers and leaders. The resources are available, and by working through interdenominational channels, its own denominational headquarters, the community council of churches, and its own parish leadership training program it should seek to clarify these needs and to find the answers.

Bold and imaginative leadership at the top level, working through the dynamic group procedures and planning of the church school workers themselves, can provide a tailor-made program. If the standards of recruiting have been high enough, it will be possible to insist that proper leadership training is one of the basic requirements; and if the leadership training is oriented to the real needs of the teachers, they will respond with their full cooperation.

SUPERVISION

Supervision is an essential part of leadership and teacher training. Ralph D. Heim defines supervision as having "the purpose of improving the acts which occur when a learner meets a leader. More narrowly, it is personal guidance of workers, on the job, for the improvement of their work and results." [8]

The supervisor may be the pastor, the director of Christian education, the general superintendent, an assistant teacher, or a specialist chosen for the specific purpose. Frequently a competent public school teacher or administrator may prefer to contribute his skills through supervising the educational procedures rather than through teaching a class.

Supervision may be helpful at any point in the total program, including worship, assemblies, youth meetings, and educational activities in the organizations, but it normally is applied to the classroom situation. It is most effective when asked for by the teacher, but if the procedure is taken for granted as part of the total program even the most sensitive teacher will accept it as routine procedure.

A complete program of supervision in a class might have the following steps:

(1) A conference between the supervisor and the teacher to establish a relationship, anticipate problems, and make arrangements for the class visit.

(2) The visitation of the class, made as unobtrusive as possible, but including note-taking and sometimes the use of a tape recorder.

(3) Development of check sheets and schedules by which the supervisor may become sensitive to the real trouble points and aid the teacher in the next conference.

---

[8] Ralph D. Heim, *Leading a Sunday Church School* (Philadelphia: Muhlenberg Press, 1950), p. 145.

(4) A follow-up conference with the teacher.

(5) A meeting with the teachers in the department, and then with the total staff, after completion of supervising classes in that department.

The supervisor considers many factors in the class, department, church school, and total life of the congregation. The conditions in the class may be outside the control of the teacher because of what happens on some other level. Among the specific classroom factors are the following:

(1) Classroom condition and equipment.

(2) The general routine of the class.

(3) Elements in the personality of the teacher.

(4) The way the pupils respond.

(5) Teaching techniques, lesson plan, degree of preparation, consideration of pupils' feelings, pupils' participation.

(6) Resources used, including lesson materials, outside resources, visual aids, materials familiar to the pupils.

(7) Degree to which pupils work between classes to provide information.

(8) An analysis of the results of the class session. This involves a subjective judgment on the part of the supervisor, who should look for emotional attitudes, motivation, relevance of the factual content and interpretation, decisions, and depth of Christian conviction on the part of both teacher and pupils.[9]

Supervisions is the most individualized form of leadership education. The crux of the matter, apart from the supervisor's ability to be an objective critic, is the relationship established between the supervisor and the individual teacher. When it becomes a counseling relationship, a great deal of criticism and guidance is possible, and the teacher will be led to new insights.

A special form of supervision comes from the work of the assistant teacher who works closely with the teacher as an observer at every session. The assistant teacher shares with the teacher the planning for the course and the specific sessions, watches the responses of the pupils from week to week, occasionally teaches the class or catches a point for discussion, takes notes for post-class conferences and evaluation, and helps the teacher discover the points at which the resources

---

[9] See Ernest J. Chave, *Supervision of Religious Education* (Chicago: University of Chicago Press, 1931).

may become more relevant to the pupils. In many cases, a husband and wife team takes the class, and during the week they have opportunities to work out together the answers to their teaching problems. They serve as a check on each other, find that they both are growing in their Christian faith and in their own relationships, and become an effective team in their work with their pupils.

CONCLUSION

All that we have said about methods, techniques, knowledge of age groups, home cooperation, and the training of leaders and teachers is important. But the character and devotion of the leaders is of even greater importance. All the expert techniques in the world do not channel the Christian faith unless there is faith in the teacher or leader to be channeled. Unless there is a contagious enthusiasm for Christian living, it will not be attractive to the learners. A quality of radiance in the face of life's decisions is essential.

A teacher was once described as follows: "But there he was; a strong man talking with knowledge and a sort of dark enthusiasm: and sentence by sentence he enforced a high contagion." [10] The enthusiasm of the teacher must be a combination of contagious interest in his subject and loving concern for his pupils. This cannot be compelled; it does not result from training in leadership techniques, important as these are; either it is there, or it isn't. It is the prerequisite for all training for Christian teaching.

In the last analysis, God makes possible the acceptance of the saving knowledge of Jesus Christ that is offered in a curriculum of Christian education.[11]

---

[10] Houston Peterson, ed., *Great Teachers* (New Brunswick: Rutgers University Press, 1946), p. 342.

[11] See my *A Symphony of the Christian Year* (Greenwich: Seabury Press, 1954), p. 172.

CHAPTER 22

CHOOSING LESSON MATERIALS

LESSON materials are resources for learning to live within the fellowship of the church. The local parish has its ways of worship, its manner of interpreting doctrine, its approach to the Bible and history, its ideals of ethical and social behavior, and its ethos or atmosphere of faith. The program of Christian education is the product of the church's life, and though educational processes lead students to make a critical appraisal of the church's life and doctrines, they also lead them to loyalty to the church as an institution and to Jesus Christ as the foundation of their fellowship. Christian education leads its students into an experience and appreciation of the redemptive and sustaining grace of God within the community *now,* and it is relevant to their basic needs.

Sometimes the lesson materials are spoken of as "the curriculum," but actually they are the guides and resources for the curriculum, and curriculum as such is the runway or path followed by the students. In the last analysis, every parish makes its own curriculum, and the use it makes of lesson materials is significant in developing an appreciation of the quality of life that results from Christian faith.

One of the most important recent developments in the field of Christian education is the better kind of materials prepared by many denominations and by interdenominational cooperation. *The Christian Faith and Life* Series of the Presbyterian Church, U.S.A., has been widely used by parishes of many denominations. The emphasis on the language of relationships and the redemptive community in *The Seabury Series* of the Protestant Episcopal Church has opened new channels of Christian education for many churches. The use of such older books as Walter Russell Bowie's *The Story of the Bible,* Roland Bainton's *The Church of Our Fathers,* and John Oxenham's *The Hidden Years* in church schools indicates the power of content when used as resource material.

Many types of lesson material are available. The *uniform lessons,* providing the same Bible passage for everyone but a variety of approaches for different age groups, retain their popularity year after year.

Group-graded lessons have a three-year age span, covering a department, so that all classes in the primary, junior, junior high, or senior high departments have the same lesson, and the teacher adapts it to the particular grade. In some series this has been altered to a two-year span for the elementary grades.

Closely graded lessons match the one-year grading of the public schools and seek to achieve balance in terms of the topics of the courses throughout the whole school.

Another variation is to use the group-graded principle combined with a *unified curriculum,* so that the entire church emphasizes the same topic for the year, although each department has its own specific area of study.

Other schools go to the opposite extreme of a *free curriculum,* in which the teachers are encouraged to follow up any area of concern that appears, regardless of the suggested outline of the course, digging up resources for the unit as it develops.

Electives, especially in the junior high and high school groups, are freely offered. Weekday and vacation church school texts are often popular in the Sunday church school. Youth fellowship programs are sometimes used in church school classes, and regular church school texts are sometimes adapted to evening meetings of youth fellowships.

There are many materials prepared for all kinds of adult classes, with the most recent development being the adaptation of group dynamics and workshop methods in the informal teaching of adults. Many courses now have special materials for parents to use during the week.[1]

[1] See Paul H. Vieth, *The Church and Christian Education,* pp. 136-38; C. A. Bowen, "Curriculum Patterns for the Church School," in *Orientation in Religious Education,* ed. Philip Henry Lotz, pp. 101-5; and *A Guide for Curriculum in Christian Education* (Chicago: National Council of Churches, 1955), pp. 113-143, 152-167.

PRINCIPLES OF SELECTION

Many parishes feel that they are bound to use the official publications of their denomination, but there is still some freedom of choice. Some parishes select their lesson materials from other denominations, from interdenominational publishers, or from a combination of sources, or prepare their own materials.

Although denominational loyalty is important, and therefore denominational materials should be used if they are satisfactory, the selection of lesson materials should be on the basis of sound principles and of a wide acquaintance with what is available. Even when the decision is to stick with denominational materials, this process makes the decision intelligible and provides many resource materials otherwise unavailable. For example, the Presbyterian readers in the Christian Faith and Life Series provide resource materials for courses on the life of Christ, the Bible, and the church that are interesting and exciting and suitable to most denominations, and they may be used in units on these subjects along with lesson materials of almost any publisher. Books by independent publishers, written especially for children and youth, are often equally suitable.

Many factors are involved in the selection of lesson materials. The needs of the pupils, the capacities of the teachers, the use made of parents, the space and equipment, the cost, the content, and the methods are the most significant.

THE PUPILS

Lesson materials are chosen for the use of a specific group of pupils. They are written for the age group in general, but unless they meet the growing edge of the particular students in the class they are not valuable for their purposes.

This criterion of pupils' needs must be understood. The place to begin is with the age group characteristics. A book such as *These Are Your Children,* by Gladys Gardner Jenkins, Helen Shacter, and William W. Bauer,[2] covers the ground of our secular knowledge. We need to understand the pupils psychologically and sociologically as

[2] Chicago: Scott, Foresman, and Co., 1953.

well as religiously. We need to understand the process of growth in religion,[3] and see how the total personalities develop within the various communities that demand the pupils' loyalties. As we come to an understanding of their basic needs, their common interests, their capacities to understand concrete instances, historical developments, and abstract concepts, their opportunities to develop, and their education from other sources, we are ready to look at the individual students in our classes.

The general knowledge about age groups never applies directly to individuals, because age group information is statistical. A certain percentage of children learn to read in the third grade, but the particular children in a third grade class may read well or not at all. Most children can think historically by the time they reach the fifth grade, but your fifth grade class may include one child who knows all about the battles of Robert E. Lee and another who thinks St. Paul founded the local St. Paul's Church. The children may attend various public, private, and parochial schools.

This particularizing of our general information is based to some extent upon the teacher's experience with previous classes, but no two classes are the same even if they come from the same neighborhood. Furthermore, the changes during the summer may throw out all estimates of the "growing edge" of a particular group of children.

Even when we have some grasp of the pupils' capacities for learning, there are widespread differences in their religious knowledge and aptitudes. One child coming from a pagan home enters a Sunday school for the first time and is placed in the fifth grade, which includes another child who has grown up in a Christian home where knowledge of the Bible is due to constant exposure to the King James version. Another child identifies religion with church and has had no experience of its relationships in daily life. Another one sees religion in terms of relationships but has not acquired the vocabulary to communicate it.

TEACHERS

Lesson materials are taught by individuals. Teachers represent a wide variety in personality, devotion, training, and willingness to prepare. Some have no aptitude for creative methods and yet transmit the faith because of their own contagious enthusiasm. Others are bungling

---

[3] See above, Chapter 5.

in almost every way, and yet they are kept on because someone recognizes that the teacher's psychological needs are being met. Others have excellent training in techniques, but somehow the children do not catch fire.

A realistic appraisal of the teaching staff is essential, for lesson materials, no matter how excellent from every other standpoint, have no value unless the teacher can use them to communicate the faith.

The lesson materials must include the resources and practical help needed by the particular teachers on the staff. Unless this includes good supervision and leadership training, the lesson plans must be carefully outlined and followed closely and without much imagination. Competent teachers always prepare their own lesson plans and depart from the routine to meet the needs of their pupils, but the less competent ones cannot do this and they need help. The freer type of curriculum should be used with trained teachers, careful supervision, and meetings to work out lesson plans.

There is a direct correlation between the time needed for preparation and success in teaching. To a great extent, this depends on the devotion of the teacher, the guidance provided, and the standards set. If the teachers have been recruited on the basis of spending at least two hours in preparation, or attending all workers' conferences, and of accepting supervision, a higher type of lesson materials may be used. Much depends on the continuing high morale of the staff and the church school at this point.

PARENTS

Parents have much to do with the success of the church school program. Lesson materials in many denominations are prepared with the expectation that parents will provide some kind of Christian teaching and guidance in the home. The preparation of materials for parents of infants, the use of family worship, the popularity of parents' classes, and the recognition of the responsibilities of parents indicate that this direction of activity will become more common.

If the program of Christian education includes the parents, lesson materials should be chosen accordingly. Some materials now being prepared will not work without parental cooperation, and it is a mistake to choose such materials unless the church is going to work out a sound home-church relationship. For churches that prefer to minister to individuals, there are good materials available that ignore parents.

The selection of lesson materials for the parents' classes should be consistent with the materials for their children. The correlation at this point is not on a Sunday-to-Sunday basis, but on a study of a similar area of concern.

SPACE, EQUIPMENT, AND COST

Some lesson materials assume an amount of space and equipment beyond the scope of the local parish. A creative activities program is not effective in cramped space. Reliance on audio-visual aids is impossible when several classes meet in the same room, or when the necessary projectors and screen are unavailable.

In some parishes these problems are not insurmountable, and a certain amount of imaginative planning and willingness to shift about improves the whole program. But some small parishes are so limited in space and equipment that their lesson materials must be adaptable to cramped quarters.

Space and equipment are often wasted. A parish with individual classrooms, proper seating and table sizes, and equipment for activities may use such poor materials that nothing of value happens.

The story is told of a church treasurer looking at a group of about 25 children and making the comment, "There's not five dollars in the whole bunch of them." This attitude, more than anything else, leads to the penny-pinching financial outlook of many church school programs. There are cheap lesson materials, crudely written, educationally wide of the mark, badly printed and bound, used in many parishes with a false sense of economy. Good materials cost money, because they are written and illustrated by experts, are well printed and bound, and are available for every pupil.

Although it is possible to run a Sunday school program at a cost of less than one dollar per child per year, the best materials will cost about three dollars per child per year. When the cost of resource materials for creative activities, filmstrips, and other aids is added, it is reasonable to suppose that a budget of $500 is necessary for an enrollment of one hundred, not counting salaries and maintenance.

A THREE-FOLD TEST

The content of the curriculum is not limited to the lesson materials, for the worship services, assembly programs, and other resources provide much content along with their direction of attitudes and actions.

There is a three-fold test for the selection of lesson materials. Are they sound, adequate, and relevant? To be sound, they must be correct as far as they go from the point of view of the congregation and its leaders. To be adequate, they must be balanced and selective in terms of the needs of the pupils and the goals of the parish educational program. To be relevant, they must contribute to the immediate purpose at hand.

This three-fold test [4] is applied to six areas, two of which specifically relate to content, three to methods, and one to local conditions.

(1) The *theology* of the lesson materials must be sound from the standpoint of the local congregation. A perusal of some widely used series of lesson materials will shock those who are acquainted with the best of contemporary theology. The principle is a simple one: *We must never teach a child anything that he will need to unlearn.* Our protection is having lesson materials and books of doctrine for teachers that are theologically sound. This is just as important at the kindergarten level as at the high school age. In order to be adequate, what is taught must be balanced, no matter how elementary the presentation may be. Simplification often leads to actual misrepresentation of the Gospel, avoiding death and suffering and sentimentalizing the God of the bird and the bees, giving false views of the Biblical characters and their problems, and distorting the redemptive factors of Christian faith.

Theological views that are irrelevant to the child should not be taught. The time will come when these views are relevant, and in the meantime through the language of relationships we can communicate what has meaning for his daily living. This is particularly true of Bible teaching. No one is more in favor of teaching the Bible than James D. Smart, but he writes that "there is good reason to believe that many children have been psychologically conditioned against the Bible by overzealous teachers who have tried to teach them too much of it too soon. . . . *Nothing* in the Bible was written specifically for children." [5] The teacher needs to know the theological implications for adults of any Bible story, and then he needs to know how to make

---

[4] See G. Gardner Monks, *The Church Looks Ahead to the New Curriculum: Specifications.* (Greenwich: Seabury Press), pp. 40-47.

[5] From *The Teaching Ministry of the Church* by James D. Smart. The Westminster Press, Philadelphia. Copyright by W. L. Jenkins, 1954, pp. 147, 148. Used by permission.

it relevant without distorting it. If this cannot be done, the story does not belong among the resources for that age. In this way, we need to examine the Biblical references in the lesson materials as well as the theological concepts to see if they meet the test of relevance.

(2) *Church history and Biblical history* must meet these same tests. Probably most general church histories and Biblical histories meet the standards of historical accuracy, although frequently there is a tendency to hedge in historical incidents involving denominational doctrines. But this is not always true of lesson materials. To be sound, they must be checked for historical, factual accuracy. The purpose of teaching history in the church's educational program is primarily religious, but ignoring the best historical and Biblical scholarship is not the way to meet religious or scientific needs.

The tendency to use anecdotes threatens the adequacy of historical presentations, whereas the use of historical and biographical incidents tends to make the material relevant. At this point, the writer of lesson materials faces a dilemma. The desire to be interesting and dramatic and to relate experiences of earlier times to our own contemporary scene tempts the author to skimp on an adequate picture in favor of relevance.

Events from the past can be presented only as "once upon a time" incidents to younger children because they lack a sense of historical time. Yet there is a strong feeling that traditional stories should be told. When children are old enough to appreciate time sequences, they are still primarily interested in biography, but the personal history must be related to the ongoing drama of God's redemption of mankind through Jesus Christ in history. Later on, they come to understand movements of history and cultural developments.

(3) Not only content but the *insights into the nature of the learner* and how he learns must be sound, adequate, and relevant. The learner must be understood *psychologically*. The view of the pupil expressed in the lesson materials must reflect the Christian doctrine of man as it is supplemented and illuminated by psychological research.

The child's own self-understanding is at stake. If he is treated as a little adult, as a naturally good animal who must go through stages of development, or as a helpless and hopeless sinner, he will not learn the essential teaching of the Gospel about his own nature.

The growth of special agencies for children and the number of books dealing with all aspects of child care indicate the importance of all aspects of our study of the nature of the child. Unless these discoveries are written into the lesson materials, there is much doubt about their validity as educational resources or as means of developing Christian faith.

(4) The next requirement for lesson materials is the *teaching methods*. "It is a false antithesis," says Gardner Monks, "to set subject-centered against pupil- (or experience-) centered curricula. A more helpful analogy is an ellipse with God at one focus and the child at the other. Every point on an ellipse must have its definite reference to both God and the child." [6]

The methods recommended in the guidance to teachers should be those developed through experiments in teaching. All that we have learned about sound methods applies here. They must be adequate for the purposes of teaching the subject matter. They must be relevant to the abilities and experiences of the learners.

Many lesson materials show lack of imagination in the selection of methods. Because a routine lesson plan works once, the teacher may not assume that it will work every time. Variety of method is essential, and lesson materials should be written in such a way that the teacher has many suggestions for making the best possible use of the subject matter as a resource for the learning process.

(5) Theology comes to grips with *sociology* as we consider the nature of the church. All that we have said about the quality of life in the congregation, the home, and the school comes into the picture as we consider the place of the individual in the group.

Secular educators were right when they interpreted education as a social process within the context of the classroom situation; and often they saw the relation of religious attitudes to the community, but they failed to see that the social process of Christian education is provided by the congregation. A sociology of education is not sufficient to provide a social theology of Christian education.[7]

Lesson materials should include an understanding of sociology and its relation to Christian learning. They should be adequate for the

[6] G. Gardner Monks, *The Church Looks Ahead to the New Curriculum: Specifications* (Greenwich: Seabury Press), p. 43.

[7] See "Christian Education as a Theological Discipline and Method," *Religious Education* (November-December 1953), p. 409.

guidance of Christian learning and living. They should be relevant to actual social conditions of children, taking into account the influences of home and school, of community activities, of radio and television, of reading and other leisure-time activities. They should recognize the existence of other organizations, such as the Young Men's and Young Women's Christian Associations and the Scouts, which serve the same age groups. The relation of education in the church to all these other agencies in the community is basic to an understanding of lesson materials as resources for teaching the Christian faith.[8]

(6) A final test of curriculum materials is in terms of the *conditions of the local parish.* It means that we must recognize the limitations of the personnel and program of the congregation, while at the same time we have a realistic appraisal of its performance and potentialities. It means that we recognize the attendance records of the students, the number who have transferred from other parishes or from no parish, the backgrounds of all the students in the parish education program. This realistic survey must be sound, adequate, and relevant.

We need then to make an over-all check on the curriculum. In the light of the aims and purpose of the parish educational program, we need to make sure that all topics and problems are covered adequately and relevantly for every age group. Not only in the church school but in the ministry to the church to all its people, there needs to be a balanced curriculum that brings the Gospel to each of them.

SOURCES

There are various sources of lesson materials available for every parish. Some denominations publish several series, often providing their own versions of the uniform, group-graded and closely graded outlines prepared by the Division of Christian Education of the National Council of Churches. The denominational lessons, however they are planned, may not be intended for mixing within the same church, and the pattern of the over-all curriculum may be spoiled by tinkering with the series. Careful study by the parish committee is essential if such mixing is to be successful.

Because these outlines prepared by the Division of Christian Edu-

---

[8] See pp. 146-51.

cation of the National Council of Churches are used by several denominations, the actual results in terms of writing vary a good deal. It is possible to mix these, using one's own denominational version in some grades and the same outlines with different approaches prepared by another denomination in other grades. The pattern of the curriculum is not disturbed and the best of this kind of material is made available.

Another combination is to use a variety of series, combining group-graded and closely graded materials from several denominations or from one's own denomination. This involves the difficulties mentioned above in mixing series conceived on different outlines.

Specific units are sometimes substituted at a particular point in a course, the teachers drawing on other sources for these units. Elective units are frequently used in this way whenever a special interest develops, but sometimes they are taken out of other courses. In such cases, the original lesson material needs to be edited, or a unit shortened or dropped to make room for the inserted unit.

Many courses are planned for the whole year, and the summer material is on a different subject. It is possible to substitute the summer unit for the one planned for another season, although this must be done with care, especially when it eliminates the treatment of Christmas or Easter at the proper time.

Church schools that run in the summer have the choice of continuing with their around-the-year materials if they have them, or of providing special materials adapted to the smaller enrollment during the summer months.

Another entirely different approach is to outline a curriculum in terms of topics or areas of concern for each age group, and then to seek among all the lesson materials for the best course on each topic at that age level. So much material is interchangeable as far as denominational teachings are concerned that sometimes a series from another denomination may be taken over in its entirety. The successful adaptation of the Christian Faith and Life Series, which makes full use of its Presbyterian traditions and doctrine, in Episcopal, Methodist, Congregational, and other churches is evidence of the ease with which this may be done. Another system is to select from all publishers those courses that fit the plans of the congregation, selecting the materials in terms of the standards we have suggested and working out a balanced curriculum.

ADMINISTRATION OF SELECTION

The point at which all groups begin is the series of lesson materials being used. Within the board of Christian education a subcommittee on lesson selection should be appointed. It should include representation from the teachers, the superintendent, the director of Christian education, and the pastor. This group should receive recommendations from the teaching staff and from the interested members of the board.

The materials being used should be evaluated according to the standards we have listed. There should be opportunity to examine other lesson materials published by the denomination, plus materials that have been recommended. When all conditions and needs of the parish educational program have been checked, the group is ready to make its recommendations to the board. Normally, the pastor and the director of Christian education will have a good deal of authority, depending on the traditions of the congregation, on the philosophy of leadership, and on their expertness in the field.

The most valuable help for this process is *A Guide for Curriculum in Christian Education*[9] of the Division of Christian Education of the National Council of Churches. Many denominations provide recommendations for the selection of lesson materials, although publishing houses normally list their own publications as preferable.

There is no substitute for wide acquaintance with the best theories of curriculum and with the actual materials. The committee needs to read through the materials with the agreed-upon standards in mind, then it needs to check with the teachers on the suitability of the materials for their own classes; the final test is the first experimental year to see how they work in practice.

When a new series is adopted, special pains must be taken to acquaint the teachers with the principles, theology, and methods of their new resources. Additional help must be provided through conferences and supervision during the first months. Evaluation of the program at the end of the first year should indicate whether the changes were satisfactory.

But there is no sense in changing just for the sake of novelty. The committee must be sure that the new materials are enough of an

[9] Chicago: National Council of Churches, 1955.

improvement to justify the effort and expense of the change-over. There is no doubt that in many parishes, the materials being used are one of the major handicaps in achieving the goals of Christian education, and there the change should be made no matter how much trouble is involved. Lesson materials are tools, and all workmen need good tools to do the best job of which they are capable.

DEVELOPING YOUR OWN MATERIALS

Unless you are convinced that your educational staff can prepare materials that are better than those already in existence, it is better not to attempt the task. But in some situations, such as in rural locaions, in the mission field, and in laboratory schools, it may be wise to prepare your own materials.

Because they are your own materials you will know how to use them, and your staff will share your enthusiasm and therefore put much effort into the operation. But usually such materials prove of no value to anyone else.

The Curriculum Guide for the Local Church[10] has a chapter outlining the procedures to be followed if such an endeavor seems wise. It takes the same detailed care to prepare materials for a local situation as for a church-wide series of lesson materials.

---

[10] International Council of Religious Education, 1950, pp. 50-59.

CHAPTER 23

EVALUATING THE EDUCATIONAL PROGRAM

EVALUATION is in two steps: the establishment of objectives, goals, and standards, and the technique of evaluating the process of education in the light of these objectives.

The educational agency is the total parish. The congregation is responsible for its educational objectives, policy, and program. This program exists whether the congregation's members are conscious of it or not, and the question is simply whether it is a poor, mediocre, or good program. There is a curriculum even when there is no Sunday church school or youth organization or parents' class or ladies' aid society, for the experience of the members of the congregation, however they come together, is its curriculum.

The curriculum should have specific objectives, means of functioning, and wholeness of impact on its learners.

OBJECTIVES

The objectives of the curriculum might be those developed by the International Council of Religious Education: a consciousness of God, loyalty to Jesus Christ as Lord and Savior, development of Christlike character, participation as a Christian in the social order, membership in the church, appreciation of the meaning of Christian family life, a life philosophy based on a Christian interpretation of life, and acquaintance with the Bible and other religious literature.[1]

Another familiar division of objectives is into the areas of content in the teaching schedule: the Bible, personal experiences and faith,

[1] *The Curriculum Guide for the Local Church* (Chicago: International Council of Religious Education, 1950), p. 8.

the family, church life, social problems, world relations, and service and Christian leadership.[2]

Another way of stating our purpose is "to provide those experiences which, with the help of God's grace, are best calculated to develop in the young the ideas, the attitudes and the habits that are demanded for Christ-like living in our American democratic society." [3]

INTEGRATION

The program of Christian education should be an integrated one. At every point its aim is to produce disciples of Christ, who will seek to share their faith with others, to live together in a genuine Christian fellowship, and to have a Christian influence upon their environment.

This element of *integration* is of the greatest significance. It means that all elements in the curriculum are arranged harmoniously and in proper order in relation to the basic goals. "The first principle of an integrated curriculum therefore is this: Educational agents must have clear understanding of the ends to be achieved, they must choose means which lead most directly to those ends, and they must avoid all instruments which lead in the opposite direction or which tend to retard progress." [4]

THE PROCESS OF EVALUATION

The local parish, through its board of Christian education, works out its own objectives and goals according to such standards as these. When it has formed its standards, which is an important but not too difficult a task in the light of all the help available, it proceeds to the second step: the evaluation of the educational processes of the parish in the light of these standards. This is where the difficulties begin. The board determines whether the major objectives have been translated into concrete ways of behavior for individuals according to their age groups, whether students actually have learned to think and behave as expected, whether one aspect of the curriculum is more effective

---

[2] *Ibid.*, p. 9.

[3] Commission on American Citizenship, *Guiding Growth in Christian Social Living* (Washington: Catholic University Press, 1946), p. 5.

[4] Sister Mary Janet Miller, *Building the Integrated Curriculum* (Washington: Catholic University Press, 1953), p. 26.

than another, whether the curriculum is flexible enough to be adapted when necessary, whether what goes on in church is tied in with home, school, and daily life experiences,[5] whether the teaching quality is good, whether the general standards are maintained, and whether the theological implications of all that happens are sound, adequate, and relevant.

ADAPTING THE OBJECTIVES

The first step is to find out how goals and objectives are applied to specific age groups. Teachers' manuals frequently provide assistance in adapting general educational objectives to the level of the age group. *Goals for the Christian Education of Children* applies the objectives of the Division of Christian Education of the National Council of Churches to the elementary ages. Help in understanding growth in religion is available from various secular and religious studies of the psychology of childhood. The parish board of Christian education, with help from age group specialists or teachers, then formulates clearly and concretely what can be expected of the particular children as they deal with the problems, situations, and issues that face them. This is checked against the lesson materials to be sure that the teacher and other leaders have the resources to guide the pupils in these directions.

CHECKING ACHIEVEMENTS

The next step is to find out if the concrete age group goals are being achieved. There are various techniques to determine changes in knowledge, attitudes, and behavior.

Profile sheets on the students at the beginning of a term may be checked against actual behavior recorded during and at the end of the term. Changes in cooperation, sociability, confidence, dominance of the group, self-control, and other attitudes are recorded against the background of the pupils' home and school environment, native intelligence, and other factors.

---

5 Adapted from "Evaluation in Relation to Integration," in *The Integration of the Catholic Secondary School Curriculum,* ed. Mary Janet Miller (Wash-

Anecdotal reports included in an observer's notes provide spot evaluations of individual members of the class from time to time, and over the period of a term these indicate changes in attitudes.

Personal interviews with individual students by the teacher often provide information otherwise unavailable. Pupils are encouraged to tell their reactions to the class sessions and to indicate areas of concern and activities that are appreciated.

Personal interviews with parents by the teacher often provide observations concerning attitudes and behavior that help in evaluating the program. When these are combined with *parents' reports,* as in the Character Education Project of Ernest M. Ligon,[6] the results are extremely valuable.

Information from parents, secular school teachers, leaders of various organizations, and that volunteered by playmates helps to analyze the influence of the student in the community. A parent may report, "I don't know what has happened to John, but suddenly he became interested in the Gra-Y program and now he is one of the leaders of the group. He simply wasn't interested until they had that unit on community resources for young people at the church."

This information needs to be supplemented by *tests*. There are more tests available than might be expected, and most students are used to them. They may be impatient with written examinations, but they will submit to objective tests. Ralph D. Heim suggests that these may be used to determine many of the desirable results of Christian education, such as attitudes, Biblical knowledge, Christian practices, Christian conduct, knowledge of the church's history and organization, appreciation of worship, personality factors, psychological status, and religious ideas and beliefs. All such tests should be corrected and handed back to the pupil, so that he will know what mistakes he has made. A number of devices are available: best answer, completion, expression of attitude or belief, matching questions and answers, multiple choice, rating or ranking, scale of values, simple recall, true-false, cross-out, and many other devices.[7]

Tests are used in many parishes to determine if members of the class are adequately prepared for confirmation.

---

[6] See Ernest M. Ligon, *A Greater Generation* (New York: The Macmillan Company, 1948), pp. 90-93, 113-16, 121-22.

[7] See Ralph D. Heim, *Leading a Sunday Church School* (Philadelphia: Muhlenberg Press, 1950), pp. 316-23; also "Educational Measurements," by Edward A. Lincoln, in *Educational Psychology,* 3rd ed., ed. Charles E. Skinner (New York: Prentice-Hall, Inc., 1951), pp. 663-89.

These objective tests do not provide all the information we need. They tell us where our children and adults stand in relation to one another, and the standardized tests provide statistical information about how they compare with those in other parishes. But even these facts must be used with extreme care. They do not get to the bottom of the matter, for we are primarily concerned with interior attitudes, relationships with the unseen as well as with people, and mental and spiritual health.

Supervisors' reports are extremely helpful at this point. They are based on the observation of actual classroom behavior, and though this does not give the information about everyday Christian living that comes from other forms of investigation and observation, it provides a diagnosis of what is happening.[8]

EFFECTIVE PHASES

Specific information is needed concerning the particular phases of the curriculum that affect the students in their changing behavior. By means of the same techniques that are described above, we can discover which classroom experiences have been favorable, how worship and the pastor's sermonette or story have influenced the students, what the fellowship of the congregation means to them, and whether cooperation in service projects has made a difference. In this way, we are able to discover how the quality of life of the congregation enrolls students' loyalty and influences their attitudes and behavior. The total curriculum has weak spots in it, and this helps us get at our strength and weaknesses.

FLEXIBILITY

When it is discovered that certain aspects of the curriculum are weak or strong, it is essential that the curriculum be flexible enough to make the alterations. A high school class may be enthusiastic about its worship program, may accept its teacher, and may be utterly bored with a course that is neither adequate nor relevant to their interests and needs. If elective courses are available as alternates, the problem may be solved quite simply; but if the students are coerced into continuing with uninteresting materials they will in all probability stop

[8] See Kimball Wiles, *Supervision for Better Schools* (New York: Prentice-Hall, Inc., 1950), pp. 249-66.

attending the class or even drop away from the church. This is a common problem with the high school age, and some churches lack the flexibility to meet it.

On a younger level, when obedience to parents guarantees attendance, the church faces the same responsibility to provide a total program that meets the learners' needs and therefore has an influence at every point on their appreciation of the Gospel. They are to be members of the redemptive community *now,* and the channels of God's grace are effectively blocked by weak spots in the curriculum.

INTEGRATION WITH OTHER EDUCATION

The curriculum of Christian education needs to be integrated with other forms of education. With children, the church school and the grade school should be fitted together, so that the youngsters see a connection. With adults, whose education continues through their daily experiences, reading programs, organizations, and family life, the curriculum in the church must be integrated with their other activities.

Information about children's grade school programs is not difficult to obtain. The church is aware of their school programs, even when they attend a number of different public, private, or parochial schools, and the integration can be accomplished in terms of their vocabulary, reading abilities, and other school subjects and activities. With adults, this is a far more difficult task, but through the use of group procedures they make their own integration.

CHECKING THE TEACHERS

The quality of teaching is judged primarily by the results in the lives of the students. The effectiveness of teaching depends on the shared fellowship of the congregation and the ability of the teaching staff. The continuing problem in attaining an adequate educational program turns on the teachers. Good standards of recruiting and of leadership education are fundamental. Part of the evaluating process will always turn on the means of enlistment and the standards that are set. These can be checked through the use of assistant teachers', supervisors', and teachers' reports.

Teachers may check themselves by means of self-rating scales, and superintendents or supervisors may double-check them with rating scales. Such categories as personal qualities, social and professional abilities, capacities for management, techniques of teaching, Christian conviction, and observed results should be included.[9]

STANDARDS FOR THE CHURCH SCHOOL

The International Standard for the Sunday Church School, published by the Division of Christian Education of the National Council of Churches, provides a list of requirements for a church school and a score sheet with a point system. By the use of this standard, it is possible to see what gaps there are in the curriculum, organization, administration, and personnel of the Sunday church school. The major items are curriculum, leadership, organization and administration, and housing and equipment. They deal with quantitative questions, such as whether class periods last more than 30 minutes, whether there is a single budget for the entire parish, whether a magazine on religious education is made available, whether there is a study group for parents. But the Standard also asks questions about the leadership that require subjective evaluations. It provides a total picture that is essential for an evaluation of the total program.

Criteria for parish education may be worked out by the local parish. The literature is so diverse that it is difficult to work out a specific plan, but when a parish makes use of competent jurors for evaluating its criteria it may discover which are applicable in terms of good standards and reasonable expectations. A group in Corpus Christi, Texas, under the direction of Richard C. Schneider submitted a proposed list of criteria to representative religious educators, revised the list, and then submitted it to officials of local parishes. This offered a check on the validity of the basic objectives, organization and administration, curriculum, and physical facilities. Among the most significant of the selected criteria were the following:

I. BASIC OBJECTIVES

Parish education:

1. Leads to a personal consciousness of God as a reality.
2. Leads to progressive and continuous development of Christlike character.
3. Leads to brotherhood and participation in community life.
4. Takes place through fellowship in Christian living and in the sharing of the Christian faith.

---

[9] See George H. Betts and Marion O. Hawthorne, *Method in Teaching Religion* (New York: Abingdon Press, 1926), pp. 248-72, for sample score cards.

5. Is for all colors, classes, and nationalities.
6. Is the responsibility of the whole congregation.
7. Motivates a deep concern for human welfare.
8. Is vitally concerned with contemporary issues facing people.
9. Focuses on the home as the primary functionary in Christian nurture.
10. Is built around the needs of its constituents.
11. Fosters and nurtures the Christian community as the "Body of Christ."
12. Is persuasive, not coercive.

(Some of these overlap, and there were others with a lower degree of preference.)

II. ORGANIZATION AND ADMINISTRATION

1. Parish education is integrated into the whole parish program so that it is related to other areas and is a part of the total church.
2. Responsibility is shared and delegated.
3. There is continuous nurturing and recruiting of leadership personnel.
4. The personnel are suited to the work and capable of carrying out the program.
5. There are enough teachers and staff to carry on effectively the educational program.
6. Parish education facilities are utilized as belonging to the entire congregation, rather than to a particular group.
7. There is continuity of program regardless of personnel changes.
8. The parish education committee
   a. Cooperates with the home and other groups of the church.
   b. Plans and develops the parish education program.
   c. Develops policies for the program and curriculum.
   d. Brings education to the attention and concern of the congregation.
   e. Participates in denominational and interdenominational organizations for education.
   f. Carries on a continuous evaluation of the educational program.
9. There is a regular system to prevent and recover drop-outs.
10. Records that are adequate and useful are kept.
11. Personnel quality is improved and maintained through workshops, conferences, courses, and supervision.
12. The pastor is trained in educational theory and practice.

(These are in order of preference, and there were other criteria with a lower degree of importance.)

III. CURRICULUM

1. The parish education program includes a program that encompasses all ages.
2. Curriculum materials are used creatively, not slavishly.

3. The curriculum and its related activities center about:
   a. Man, as a creature of God, is responsible to God.
   b. Christ, as the Son of God, is Lord and Savior.
   c. The story and the message of the Bible are significant for daily living.
   d. The church, as an organ of Christianity, makes possible belonging to and participating in the Christian fellowship.
   e. God, as Creator and Father, is to be worshipped as Sovereign.
   f. Society, as the brotherhood of man, is responsible for human welfare.
4. Provision is made in the curriculum for:
   a. An intensive study of the Bible and its message.
   b. Good citizenship practices.
   c. The encouragement of giving to benevolent causes.
   d. An acquaintance with the heritage of the church (as history, doctrine, movements, trends, and the arts).
   e. Social service projects.
   f. Vocations in the church.

5. There are optional curricula plans, and materials are varied for selectivity.

6. Parents are responsible for making the home a Christian unit by demonstrating and encouraging Christian practices.

7. Interest groups for youth and adults have flexibility of program.

8. Resources and reference materials are available (as commentaries, atlases, religious bibliographies, books, periodicals, manuals).

9. Pupils are visited in their homes by their teacher.

10. The nature of the learner (needs, experience, life style) determines the approach to the curriculum.

(There is no reference to worship as part of the curriculum, nor is there any emphasis on the development of group relationships under 4.)

IV. PHYSICAL FACILITIES

1. Classrooms conform physically to educational standards for the age group served.

2. Tables, chairs, and desks are movable to allow for flexible arrangements.

3. The size and construction of chairs, tables, and other equipment are right for the pupils using them.

4. Over-crowding is avoided (as through multiple schedules).

5. Classrooms or class areas are so arranged that class activities do not interfere with one another.

6. Some rooms are easily adaptable to a variety of uses (as for dramatics, audio-visual aids, recreation, classes).

7. Facilities for recreation and special activities are provided.

8. Assembly facilities are available.

9. There are ample utility and store rooms.

(Again there is no mention of available places for worship.)

The above schedule of criteria is an example rather than a model, and many groups might supplement it with requirements for family worship, parents' classes, or some other activities they believe are as important as the ones listed here. The point is that it is possible to set up criteria that are relevant to the goals of a particular congregation so that the educational program may be evaluated on these terms. When fitted in with the other kinds of measurements we have mentioned, a fairly accurate picture of the comprehensive educational program of the parish may be obtained.

THEOLOGICAL EVALUATIONS

The final check on the program is a theological one. This is avoided in most rating scales, but it is essential to the educational philosophy we have presented. Theology is the source of the curriculum, provided theology is understood as the truth-about-God-in-relation-to-man. If Christian truth is consistent with all other data gleaned from all the sources of knowledge known to man, and if the Christian theologian takes this other knowledge into account as he constructs an educational philosophy and method, then theology stands behind every curriculum of Christian education as the source of it and the means of evaluating it.

James D. Smart puts it clearly:

> The function of theology is to be constantly exercising a critique upon the doctrines and practices that exist within the Church, holding them against the criterion of what God has shown us in his Word to be the true nature of the Church, and so enabling us to see what ought to be and what ought not to be.[10]

By this, I understand that we are to use our theological insights to evaluate the doctrines that are implied and the methods that are used in our teaching. Our expectations concerning what children and adults can learn, how they will behave, and whether they may become reconciled with one another and with God, depend on our theological analysis. The Christian doctrine of man makes use of psychological insights, but it is based on revelation and therefore points to a deeper

---

[10] From *The Teaching Ministry of the Church* by James D. Smart. The Westminster Press, Philadelphia. Copyright by W. L. Jenkins, 1954. Used by permission, p. 70.

truth. The Christian doctrine of the church makes use of sociological insights, but education in the church is more than a social process. Christian truth makes use of all the ideas of modern science, but though modern science illuminates aspects of the Christian revelation it does not replace it.

We need to ask, then, whether what is happening in the church's educational program is consistent with Christian truth. Much has passed for Christian education that has been respectable moral training, or indoctrination in theological tenets, or knowledge of Biblical facts. We have been satisfied with morsels of moralism, with tidbits of theology, and with *hors d'oeuvres* of Biblical verses. But the task of Christian education is to work through the institution of the church to incorporate boys and girls, men and women, into the redemptive and sustaining community that is the true church of which Jesus Christ is the foundation.

When all the facts are in from tests and score cards and observations, the evaluation of these facts must be from a theological perspective. A conference of the evaluating committee or of the board of Christian education, with time enough to sift the evidence and to get at the theological roots, should be conducted by a leader who understands the relation of theology to Christian educational methods and testing devices.

The essence of Christian learning is a faith-grace relationship. Christian nurture takes place when the believer trusts in God and in turn God's gracious favor comes to him, because that grace was there all the time awaiting the act of faith. Therefore, the application of theology to education leads to a dynamic personal relationship of faith and grace, and the ideas of theology arising from the relationships of men to God are the guides to a greater and deeper experience of God. A relevant theology stands in the background as a guide to the whole process, so that we know where we are going.[11]

All of our scientific knowledge about means is to be used, especially our knowledge of the learning process and of teaching techniques. But the theological categories are primary and the scientific categories are secondary. Too often in the past, theology has been at best a footnote to scientific conclusions, and this needs to be reversed. Theol-

---

[11] See "Christian Education as a Theological Discipline and Method," *Religious Education* (November-December 1953), p. 410.

ogy is mediated through relationships in the home and in the community, but chiefly through the theological community or fellowship (*koinonia*).[12]

The Gospel centers in Jesus Christ as he appeared in history as the focal point in the drama of redemption, and its story is the traditions of the Christian church coming down to us through the ages. We can adapt it and make it relevant, but we cannot expect to find it in the mind of a child.

CONCLUSION

From the standpoint of our understanding of the Christian faith, we evaluate the factual information about the parish educational program. Ultimately, we are training children, young people, and adults "*to be* the Church in the world of today." [13] The church is made up of people and people are the church, the community of the covenant with the lord of history.

Theodore O. Wedel writes that a man who has never seen Yale University might have full knowledge of its history, curriculum outlines, budget, and faculty, but this would not make him a Yale man. Any freshman, no matter how ignorant and irresponsible, would possess more of the Yale spirit than he. So it is, he says, with the Holy Spirit. It is the *esprit de corps,* for the church is the Spirit-bearing body. *Esprit de corps* is a social possession that must be imparted. It is a gift that comes by grace to those who belong to the fellowship. Whereas Yale can create the spirit of *alma mater,* people do not create the Holy Spirit. God founded the Christian community of the Holy Spirit, which we enter by baptism and a confession of faith. The people are the church, and yet the church is the gift of God.[14]

Christian education is the process of growing up within the life of the Christian church, and it goes on all the time.[15] The atmosphere

---

[12] See "Theology in Religious Education," *Religious Education* (March-April 1954), pp. 168-72.

[13] James D. Smart, *The Teaching Ministry of the Church,* p. 129.

[14] See Theodore O. Wedel, *The Coming Great Church* (New York: The Macmillan Company, 1945), pp. 62-63.

[15] "If education is considered as a process of growing up within the life of the group, it is immediately clear that this goes on all the time." Marjorie Reeves, *Growing Up in a Modern Society* (London: University of London Press, 1952), p. 11.

in which grace flourishes is the environment of Christian education. With all of our plans and standards and techniques and theological insights, it is God who does the educating. We are channels of his grace, doing the planting and the watering, and the increase is a gift of God.

A BASIC BIBLIOGRAPHY

THESE books provide a systematic coverage of the main items in Christian education. The list is limited to less than 50 volumes. They are more or less in agreement with the fundamental thesis of this book. Those marked with an asterisk (*) are especially suitable for church school teachers, and all of them may be read with profit by college and divinity school students.

I. THEORY OF CHRISTIAN EDUCATION

**Christian Education Today*. Chicago: International Council of Religious Education, 1945.

A committee under the chairmanship of Luther A. Weigle reworked the basic educational philosophy of the churches now belonging to the Division of Christian Education of the National Council of Churches of Christ in the United States of America.

*Howe, Reuel, *Man's Need and God's Action*. Greenwich: Seabury Press, 1953.

Applies the "language of relationships" in a radical way to the life situations of those in churches, with especial attention to baptism. Fits in with the Seabury Series.

*Lotz, Philip Henry, ed., *Orientation in Religious Education*. Nashville: Abingdon-Cokesbury Press, 1950.

Covers the whole subject with brief articles, averaging ten pages each, by experts. It is spotty, but it is the best over-all treatment.

*Miller, Randolph Crump, *The Clue to Christian Education*. New York: Charles Scribner's Sons, 1950.

Represents the kind of thinking that resulted in this introduction to Christian education.

Smart, James D., *The Teaching Ministry of the Church*. Philadelphia: Westminster Press, 1954.

The best attempt to bring theology and Christian education together, by a man who was for six years editor of the Presbyterian Christian Faith and Life Series.

Vieth, Paul H., *The Church and Christian Education.* St. Louis: Bethany Press, 1947.

The report of a committee organized to study the relationship of educational theory to the thinking of the churches in the 1940's, put into a systematic form by one of the leading thinkers in the field.

II. HISTORY OF RELIGIOUS EDUCATION

*Benson, C. H., *A Popular History of Christian Education.* Chicago: Moody Press, 1943.

A simple treatment from a conservative point of view.

Brubacher, John S., *A History of the Problems of Education.* New York: McGraw-Hill Book Co., 1947.

Covers the whole subject of education, with frequent references to religion.

Sherrill, Lewis J., *The Rise of Christian Education.* New York: The Macmillan Company, 1944.

An authoritative treatment of Jewish and Christian education up to the beginning of the fifteenth century.

III. GROWTH IN RELIGION

*Jenkins, Gladys Gardner, Helen Schacter, and William W. Bauer, *These Are Your Children,* expanded ed. Chicago: Scott, Foresman and Co., 1953.

The best popular presentation of the development of children, with plenty of illustrations but with no references to religion.

*Parkhurst, Helen, *Exploring the Child's World.* New York: Appleton-Century-Crofts, Inc., 1951.

A fascinating account of the way children respond to someone who is really interested in what they think and how they feel.

*Sherrill, Lewis J., *The Opening Doors of Childhood.* New York: The Macmillan Company, 1939.

An interpretation of the growth of religion in childhood.

*Sherrill, Lewis J., *The Struggle of the Soul.* New York: The Macmillan Company, 1951.

One of the best accounts of religion, traced from the cradle to the grave in terms of encounter with God.

Yeaxlee, Basil A., *Religion and the Growing Mind,* 3rd ed. Greenwich: Seabury Press, 1952.

Combining psychological and theological interests, the author provides us with an accurate picture of the development of religion in the individual. Parents and teachers with more than usual education will find this among their most helpful resources.

IV. CHURCH AND HOME

Bushnell, Horace, *Christian Nurture.* New Haven: Yale University Press, 1947.

Provides an organic view of the family as the center of sound Christian nurture. As relevant today as it was one hundred years ago. This edition has historical introductions by Williston Walker and Luther A. Weigle.

*Chaplin, Dora P., *Children and Religion.* New York: Charles Scribner's Sons, 1948.

Good theology, method, and common sense combined to provide guidance for parents and teachers.

*Fallaw, Wesner, *The Modern Parent and the Teaching Church.* New York: The Macmillan Company, 1946.

This is the most significant of all the recent books showing how the church can work with families.

Ligon, Ernest M., *A Greater Generation.* New York: The Macmillan Company, 1948.

Provides evidence of the ways in which parents cooperate when a program of Christian character education is taken seriously.

V. CHURCH AND SCHOOL

Linton, Clarence, *The Function of Public Schools in Dealing with Religion.* Washington: American Council on Education, 1953.

A statement that points out difficulties and possibilities.

*Williams, J. Paul, *The New Education and Religion.* New York: Association Press, 1945.

Literature in this field is constantly appearing. This is as good a summary of the various options and the reasons for them as may be found.

VI. CHURCH AND COMMUNITY

Lippitt, Ronald, *Training in Community Relations.* New York: Harper & Brothers, 1949.

Group procedures at work to create relationships.

*Reeves, Marjorie, *Growing Up in a Modern Society,* 3rd ed. London: University of London Press, 1952.

Admirable for its insights into the nature of community both inside and outside the church.

Swearington, Tilford T., *The Community and Christian Education.* St. Louis: Bethany Press, 1950.
Based on a committee study, this book gets at some of the fundamental problems in an American community.

VII. THE CHURCH AND THE CHURCH SCHOOL

*Lobinger, John Leslie, *The Better Church School.* Boston: Pilgrim Press, 1952.
An elementary treatment of the over-all educational task of the church. Excellent to use for leadership training.

*Miller, Randolph Crump, *A Guide for Church School Teachers,* 2nd ed. Greenwich: Seabury Press, 1947.
An elementary approach to Christian education, helpful to church school teachers and staff. Appendix contains selected lesson materials and suggestions for parish library.

*Young, Frances M., *An Almanac for Church School Superintendents.* Greenwich: Seabury Press, 1953.
Through the church year with all the important tasks mapped out and with plenty of help.

VIII. TEACHING METHODS

Betts, George Herbert, and Marion O. Hawthorne, *Method in Teaching Religion.* New York: Abingdon Press, 1925.
Still the most thorough coverage of all teaching methods in relation to religion. Probably out of print, but available in libraries or second-hand bookstores.

*Eakin, Mildred Moody, and Frank Eakin, *The Church School Teacher's Job.* New York: The Macmillan Company, 1949.
Gives the larger framework of the teacher's task, with plenty of specific help and illustrations.

*Haas, Kenneth B., and Harry Q. Packer, *Preparation and Use of Audio-Visual Aids.* New York: Prentice-Hall, Inc., 1950.
Practical helps for every kind of showing.

*Rogers, William L., and Paul H. Vieth, *Visual Aids in the Church.* Philadelphia: Christian Education Press, 1946.
Good theory and practice are suggested throughout.

*Vieth, Paul H., *How to Teach in the Church School.* Philadelphia: Westminster Press, 1935.
A standard textbook for teachers. It is clear, simple, and to the point.

*Wiles, Kimball, *Teaching for Better Schools.* New York: Prentice-Hall, Inc., 1952.

A study of skill in human relations, group work, evaluation, individualizing instruction, cooperation, and self-improvement. Can be adapted to Reuel Howe's "language of relationships." (See *Man's Need and God's Action,* above.)

IX. THE USE OF THE BIBLE

*Anderson, Bernard W., *The Unfolding Drama of the Bible.* New York: Association Press (Haddam House), 1953.

By far the best pamphlet to guide teachers, parents, and other adults in understanding the Biblical drama of redemption. To be used with his *Rediscovering the Bible,* 1951.

*Dentan, Robert C., *The Holy Scriptures.* Greenwich: Seabury Press, 1949.

An interpretation of the Bible as "the mighty acts of God in history." May be used in the same way as Anderson's book, with a study guide, *Redemption and Revelation,* 1951.

*Smither, Ethel L., *The Use of the Bible with Children.* Nashville: Abingdon-Cokesbury Press, 1937.

Although this book does not share the theological outlook of Anderson or Dentan, it is a reliable guide to the limitations of children through the sixth grade.

X. ADMINISTRATION

Conover, Elbert M., *The Church School and Parish House Building.* Chicago: National Council of Churches, 1949.

The only reliable guide to building or making alterations for effective Christian learning.

*Crawford, Donald W., ed., *A Parish Workshop in Christian Education.* Greenwich: Seabury Press, 1953.

Brings out in the congregation a realization of the need for a quality of life that provides resources for the education of children and adults.

*Eakin, Mildred Moody, and Frank Eakin, *The Pastor and the Children.* New York: The Macmillan Company, 1947.

The only book that makes clear the pastor's function in relation to the children and the educational program of the parish.

*Heim, Ralph D., *Leading a Sunday Church School.* Philadelphia: Muhlenberg Press, 1950.

This is the best single book dealing with administrative and organizational problems.

Kean, Charles D., *The Christian Gospel and the Parish Church.* Greenwich: Seabury Press, 1953.

Goes a step beyond the workshop (see Crawford, above) and may be used with a study guide for adults, *The Gospel and the Parish,* 1953.

*Vieth, Paul H., *Improving Your Sunday School.* Philadelphia: Westminster Press, 1930.

Shows the responsibilities of the superintendent as administrator, organizer, and especially as supervisor.

*Wiles, Kimball, *Supervision for Better Schools.* New York: Prentice-Hall, Inc., 1950.

Written for secular schools, this book provides more help for church school supervisors than any written specifically in the field of Christian education.

XI. CHILDREN, YOUTH, AND ADULTS

Bowman, Clarice M., *Ways Youth Learn.* Nashville: Abingdon-Cokesbury Press, 1952.

This book reflects the actual behavior of young people today. Should be used in conjunction with Roberts, Dorothy M., *Leadership of Teen-Age Groups.* New York: Association Press, 1950.

Chamberlain, J. Gordon, *The Church and Its Young Adults.* Nashville: Abingdon-Cokesbury Press, 1943.

How to minister to a group often neglected by the churches.

Knowles, Malcolm S., *Informal Adult Education.* New York: Association Press, 1950.

The first half of this book is particularly helpful in setting up an adult program in the church. May be used with *How to Teach Adults,* Greenwich: Seabury Press, and Gorham, Donald, *Understanding Adults,* Philadelphia: Judson Press, 1948.

*Manwell, Elizabeth M., and Sophia L. Fahs, *Consider the Children: How They Grow,* rev. ed. Boston: Beacon Press, 1951.

Remarkable insights into children during the first five years.

Maves, Paul, and J. Lennart Cedarleaf, *Older People and the Church.* Nashville: Abingdon-Cokesbury Press, 1949.

The church's program to meet the needs of older people rounds out the mission from birth to the grave.

More Than Words. Greenwich: Seabury Press, 1955.

A theological word book for 12-year-olds. An excellent resource book for teachers.

XII. MAGAZINES AND PERIODICALS

**Child Study.* Child Study Association of America.
Deals occasionally with religious problems.

**Children's Religion.* Boston: Pilgrim Press.
Published by Congregationalists and widely used by Christian teachers and parents.

**The Christian Home.* Nashville: Methodist Publishing House.
Has a large interdenominational clientele.

**International Journal of Religious Education.* Chicago: Division of Christian Education, National Council of Churches.
Should be in every parish library and, preferably, in every leader's home. The one sure way of keeping up to date.

Pastoral Psychology. Great Neck, N. Y.: Pulpit Digest Publishing Co.
Frequently has articles on Christian education and related subjects. Likely to be technical.

Religious Education. New York: Religious Education Association.
Published bi-monthly. Has articles by Protestants, Roman Catholics, and Jews on every aspect of religious education. Indispensable for the college and seminary student.

**World Christian Education.* New York: World Council of Religious Education.
A quarterly journal reflecting opinions from all over the world.

Most of the denominations publish excellent magazines, and some teacher-parent quarterlies carry articles of general interest. Many other journals, such as *Religion in Life,* carry occasional articles of real importance.

FOR MORE INFORMATION

CHAPTER 1. THE SIGNIFICANCE OF RELIGIOUS EDUCATION

The theory of Christian education underlying this book has an earlier foundation in my *The Clue to Christian Education* (New York: Charles Scribner's Sons, 1950), the first chapter of which is particularly relevant. Paul H. Vieth approaches the same problems from the position of a large committee that studied the situation, in *The Church and Christian Education* (St. Louis: Bethany Press, 1947). James D. Smart provides another step toward a theological synthesis in *The Teaching Ministry of the Church* (Philadelphia: Westminster Press, 1954).

The treatment of revelation in this chapter is found in more detail in William Temple, *Nature, Man and God* (London: Macmillan & Co., Ltd., 1934), pp. 301–327, and in A. E. Baker, ed., *William Temple's Teaching* (Philadelphia: Westminster Press, 1950), pp. 36–42.

The ecumenical movement is summarized in William Adams Brown's *Toward a United Church* (New York: Charles Scribner's Sons, 1946). See also Henry P. Van Dusen, *World Christianity* (Nashville: Abingdon-Cokesbury Press, 1947); Robert Bilheimer, *The Quest for Christian Unity* (New York: Association Press, 1952); Lesslie Newbigin, *The Reunion of the Church* (New York: Harper & Bros., 1948); Charles Clayton Morrison, *The Unfinished Reformation* (New York: Harper & Bros., 1953).

The modern scope of education is covered adequately in John S. Brubacher, *Modern Philosophies of Education* (New York: McGraw-Hill Book Co., 1950), especially, for our purposes, in his chapter 13; in a scheme of three major systems in John P. Wynne, *Philosophies of Education* (New York: Prentice-Hall, Inc., 1950); and in J. Donald Butler, *Four Philosophies and Their Practice in Education and Religion* (New York: Harper & Bros., 1951).

The relation of education to community is brought out clearly by Marjorie Reeves in *Growing Up in a Modern Society,* 3rd ed. (London: University of London Press, 1952), a book remarkable in that it deals with public education from the standpoint of a Christian world view. On group processes see Ronald Lippitt, *Training in Community Relations* (New York: Harper & Bros., 1949).

The March-April 1954 issue of *Religious Education* is especially valuable as an example of the latest thinking in the field and could serve as a syllabus for a discussion of basic issues.

CHAPTER 2. HISTORICAL DEVELOPMENT OF CHRISTIAN EDUCATION

A thorough treatment of Jewish and Christian education to the year A.D. 1400 is in Lewis J. Sherrill, *The Rise of Christian Education* (New York: The Macmillan Company, 1944). A less detailed treatment bringing the story down to date is *Popular History of Christian Education,* by C. H. Benson (Chicago: Moody Press, 1943). Brief chapters on the subject are in John S. Brubacher, *A History of the Problems of Education* (New York: McGraw-Hill Book Co., 1947), chap. 11; Lewis J. Sherrill, "A Historical Study of the Religious Education Movement," in *Orientation in Religious Education,* ed. Philip Henry Lotz (Nashville: Abingdon-Cokesbury Press, 1950), pp. 13–24; Randolph C. Miller, *A Guide for Church School Teachers,* rev. ed. (Greenwich: Seabury Press, 1947), pp. 3–16; Mildred Moody Eakin and Frank Eakin, *The Church School Teacher's Job* (New York: The Macmillan Company, 1949), pp. 188–205.

The history of American Sunday schools is found in *A History of Religious Education in Recent Times,* by A. A. Brown (New York: Abingdon Press, 1923). Specific areas are covered in detail in George Stewart, Jr., *A History of Religious Education in Connecticut to the Middle of the Nineteenth Century* (New Haven: Yale University Press, 1924); Sandford Fleming, *Children and Puritanism* (New Haven: Yale University Press, 1933); Clifton H. Brewer, *A History of Religious Education in the Episcopal Church to 1835* (New Haven: Yale University Press, 1924). To appreciate the significance of Horace Bushnell, see Luther A. Weigle's introduction to the centenary edition of *Christian Nurture* (New Haven: Yale University Press, 1947).

The story of the past fifty years, with special attention to George A. Coe, is in H. Shelton Smith's chapter on "Christian Education," in *Protestant Thought in the Twentieth Century,* ed. Arnold S. Nash (New York: The Macmillan Company, 1951), pp. 225–46. Excellent brief articles are in *Encyclopedia of Religion,* ed. Vergilius Ferm (New York: Philosophical Library, 1945), pp. 649–50, 744–49. The story of interdenominational cooperation is covered by William Clayton Bower and Percy Roy Hayward in *Protestantism Faces Its Educational Task Together* (Chicago: National Council of Churches, 1949), and by Paul H. Vieth in *The Church and Christian Education* (St. Louis: Bethany Press, 1947), pp. 263–92.

The rise of psychology of religion can be best understood in William James' *Varieties of Religious Experience* (New York: Longmans, Green and Co., 1902), available in a special Modern Library edition, and in George A. Coe's *The Psychology of Religion* (Chicago: University of Chicago Press, 1916). The best recent book is Paul E. Johnson's *Psychol-*

ogy of Religion (Nashville: Abingdon-Cokesbury Press, 1945), which also has an excellent bibliography. *Reality in Worship,* by Willard L. Sperry (New York: The Macmillan Company, 1925), continues to be a remarkable combination of psychological and religious insight in the field of worship. George Hedley's *Christian Worship* (New York: The Macmillan Company, 1953) indicates the status of recent thinking on the subject, with many helps for religious educators on the high school and college level.

Contemporary American Theology, two volumes edited by Vergilius Ferm (New York: Round Table Press, 1932, 1933), comes nearest to providing the flavor of theological thinking before the impact of Karl Barth on American thought. Thomas S. Kepler's anthologies, *Contemporary Religious Thought* and *Contemporary Thinking about Jesus* (Nashville: Abingdon-Cokesbury Press, 1941 and 1944), let the scholars speak for themselves. *Types of Modern Theology,* by Hugh Ross Mackintosh (New York: Charles Scribner's Sons, 1937), gives a fine evaluation of continental theology. *Protestant Christianity,* by John Dillenberger and Claude A. Welch (New York: Charles Scribner's Sons, 1954), covers a wider period of history. *A Layman's Guide to Protestant Theology,* by William Hordern (New York: The Macmillan Company, 1955), is excellent for church school teachers.

The reactions of religious educators to the changing theological climate can be seen in George A. Coe's *What Is Christian Education?* (New York: Charles Scribner's Sons, 1929), Harrison S. Elliott's *Can Religious Education Be Christian?* (New York: The Macmillan Company, 1940), H. Shelton Smith's *Faith and Nurture* (New York: Charles Scribner's Sons, 1941), Paul H. Vieth's *The Church and Christian Education,* (St. Louis: Bethany Press, 1947), pp. 19–87, Randolph C. Miller's *The Clue to Christian Education* (New York: Charles Scribner's Sons, 1950), and James D. Smart's *The Teaching Ministry of the Church* (Philadelphia: Westminster Press, 1954). Wesner Fallaw's *Modern Parent and the Teaching Church* (New York: The Macmillan Company, 1946) is the most significant of a number of books dealing with the place of the home in Christian education.

CHAPTER 3. WHAT IS CHRISTIAN EDUCATION?

For further understanding of the nature of education and the curriculum from the standpoint of history, see John S. Brubacher, *A History of the Problems of Education* (New York: McGraw-Hill Book Co., 1947), pp. 96–317. John P. Wynne, in *Philosophies of Education* (New York: Prentice-Hall, Inc., 1947), compares three basic educational theories.

Much can be learned about the learning process from John Dollard and Neal E. Miller, *Personality and Psychotherapy* (New York: McGraw-Hill Book Co., 1950), pp. 25–97, and *Social Learning and Imitation* (New Haven: Yale University Press, 1941), pp. 1–90. John S. Brubacher has two chapters on "The Educative Process" in *Modern Philosophies of Edu-*

cation (New York: McGraw-Hill Book Co., 1950). The subject is treated in popular form by Harold Spears, *Principles of Teaching* (New York: Prentice-Hall, Inc., 1951), pp. 93–182. Kimball Wiles' *Teaching for Better Schools* (New York: Prentice-Hall, Inc., 1952), pp. 3–29, is extremely effective in making the picture of the learning process simple.

The problem of curriculum from a religious perspective is best seen in William Clayton Bower, *Curriculum of Religious Education* (New York: Charles Scribner's Sons, 1925). *The International Curriculum Guide, Book I: Principles and Objectives of Christian Education* (Chicago: International Council of Religious Education, 1932, 1935) is of great value for understanding ways in which religious educators have made use of new educational insights. *Christian Education Today* (Chicago: International Council of Religious Education, 1940, 1945) shows the changes that took place in a decade. *Curriculum Guide for the Local Church* (Chicago: International Council of Religious Education, 1950) has gone through several revisions, but this edition summarizes the viewpoint for 1950. *A Guide for Curriculum in Christian Education* (Chicago: National Council of Churches, 1955), brings this line of thought up to date.[1]

To know John Dewey at first hand, one should read his *Democracy and Education* (New York: The Macmillan Company, 1916), *How We Think* (Boston: D. C. Heath & Co., 1933), *A Common Faith* (New Haven: Yale University Press, 1934), which is his only book on religion, and *Experience and Education* (New York: The Macmillan Company, 1938).

On the nature of philosophy, Vergilius Ferm's *First Adventures in Philosophy* (New York: Charles Scribner's Sons, 1936), pp. 1–101, provides essential information. J. V. Langmead Casserley treats the problem of *The Christian in Philosophy* (New York: Charles Scribner's Sons, 1951) in an unusual manner.

The Nature of Religion, by Georg Wobbermin (New York: Thomas Y. Crowell Co., 1933) is a thoroughgoing treatment of the subject. Edgar Brightman's *A Philosophy of Religion* (New York: Prentice-Hall, Inc., 1940), summarizes the findings of various scholars on pages 13–18. Henry H. Shires' "An Inquiry into the Origin of Religion," in *Christianity and the Contemporary Scene* (New York: Morehouse-Gorham Co., 1943), eds. Randolph C. Miller and Henry H. Shires, pp. 61–72, summarizes the most important theories.

Harris Franklin Rall deals with the nature of both religion and Christianity in *Christianity* (New York: Charles Scribner's Sons, 1940), pp. 3–86. D. M. Baillie's *God Was in Christ* (New York: Charles Scribner's Sons, 1948) is one of the classic statements of faith. Karl Barth's *Dogmatics in Outline* (New York: Philosophical Library, 1950) is probably

---

[1] The International Council of Religious Education became the Division of Christian Education of the National Council of the Churches of Christ in the United States of America in 1950. Its catalog of publications may be ordered from 257 Fourth Avenue, New York 10, New York.

the simplest introduction to his thought. The Lundensian emphasis is clearly treated in Gustaf Aulén's *Faith of the Christian Church* (Philadelphia: Muhlenberg Press, 1948). Daniel Day Williams' *God's Grace and Man's Hope* (New York: Harper & Bros., 1949) is an example of theology that maintains the values of both liberalism and neo-orthodoxy, and his *What Present-Day Theologians Are Thinking* (New York: Harper & Bros., 1952) is an admirable interpretation of the current scene. John Dillenberger and Claude A. Welch have provided a sound treatment of the development of *Protestant Christianity* (New York: Charles Scribner's Sons, 1954). Julian N. Hartt's *Toward a Theology of Evangelism* (Nashville: Abingdon Press, 1955), provides a background for both evangelism and education.

The best introduction to George A. Coe's thought is his *What Is Christian Education?* (New York: Charles Scribner's Sons, 1929). The March-April 1952 issue of *Religious Education* is dedicated to him. An evaluation of Coe by H. Shelton Smith appears in *Protestant Thought in the Twentieth Century,* ed. Arnold S. Nash (New York: The Macmillan Company, 1951), pp. 225–241. Ernest Chave's *A Functional Approach to Religious Education* (Chicago: University of Chicago Press, 1947) treats religion from a naturalist's point of view.

The changing scene is illustrated by Dora P. Chaplin in *Children and Religion* (New York: Charles Scribner's Sons, 1948). Paul H. Vieth's *The Church and Christian Education* (St. Louis: Bethany Press, 1947) is representative of the thinking of the leaders in the field, and pages 19–87 are particularly significant. James D. Smart's *The Teaching Ministry of the Church* (Philadelphia: Westminster Press, 1954) carries the theological emphasis even further. *Religious Education* (November–December, 1953), pp. 371–79, 409–21, (March-April 1954), pp. 168–72, indicates this same concern. The emphasis on community in relation to Christian demands is found in Marjorie Reeves' *Growing Up in a Modern Society,* 3rd ed. (London: University of London Press, 1952). For perspective, one should turn back to *Christian Nurture* (New Haven: Yale University Press, 1947), by Horace Bushnell, who foresaw many recent developments over a century ago.

CHAPTER 4. THEOLOGY AND CHRISTIAN EDUCATION

The simplest summaries of the point of view in this chapter concerning the Bible are to be found in Bernhard Anderson's *Rediscovering the Bible* (New York: Association Press–Haddam House, 1951), and the summary of it in his *The Unfolding Drama of the Bible* (New York: Association Press–Haddam House, 1953). Robert Dentan's *The Holy Scriptures* (Greenwich: Seabury Press, 1949) is of equal value. More advanced students will especially want to read G. Ernest Wright's *The God Who Acts* (Chicago: Henry Regnery Co., 1952), Millar Burrows' *Outline of*

Biblical Theology (Philadelphia: Westminster Press, 1946), Emil Brunner's *The Christian Doctrine of Creation and Redemption* (Philadelphia: Westminster Press, 1952), Alan Richardson's *Theological Word Book of the Bible* (New York: The Macmillan Company, 1950), and H. H. Rowley's *The Relevance of the Bible* (New York: The Macmillan Company, 1944). For a critical appraisal of this view, see Sophia Fahs' *Today's Children and Yesterday's Heritage* (Boston: Beacon Press, 1952), pp. 59–100.

Current theology can best be understood by reading Walter Marshall Horton's *Christian Theology: An Ecumenical Approach* (New York: Harper & Brothers, 1955), Charles D. Kean's *Making Sense Out of Life* (Philadelphia: Westminster Press, 1954), William A. Spurrier's *Guide to the Christian Faith* (New York: Charles Scribner's Sons, 1952), Henry H. Farmer's *God and Men* (Nashville: Abingdon-Cokesbury Press, 1946), Robert E. Fitch's *The Kingdom Without End* (New York: Charles Scribner's Sons, 1950), Gustaf Aulen's *The Faith of the Christian Church* (Philadelphia: Muhlenberg Press, 1948), Daniel Day Williams' *What Present Day Theologians Are Thinking* (New York: Harper & Brothers, 1952), and Reinhold Niebuhr's *The Nature and Destiny of Man* (New York: Charles Scribner's Sons, 1948). An attempt to translate this information into the language of seventh graders is found in *More Than Words* (Greenwich: Seabury Press, 1955).

On the relation of theology to life, the opening chapter of my *The Clue to Christian Education* (New York: Charles Scribner's Sons, 1950) presents the viewpoint of this book. A contrast in approaches can be studied in Harrison Elliott's *Can Religious Education Be Christian?* (New York: The Macmillan Company, 1940) and H. Shelton Smith's *Faith and Nurture* (New York: Charles Scribner's Sons, 1941); a study of these two books makes an excellent term paper for a seminary course. See also James D. Smart's *The Teaching Ministry of the Church* (Philadelphia: Westminster Press, 1954).

Emil Brunner's *The Misunderstanding of the Church* (Philadelphia: Westminster Press, 1953) is an excellent picture of the New Testament concept. A broader view is found in J. Robert Nelson's *The Realm of Redemption* (Greenwich: Seabury Press, 1951). The practical application is found in Charles Kean's *The Christian Gospel and the Parish Church* (Greenwich: Seabury Press, 1953).

My article on "Theology and the Understanding of Children," *Pastoral Psychology* (June 1952), may prove helpful. Basil A. Yeaxlee's *Religion and the Growing Mind* (Greenwich: Seabury Press, 1952), although essentially psychological in its orientation, has theological assumptions. More liberal theological assumptions underlie Mildred Moody Eakin and Frank Eakin's *Your Child's Religion* (New York: The Macmillan Company, 1942). Ernest M. Ligon's *Their Future Is Now* (New York: The Macmillan Company, 1939) shows how character education develops. Lewis J. Sherrill's *The Struggle of the Soul* (New York: The Macmillan Company, 1951) combines the theological and psychological interests.

CHAPTER 5. GROWTH IN RELIGION

The most helpful book for understanding the psychology of religious development for all age groups is Basil A. Yeaxlee, *Religion and the Growing Mind,* 3rd ed. (Greenwich: Seabury Press, 1952). Two books by Lewis J. Sherrill that are somewhat easier reading are *The Opening Doors of Childhood* (New York: The Macmillan Company, 1939) and *The Struggle of the Soul* (New York: The Macmillan Company, 1951). Mildred Moody Eakin and Frank Eakin relate theology to various age groups in *Your Child's Religion* (New York: The Macmillan Company, 1942). Ernest M. Ligon deals with character education in terms of age groups in *Their Future Is Now* (New York: The Macmillan Company, 1939).

The study of age groups in terms of their religious development is traced through the first five years in *Consider the Children—How They Grow,* rev. ed., by Elizabeth M. Manwell and Sophia L. Fahs (Boston: Beacon Press, 1953). Ruth Davis Perry deals with the pre-school age in *Children Need Adults* (New York: Harper & Bros., 1943). Marguerite Harmon Bro, in *When Children Ask* (New York: Harper & Bros., 1940), shows many ways of dealing with childrens' questions. *Teen-Agers—Their Days and Ways,* by Rowena Ferguson (Chicago: National Council of Churches, 1952), is an excellent pamphlet. Some help may be found in my " 'Bobby-Sox' Religion," *Religious Education* (March–April 1946). Dora P. Chaplin, in *Children and Religion* (New York: Charles Scribner's Sons, 1948), provides many insights for all age groups. *More Than Words* (Greenwich: Seabury Press, 1955)is an approach to religious vocabulary for intermediates.

The difficulty that children face in dealing with abstract concepts is brought out vividly in a statistical survey by John B. McDowell, *The Development of the Idea of God in the Catholic Child* (Washington: Catholic University Press, 1952). *Building the Integrated Curriculum,* ed. Sister Mary Janet Miller (Washington: Catholic University Press, 1953), shows what is being done with secondary education in Roman Catholic schools.

Other age-groups are treated adequately by J. Gordon Chamberlain, *The Church and Its Young Adults* (Nashville: Abingdon-Cokesbury Press, 1943); Donald Graham, *Understanding Adults* (Philadelphia: Judson Press, 1948); Paul Maves and J. Lennart Cedarleaf, *Older People and the Church* (Nashville: Abingdon-Cokesbury Press, 1949).

These Are Your Children, expanded ed., by Gladys Gardner Jenkins, Helen Shacter, and William W. Bauer (Chicago: Scott, Foresman, and Co., 1953), gives an over-all picture of children's development with no reference to religion. Robert J. Havighurst's *Developmental Tasks and Education* (New York: Longmans, Green & Co., 1952), is a brief pamphlet summarizing the most important age group tasks. Arthur T. Jersild, *Child Psychology,* 4th ed. (New York: Prentice-Hall, Inc., 1954), offers complete coverage of the subject. Helen Parkhurst, *Exploring the Child's*

World (New York: Appleton-Century-Crofts, Inc., 1951), is unusual in that it reports the children's own comments and reactions.

More details for specific age groups may be found in the books by Arnold Gesell and others, *Infant and Child in the Culture of Today* (New York: Harper & Bros., 1943), *The First Five Years of Life* (New York: Harper & Bros., 1940), *The Child from Five to Ten* (New York: Harper & Bros., 1946). *Growth and Development of the Preadolescent,* by Arthur Witt Blair and William H. Burton (New York: Appleton-Century-Crofts, Inc., 1951), is the only full treatment of ages nine through eleven. There are many good books on adolescence, among which may be recommended *The Adolescent Years,* by William W. Wattenberg (New York: Harcourt, Brace and Company, Inc., 1955). Teen-age boys are discussed in *Rediscovering the Adolescent,* by Hedley Seldon Dimock (New York: Association Press, 1947).

CHAPTER 6. RELIGIOUS EDUCATION IN THE HOME

On the nature of Christian marriage, Derrick Sherwin Bailly's *The Mystery of Love and Marriage* (New York: Harper & Brothers, 1952) is probably the best single treatment of the subject. Help will be found in *The Divine Imperative,* by Emil Brunner (Philadelphia: Westminster Press, 1937), pp. 340–83; and in *Christian Nurture,* by Horace Bushnell (New Haven: Yale University Press, 1947), pp. 74–101; see also pp. 102–20, 194–351, on family living.

The most thoroughgoing sociological approaches to the family, including religion, are found in *The Family,* by Ernest W. Burgess and Harvey J. Locke (New York: American Book Co., 1953), and *Marriage and the Family in American Culture,* by Andrew Truxal and Frances E. Merrill (New York: Prentice-Hall, Inc., 1952). For success in marriage, the basic book is by Ernest W. Burgess and Leonard S. Cottrell, *Predicting Success or Failure in Marriage* (New York: Prentice-Hall, Inc., 1939).

The best book for clergy concerning premarital instruction is *Education for Christian Marriage,* ed. Arnold S. Nash (London: Student Christian Movement, 1939). W. Norman Pittenger's *A Christian View of Sex* (Greenwich: Seabury Press, 1954) is a clear and elementary approach. *When You Marry,* by Eleanor Duvall and Reuben Hill (New York: Association Press, 1945), and *Harmony in Marriage,* by Leland Foster Wood (New York: Round Table Press, 1939), are as good as any books to place in the hands of those contemplating marriage.

Reuel Howe's *Man's Need and God's Action* (Greenwich: Seabury Press, 1953), pp. 51–61, is a good, brief introduction to infant baptism. E. W. Southcott's *Receive This Child* (London: A. A. Mowbray & Co., Ltd., 1951) tells how one clergyman implemented this program.

On the relation of the family to the church, there are a number of good books. Wesner Fallaw's *The Modern Parent and the Teaching Church* (New York: The Macmillan Company, 1946) and Ernest Ligon's *A Greater Generation* (New York: The Macmillan Company, 1948) show two significant approaches with quite different underlying philosophies. (The former is also excellent from the standpoint of administration.) Wesner Fallaw's brief article, "Home and Parent Education," in *Orientation in Religious Education,* pp. 236–46, ed. Philip Henry Lotz (Nashville: Abingdon-Cokesbury Press, 1950), is worth looking at. Luther Allen Weigle's *The Training of Children in the Christian Family* (Boston: Pilgrim Press, 1922), has some good material not available elsewhere. Basil Yeaxlee's *Religion and the Growing Mind* (Greenwich: Seabury Press, 1952) has a chapter for parents, pp. 178–97. Several chapters in my books may prove helpful: *Religion Makes Sense* (Greenwich: Seabury Press, 1950), pp. 96–112, and *A Symphony of the Christian Year* (Greenwich: Seabury Press, 1954), pp. 140–53, 207–12. Paul H. Vieth's *The Church and Christian Education* (St. Louis: Bethany Press, 1947) has a chapter on "The Family in Christian Education," pp. 168–92.

Some good books for parents are Donald M. Maynard, *Your Home Can Be Christian* (Nashville: Abingdon-Cokesbury Press, 1952); Marguerite Harmon Bro, *When Children Ask* (New York: Harper & Brothers, 1940); Dora P. Chaplin, *Children and Religion* (New York: Charles Scribner's Sons, 1948); Mary Alice Jones, *Guiding Children in Christian Growth* (Nashville: Abingdon-Cokesbury Press, 1949); Mildred Moody Eakin and Frank Eakin, *Your Child's Religion* (New York: Macmillan Co., 1942); John Charles Wynn, *How Christian Parents Face Family Problems* (Philadelphia: Westminster Press, 1955); Pearl R. Rosser, *Your Child Grows Toward God* (Philadelphia: Judson Press, 1944); Ethel Smither, *The Use of the Bible with Children* (Nashville: Abingdon-Cokesbury Press, 1937); Mazelle W. Thomas, *The Family Worships Togther* (Boston: Pilgrim Press, 1949); Anita Wheatcroft, *Preface for Parents* (Greenwich: Seabury Press, 1955); Randolph C. Miller, *The Clue to Christian Education* (New York: Charles Scribner's Sons, 1950). *The Growing Family,* ed. Maxwell S. Stewart (New York: Harper & Brothers, 1955), carries reprints of some Public Affairs pamphlets. *Our Children Today,* ed. Sidonie Matsner Gruenberg (New York: Viking Press, 1952), contains some excellent articles on all major problems, and has a good bibliography of secular books. Another good bibliography is in *These Are Your Children,* by Gladys Gardner Jenkins, Helen Shacter, and William W. Bauer (Chicago: Scott, Foresman and Co., 1953), which is a readable book for all parents.

A good deal of technical information has appeared in *Pastoral Psychology,* especially the issues of May, September, and October 1952, February and March 1953; and in *Sex and Religion,* ed. Simon Doniger (New York: Association Press, 1954).

The baffling problem of interreligious marriages is handled with expertness by James A. Pike in *If You Marry Outside Your Faith* (New York: Harper & Bros., 1954). *If I Marry a Roman Catholic* (New York: National Council of Churches) is a brief pamphlet for the literature rack. A less temperate view is found in Paul Blanshard, *American Freedom and Catholic Power* (Boston: Beacon Press, 1949), pp. 132–79.

Some books written in popular style have value. Neil Hart's *Home and Church Working Together* (Nashville: Abingdon-Cokesbury Press, 1951) has much practical wisdom. Ann Proctor's two books, *The Christian Household* and *Background to Marriage* (New York: Longmans, Green and Co., 1950, 1953), have much frank and homely advice. Among James Ellenwood's books, all of which are delightful, *It Runs in the Family* (New York: Charles Scribner's Sons, 1942), is as captivating as any.

A few outstanding books for children's use in the home should be mentioned: For very young children, the story books in the curriculum materials are among the best. Three-year-olds will enjoy the *Martin and Judy Stories,* Vol. I, by Verna Hills and Sophia Fahs (Boston: Beacon Press, 1939), and the later volumes in this series will please four and five year olds. *A Small Child's Bible,* by Pelagie Doane (New York: Oxford University Press, 1946), retells some of the best stories for children from six to eight. For this same age, Mary Alice Jones has written four books: *Tell Me About God, Tell Me About Jesus, Tell Me About Prayer,* and *Tell Me About the Bible* (Chicago: Rand, McNally & Co.). Her *Bible Stories* (Rand, McNally & Co., 1952) are excellently presented. Dorothy Kunhardt's *Once There Was a Little Boy* (New York: Viking Press, 1946) is a fascinating account of Jesus' boyhood for primary children. Juniors and junior highs are fascinated by *One God: The Ways We Worship Him,* by Florence Mary Fitch (New York: Lothrop, Lee and Sheperd, 1944), with its pictures and text illustrating the Jewish, Roman Catholic and Protestant customs of worship. Walter Russell Bowie's *The Bible Stories for Boys and Girls* (Nashville: Abingdon-Cokesbury Press, 1951, 1952) has a volume on the Old Testament and another on the New Testament for those about nine to thirteen. Hulda Niebuhr's *The One Story* (Philadelphia: Westminster Press, 1950) is an excellent treatment of the Bible story for those eleven to fourteen. Roland Bainton's *The Church of Our Fathers* (New York: Charles Scribner's Sons, 1940) works best at about the ninth grade and up. *The King Nobody Wanted,* by Norman Langford (Philadelphia: Westminster Press, 1949), is one of the best lives of Christ for juniors, and *Men Called Him Master,* by Elwyn Allen Smith (Philadelphia: Westminster Press, 1949), is equally good for junior highs. John Oxenham's *The Hidden Years* (New York: Longmans, Green, and Co., 1925) is an exciting fictional approach to the life of Jesus, and is suitable for junior high and adults. Mary McNeer and Lynd Ward have written and illustrated lives of *John Wesley* (Nashville: Abingdon-Cokesbury Press, 1951) and of *Martin Luther* (Nashville: Abingdon-Cokesbury Press, 1953) which are good for boys and girls from ten through fourteen. There are many children's bible books and books of prayers which are beautifully illustrated. *I Believe,* by Nevin C. Harner (Philadelphia: Christian Education Press, 1950), is an excellent approach to doctrine for high school students. *Great Ideas of the Bible,* 2 vols., by Ryllis Goslin Lynip (New York: Harper & Brothers, 1954, 1955), presents the Moffatt translation to modern youth with an interesting commentary.

Parents who want a guide to their children's reading in every field from religion to comics should read Josette Frank's *Your Child's Reading Today* (New York: Doubleday and Co., Inc., 1954). Recommended comics are listed by the Committee on Evaluation of Comic Books (Box 1486, Cincinnati 1, Ohio, 10 cents).

CHAPTER 7. RELIGIOUS EDUCATION IN THE SCHOOLS

For a general discussion of all the possibilities in the relation of religion to public education, see J. Paul Williams, *The New Education and Religion* (New York: Association Press, 1945). *American Democracy and Religion,* ed. F. Ernest Johnson (New York: Harper & Brothers, 1952), deals with Jewish, Catholic, and Protestant points of view, and with the problem as it exists in all kinds of educational institutions. Anson Phelps Stokes' three-volume survey of *Church and State in the United States* (New York: Harper & Brothers, 1950) is an encyclopedic reference dealing with the status of churches and synagogues. Brief treatments are found in chapters by Luther A. Weigle, Ray Gibbons, and J. Paul Williams in *Orientation in Religious Education,* ed. Philip Henry Lotz (Nashville: Abingdon-Cokesbury Press, 1950), pp. 87–97, 479–89, 491–99.

Vivian T. Thayer, in *The Attack upon the American Secular School* (Boston: Beacon Press, 1951), defends secularism but admits that some form of objective teaching about religion is legal. See also his *Religion in Public Education* (New York: Viking Press, 1947). R. Freeman Butts, in *The American Tradition in Religion and Education* (Boston: Beacon Press, 1950), takes a negative position, as does Conrad H. Moehlman in *The Wall of Separation between Church and State* (Boston: Beacon Press, 1951).

The Public Schools and Spiritual Values, ed. John S. Brubacher (New York: Harper & Brothers, 1944), presents the views of outstanding educators who believe that an approach to spiritual values on a naturalistic basis is the best for American life. William Clayton Bower presents the Kentucky experiments in teaching moral and spiritual values in *Moral and Spiritual Values in Education: A Challenge to Every American* (Lexington, Ky.: University of Kentucky Press, 1952). See also his *Church and State in Education* (Chicago: University of Chicago Press, 1944). A nonsectarian approach to religion is suggested by Ward Madden, *Religious Values in Education* (New York: Harper & Brothers, 1951), and by W. S. Fleming, *God in Our Public Schools* (Pittsburgh: National Reform Association, 1943).

The Roman Catholic point of view is presented by George Johnson, *Better Men for Better Times* (Washington: Catholic University Press, 1943); J. M. O'Neill, *Religion and Education under the Constitution* (New York: Harper & Brothers, 1949); Sister Mary Bernard McGrath, *The Compatibility of Catholic Schools and Democratic Standards* (Washington: Catholic University Press, 1948); Pope Pius XI, *Christian Education of Youth* (Washington: National Catholic Welfare Conference, 1930);

Edward J. Heffron, "Roman Catholic Religious Education," in *Orientation in Religious Education,* ed. Philip Henry Lotz (Nashville: Abingdon-Cokesbury Press, 1950), pp. 519–32.

Jewish education is treated by Leo L. Honor, "Jewish Education in the United States," in *The Jewish People, Past and Present,* Vol. II (New York: Central Yiddish Culture Association, 1948), p. 151; Israel S. Chipkin, "Jewish Education in America," in *Orientation in Religious Education,* ed. Philip Henry Lotz (Nashville: Abingdon-Cokesbury Press, 1950), pp. 501–518. Issues of *Jewish Education Magazine* (New York: National Council for Jewish Education) provide accurate information. Views of Catholics, Protestants, and Jews are reflected in issues of *Religious Education;* see especially those of July-August 1951, March-April and November-December 1953.

The approach to the factual teaching of religion in the schools is carefully treated in three reports of the Committee on Religion and Education of the American Council on Education, *Religion and Public Education* (1944), *The Relation of Religion to Public Education: Basic Principles* (1947), *The Function of Public Schools in Dealing with Religion* (1953) (Washington: American Council on Education, 1944, 1947, 1953). A report by the Educational Policies Commission of the National Education Association and the American Association of School Administrators, *Moral and Spiritual Values in the Public Schools* (Washington: Educational Policies Commission, 1951), is extremely important. Virgil Henry, in *The Place of Religion in Public Schools* (New York: Harper & Brothers, 1950), provides a practical experimental program for a community. Nevin C. Harner, *Religion's Place in General Education* (Richmond: John Knox Press, 1949), includes as an appendix the 1947 report of the American Council on Education.

On the college level, see Marcus Bach, *Of Faith and Learning: The Story of the School of Religion at the State University of Iowa* (Iowa City: School of Religion, State University of Iowa, 1952). Merrimon Cuninggim's *The College Seeks Religion* (New Haven: Yale University Press, 1947) notes the relevant trends in four-year colleges. *The Crisis in the University,* by Sir Walter Moberly (London: Student Christian Movement Press, 1949), is an analysis of higher education in Great Britain that is relevant for the United States. *Religion in State Teachers Colleges* (New Haven: Yale Divinity School, 1952) is a brief report of a conference held at Yale Divinity School. See also Clarence Shedd, "The Movement of Religion in American Higher Education," in *Journal of the American Association of Collegiate Registrars* (October 1945), and his "The Agencies of Religion in Higher Education," in *Religious Education* (September-October 1943), pp. 287–98; Edward R. Bartlett, "Religious Education in Church Colleges and Theological Schools," and Edward W. Blakeman, "Religious Education in Tax-Supported Colleges and Universities," in *Orientation in Religious Education,* ed. Philip Henry Lotz (Nashville: Abingdon-Cokesbury Press, 1950), pp. 352–63, 365–76.

The legality of weekday released time education is discussed authoritatively by Erwin L. Shaver, "Weekday Religious Education Secures Its Charter and Faces a Challenge," *Religious Education,* January–February, 1953, pp.38–43. Erwin L. Shaver's article, "The Weekday Church School," in *Orientation in Religious Education,* ed. Philip Henry Lotz (Nashville: Abingdon-Cokesbury Press, 1950), is a good brief summary of the movement. See for more details Minor Miller's *Teaching the Multitudes* (Bridgewater, Va.: Beacon Publishers, 1944), Paul H. Vieth's *The Church and Christian Education* (St. Louis: Bethany Press, 1947), pp. 38–42, and *Protestantism Faces Its Educational Task Together,* by William Clayton Bower and Percy Roy Hayward (Chicago: National Council of Churches, 1949), pp. 174–84.

The most complete discussion of vacation church schools is found in W. Dyer Blair's *The New Vacation Church School,* rev. ed. (New York: Harper & Brothers, 1939). Ethel Ristine's *The Vacation Church School* (Nashville: Abingdon-Cokesbury Press, 1947) provides practical guidance. "The Vacation Church School," by Ruth Elizabeth Murphy, in *Orientation in Religious Education,* ed. Philip Henry Lotz (Nashville: Abingdon-Cokesbury Press, 1950), is a brief introduction. See also *Protestantism Faces Its Educational Task Together,* by William Clayton Bower and Percy Roy Hayward (Chicago: National Council of Churches, 1949), pp. 166–74.

CHAPTER 8. RELIGIOUS EDUCATION AND THE COMMUNITY

The most significant book covering this field is *The Community and Christian Education,* by Tilford T. Swearington (St. Louis: Bethany Press, 1950), which deals with all kinds and sizes of communities. *Community Organization in Religious Education,* ed. Hugh Hartshorne (New Haven: Yale University Press, 1932), is old but sound. A brief treatment may be found in Helen Marie Edick's "The Community as a Unit of Religious Education," and Paul M. Limbert's "Agencies of Recreation and Group Services," in *Orientation in Religious Education,* ed. Philip Henry Lotz. (Nashville: Abingdon-Cokesbury Press, 1950), pp. 312–37.

Specialized studies include *Church Work in the City,* by Frederick A. Shippey (Nashville: Abingdon-Cokesbury Press, 1952), which has information about taking a census, resources, and the areas that churches serve. Wyndham B. Blanton's *Making of a Downtown Church* (Richmond: John Knox Press, 1945) is more specialized. The problem of meeting people's needs is treated concretely by Charles Kean in *The Christian Gospel and the Parish Church* (Greenwich: Seabury Press, 1953). *Religious Education,* January–February 1955, deals with church, synagogue, and community.

Growing Up in a Modern Society, by Marjorie Reeves (London: University of London Press, 1952), is a magnificent but simple treatment of what happens to people in a community; see especially chapter 6 on

"Young People in a Mass Society." The relation of the churches to society is treated in a classic manner in *Social Sources of Denominationalism,* by H. Richard Niebuhr (New Haven: Shoestring Press, 1954). Another angle comes from Reinhold Niebuhr's *Contribution of Religion to Social Work* (New York: Columbia University Press, 1932).

The ethical implications of Christian faith for theology and for Christian education are brought out strongly in "The Interseminary Series," especially Volume I, *The Challenge of Our Culture,* ed. Clarence Tucker Craig, and Volume II, *The Church and Organized Movements,* ed. Randolph Crump Miller (New York: Harper & Bros., 1946). Something of the church's responsibility for society is clarified in *Christian Faith and Social Action,* ed. John A. Hutchison (New York: Charles Scribner's Sons, 1953). One of the classics in this field is William Temple's *Christianity and Social Order* (London: Student Christian Movement Press, 1942). H. Richard Niebuhr's *Christ and Culture* (New York: Harper & Bros., 1951) provides a theological perspective for the relation of the church to society. Liston Pope's *Millhands and Preachers* (New Haven: Yale University Press, 1942) shows the impact of social changes in the community on the thinking of the churches. Christian educators need to come to terms with the thesis of John C. Bennett's *Christian Ethics and Social Policy* (New York: Charles Scribner's Sons, 1946) and *Christianity and Communism* (New York: Association Press–Haddam House, 1948). Emil Brunner's *Justice and the Social Order* (New York: Harper & Bros., 1945) gets down to specific questions of wages and property, family life, the mass man, the political and international order. Walter G. Muelder concerns himself with the Christian attitude to economics in *Religion and Economic Responsibility* (New York: Charles Scribner's Sons, 1953). *In An Age of Revolution,* by Cyril Garbett (New York: Oxford University Press, 1952) covers the competing ideologies of our time.

Religious Education, November–December 1954, contains ten articles on mass media of communication. The simplest approach to one aspect of mass communications is Josette Frank's *Comics, Radio, Movies—and Children* (New York: Public Affairs Pamphlets No. 148, 1949). See also her *Your Child's Reading Today* (New York: Doubleday & Co., Inc., 1954), pp. 25–27, 245–56, 294–95, and her chapter in *Our Children Today,* ed. Sidonie Matsner Gruenberg (New York: Viking Press, 1952), pp. 310–22. For a violent attack on the comics, see Frederic Wertham, *Seduction of the Innocent* (New York: Rinehart & Co., 1954). Charles A. Siepmann's *Radio, Television and Society* (New York: Oxford University Press, 1950) gives some careful evaluations of these media. Lancelot Hogben's *From Cave Dwelling to Comic Strip: A Kaleidoscope of Human Communication* (New York: Chanticleer Press, 1949) is important. The most comprehensive treatment is *Reader in Public Opinion and Communication,* ed. Bernard Berelson and Morris Janowitz (Glencoe, Ill.: Free Press, 1950).

CHAPTER 9. RELIGIOUS EDUCATION AND THE CHURCH

Very few books deal with the over-all life of the church and its relation to Christian education. The best is Charles D. Kean's *The Christian Gospel and the Parish Church* (Greenwich: Seabury Press, 1953). Donald Crawford's *A Parish Workshop* (Greenwich: Seabury Press, 1953) provides a possible approach to the solution on the local level.

On the nature of the church, Emil Brunner's *The Misunderstanding of the Church* (Philadelphia: Westminster Press, 1953) is excellent, but a more comprehensive treatment is to be found in J. Robert Nelson's *The Realm of Redemption* (Greenwich: Seabury Press, 1951). See also Daniel Jenkins, *The Strangeness of the Church* (New York: Doubleday & Co., Inc., 1955).

The relation of the church to the community is treated theologically and ethically in H. Richard Niebuhr's *Christ and Culture* (New York: Harper & Bros., 1951), and in his *Social Sources of Denominationalism* (New Haven: Shoestring Press, 1954). See also *Christianity and the Cultural Crisis,* by Charles Duell Kean (New York: Association Press, 1945), and *In an Age of Revolution,* by Cyril Garbett (New York: Oxford University Press, 1952). See books listed for Chapters 6, 7, and 8.

On the church and education see A. Victor Murray's *Education into Religion* (New York: Harper & Bros., 1954), Nevin C. Harner's *Educational Work in the Church* (Nashville: Abingdon-Cokesbury Press, 1939), Paul H. Vieth's *The Church and Christian Education* (St. Louis: Bethany Press, 1947), Dora P. Chaplin's *Children and Religion* (New York: Charles Scribner's Sons, 1948), and Harry Thomas Stock, "The Sunday Church School," in *Orientation in Religious Education,* ed. Philip Henry Lotz (Nashville: Abingdon-Cokesbury Press, 1950), pp. 248–58.

CHAPTER 10. GOOD CLASSROOM PROCEDURE

Kimball Wiles, in *Teaching For Better Schools* (New York: Prentice-Hall, Inc., 1952), deals in detail with the skills in human relations and group work that are essential in attaining a dependable classroom response. His public school approach is easily adapted to church school situations.

The best book on *Method in Teaching Religion* is by George Herbert Betts and Marion O. Hawthorne (New York: Abingdon Press, 1925), which contains a fine chapter on "Control of Class Room Response," pp. 185–209. It is out of print but can be found in most libraries and in some second-hand book stores. John Dewey's classic treatment is found in *Democracy and Education* (New York: The Macmillan Company, 1916), especially pp. 117–211; his treatment of "The Nature of Subject Matter," pp. 212–27, is also of importance.

Henry P. Smith has a chapter on "Learning in the Classroom" in *Psychology in Teaching* (New York: Prentice-Hall, Inc., 1954), pp. 240–68, followed by an equally important chapter on "Individual Differences in Ability to Learn," pp. 270–95.

Suggestions for improvement in teaching will be found in *Learning and Instruction,* the Forty-Ninth Yearbook, Pt. I, of the National Society for the Study of Education (Chicago: University of Chicago Press, 1950), pp. 256–348.

"The Teacher's Classroom" is discussed in an informal way by Harold Spears in *Principles of Teaching* (New York: Prentice-Hall, Inc., 1951), pp. 115–36.

CHAPTER 11. TYPES AND SELECTION OF METHOD

One of the finest books for obtaining an understanding of the over-all task of the teacher is *Teaching for Better Schools,* by Kimball Wiles (New York: Prentice-Hall, Inc., 1952). Although he does not deal with religious teaching, his interpretation of relationships in the class and school, of group work, and of concern for the individual is consistent with the aims and goals of Christian education. *Learning and Instruction,* Pt. I, the Forty-ninth Yearbook of the National Society for the Study of Education (Chicago: University of Chicago Press, 1950), pp. 192–215, 217–53, is more technical, but helpful. See also *Educational Psychology,* ed. Charles E. Skinner (New York: Prentice-Hall, Inc., 1951), pp. 764–75, steps in teaching; Henry P. Smith, *Psychology in Teaching* (New York: Prentice-Hall, Inc., 1954), pp. 240–68, for a description of learning in the classroom; John P. Wynne, *Philosophies of Education* (New York: Prentice-Hall, Inc., 1947), for three approaches to general method of teaching.

Paul H. Vieth's *How to Teach in the Church School* (Philadelphia: Westminster Press, 1935) is written specifically for church school teachers. My *A Guide for Church School Teachers,* 2nd ed. (Greenwich: Seabury Press, 1947), pp 38–58, does the same thing more briefly. George Herbert Betts and Marion O. Hawthorne, in *Method in Teaching Religion* (New York: Abingdon Press, 1925), pp. 213–38, 285–301, deal with the problem of method in more detail.

CHAPTER 12. TELLING

The "cone of experience" is described in Edgar Dale's *Audio-Visual Methods in Teaching* (New York: The Dryden Press, Inc., 1946), pp. 37–52.

Jeanette Perkins Brown's *The Storyteller in Religious Education* (Boston: Pilgrim Press, 1951) is the best recent book in the field. Raimundo de Ovies, in *The Church and the Children* (New York: Morehouse-Gorham Co., 1941), provides both advice and excellent samples. See also George Herbert Betts and Marion O. Hawthorne, *Method in Teaching Religion* (New York: Abingdon Press, 1925), pp. 325–50; and Paul H. Vieth, *How to Teach in the Church School* (Philadelphia: Westminster Press, 1935), pp. 123–30. Sample stories may be found in *Story Sermons for*

Juniors, by Alice Greer Kelsey (Nashville: Abingdon-Cokesbury Press, 1954), and in *Worship Programs for Intermediates,* by Alice A. Bays (Nashville: Abingdon-Cokesbury Press, 1942).

Two different approaches to Bible stories may be found in James D. Smart, *The Teaching Ministry of the Church* (Philadelphia: Westminster Press, 1954), pp. 131–53, and Sophia Lyon Fahs, *Today's Children and Yesterday's Heritage* (Boston: Beacon Press, 1952), pp. 59–100. For a third point of view, see Lois E. Le Bar, *Children in the Bible School* (Westwood, N. J.: Fleming H. Revell Co., 1952), pp. 223–65. "The Bible in the Literature for Christian Education," by Ralph D. Heim, *Religious Education* (November–December 1952), pp. 402–20, indicates how much material appears in the curriculum.

Bible stories appear for all ages. Some samples are Pelagie Doane's *A Small Child's Bible* (New York: Oxford University Press, 1946) for ages 6–8; Walter Russell Bowie's *Bible Story for Boys and Girls* (Nashville: Abingdon-Cokesbury Press, 1951, 52), with a volume each for the Old Testament and the New Testament, for ages 9–13; Dorothy Kunhardt's *Once There Was a Little Boy* (New York: Viking Press, 1946) for ages 5–8. Hulda Niebuhr's *The One Story* (Philadelphia: Westminster Press, 1950) is magnificent for ages 11-14; E. Jerry Walker's *Five-Minute Stories from the Bible* (Nashville: Abingdon Cokesbury Press, 1947) are vivid and exciting for those 9–14. Ethel Smither's *The Use of the Bible with Children* (Nashville: Abingdon-Cokesbury Press, 1937) provides a basis for selection up to the age of 12.

The chart on p. 40 of *Informal Adult Education,* by Malcolm S. Knowles (New York: Association Press, 1950), is helpful, as is his brief treatment of the lecture method on pp. 39–45. See also Rudolf Flesch, *The Art of Plain Talk* (New York: Harper & Bros., 1946).

For the use of audio aids, see Kenneth B. Haas and Harry Q. Packer, *Preparation and Use of Audio-Visual Aids,* 2nd ed. (New York: Prentice-Hall, Inc., 1950), pp. 189–218.

CHAPTER 13. SHOWING

Standard texts dealing with most of the aspects of audio-visual instruction include Edgar Dale, *Audio-Visual Methods in Teaching* (New York: The Dryden Press, Inc., 1946), which includes some valuable theory of learning based on the "cone of experience," and many suggestions for the teaching of specific secular subject matter. *Preparation and Use of Audio-Visual Aids,* 2nd ed., by Kenneth B. Haas and Harry Q. Packer (New York: Prentice-Hall, Inc., 1950), is a practical "how to" book, containing lists of sources for recordings (p. 199), wire and tape recorders (pp. 201, 203), and audio-visual aids (pp. 2–3, 285–320), as well as practical advice on every aspect of the subject. Suggested lists of films and filmstrips for understanding children may be found in *Effective Home-School Relations,* by James L. Hymes, Jr. (New York: Prentice-Hall, Inc., 1953), pp. 243–45, 253–56.

William L. Rogers and Paul H. Vieth's *Visual Aids in the Church* (Philadelphia: Christian Education Press, 1946) is among the best of the books in the religious field. See also William S. Hockman, *Projected Visual Aids in the Church* (Boston: Pilgrim Press, 1947); Howard E. Tower, *Church Use of Audio-Visuals* (Nashville: Abingdon-Cokesbury Press, 1940); *Visual Method in the Church* (Chicago: International Council of Religious Education, 1940); F. A. Peake, *Seeing Is Believing* (Toronto: General Board of Religious Education, Church of England in Canada, 1950).

Religious Education (November–December 1946) has articles on religious radio and audio visuals (pp. 321–40). Paul H. Vieth's "Audio-Visual Method and Content," in *Orientation in Religious Education,* ed. Philip Henry Lotz (Nashville: Abingdon-Cokesbury Press, 1950), pp. 150–62, is the best brief summary of the topic.

CHAPTER 14. EXCHANGING IDEAS

Teaching through discussion and questions is covered briefly by Paul H. Vieth in *How to Teach in the Church School* (Philadelphia: Westminster Press, 1935), pp. 113–22, 132–39. See also George Herbert Betts and Marion O. Hawthorne, *Method in Teaching Religion* (New York: Abingdon Press, 1925), pp. 219–26, 407–18; Le Roy E. Bowman, *How to Lead a Discussion* (New York: The Woman's Press, 1947); Harrison S. Elliott, *Group Discussion in Religious Education* (New York: Association Press, 1946).

For understanding group procedures see Ronald Lippitt, *Training in Community Relations* (New York: Harper & Bros., 1949), which is one of the best books in the field; Kurt Lewin, *Resolving Social Conflicts* (New York: Harper & Bros., 1948); Malcolm S. Knowles, *Informal Adult Education* (New York: Association Press, 1950), especially pp. 55–83; Leland P. Bradford and Ronald Lippitt, *Group Dynamics and Education* (Washington: National Education Association, 1949); Harrison S. Elliott, *The Process of Group Thinking* (New York: Association Press, 1932); Bert and Frances Straus, *New Ways to Better Meetings* (New York: Viking Press, 1951), which is an excellent guide for those conducting parents' and adult classes; Rudolph Wittenberg, *The Art of Group Discipline* (New York: Association Press, 1951); *How to Teach Adults* (Greenwich: Seabury Press, n.d.), a pamphlet containing essentials of the process for leaders; Dorwin Cartwright and Alvin Zander, *Group Dynamics, Research and Theory* (Evanston, Ill.: Row, Peterson and Co., 1953); Earl C. Kelley, *The Workshop Way of Learning* (New York: Harper & Bros., 1951).

Religious Education has some excellent articles on this subject, beginning with the issue of November–December 1951, pp. 323–45; November–December 1952, pp. 371–401; January–February 1954, a bibliography on pp. 52–54; July–August 1954, pp. 291–93, an article on staff-congregation dynamics.

CHAPTER 15. GROUP PLANNING AND ACTIVITY

Method in Teaching Religion, by George Herbert Betts and Marion O. Hawthorne (New York: Abingdon Press, 1925), pp. 304–22, 354–73, 378–403, 421–42, covers in detail many of the problems presented in this chapter. *The Church School Teacher's Job,* by Mildred Moody Eakin and Frank Eakin (New York: The Macmillan Company, 1949), contains many illustrations of projects. Dorothy M. Roberts' *Leadership of Teen-age Groups* (New York: Association Press, 1950), has a section on program planning, pp. 119–89. A more technical approach to the problems of high school age is found in *Learning and Instruction,* Pt. I, Forty-ninth Yearbook of the National Society for the Study of Education (Chicago: University of Chicago Press, 1950), pp. 304–33. Kimball Wiles' *Teaching for Better Schools* (New York: Prentice-Hall, Inc., 1952), especially pp. 99–183, is the most helpful for church school teachers in presenting practical ways of achieving group planning.

Rebecca Rice, *Creative Activities* (Boston: Pilgrim Press, 1947) and Elizabeth M. Lobingier, *Activities in Child Education* (Boston: Pilgrim Press, 1950), are two of the most helpful guides to handwork and projects for younger children. For missionary projects see Nevin C. Harner and David D. Baker, *Missionary Education in Your Church* (New York: Friendship Press, 1950). The Friendship Press publishes annually special missionary education resources for use of all churches.

On the use of creative arts see Amy Goodhue Loomis, "The Creative Arts in Religious Education," in *Orientation in Religious Education,* ed. Philip Henry Lotz (Nashville: Abingdon-Cokesbury Press, 1950), pp. 137–48. See also Esther Bates, *The Church Play and Its Production* (Boston: Walter Baker Co., 1938); Harold Ehrensperger, *Conscience on Stage* (Nashville: Abingdon-Cokesbury Press, 1947); Thelma Sharman Brown, *A Treasury of Religious Plays* (New York: Association Press, 1947); Mildred B. Hahn, *Best Plays for the Church* (Philadelphia: Christian Education Press, 1947); Fred Eastman, *Christ in the Drama* (New York: The Macmillan Company, 1947); Mona Swann, *An Approach to Choral Speech* (Boston: The Expression Co., 1934).

The Recreation Leader, by E. O. Harbin (Nashville: Abingdon-Cokesbury Press, 1952), is full of suggestions for all ages and has many resources listed according to availability; the age-group chart on pp. 58–60 is valuable; the resources listed on pp. 114–17 cover camps, crafts, drama, games, music, nature lore, art, and music. The same author's *Fun Encyclopedia* (Nashville: Abingdon-Cokesbury Press, 1940) has many suggestions; he also has a booklet, *Recreation for Youth* (Nashville: Abingdon-Cokesbury Press, 1941). Nina Millen's *Children's Games from Many Lands* (New York: Friendship Press, 1943) has missionary educational values. James P. Lincoln's *Please Take Me Back* (West Point, Va.: Tidewater Press, 1952) has suggestions and a list of books on pp. 42–48.

CHAPTER 16. METHODS OF WORSHIP

General books on worship include George Hedley's *Christian Worship* (New York: The Macmillan Company, 1953) with its full treatment of all aspects of worship. Written against the background of a college chapel, it expresses the ethos of our Protestant heritage and includes a bibliography that is satisfying. Massey H. Shepherd, Jr., in *The Worship of the Church* (Greenwich: Seabury Press, 1952), deals more explicitly with the *Book of Common Prayer* and provides a full bibliography. Henry Sloane Coffin, in *The Public Worship of God* (Philadelphia: Westminster Press, 1946), discusses a freer type of service.

Chapters on worship in my *A Guide for Church School Teachers,* 2nd ed. (Greenwich: Seabury Press, 1947), pp. 59–70; in Sophia Lyon Fahs' *Today's Children and Yesterday's Heritage* (Boston: Beacon Press, 1952), pp. 198–218; in Paul H. Vieth's *How to Teach in the Church School* (Philadelphia: Westminster Press, 1935), pp. 106–12; in *Method in Teaching Religion,* by George Herbert Betts and Marion O. Hawthorne (New York: Abingdon Press, 1925), pp. 444–83, provide insights into the general principles of worship for children. See also Marie Cole Powell, "Worship in Religious Education," in *Orientation in Religious Education,* ed. Philip Henry Lotz (Nashville: Abingdon-Cokesbury Press, 1950), pp. 126–36.

Jeannette Perkins Brown's *Children's Worship in the Church School* (New York: Harper & Brothers, 1939) and *As Children Worship* (Boston: Pilgrim Press, 1936); Marie C. Powell's *Boys and Girls at Worship* (New York: Harper & Brothers, 1943); Irwin Paulsen's *The Church School at Worship* (New York: The Macmillan Company, 1940); and Estelle Barbar's *Guiding Intermediates in Worship* (Nashville: Abingdon-Cokesbury Press, 1946) provide help for those leading departmental worship.

The importance of music is brought out by Donald Kettring in *Steps Toward a Singing Church* (Philadelphia: Westminster Press, 1948) and by Elizabeth Shields in *Music in the Religious Growth of Children* (Nashville: Abingdon-Cokesbury Press, 1943). *Church Music in History and Practice,* by Winfred Douglas (New York: Charles Scribner's Sons, 1937), is probably the best single volume on theory and practice.

Percy Dearmer's *Songs of Praise for Boys and Girls* (New York: Oxford University Press, 1929–30) and *Songs of Praise for Little Children* (New York: Oxford University Press, 1932) provide selections that are in good taste and suitable for the age groups. *New Hymnal for American Youth,* ed. Henry Augustine Smith (New York: Century Co., 1930), has many fine selections.

Religious Education (September–October 1949), pp. 259–287, has a symposium on "Music and Religious Education," including the choir, organization, and sources.

Many books of worship services and stories and sermonettes are available. They are related to the age levels and may be used in department worship or adapted for family worship.

CHAPTER 17. A COMPREHENSIVE PROGRAM OF RELIGIOUS EDUCATION

The theory of a Christian parish in action, based on good theology and related to Christian education, is found in Charles D. Kean, *The Christian Gospel and the Parish Church* (Greenwich: Seabury Press, 1953). Although written from the standpoint of the Protestant Episcopal Church, it is suitable for all who share the insights of reformed theology.

See *Organization and Administration of Christian Education in the Local Church* (Chicago: International Council of Religious Education, 1935, 1940); also, Donald M. Maynard, "The Total Church as an Agency of Religious Education," in *Orientation in Religious Education,* ed. Philip Henry Lotz (Nashville: Abingdon-Cokesbury Press, 1950), pp. 221–27. Chapters 5, 6, and 17 of *Leading a Sunday Church School,* by Ralph D. Heim (Philadelphia: Muhlenberg Press, 1950), are related to this chapter. Wesner Fallaw, in *The Modern Parent and the Teaching Church* (New York: The Macmillan Company, 1946), has a chapter on "The School of the Church," pp. 78–89, which indicates something of the view developed here. See also Paul H. Vieth, *The Church and Christian Education* (St. Louis: Bethany Press, 1947), pp. 88–133.

Ideas for promotion may be found in two books by Willard A. Pleuthner, *Building Up Your Congregation* (Greenwich: Seabury Press, 1950, 1951) and *More Power to Your Church* (New York: Farrar, Straus & Young, 1952).

For the rural minister, Rockwell C. Smith, *Rural Church Administration* (Nashville: Abingdon-Cokesbury Press, 1953), is essential; see also *Religious Education,* March–April 1945, pp. 67–91, for a symposium on "Religious Education in Rural America."

CHAPTER 18. THE CHURCH ORGANIZED FOR RELIGIOUS EDUCATION

On the general question of administration of an educational program in the church, the most comprehensive treatment is in Ralph D. Heim's *Leading a Sunday Church School* (Philadelphia: Muhlenberg Press, 1950). Help will be found in Paul H. Vieth's *Improving Your Sunday School* (Philadelphia: Westminster Press, 1930). Verdia Burke's *Building a Better Sunday School* (St. Louis: Bethany Press, 1950), Nevin Harner's *The Educational Work of the Church* (Nashville: Abingdon-Cokesbury Press, 1939), and John Leslie Lobingier's *The Better Church School* (Boston: Pilgrim Press, 1952). Background and theory behind such organization is clearly brought out in Charles D. Kean's *The Christian Gospel and the Parish Church* (Greenwich: Seabury Press, 1953).

The best book on the responsibility of the pastor is *The Pastor and the Children,* by Mildred Moody Eakin and Frank Eakin (New York: The Macmillan Company, 1947), which should be required reading for every minister. Raimundo de Ovies' *The Church and the Children* (New York: Morehouse-Gorham Co., 1941) and Frank A. Lindhorst's *The Minister Teaches Religion* (Nashville: Abingdon-Cokesbury Press, 1945) have many good suggestions. "Pastoral Psychology and Christian Education," in *Religion and Human Behavior,* ed. Simon Doniger (New York: Association Press, 1954), pp. 217–33, indicates the significance of the pastor within the redemptive community.

Harry C. Munro's *The Director of Religious Education* (Philadelphia: Westminster Press, 1930) is one of the few books on the subject. *Religious Education* for November–December 1946, pp. 345–73, contains the results of a survey of directors of religious education; "The Roles of Ministers and Directors in Christian Education" are described by Wesner Fallaw in the issue of January–February 1950, pp. 41–47; Dorotha Lawshe discussess "The Effective Functioning of the Director of Religious Education," and Mary Anderson Tully describes "Laboratory or Field Experiences in the Professional Training of Directors of Religious Education" in the issue of May–June 1952, pp. 181–92, 193–97. Marcella Prugh has written a pamphlet on *The Parish Director of Christian Education* (Greenwich: Seabury Press, 1953). See also Nevin C. Harner, "The Educational Ministry of the Church," in *Orientation in Religious Education,* ed. Philip Henry Lotz (Nashville: Abingdon-Cokesbury Press, 1950).

The Church School Superintendent, by Philip Cowell Jones (New York: Abingdon Press, 1939), is the fullest treatment of the subject. *An Almanac for Church School Superintendents,* by Frances M. Young (Greenwich: Seabury Press, 1953), is the most practical booklet on the subject. *Sunday School Superintendent's Problem* (Chicago: National Council of Churches of Christ in America) is a tract that raises many questions. Of the books in the opening paragraph see Vieth, pp. 11–22, Heim, pp. 104–07, and Lobingier, pp. 139–42. Some other helpful books are *The Superintendent Faces His Task,* by Charles Marion Ross and Glenn McRae (St. Louis: Bethany Press, 1947), and *The Superintendent Wants to Know* (Philadelphia: Judson Press, 1937).

The Church School and Parish House Building, by E. M. Conover (Chicago: National Council of Churches, 1949) is one of the few books dealing with the problem of church architecture while keeping in mind the educational requirements. John R. Scotford's *The Church Beautiful* (Boston: Pilgrim Press, 1946), has a chapter on the church school, and he has written a chapter on "Building for Religious Education" in *Orientation in Religious Education,* ed. Philip Henry Lotz (Nashville: Abingdon-Cokesbury Press, 1950).

CHAPTER 19. CHILDREN, YOUTH, AND ADULTS

"From Age to Age," in *The Better Church School,* by John Leslie Lobingier (Boston: Pilgrim Press, 1952), pp. 14–30, has a good description of the way in which the departments in this chapter should be understood.

Some of the best information concerning departments is found in teachers' manuals published by the various denominations. In some cases there are manuals for departmental and general superintendents. Such magazines as *Children's Religion* (Boston: Pilgrim Press, monthly) are helpful.

Nursery Children in the Church, by Gertrude E. Andon (Boston: Pilgrim Press, 1945), *The Primary Church School,* by Hazel A. Lewis (St. Louis: Bethany Press, 1951), *Teaching Juniors,* by Florence E. Norton (Philadelphia: Judson Press, 1937), *Junior High Boys and Girls in the Church,* by Louise B. Griffiths (Boston: Pilgrim Press, 1944), *Youth Work in the Church,* by Nevin C. Harner (Nashville: Abingdon-Cokesbury Press, 1942), and *Please Take Me Back: A Youth Manual,* ed. James P. Lincoln (West Point, Va.: Tidewater Press, 1953), are among the best material available.

George Gleason has written two excellent booklets, *Single Young Adults in the Church* (New York: Association Press, 1952) and *Church Activities for Young Couples* (New York: Association Press, 1949). *The Modern Parent and the Teaching Church,* by Wesner Fallaw (New York: The Macmillan Company, 1946), remains the best book in this field.

Our Church Plans for Adult Education, by Idris W. Jones (Philadelphia: Judson Press, 1952), has some good suggestions. *Informal Adult Education* by Malcolm S. Knowles (New York: Association Press, 1950), contains insights into a more dynamic adult program. See also Edward P. Westphal's *The Church's Opportunity in Adult Education* (Philadelphia: Westminster Press, 1941).

Older People and the Church, by Paul Maves and J. Lennart Cedarleaf (Nashville: Abingdon-Cokesbury Press, 1949) deals with an increasing responsibility of the church.

CHAPTER 20. VACATION AND WEEKDAY CHURCH SCHOOLS; SUMMER CAMPS AND CONFERENCES

W. Dyer Blair's *The New Vacation Church School* (New York: Harper & Brothers, 1939) is still the best and most complete description of this work. Some specific helps are found in Ethel Ristine's *The Vacation Church School* (Nashville: Abingdon-Cokesbury Press, 1947). Ruth Elizabeth Murphy's "The Vacation Church School," in *Orientation in Religious Education,* ed. Philip Henry Lotz (Nashville: Abingdon-Cokesbury Press, 1950), pp. 260–72, is brief and concise.

The Division of Christian Education of the National Council of the Churches of Christ has some pamphlets that are excellent, especially *How to Plan and Conduct a Vacation Church School* and *The How of Vacation Church School* (Chicago: International Council of Religious Education, 1947). *Protestantism Faces Its Educational Task Together,* by William Clayton Bower and Percy Roy Howard (Chicago: National Council of Churches, 1949), has a chapter on the history of vacation and weekday religious education, pp. 166–84.

Minor Miller's *Teaching the Multitudes* (Bridgewater, Va.: Beacon Publishers, 1944), Alleen Moon's *Planning for the Weekday Church School* (Nashville: Methodist Publishing House, 1942), and Erwin L. Shaver's "The Weekday Church School," in *Orientation in Religious Education* (Nashville: Abingdon-Cokesbury Press, 1950) have most of the information available on the subject. The legal angle is treated concisely in "Weekday Religious Education Secures Its Charter and Faces a Challenge," by Erwin L. Shaver, in *Religious Education* (January–February 1954), pp. 38–43. *Choosing a Course of Study for Your Weekday Church School* (Chicago: International Council of Religious Education, 1945) indicates the possibilities of curriculum materials, although the recommendations are mostly out of date.

There is very little material on summer conferences, and not very much material on church summer camps, particularly in relation to the local church administration. *Administration of the Modern Camp,* ed. Hedley Dimock (New York: Association Press, 1948), is excellent. Two pamphlets, *When Juniors Go Camping* (Chicago: International Council of Religious Education, 1947) and *Going Camping with Junior High Boys and Girls* (Chicago: International Council of Religious Education, 1949), are good. *Day Camping for Your Church,* by Reynold Carlson (Philadelphia: Judson Press, 1948), covers a specific kind of camping. *Spiritual Values in Camping,* by Clarice M. Bowman (New York: Association Press, 1954), shows the religious value of relationships in camps and conferences.

CHAPTER 21. RECRUITING AND TRAINING LEADERS

"The Education of Lay and Professional Religious Education Leaders," by Herman J. Sweet, in *Orientation in Religious Education,* ed. Philip Henry Lotz (Nashville: Abingdon-Cokesbury Press, 1950), pp. 392–402, is the best brief treatment. See also Paul H. Vieth, *The Church and Christian Education* (St. Louis: Bethany Press, 1947), pp. 193–224; Frank M. McKibben, *Christian Education through the Church* (Nashville: Abingdon-Cokesbury Press, 1947), pp. 132–43; William Clayton Bower and Percy Roy Hayward, *Protestantism Faces Its Educational Task Together* (Chicago: National Council of Churches, 1949), pp. 148–65, for the work of the International Council of Religious Education; Ralph D. Heim, *Leading a Sunday Church School* (Philadelphia: Muhlenberg Press, 1950), pp. 130–49.

See also Gaines S. Dobbins, *The Improvement of Teaching in the Sunday School* (Nashville: Broadman Press, 1943); Forrest L. Knapp, *Leadership Education in the Church* (New York: Abingdon Press, 1933); *A Philosophy of Leadership Education* (Chicago: International Council of Religious Education, 1950); Frances C. McLester, *Teaching in the Church School* (Nashville: Abingdon-Cokesbury Press, 1940); Mildred Moody Eakin and Frank Eakin, *The Church School Teacher's Job* (New York: The Macmillan Company, 1949).

On supervision, see Paul H. Vieth, *Improving Your Sunday School* (Philadelphia: Westminster Press, 1930), which ties in supervision with the work of the superintendent. Ernest J. Chave, in *Supervision of Religious Education* (Chicago: University of Chicago Press, 1931), has the most complete discussion of the procedures. Frank M. McKibben, in *Improving Religious Education through Supervision* (New York: Methodist Book Concern, 1931), has many helpful suggestions. "Can You Supervise a School?" is addressed to ministers in *The Pastor and the Children,* by Frank Eakin and Mildred Moody Eakin (New York: The Macmillan Company, 1947), pp. 80–89. *Supervision for Better Schools,* by Kimball Wiles (New York: Prentice-Hall, Inc., 1950), can be adapted to church school problems.

BASIC BOOKS FOR TEACHERS

A library for teachers might be selected out of the following:

For the understanding of the teaching task, they might read *Children and Religion,* by Dora P. Chaplin (New York: Charles Scribner's Sons, 1948); *The Church School Teacher's Job,* by Frank Eakin and Mildred Moody Eakin (New York: The Macmillan Company, 1949); *A Guide for Church School Teachers,* by Randolph C. Miller, rev. ed., (Greenwich: Seabury Press, 1947); *Guiding Children in Christian Growth,* by Mary Alice Jones (Nashville: Abingdon-Cokesbury Press, 1949); *How to Teach in the Church School,* by Paul H. Vieth (Philadelphia: Westminster Press, 1935). *Teaching for Better Schools,* by Kimball Wiles (New York: Prentice-Hall, Inc., 1952), gives teachers a good interpretation of relationships.

The Use of the Bible with Children, by Ethel L. Smither (Nashville: Abingdon-Cokesbury Press, 1937), is the best book on the use of the Bible by children through the sixth grade. There are chapters on this subject in the books listed in the first paragraph of this bibliography.

The understanding of the whole church school is found in *The Better Church School,* by John Leslie Lobingier (Boston: Pilgrim Press, 1952). Frank M. McKibben's *Christian Education through the Church* (Nashville: Abingdon-Cokesbury Press, 1947) covers many administrative problems in an elementary way.

Superintendents should read Paul H. Vieth's *Improving Your Sunday School* (Philadelphia: Westminster Press, 1930), Philip Cowell Jones' *The Church School Superintendent* (New York: Abingdon Press, 1939); and Frances M. Young's *An Almanac for Church School Superintendents* (Greenwich: Seabury Press, 1953).

The understanding of Christian faith in popular form may be found in Ralph B. Knudson's *Christian Beliefs* (Philadelphia: Judson Press, 1947); Aaron J. Ungersma's *Handbook for Christian Believers* (Indianapolis: Bobbs-Merrill Co., Inc., 1953); William A. Spurrier's *Guide to the Chris-*

tian Faith (New York: Charles Scribner's Sons, 1952); James D. Smart's *What a Man Can Believe* (Philadelphia: Westminster Press, 1943); Charles D. Kean's *Making Sense Out of Life* (Philadelphia: Westminster Press, 1954); William Hordern's *A Layman's Guide to Protestant Theology* (New York: The Macmillan Company, 1955); or my *Religion Makes Sense* (Greenwich: Seabury Press, 1950).

On the Bible let them read Bernhard Anderson's *Unfolding Drama of the Bible* (New York: Association Press-Haddam House, 1953) and *Rediscovering the Bible* (New York: Association Press-Haddam House, 1952); Robert Dentan's *The Holy Scriptures* (Greenwich: Seabury Press, 1949); Edgar J. Goodspeed's *The Story of the Bible* (Chicago: University of Chicago Press, 1934).

To bring their beliefs and their methods together, they should read James D. Smart's *The Teaching Ministry of the Church* (Philadelphia: Westminster Press, 1954) or my *The Clue to Christian Education* (New York: Charles Scribner's Sons, 1950). Some will want to read Reuel L. Howe's *Man's Need and God's Action* (Greenwich: Seabury Press, 1953), especially for its insights into the "language of relationships."

These will be enough to get a library under way, and they are among the easier books to understand.

CHAPTER 22. CHOOSING LESSON MATERIALS

A Guide for Curriculum in Christian Education (Chicago: National Council of Churches, 1955) should be available to every committee working on the selection of lesson materials.

For background see C. A. Bowen, "Curriculum Patterns for the Church School," in *Orientation in Religious Education,* ed. Philip Henry Lotz (Nashville. Abingdon-Cokesbury Press, 1950), pp. 101–12; Paul H. Vieth, *The Church and Christian Education* (St. Louis: Bethany Press, 1947), pp. 134–67; William Clayton Bower and Percy Roy Hayward, *Protestantism Faces Its Educational Task Together* (Chicago: National Council of Churches, 1949), pp. 66–88; John Leslie Lobingier, *The Better Church School* (Boston: Pilgrim Press, 1952), pp. 41–47.

The September–October 1952 issue of *Religious Education* is concerned with the curriculum of Christian education.

CHAPTER 23. EVALUATING THE EDUCATIONAL PROGRAM

Ralph D. Heim, in *Leading a Sunday Church School* (Philadelphia: Muhlenberg Press, 1950), has chapters on "Securing, Reporting, and Using Data," and "Measuring in the Sunday Church School," pp. 286–96, 310–27. *The Curriculum Guide for the Local Church* (Chicago: International Council of Religious Education, 1950) has a chapter on "Testing the Outcomes," pp. 60–73. An excellent treatment of "Evaluation in Relation to Integration," by William E. McManus, is found in *The Integration of the Catholic Secondary School Curriculum,* ed. Sister Mary

Janet Miller (Washington: Catholic University Press, 1951), pp. 103–115; see also the chapter by Sister Mary Janet Miller on "Christian Principles as Integrating Elements," pp. 7–16.

Tests of teaching efficiency are suggested by George H. Betts and Marion O. Hawthorne, *Method in Teaching Religion* (New York: Abingdon Press, 1925), pp. 247–81.

Much help in evaluating the educational process that can be adapted to the church's program is found in Kimball Wiles, *Teaching for Better Schools* (New York: Prentice-Hall, Inc., 1952), pp. 187–236, and in his *Supervision For Better Schools* (New York: Prentice-Hall, Inc., 1950), pp. 249–81; see also Edward A. Lincoln's chapter, "Educational Measurements," and Walter J. Gifford's "Teacher-Made Examinations and Other Techniques of Evaluation," in *Educational Psychology,* ed. Charles E. Skinner (New York: Prentice-Hall, Inc., 1951), pp. 663–89, 692–719. Suggestions for parent education can be adapted from James L. Hymes, Jr., *Effective Home-School Relations* (New York: Prentice-Hall, Inc., 1953), pp. 225–32.

For the place of theology in the evaluation of the parish educational program, see Charles D. Kean, *The Christian Gospel and the Parish Church* (Greenwich: Seabury Press, 1953), and the study booklet that goes with it, *The Gospel and the Parish: A Study Outline;* Donald Crawford, *A Parish Workshop* (Greenwich: Seabury Press, 1953); James D. Smart, *The Teaching Ministry of the Church* (Philadelphia: Westminster Press, 1954); my *The Clue to Christian Education* (New York: Charles Scribner's Sons, 1950).

Several new books have appeared recently which deal with the problem of theology in Christian education. Lewis J. Sherrill, in *The Gift of Power* (New York: The Macmillan Company, 1955), brings to bear on the theory of Christian education his insights into theology and psychology in a way that is unique and significant. My *Biblical Theology and Christian Education* (New York: Charles Scribner's Sons, 1956) seeks to make clear the Bible as an unfolding drama which illuminates the relationships of daily living, with attention to various age-groups. Howard Grimes, in *The Church Redemptive* (Nashville: Abingdon Press, 1958), has dealt seriously with the nature of the church and the educational responsibilities that result when one understands what the church is. Paul H. Vieth has written *The Church School* (Philadelphia: Christian Education Press, 1958), which deals with administrative problems of interest to all leaders in the church. *Learning Together in the Christian Fellowship,* by Sara Little (Richmond: John Knox Press, 1956), is the best guide for group study of the Bible for young people and adults. Issues of *Religious Education* which are valuable include "The Church and Family" (January-February 1957), "The Images of Man" (March-April 1958), "Theology and Religious Education" (September-October 1958).

INDEX

The main treatments of the more important topics are indicated by **boldface** type.